Praetorian Politics in Liberal Spain

Praetorian Politics in Liberal Spain

by Carolyn P. Boyd

The University of North Carolina Press
Chapel Hill

© 1979 The University of North Carolina Press
All rights reserved
Manufactured in the United States of America
Library of Congress Catalog Card Number 79-300
ISBN 0-8078-1368-0

Library of Congress Cataloging in Publication Data

Boyd, Carolyn P   1944–
    Praetorian politics in liberal Spain.

    Bibliography: p.
    Includes index.
    1. Spain—Politics and government—1886–1931.
2. Spain. Ejército—Political activity.   3. Civil
supremacy over the military—Spain.   I. Title.
DP243.B6   322′.5′0946   79-300   16 Jan'80
ISBN 0-8078-1368-0

To Frank

Contents

Preface

Until recently, Spanish historiography has been dominated by political history. Yet there have been surprisingly few analytical studies of the failure of parliamentary government in Spain. The same is true of Spanish praetorianism, even though military intervention in the political process has been the most obvious fact of Spanish political life for nearly two centuries.[1] This book attempts to explain the relationship between these two phenomena during the critical seven years between the emergence of the military defense juntas in 1917 and the *pronunciamiento* of General Miguel Primo de Rivera in 1923.

In general, studies of Spanish civil-military relations—whether by historians, sociologists, or political scientists—have been unidimensional and static, rather than multidimensional and dynamic in focus. One approach has emphasized the disposition of the army to intervene, analyzing the institutional characteristics that induced officers (perhaps inevitably) to feel isolated from and often superior to the society around them. In this view, the case of Spanish praetorianism is not unique, but merely an exaggerated form of the corporate military mentality that developed along with the professionalization of European armies in the late nineteenth and early twentieth centuries. Everywhere that traditional society underwent modernization, officers responded to the growing complexity and conflicts of political life by claiming to be the sole representatives of the national will, with not only a right, but a duty to intervene when that will was in danger of perversion or neglect by the state. This interpretation has been reinforced by Spanish officers themselves, who have never exalted what they consider to be "servile" obedience in the manner of, say, the French army of the nineteenth century. In Spain, military coups have usually been the work of soldiers professing to represent the true interests of the nation. Pronunciamiento literature of the nineteenth century is rich in examples; military rhetoric in the twentieth century has kept alive the image of the army as "the guardian of all the *values and historical constants* of the people to which it belongs."[2]

Studies that stress the structural or moral peculiarities of the military, however, explain only the disposition to intervene, whereas a satisfactory model of praetorianism must account for provocation and opportunity as well. As the Spanish case illustrates, civilian weakness seems to be a necessary precondition of praetorian involvement. The origins of Spanish militarism lie in the prolonged search for constitutional legitimacy after the collapse of the old regime during the Napoleonic wars. After playing a fundamental role in the creation of the liberal state in a nation socially and economically underdeveloped by European standards, the army then acted as the moderating power within this artificial political system, providing the mechanism for the rotation of political parties—the pronunciamiento—in the absence of a responsible Crown or an agreement on constitutional principles. A handful of military politicians successfully exploited the functional role of the military—and the endemic factionalism of the officer corps—to satisfy personal ambitions for political power and social status. But the majority of officers, victimized by the favoritism and professional insecurity of the pronunciamiento era, were less satisfied with the army's political role and welcomed the settlement of 1875, which eliminated the pronunciamiento as a device for maintaining the two-party system by establishing a consensus among the great political interests. Under the Restoration, the army became the instrument by which the dynastic parties maintained their supremacy over the working classes and the peripheral nationalities. In return, the army was protected from the full rigors of professionalization and was encouraged to identify with a particular set of constitutional arrangements and class interests.

Impressed by the absence of military intervention during the last quarter of the nineteenth century, historians have overlooked the fact that the "civilianized" parliamentary monarchy contrived by Antonio Cánovas del Castillo in 1875 was indebted to the army for both its existence and its continuity; the professional and apolitical officer corps that he claimed to have created was a fiction maintained only by the assiduous neglect of military reform and by the relative tranquility of the Restoration era. Ironically, the policies adopted by Cánovas to insure the neutrality of the army in fact guaranteed that it would become a disruptive force in the political system. Limited military professionalization intensified factionalism and alienated many officers from the state. At the same time, after the turn of the century, the political leverage of this dissatisfied army was enhanced. As the gradual modernization of the Spanish economy enlarged both the industrial bourgeoisie and the urban working class (groups previously excluded from political power), the financial and agrarian oligarchy relied increasingly on force to retain its hegemony. By 1917 the parliamentary monarchy once again began to resemble a praetorian regime, characterized by a lack of constitutional legitimacy, the mobilization of hitherto weak or indifferent social classes, and the willingness of all civilian groups to appeal to the army—or to one of the factions within it—for support.

As even contemporary observers could perceive,[3] 1917 marked a turning point in the history of the parliamentary monarchy. During the summer of 1917, three political groups—junior army bureaucrats, the Catalan bourgeoisie, and the organized working-class left—attacked the regime, demanding a redistribution of political and economic power more in line with their interests. Although the parliamentary system survived this onslaught, it would never again assume its customary complacency. After 1918, Wilsonian idealism, the Russian Revolution, and economic dislocation mobilized the Spanish working classes and encouraged peripheral nationalists to challenge the political hegemony of Madrid; then in 1921, the failure of the army and of Spanish colonial policy in Morocco aroused the usually apathetic middle classes to demand an accounting for the disaster, together with constitutional reform to prevent its recurrence. Bereft of the popular indifference to politics that had eased their rule since 1875, the dynastic parties experienced a severe crisis of confidence.

Their initial response was to strengthen their alliance with the military. But intercorps rivalries and the conflicting interests of peninsular bureaucrats and colonial officers—all exacerbated by the lack of military reform—made an appeal to "the army" impossible. By 1922 the dynastic politicians had discovered that the survival of the parliamentary monarchy depended on a redefinition of civil-military relations wherein the power of the state rested on popular consent rather than military force. In 1922–23, first the Conservatives, then the Liberals, cautiously introduced measures to curb military factionalism and to impose civilian control over areas in which the army had traditionally operated autonomously—in particular, over social policy in Barcelona and colonial policy in Morocco. Their efforts to free themselves from the yoke of military dependence and to democratize Spanish political life were cut short, however, in September 1923 by the coup of General Primo de Rivera and the negative pronunciamiento of the officer corps, which temporarily united to protect the privileged position of the army within the state. The pronunciamiento was successful because the regime lacked widespread civilian support in the country as a whole.

In this sense, the politicians—not the army—were responsible for the collapse of parliamentary government in 1923. Spanish praetorianism was a by-product, rather than a cause, of civilian weakness.

In this study I have tried to emphasize the relationship between political modernization and military professionalization. The latter is a process that involves the formation of a corporate and institutionally autonomous body of military experts, selected on the basis of merit rather than birth or social class, and isolated from the rest of society, including the civilian elites, by virtue of its social function. Its relationship with political modernization is a dynamic one. Complete military professionalization seems largely to depend on the extent to which government rests on the principle of popular sovereignty—that is, on the extent to which a government does not rely on the army to remain in power. At the same time, incomplete professionalization may encourage praetorian tendencies in the military, which may then intervene to obstruct political modernization. The result is a kind of vicious circle from which it is difficult to emerge. In the Spanish case, the development of representative government was forcefully opposed first by a ruling elite unreconciled to the democratization of Spanish political life, then later by a military establishment whose interests were bound to suffer in any alteration of the status quo. Put in the simplest terms, the parties of the parliamentary monarchy created the praetorian army that later destroyed them.

The purpose of this book is to analyze the role of the military in the breakdown of parliamentary government in Spain between 1917 and 1923. Nevertheless, I hope that it also deepens our understanding of the general phenomenon of military intervention in contemporary Spain. The process that led to military dictatorship in 1923 in some ways prefigured the pattern of events that led to civil war in 1936. In the first place, Spanish governments after 1923 remained weak and narrowly based. Neither the seven-year dictatorship of General Primo de Rivera nor the short-lived Second Republic, proclaimed in 1931, succeeded in forging a national consensus on the extent and pace of political and social reform. In the second place, despite a major effort at military reform in 1931–32, the process of professionalization was not yet complete in 1936. As General Francisco Franco pointed out in his last letter to the Republican government before the military rebellion of 1936, the internal conflicts and institutional defects that had plagued the army since 1917 were still unresolved.[4] When over half the officer corps supported the military conspirators against the government a month later, their professional grievances were largely those that had motivated their support for Primo de Rivera in 1923. By illuminating the historical background of those grievances, this book should make the military origins of the Spanish civil war more intelligible.

It should be clear that my own view frankly favors liberal, democratic government and civilian supremacy over the military. I interpret Spanish history in the nineteenth and twentieth centuries as essentially a search for legitimate representative government, a quest complicated by the heterogeneous and somewhat tardy modernization of Spanish economic and social life. In these circumstances, civilian government has found it difficult to provide a countervailing force to the force inherent in military institutions. The Spanish army has shown little regard for the principle of civil supremacy when it has felt its basic interests to be threatened. But Spanish praetorianism cannot be laid exclusively at the door of an ambitious and arrogant military establishment. Militarism has also been nurtured by the failure of Spain's traditional elites to accommodate themselves to social and economic change. The complex relationship between military discontent and civilian weakness is the subject of this study.

Acknowledgments

At the end of any scholarly project, the author is faced with the difficulty of adequately expressing gratitude for the assistance received along the way. In my own case, the list of helpful persons and institutions is long and the gratitude profound. I would like to begin by thanking Joan Connelly Ullman of the University of Washington, who has given generously of her time, knowledge, and friendship at every stage of this project. The manuscript has benefited enormously from her critical insight and her unflagging attention to detail. I am also indebted to Stanley Payne, Standish Meacham, Richard Graham, and Edward Malefakis, and to Lewis Bateman of The University of North Carolina Press, who read all or parts of the manuscript and offered helpful comments and suggestions for revision. All remaining errors of fact or deficiencies of interpretation are of course my own.

Special thanks are due the Marqués de Santo Floro, who generously allowed me to consult the archive of his father, the Conde de Romanones, and the Fundación Antonio Maura, which gave me permission to use the papers in its possession. I would also like to thank Burnett Bolloten for his bibliographic assistance at an early stage of the project; Shannon Fleming for sharing his expert insights into the Moroccan problem; Ricardo de la Cierva, José Antonio Maravall, Julio Busquets Bragulat, Amando de Miguel, Captain Miguel Alonso Baquer, Colonel Ramón Salas Larrazábal, Colonel José María Gárate Córdoba, and other Spanish scholars for their advice and assistance during several research trips to Spain; the officers and staff at the Servicio Histórico Militar, and the staffs of the Biblioteca Nacional and the Hemeroteca Municipal for their cooperation and attentiveness. The manuscript was ably and efficiently typed by Mrs. R. C. Stephenson. David Ridner prepared the map; Lorraine Mills, the index. I would like to thank them, along with Martha Dukas and Judith Gran of the Middle Eastern Collection at The University of Texas, who helped me resolve the difficult problem of transliteration of North African proper names and place-names.

Portions of the research were supported by grants from the American Association of University Women, the University of Texas Research Institute, and the American Council of Learned Societies. I would like to express my appreciation to each of these granting agencies.

My deepest gratitude, however, is reserved for my husband, Frank Bean, whose editorial advice, moral support, and endless patience made it possible for me to complete this study. This book is dedicated to him.

A Note on Transliteration

The transliteration of North African proper names and place names in this book has posed some special problems. The Spanish and French transliterations found in the historical literature to date did not seem appropriate for English readers; on the other hand, well-established English forms of these names do not exist in many cases. The method I have followed is a compromise. Arabic terms and proper names have generally been given English transliterations according to a modified Library of Congress system in which most special diacritics have been eliminated, with the exception of *ain* (rendered by ᶜ) and *hamza*, indicated by an apostrophe where it appears in the middle of a word. The Library of Congress makes an exception for the name of the Riffian leader Abd el-Krim, who is better known by the French and Spanish versions of his name than by the classical Arabic ᶜAbd al-Karim. I have followed their practice in this account. In addition, North African place-names have been given the spelling conventional on Spanish maps of northern Morocco in those cases where no well-established English form exists, in order to avoid unnecessary confusion in the historical account.

Except where otherwise indicated, all translations in the text are my own. Where English usage demands, Spanish place-names have been anglicized and the accents have been omitted.

Praetorian Politics in Liberal Spain

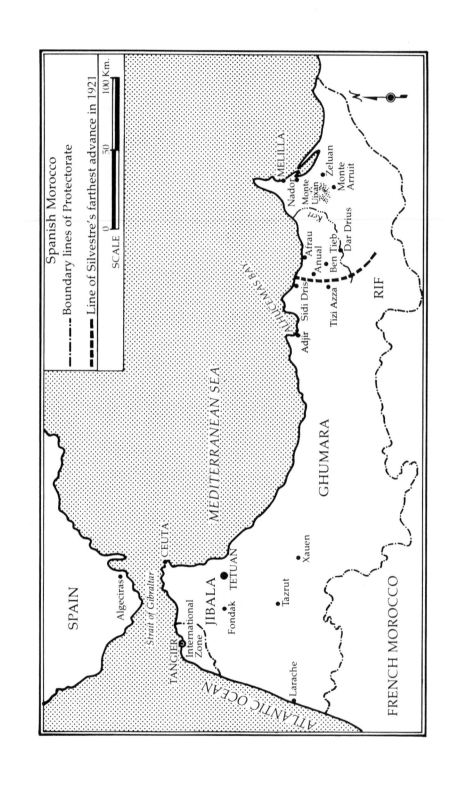

SPAIN

Algeciras •

Strait of Gibraltar

CEUTA

MEDITERRANEAN SEA

TANGIER
International
Zone

JIBALA
Fondak TETUAN

Tazrut •

Xauen •

ATLANTIC OCEAN

Larache •

GHUMARA

FRENCH MOROCCO

ALHUCEMAS BAY

Adjir

Sidi Dris

Tizi Azza

Afrau
Anual
Ben Tieb
Dar Drius

Kert

Monte
Uixan

Nador

MELILLA

Zeluan •
Monte
Arruit

RIF

Spanish Morocco
—·—·— Boundary lines of Protectorate
▬ ▬ ▬ Line of Silvestre's farthest advance in 1921

SCALE
0   50   100 Km.

N

The Breakdown of the Restoration Settlement

In twentieth-century Spain, the army has been an active agent of political crisis and change. The explanation for this phenomenon lies as much with the weakness of civilian governments as with the inclination of the military to intervene. The pattern began at the turn of the century. Their confidence shaken by a humiliating defeat in the War of 1898 and by the loss of the remnants of the colonial empire, Spain's ruling elites were unable to respond positively to the national demand for political reform or to the rising strength of groups previously excluded from the Restoration settlement of 1875. Instead, they turned to the army to maintain the status quo. In this fashion, the army, as the tacit guarantor and privileged beneficiary of the Restoration system, was drawn into the struggle to reshape Spanish political life.

The Restoration Settlement

The emergence of the army as an independent political factor contrasted sharply with its quiescence during the last quarter of the nineteenth century. The architect of the Restoration system, Antonio Cánovas del Castillo, had been obsessed by the necessity of "returning the army to the barracks," especially since the restored Bourbon monarchy owed its existence to the military pronunciamiento of General Arsenio Martínez Campos in December 1874. Encouraged by the weakness of civil institutions and by the proclivity of civilian politicians to seek military support, the army had been the moderating power in Spain for most of a century. As a result, in 1875 the officer corps was heavily politicized, burdened with factionalism, and dangerously tolerant of insubordination. Cánovas correctly perceived that a successful remedy must be at once political and military: the new political regime must be stable enough to function without military intervention, and military policy must encourage the development of a professional, politically neutral officer corps.

The first step was the creation of a political system that could function without the aid of military pronunciamientos. Under the Isabelline monarchy, the absence of an educated electorate and the refusal of the Crown to recognize the legitimacy of the Progressive opposition had robbed parliamentary government of its natural dynamics, making appeals to military force irresistible. Cánovas could not manufacture an educated public; he did, however, create a system that could function without the aid of the army by providing for the peaceful and automatic rotation of two parties in office—the *turno pacífico*.[1] Replacing the army as the moderating power between the parties was the king, who was given the right to dissolve the Cortes and to appoint a new prime minister. Once in office, the prime minister called elections in order to construct a parliamentary majority.

There was no risk involved in the elections, which were "made" from Madrid by the Minister of the Interior with the aid of local notables and party bosses known as *caciques*.[2] In rural areas, voter apathy, along with the influence of the cacique, insured an uncontested victory; in the cities, where urban workers and lower-middle-class radicals were likely to be less manageable, bribes, falsifications, and violence provided majorities for the first twenty years of the regime. An admittedly cynical method for achieving rotation in office, it was nonetheless effective in a society in which political immaturity and illiteracy made a mockery of parliamentary democracy.

Moreover, Cánovas's system included the most important political, economic, and social forces in Spain in 1875. Suspicious as he was of liberalism, Cánovas recognized the need to open the system to all political groups willing to accept the dual sovereignty of king and Cortes. While his Conservative party appeased Neo-Catholics on the right, the Liberals of Práxedes Mateo Sagasta attracted the hostile forces on the left by incorporating the so-called liberal conquests into the constitution: universal suffrage, freedom of association, civil marriage, and trial by jury. By the 1890s, only the ultraconservative Carlists, the working classes, and the regionalists remained outside the Restoration settlement.

Carlism was fighting a losing battle against history; organized labor and regionalism were still only embryonic movements. Cánovas claimed his system represented all the "live forces" in Spain, and in all fairness, it did. Critics complained that the Cortes favored the interests of Andalusian landowners, Castilian wheat growers, and the civil and military bureaucracies, but this, while true, meant only that the Restoration system accurately reflected the dominant economic and social forces of a still underdeveloped agricultural and financier economy, whose feeble middle classes were dependent on the state for their position and income. In a largely traditional society, *caciquismo* and party rotation (the *turno*) provided stable government by eliminating internal conflict among the ruling elites. In a crude way, caciquismo also allowed for a measure of local control in an otherwise highly centralized regime.

This system largely removed the opportunities for military intervention in politics. But equally important to the success of the Canovite system was the curbing of the army's long-standing disposition to intervene. The army's inclination toward political activism sprang from two sources. One was the political ambitions of the senior generals, who had exploited civilian weakness to further their own careers. The other, and more important, source of praetorianism was the professional dissatisfaction within the lower ranks of the officer corps, where support for rebellious generals sprang from a desire for promotions and higher salaries. The inherent weakness of the Restoration civil-military settlement was that it removed the first, but not the second, of these potential sources of disruption.

Cánovas accommodated the political generals without violating the principle of civilian rule by incorporating them into the party system that controlled the parliamentary monarchy. The linchpin in the institutional framework that united the army, the government, and the Crown was the Minister of War. The appointment always followed the turno, each party placing its most trusted generals in this key position of patronage and power. The other politically sensitive military posts also reflected party politics, thus assuring domestic tranquility and a turnover in patronage spoils.

The Constitution of 1876 also provided for political participation by officers in both the Congreso de los Diputados and in the Senate. Army and navy officers of all ranks were eligible for election to the Congress, while membership in the Senate was restricted to senior officers. All officers with the rank of captain general (the highest rank in the army) or admiral (the corresponding rank in the navy) were members of the Senate by right;[3] lieutenant generals and vice-admirals were eligible for appointment to lifetime Senate seats or could run for election. A Senate seat represented the culmination of a political career often initiated by election to a safe seat in the Congress, the parties' reward for political loyalty.

Figure 1. The Chain of Command in the Spanish Army

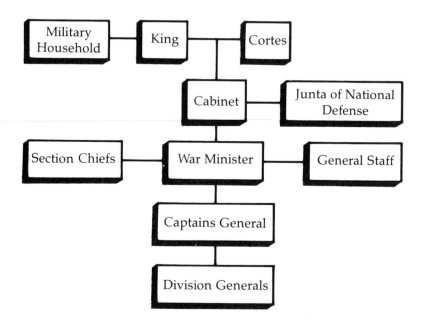

Some general conclusions about military membership in the Cortes can be derived using biographical data for the Cortes of 1907.[4] Given the political significance of the army, the most surprising characteristic of military membership was that it was so small—about 8 percent in the Senate and 6 percent in the Congress, including several no longer actively serving in the armed forces.[5] Equally important was the advanced age of the majority of officers, many of whom had actively supported the Bourbon Restoration in 1875. The younger military deputies were often men of wealth and birth whose personal attributes coincidentally included a neglected military rank. Neither group was in touch with the vast majority of middle-class officers in the middle and lower ranks. As an institutional outlet for the political ambitions of the military elites, the system was a success, but it did not guarantee responsive representation for lower-ranking officers. In 1917 the politicians would be confronted by junior officers disaffected from both the hierarchy and the parliamentary system.

On the whole, the parliamentary participation of the military, like its representation, seems to have been minimal. If the interests of the army were protected in the Cortes during the Restoration, it was due primarily to the civilian politicians, who were determined to keep the army apolitical by anticipating its demands almost before they were articulated. A few politically active generals took an interest in military reform; many more limited themselves to the defense of all existing privileges. On issues not directly bearing on military interests, officers in both chambers usually kept silence.

A more important sounding board for army opinion was the Crown. Cánovas strengthened the loyalty of the army to the restored monarchy by institutionalizing the ties between them in the Constitution of 1876. Articles 52 and 53 made the king the commander-in-chief of the armed forces with the exclusive right to award promotions and decorations. The enabling legislation, the Ley Constitutiva del Ejército of November 29, 1878, expanded the constitutional powers of the king to include both appointments and general army organization.[6] As Regent from 1886 to 1902, Queen María Cristina rarely exercised this prerogative, and appointments followed the military turno. But on coming of age in 1902, Alfonso XIII immediately took a keen interest in military appointments, disrupting the turno and loosening the strong ties between the senior generals and the dynastic parties.[7] Thus royal favoritism began to replace political affiliation as a criterion for professional advancement.

Another institutional link between the king and the army was the Military Household, an official body of officers in personal service to the king. Created by royal decree on March 29, 1875, as an advisory body during the Carlist war, the Household soon became an honorific repository for the aristocracy, members of the military dynasties, and officers whose exploits in Morocco had caught the eye of the king.[8] Because he controlled military access to the king, the head of the Military Household (a captain general or lieutenant general) wielded considerable power within the court. Between 1915 and 1930, governments used the office to separate politically controversial officers from active commands without damaging their prestige or offending their dignity.[9] Like the Cortes, however, the Military Household did not provide representation for the anonymous bulk of the officer corps, who tended to view the *palaciegos* in the Household with envy and resentment.

The contacts between the Crown and the senior hierarchy were not merely institutional. Between 1875 and 1923, the leading political generals were granted titles of nobility, as part of the general consolidation of new and old elites that characterized the Restoration.[10] A lesser distinction conferred by the king was that of gentleman of the chamber, a purely honorific title used to single out junior officers, sometimes of modest social origins, for special favor and attention.[11] Above all, both Alfonso XII, the "soldier-king," and his son surrounded themselves with military companions, with whom they shared professional and personal interests. Both the institutional and the personal contacts between the king and the army were useful in binding the military to the parliamentary monarchy. They also encouraged the army to look to the throne rather than to the Cortes to further its interests and protect its privileges. In the peaceful years of the Restoration, the danger was not perceived; later, the alliance would prove fatal.

By the mid-1880s all the leading generals had been reconciled to the regime. The days of the pronunciamiento seemed over for good. In reality, however, political neutralization of the army depended not only upon the integration of the generals into the political system, but also upon the elimination of professional dissatisfaction among the lower ranks of the officer corps. Professionalization—in particular, rationalization of the military bureaucracy and a guarantee of institutional autonomy over internal matters—was the key to military respect for civilian authority. Yet Cánovas could not countenance the thoroughgoing professionalization of the officer corps. In the first place, radical reduction of the inflated military bureaucracy would have eliminated career opportunities for thousands of middle-class officers whose loyalty to the state ultimately rested on its reliability as an employer.[12] Even though modernization of the army's equipment and training was contingent upon personnel cutbacks, no serious reform was contemplated for fear of damaging vested interests.[13] In the second place, institutional autonomy was incompatible with the incorporation of the politicized senior hierarchy into the Restoration settlement. Promotions and appointments were determined by political, rather than professional, criteria because, like its political counterpart, the military turno was based on influence and patronage. Cánovas avoided professionalization of the new officer corps for fear of diminishing military loyalty to the new regime. Ironically, his policy only encouraged professional dissatisfaction and thus, a tendency toward insubordination among the officer corps as a whole.

First Signs of Praetorianism

Until the 1890s elite consensus and the weakness of the opposition guaranteed the stability of the Restoration settlement. But after the turn of the century, the system became increasingly dysfunctional.

The domestic tranquility of the Restoration years had encouraged the growth of industry and commerce, ironically enlarging the social and economic groups originally excluded from the Canovite system, whose political failure lay less in its initial disposition than in its inflexibility once conditions had changed. Jealous of their prerogatives and comfortably attached to the benefits of electoral manipulation, the agrarian and financial oligarchy was hostile to the legitimate claims of emerging economic interests, while at the same time disturbed by the growing ineffectiveness of caciquismo in the urban areas. The repercussions of the Spanish-American War of 1898 intensified their confusion, for the loss of the empire shocked the usually apathetic middle classes out of their indifference to political issues. After 1898, the parties tried to assume the leadership of the regenerationist movement. But there was no consensus, in the nation or within the parties, as to the direction reform should take. Their former self-confidence shattered by defeat and mounting criticism, the dynastic parties took refuge in their control over the instruments of political power. Instead of broadening the system to include the new politically significant groups, they responded to the challenge of regionalism and organized labor with repression. In this way the stage was set for a return to the pronunciamiento politics of the early nineteenth century, when the intransigence of the ruling elites had forced the opposition into revolution and the army into politics.

Political instability was enhanced by the collapse of the rotation system that had regulated Spanish politics since the 1880s. The assassination of the Conservative leader Cánovas in 1897, followed by the death of the Liberal party chief, Sagasta, in 1902, left both dynastic parties leaderless at a moment when public opinion was demanding regeneration and reform. Struggles over succession sapped already feeble party energies without producing uncontested leadership for either of them. They also fostered cabinet instability and the subordination of policy to politics.[14] Symptomatic of the breakdown of party discipline—and ultimately of the disintegration of the political consensus resting on apathy and ignorance—was the growing tendency of governments to govern by decree. When real leadership for both parties finally emerged—Antonio Maura for the Conservatives and José Canalejas for the Liberals—it was short-lived; Maura was destroyed by political intransigence (not only the opposition's, but his own), Canalejas was cut down by an assassin's bullet. By 1913 the regenerationist impulse had been dissipated, both parties were divided, demoralized, and discredited, and the alienation of much of the country from the political process was greater than ever.

The failure to broaden the base of support for the parliamentary regime magnified the power of the army, which exercised its leverage to increase its privileges and to protect itself from military reform. The symbiotic relationship between the army and the dynastic politicians grew out of their common antagonism to social and economic modernization. Both the Conservative and the Liberal parties represented landowners in Andalusia and New Castile whose interests were opposed to those of the industrial and commercial bourgeoisie in the port cities in the north and east. In addition, they served as sources of patronage and employment for the underemployed urban middle class. The similar social base of the two great parties discouraged their adoption of social reforms; both parties remained unsympathetic to the demands of the urban and rural working classes. The officer corps was recruited largely from petty bourgeois and bureaucratic middle sectors whose survival was threatened by economic development.[15] As a result, officers tended to view demands for political democratization or social reform as destructive of a political and social system that guaranteed their own status and security.

If the military's violent response to the challenge of both regionalism and organized labor grew largely out of self-interest, it was also emotional and ideological. Deeply humiliated by the defeat of 1898, the officer corps entered the twentieth century with "the conviction that they would never be useful for anything."[16] Military literature of the day exalted war and martial values as the means by which nations and the human race eliminated "the weak or the poorly constituted,"[17] but for Spanish officers there was little realistic hope of another war in which to earn individual or collective redemption. Eager to be of service to the nation, they increasingly saw themselves as the defenders of a nation endangered by the divisive effects of regionalism and class conflict. As the "guardian of all the values and historical constants of the people," the army was a national institution uniquely qualified to protect the unity of the Fatherland.[18] By extending this line of reasoning, an attack on the army became, ipso facto, an attack on the nation itself. The antimilitarism characteristic of both regionalistic and labor movements was thus evidence of lack of patriotism, if not treason. The army's extreme response to the protest of regionalism and labor limited the flexibility of the dynastic parties, which, when forced to choose between appeasing the army or the protesters, invariably chose the former. Thus an already rigid political system became even less capable of evolution.

From the War of 1898 to the pronunciamiento of General Primo de Rivera in 1923, the army displayed a growing tendency to take matters into its own hands whenever the civilian politicians faltered in their determination to preserve the status quo. In the nineteenth century, military intervention in politics had been prompted by the personal and political ambitions of individual officers and their factions. In the twentieth century, the army would intervene as an injured *institution*, demanding redress for professional and political grievances while invoking a national ideal. The turbulent years of the new century exposed the flaw in the Canovite solution to the military problem—its reliance on a political consensus to guarantee the neutrality of the army. As the appearance of political dissent after 1898 made the appeasement of military demands more difficult, the army showed its willingness to resort to force—or the threat of it—to retain its favored position in the state.

The Army, Regionalism, and the Law of Jurisdictions

Military antagonism to political decentralization contributed to the prolonged isolation of the Spanish bourgeoisie from the parliamentary monarchy. It also encouraged regionalists to focus their general animosity toward the Spanish state on the army. This mutual hostility mounted to a climax in 1906, when disgruntled junior officers successfully pressured the Liberal government into passage of the "Law of Jurisdictions," which gave the army the right of censorship over journalistic attacks on its collective honor. For twenty-five years, the law insulated the army from criticism and generally limited the free expression of political and social dissent. Its approval by the Cortes in 1906 reflected the lack of self-confidence among the political elites in Madrid and marked the first major intrusion of the army into civilian politics in the twentieth century.

Spanish liberalism had always been crippled by the lack of a large and vigorous industrial bourgeoisie. But by 1900 three significant commercial and industrial regions had arisen on the periphery of the nation—in Catalonia, where textiles and light industry predominated; in the Basque provinces, home of the iron and steel industries; and in Asturias, a commercial and mining center. The industrial bourgeoisie might have attempted the creation of a third national party to challenge the hegemony of the predominantly agrarian Conservatives and Liberals of the center. But they were deflected by the seeming inviolability of the cacique system and by the emergence, in the 1890s, of local movements for regional autonomy, which had grown out of the romantic nationalism of the mid-nineteenth century. Regionalism, especially Catalanism, received a boost when the loss of Cuba and the Philippines closed the protected markets for the essentially uncompetitive Catalan textiles.[19] The failure of the government and the army to defend Spain's colonial markets seemed to confirm what regionalists had argued all along: that union with the center hindered rather than furthered the development of Catalonia.

Extensive peripheral resentment of the political hegemony of the center did not necessarily guarantee effective opposition. The protest of the bourgeoisie was weakened rather than strengthened by regionalism, which obstructed a national political alliance. Basques and Catalans divided their allegiance and their energy, while the Asturian bourgeoisie began to gravitate toward moderate republicanism. Furthermore, regionalists were separated by political and economic goals. In Catalonia, for example, the bourgeoisie wanted administrative autonomy and a higher tariff, along with political hegemony at home and a share of power in Madrid. The lower middle class, however, was divided into a minority of left Republicans and a much more potent majority of antiregionalist Radical Republicans, whose leader, Alejandro Lerroux, combined democratic radicalism with a fundamental social conservatism. The urban working class, increasingly composed of peasants from outside Catalonia, was indifferent to regionalism altogether.

Perhaps because they had accurately gauged the weakness of the opposition, the dynastic politicians were prepared to tolerate, if not encourage, the manifestations of Catalan and Basque nationalism that followed the loss of the overseas empire. But the army found the rhetorical excesses of the more ardent regional patriots intolerable. In May 1902 irate officers attacked Basque demonstrators in Bilbao and arrested three civilians for insulting the flag in Barcelona. In November officers entered the University of Barcelona in pursuit of Catalan students protesting a recent decree on instruction in Castilian, wounding several students and one of the deans in the process.[20] Although these confrontations clearly violated the civil rights of the protesters, the Liberal government took no action, preferring to offend the regionalists rather than the army.[21] This inhibition amounted to a license for military indiscipline, issued by a government unsure of the army's loyalty while at the same time dependent on it to maintain the status quo. The precedent was thus set for the *¡Cu-cut!* affair of 1905 and the Juntas de Defensa of 1917.

Regionalist antimilitarism was most pronounced in Catalonia, where the Catalanist press delighted in heaping a steady stream of abuse on the army. When regionalist candidates triumphed in the

Barcelona municipal elections of November 1905, the friction between the local garrison and the more radical separatists began to threaten public order. In Madrid, antiregionalist and pro-military groups in the Cortes pressured the Liberal government of Eugenio Montero Ríos to declare martial law in the Catalan capital. When the government refused, *El Ejército Español*, a military newspaper with ties to the Liberal party, issued a warning: "The remedy against the separatist *canaille* is in the Army. The weakness of temporizing Governments must be opposed by the firm will of the military, which cannot and must not allow these outrages against Spain."[22] Thus the army was poised for intervention. It was a small incident that provided an excuse.[23]

The provocation was a small cartoon in the Catalan humor weekly, *¡Cu-cut!*, satirically contrasting the regionalist victory in the elections with the military defeat of 1898.[24] On the evening of November 24, 1905, a group of some two hundred junior officers attacked the printing press of *¡Cu-cut!* and the offices of *La Veu de Catalunya*, the principal Catalanist daily.[25] As soon as the news became known, nearly the entire officer corps publicly united behind the Barcelona garrison. Outspoken support came from the highest military quarters, including the Captains General of Madrid, Barcelona, and Seville. The real focus of insubordination, however, was the junior officers. In Madrid and Barcelona, young extremists formed commissions to prepare an ultimatum for the king demanding suspension of the Cortes and the cabinet—in short, of the constitution—until action was taken against the separatists.[26] On November 27 *El Ejército Español* equated the government's inaction with "complicity with the evildoers" and warned that the army was ready to act in its place.[27]

What the young officers wanted was the immediate suspension of constitutional guarantees in Barcelona and the introduction of legislation in the Cortes to curb separatist attacks on the army and the nation. Their chief demand, however, was for a law placing press attacks on the army under military jurisdiction.

The honor of the army was already well protected under Spanish law. The Code of Military Justice of 1890 prohibited all oral and written "injuries or offenses" to military authorities and institutions and granted military courts jurisdiction over all attacks on the army and its honor.[28] But the Spanish Supreme Court had repeatedly ruled these provisions to be inapplicable to the constitutionally protected civilian press; in 1900 a special law had specifically excluded press offenses from the jurisdiction clauses of the Code.[29] To placate the army, the same law had denied a jury trial to those attacking civil, military, or ecclesiastical authorities. But in the event, judges in the civil courts had proved no more inclined to propitiate injured military sensibilities by finding against the army's critics.[30] The rebellious officers in 1905 were thus demanding revision of the Code of Military Justice to give the army jurisdiction over its opponents in the press. But, of course, more than a minor revision of the Code was at issue: the military rebellion represented nothing less than an attempt to modify the Constitution of 1876 by force.[31]

With so much at stake, the Liberal government agreed to resist the mounting military pressure, although it did order the declaration of martial law in Barcelona on November 29. But the cabinet's resolution was undermined by the fence-straddling of the War Minister, General Valeriano Weyler, who, like other senior generals, feared that opposition to the junior officers' demands might lead to an outright breach of military discipline. Once organized into commissions, the junior officers were displaying an alarming tendency to stray from the immediate issues into a general discussion of their professional grievances, many of which were directed against the privileged senior hierarchy. To forestall a further breakdown of military discipline, the generals had to assume leadership of the movement.[32] At a cabinet meeting on November 30, the king also announced his intention of supporting the army's demands.[33] This was tantamount to asking for the resignation of the prime minister, Montero Ríos, which was immediately forthcoming; it was also tantamount to an open invitation to further army rebellion, extended by the Crown itself.

Alfonso's decision has been characterized as a "strictly appeasing" attempt to ward off a military coup.[34] In reality, his capitulation to the officer corps was the first major betrayal of the facade of civil supremacy that had been the crowning achievement of the Canovite system. To be sure, the regime had always been vulnerable to the threat of military insubordination. But its susceptibility had been minimized by the political stability of the Restoration years. In 1905 that stability was diminished, and Alfonso increasingly viewed himself and the army as the only permanent forces in a kaleidoscopic political situation. By abandoning the government of Montero Ríos, he guaranteed that the junior officers would have their way without having to make good on their threat of force.

The new government, headed by Segismundo Moret, an anti-Catalan Liberal, accepted office prepared to placate the army. To indicate his good intentions, Moret appointed General Agustín Luque y Coca, the Captain General of Seville who had seconded the Barcelona revolt, to the War Ministry.[35] Luque's insubordination in 1905 was only the latest in a notorious career of republican conspiracy and political intrigue; at one level, his appointment was representative of the traditional method of neutralizing the political ambitions of the senior hierarchy.[36] But Luque also took office as the spokesman for the dissident young officers, who for the last time placed their confidence in the political system and the military elite. In 1917 they would bypass their superiors altogether, forming Juntas de Defensa to represent their interests directly, without intermediaries. The ¡Cu-Cut! rebellion of 1905 was the prelude to the total collapse of the civil-military settlement so carefully constructed by Cánovas in 1875.

Moret's declaration to the Senate on December 2, 1905, that the motto of the Liberal party was "always the supremacy of the civil power,"[37] did not disguise the real betrayal of that principle that was soon forthcoming. Neither did the elaborate parliamentary strategy devised to soothe the uneasy consciences of some of the cabinet members.[38] When the bill for the "Repression of Crimes Against the Fatherland and the Army" arrived in the Congress from the Senate on February 15,[39] the government supported its adoption, arguing that the bill was a temporary "compromise, . . . a labor of peace."[40] Not even its sponsors could argue that it was a progressive law; progress, one spokesman admitted, "ebbs and flows."[41] What convinced a majority of the dynastic politicians to vote the bill into law on March 20, 1906, was the argument, tentatively put forward by the Liberals, but given fullest expression by the Conservative leader, Antonio Maura, that the bill provided an immediate, albeit temporary, remedy to the disorder in Catalonia.[42] Unable to find a peaceful resolution to the conflict between regionalist demands for autonomy and the army's exaggerated sense of honor, the deputies succumbed to the logic of superior force.

In so doing, of course, they ignored the military disorder and violence that the bill sanctioned and that itself comprised the chief obstacle to negotiation with the regionalists. Only the Republican deputies were bold enough to point directly at the military pressure that had made passage of the bill a "necessity." For Melquíades Álvarez, the bill was nothing less than "the bastard fruit of a bloodless revolution, of a revolution that has not shed blood because it triumphed easily, without encountering resistance in the public power, nor in the Parliament, nor in the political parties, nor even in the individual protest of any one of us."[43]

The Law of Jurisdictions, as it was commonly known, appeared in the *Gaceta* on April 24 prefaced by an emphatic statement by Moret that the law was in no way intended to prosecute regionalism, but only the specific offenses listed in Articles 1, 2, and 3. Reminding those entrusted with implementation of the law that "our political system is based on freedom of the press and on respect for the rights of conscience," he also pointed out that the "habitual license of style and thought" characteristic of the Spanish press should not be confused with deliberate attacks on the Fatherland or on military discipline.

Despite these disclaimers, Moret and the Liberal party had sponsored a law that was used repeatedly in the next twenty-five years to stifle civilian criticism of the army, not only in Catalonia but wherever it occurred. Although the censorship rights of the army were limited to military affairs, it was a fundamental concession that abridged one of the freedoms essential to the successful functioning of representative government. To be sure, the law did not completely muzzle the press, partly because the War Ministry seems to have exercised its influence to discourage excessive use of the legislation by zealous local commanders.[44] In addition, editors quickly learned that the Cortes would protect its members by invoking parliamentary immunity; thus, articles critical of the army often bore the signature of a deputy to the Congress.[45]

Nevertheless, in intent and often in practice, the Law of Jurisdictions functioned as a permanent exception clause to the guarantee of free speech in the Constitution of 1876. Like the Code of Military Justice of 1890, the Law of Jurisdictions gave witness to the inflexibility and fear of the ruling oligarchy, which was prepared to sacrifice civilian supremacy in order to protect its economic and social position. The army would play an increasingly central role in defending the regime from internal and external threats in the years to come, a role in which it would largely fail. Ironically, that failure would be at least partly due to the immunity from criticism provided by the Law of Jurisdictions.

Also ironically, the Liberals had created a symbol around which antimilitarist and antidynastic forces could rally. After 1906 repeal of the Law of Jurisdictions became a principal plank in opposition platforms. From 1908 on, to restore the luster to its tarnished image, the Liberal party advocated repealing the law while incorporating its main provisions into the military and civil codes; this cynical maneuver, employed three times between 1908 and 1914, did little to shore up the party's sagging liberal credentials. The true contents of the law were soon forgotten by the general public; it was thought that the law had given military courts jurisdiction over all "crimes against the Fatherland and the army," when, in fact, most of the military's broad judicial powers had been acquired long before 1906. Thus, the law designed to protect the army from criticism intensified that criticism by drawing attention to military privilege and power.

Of course, the bill in no way resolved the Catalan question, as Maura had warned. The immediate response to the Law of Jurisdictions was the formation in February 1906 of Solidaritat Catalana, an electoral coalition composed of all the political forces in Catalonia except Alejandro Lerroux's Radical Republicans, who were courting the army. In the Cortes elections of April 1906, Solidaritat Catalana won forty-one of the forty-four Catalan seats, ending forever the grip of dynastic caciquismo on Catalonia. This demonstration of regionalist strength prepared the way for the eventual accommodation of the Catalan bourgeoisie within the regime (the Catalan provincial assembly, or Mancomunitat, was finally created by royal decree on March 26, 1914). The Catalan Republican left, however, only increased their attacks on the unitary state and its symbol, the army, which in turn continued to regard all forms of regionalism as the equivalent of treason.

The *¡Cu-Cut!* incident and the passage of the Law of Jurisdictions are significant because they foreshadowed the relationship between the army and politics in the twentieth century. The early capitulation of the dynastic politicians measured the extent to which they had lost faith in their own capacity and right to rule. Unable to assert civilian supremacy by an appeal to popular opinion and abandoned by the other source of constitutional sovereignty—the king—they provided the army with an opportunity to impose its demands on the state. The Liberals probably underestimated the ability of the system to withstand a military challenge. Their response—parliamentary approval of the army's bill and incorporation of General Luque into the turno—restored military discipline, since the army still largely recognized the legitimacy of the political and military turno and of the parliamentary regime. But it also contributed heavily to the further alienation of the many Spaniards excluded from the political system. When, in 1917, disillusioned junior officers would once again intervene in the political process, the dynastic parties would find themselves even less able to resist the imposition.

It was surely no coincidence that only a few years separated the *¡Cu-Cut!* crisis from the prolonged trauma of the Dreyfus affair in France. Contemporary observers in Spain were certainly aware of the parallel.[46] Both episodes reflected the fears aroused by rapid political and social change in those most concerned with the maintenance of a strong state. Military sympathizers have denounced both incidents as unwarranted civilian intrusions into military autonomy.[47] As the guarantor of national integrity, the army must be strong, free from debilitating criticism. On the other hand, for opponents of the status quo in France and Spain, the army's immunity from and hypersensitivity to criticism were vivid reminders of the decadence of the state. In both cases, the role of the military in a liberal democracy was at the vital center of all discussions concerning political and social change; resolution of this constitutional issue was, quite justifiably, considered necessary before attention could be given to economic and social reforms. There was, however, one major difference in the two affairs. In France, the principle of civil supremacy emerged victorious from the struggle.

The Army and the Social Question

The dynastic politicians surrendered their freedom of action to the army because of fear of social revolution from below. The use of the army to suppress social unrest predated the Restoration settlement, but it had intensified as the Spanish working classes gradually acquired class consciousness through their contacts with doctrines and tactics imported from the advanced industrial societies of Western Europe. In the textile centers of Catalonia, in the mining regions of the north, and in the latifundia areas of southern Spain, labor organizers and revolutionaries took advantage of the right of association granted in 1881 to test both their own strength and that of their opponents. The result was the growing dependency of the regime on the army. By 1890 Cánovas was referring to the army as "the robust support of the social order and an invincible dike against the illegal attempts by the proletariat. . . ."[48]

A series of confrontations during the 1880s and 1890s confirmed the popular image of workers fighting an implacable alliance of capitalists, politicians, and army. Urban general strikes and agrarian revolts alike were repressed by local garrisons or by Civil Guard units under army command; in severe cases, the declaration of martial law provided the captain general of the region with near-dictatorial powers and precedence over all civil authority. Under martial law, strike leaders could be prosecuted in military courts. In addition, the broad provisions of the Code of Military Justice gave military courts jurisdiction over civilian incitement to military rebellion and sedition as well as insults or attacks on military authority.[49] Since most strikes and popular protests were accompanied by antimilitaristic sloganeering or appeals for troop defections, military tribunals regularly dealt with activities that might ordinarily have fallen under the jurisdiction of civil courts. Once they had acquired jurisdiction, military courts administered harsh sentences in summary fashion, which stood as a warning to potential strikers. After 1906, the Law of Jurisdictions increased the power of military courts over the army's critics.

Undaunted, revolutionaries quickly concluded that the regime might be most effectively attacked through its army. Popular antimilitarism was a natural outgrowth of a conscription system that fell exclusively on the working classes;[50] socialism and anarchism gave it doctrinaire expression. The army was both the symbol and the servant of the bourgeois state; deprived of its means of protection, the state, and the repressive social system, would collapse. In the 1890s, revolutionaries staged a variety of assaults on the army, ranging from antimilitaristic pamphleteering to the attempted subversion of conscripted troops. In 1893 a young Anarchist in Barcelona threw a bomb at the general most identified with the stability of the Restoration system, Martínez Campos.[51] Although the general was only slightly wounded, the terrorist was tortured and executed, and Martínez Campos's replacement as Captain General of Barcelona, Valeriano Weyler, implemented a harsh antilabor policy.[52] Inexorably, the rift between the Barcelona working class and the army widened.

Recruited largely from the traditional middle class, Spanish officers did not always identify with the class interests of the ruling oligarchy. As it did elsewhere in Europe, the divorce between people and army worried conscientious officers, who recognized that a social order resting on bayonets would in the long run jeopardize national interests. They also worried that a popularly conscripted army would be crippled by the alienation of the troops from their officers. Out of their concern grew a new definition of the army as an instrument of social reconciliation. Responding both to the increase in class conflict and to the extension of democratic values, military authors argued that the army was a national institution transcending class interests.[53] The duty of the officer was to promote social unity, not only by instilling patriotism, but also by recognizing the legitimacy of some working-class grievances.[54] Implicit in much of the literature was an assumption of the essentially artificial character of class conflict. Social harmony depended on the unselfish reconciliation of both labor and capital.

A few officers stood out for their active interest in social reform. Probably the best known and respected by labor was José Marvá y Mayer, an Engineer appointed in 1905 to the Institute of Social Reforms, where he served as head of a section specializing in industrial safety. Both at the Institute and as president of the National Institute for Social Security after 1913, General Marvá advocated extensive government regulation of working conditions.[55] But officers did not need a finely tuned social conscience like Marvá's to perceive the wisdom of recognizing "legitimate" workers' demands, and on a number of occasions, commanding officers negotiated settlements favorable to strikers.[56]

Still, whatever misgivings some officers may have had about identifying the army too closely with the established social order, the army did in fact become the willing instrument of social repression. The trigger-happy governments that responded to every major strike or peasant rebellion with a declaration of martial law must bear most of the blame for this; the army was merely obeying orders. Yet as the army was thrown against workers and peasants in increasingly bloody confrontations, the patience of many officers wore dangerously thin. Their resentment was directed against both the people whom they were called on to repress and the governments that ordered them to do it. Similarly, the working classes made no distinction between those who gave the orders and those who carried them out.

The climax to this series of confrontations between the working classes and the army was the Tragic Week in Barcelona in 1909.[57] The outbreak of violence in Spain's oldest industrial center was the immediate consequence of a renewal of military activity in Morocco.[58] When fighting broke out in July 1909, the Conservative prime minister, Antonio Maura, ordered a call-up of reserve troops to be sent as reinforcements to Africa. The Minister of War, General Arsenio Linares, called up the Third Mixed Brigade of Chasseurs, composed of both active and reserve units in Catalonia, including 520 men who had completed active duty six years earlier and had not anticipated further service.[59] Furthermore, there was no enthusiasm for a Moroccan war among the Barcelona working class, who had been coached in antimilitarism and anticolonialism by Anarchist-dominated labor organizations and by the Radical Republicans of Alejandro Lerroux. The result was the Tragic Week—an antiwar protest that degenerated into riots, strikes, and convent burnings in the last week of July. By the end of a week of bloody street fighting, the army and the police had lost 8 dead and 124 wounded, while 104 civilians were reported killed. Not only the street violence, but the subsequent repression pitted the army against the working class. Over 1,700 individuals were indicted in military courts for "armed rebellion" in the wake of the Tragic Week. Although only 5 were sentenced to death and executed, 59 others received sentences of life imprisonment.[60]

The repression of the Tragic Week had repercussions long after the event.[61] Disagreement over the repression shattered the remnants of the elite consensus that had sustained the turno. The Liberals had already violated the unstated terms of the turno by forming a "bloc" with the Republicans in 1908 in order to bring down the Maura government; the executions the following year provided the bloc with a vulnerable target. But Maura and his Interior Minister, Juan de la Cierva, refused to resign, convinced of the unmitigated evil that would come from capitulation to the "forces of anarchy," whether in Spain or abroad. Forced to exercise his constitutional function as the moderating power, the king returned the Liberals to office, but at the expense of the gentlemen's agreement that had maintained the Restoration turno. Henceforth, Maura intransigently refused to rotate in office with the party whose "sordid and troublesome collaboration" with an antidynastic party (the Republicans) had brought him down.[62] The Conservative party thus lost the only man with enough personal prestige to hold the party together. The Liberals, on the other hand, were not able to develop an alternative to Maura's policy of repression. Their Republican allies quickly abandoned them in favor of an antidynastic alliance with the Socialists—the Conjunción Republicana-Socialista. After the assassination of their leader Canalejas in 1912, the Liberal party disintegrated into a gaggle of rival personalist factions.

The bitterness generated by the Tragic Week affected the army as well. The mutual distrust of the military and the working classes was deepened by the draconian repression of the general strike in Barcelona and the subsequent military trials and executions. At the same time, officers were resentful of the Liberals' alliance with the left and their exploitation of Maura's role in the repression. Instead, they sympathized with Maura and La Cierva, whose no-nonsense attitude toward law and order had generated great hostility among the left-liberal elements in Spanish society. On the whole, the Tragic Week increased military impatience with the political system, convincing many officers that only they could be relied on to resist social disintegration.

Finally, the Tragic Week was a turning point for the Spanish labor movement, the last of the spontaneous, unstructured protests that had punctuated both rural and urban labor history in the nineteenth century. Henceforth, urban workers would be both better organized and more convinced than ever of the need for a radical alteration of the political and social order. The first fruits of this new determination were the formation of the Republican-Socialist Alliance of November 7, 1909, which led to the election of the first Socialist deputy, Pablo Iglesias, the following year, and the formation of the Anarchosyndicalist labor federation, the Confederación Nacional del Trabajo (the CNT) in 1911. The determination of labor was matched and encouraged by the reaction of the propertied classes, who braced themselves after the

Tragic Week to resist all attempts at revolution from below. Thus, as Gerald Meaker has observed, "the Tragic Week was the opening gun in the social war that would increasingly dominate Spanish life in the early twentieth century."[63]

The Renewal of the Moroccan War

Equally disruptive of the Restoration political system was the renewal of the Moroccan war.[64] As we have seen, the immediate consequence was a major confrontation between the army and the Barcelona working class. The long-range consequences were even more devastating. The war soon became the special preserve of the military, consuming lives and funds without compensating the nation either politically or economically for the expense. Bitterly opposed by the working classes who were conscripted to fight and die for a cause in which they did not believe, the war was sustained by the apathy of the middle classes and the passivity of the dynastic parties, who lacked the power to act independently of the army or of the great European powers. In Morocco, the dynastic politicians irrevocably bound their fate to that of the army. In 1923 that alliance would destroy the parliamentary regime.

The Spanish army's domination of the colonial enterprise was the result of a general lack of civilian interest in the "new imperialism" that captured the European imagination from the 1880s on. In Spain, capitalism was too cautious and nationalism too weak to provide a stimulus for colonialism. In the early years, convinced imperialists were few in number: a handful of Republican "Europeanizers" led by Joaquín Costa,[65] Staff officers with a taste for exploration and cartography, and a microscopic number of businessmen. This colonial party campaigned enthusiastically for two decades without finding an echo in the rest of the country; on the contrary, a brief but humiliating military confrontation in Morocco in 1893 and the painful and costly wars in Cuba and the Philippines conclusively dampened all enthusiasm for colonial adventures among the Spanish people.

Spanish involvement in Morocco came to depend instead on the resigned acceptance by both Conservatives and Liberals of Spain's interest in the Mediterranean balance of power. A conference of interested colonial powers called by Cánovas in Madrid in May 1880 defined Spain as an interested party in any alteration of the status quo in Morocco. After 1880, however, no Spanish government was inclined to act upon that interest. The military action of 1893 was a defense of Spain's long-established garrison in Melilla, not an expansion of her sphere of influence. When the Moroccan question was finally reactivated, it was French expansionism, not Spanish imperialism, that triggered events. In fact, Spain was too underdeveloped, economically and politically, to undertake the successful colonization of North Africa. Her essentially static policy was designed to protect her interests and her reputation as a great power without effort or expense. While the other European powers expanded their empires elsewhere in Africa, this policy was possible; unfortunately, the dynastic politicians were lulled into believing they could continue it after the turn of the century, when the power vacuum in Morocco began to attract the attention of a France cut off from further expansion in East Africa. As a consequence, they allowed Spain's hitherto theoretical interest in the Sharifian Empire to be converted into a contractual obligation to protect the sultan and to maintain order in the mountainous and sparsely settled coastal areas of northern Morocco known as the Rif, the Ghumara, and the Jibala. Henceforth, Spain was committed to action not only by strategic and status considerations, but also by the "sacred obligations" contracted in the treaties of 1904, 1906, and 1907.[66]

Thus, through vanity and inertia, Spain was drawn into a colonial enterprise that aroused no enthusiasm in any sector of Spanish society and that promised few rewards for the investment required. To be sure, as Morocco became a primary source of international tension, it was difficult for Spain to withdraw from the area. Not only was this a public admission of national weakness, but Spanish diplomats were under pressure from Great Britain to forestall French domination of the area. Nevertheless, the immediate loss of international prestige would have been far less than the ultimate cost in prestige, lives, and wealth.

Although economic imperialism was never a strong motive for Spanish intervention in Morocco, protection of Spanish investments was the immediate cause of the military action of 1909. Spanish capital, never venturesome even in the peninsula, had shown no tendency to flow toward Africa, until rich iron ore and lead deposits were discovered in northern Morocco in 1906.[67] But these could not be exploited until the benevolence of the hostile local tribes could be secured. The dilemma facing the mining consortium, and by extension, the government in Madrid, was whether to deal with the de facto power in the area—a local strongman known to the Spanish as El Roghi (Abu Himara)—or to recognize the entirely fictional sovereignty of the sultan in Marrakesh, as prescribed by Spain's treaty obligations. The consortium favored an agreement with El Roghi. The Conservative government of Antonio Maura, however, was aware that failure to observe the provisions of the 1906 treaty would give the French a pretext for intervention in the Spanish zone. In 1908 Maura ordered the Military Governor of Melilla, General José Marina, to eliminate the rebel leader and to prepare to defend the mining operations with force.[68] The foreseen attack by xenophobic Riffian tribesmen came on July 9, 1909, the prelude to seventeen years of costly colonial warfare.

The immediate response in the peninsula was the Tragic Week. But despite this outburst of anticolonialism, military operations and expenses escalated rapidly in the next few years. The principal agent of this increased activity was not the government, but the Spanish officer corps, which was transformed by its dismal performance in July 1909 from a reluctant occupying force into a bellicose colonial party bent on avenging and maintaining Spain's honor against native rebellion or French ambition. "Depressed" by the policy of peaceful attraction favored by the government's Office of Native Affairs,[69] indifferent to theories of colonial action, the African army demanded, and soon got, full-scale operations against the Moroccan "enemy." In 1911 the army began a campaign to expand the Spanish sphere of influence in the east beyond the Kert River;[70] in the west, to forestall French expansion northward from Fez, they occupied Larache, a coastal city near the roughly defined frontier. A diplomatic rupture between the two powers was averted only by the unwelcome intrusion of Germany, whose presence at Agadir in July 1911 triggered the Second Moroccan Crisis.

In the feverish negotiations that followed this international crisis, Spain's interests were represented by a vigorous colonial party composed of the prime minister, José Canalejas, a regenerationist politician in the Costa mold, Alfonso XIII ("el Africano," as he was rashly dubbed by Eugenio Montero Ríos), and the Spanish army. In March 1912 the French forced the sultan to accept the Treaty of Fez, which established a French "Protectorate" over the Sharifian Empire with the exception of northern Morocco, which was assigned to Spain in an agreement signed on November 27, just two weeks after the assassination of its architect, Canalejas.[71] Within her zone, Spain was to keep the peace and, as the document stated with unintentional irony, "to lend her assistance to the Moroccan Government in introducing all the administrative, economic, financial, judicial, and military reforms that it needs." The authority of the sultan, theoretically unimpaired by the Protectorate, would be delegated to a *khalif*, a member of the royal family nominated and supervised by the Spanish, whose local representative, the High Commissioner, was entrusted with protecting and extending that authority throughout the zone. In short, Spain was committed to a policy of tutelage and development that far exceeded both her resources and her strategic necessities.

With Canalejas no longer on hand to present the case for the Protectorate, the absence of a colonial commitment in the Spanish political community was immediately and obviously felt. Despite the government's assurance that it would "reconcile and harmonize [the] action in Africa with necessities in the Peninsula,"[72] debate in the Cortes over the ratification of the treaty produced serious reservations from both Conservatives and Liberals. Viewing the treaty as the "liquidation" of a decade of diplomacy,[73] a huge majority ratified it unenthusiastically and hoped unrealistically for a return to the status quo.[74] As a result, they effectively abandoned the field to the African army in Morocco and left themselves vulnerable to attacks from the left, which quite naturally seized upon the Moroccan adventure as the weakest point in the regime's defenses. As early as May 1914, Pablo Iglesias, the lone Socialist deputy in the Cortes, was expertly dissecting the contradictory and vacillating colonial policy of the dynastic parties, who lacked the courage to abandon Morocco and the conviction to pacify it effectively.[75] Morocco symbolized the anemic political authority of the regime, which had been maneuvered by the great powers, the king, and the army into a project for which no one else had any enthusiasm and over which they seemingly had little control. Morocco was the prime justification for revolutionary politics.

Above all, it was military action in Morocco that drew fire, if only because there was little action of any other kind. To defend its colonial policy, the regime was forced to defend the army, which was increasingly intolerant, however, of civilian supervision of its affairs, whether in the peninsula or in Morocco. Either from lack of interest or out of fear of challenging the army, successive governments refrained from establishing civilian checks on unauthorized military actions and watched impassively as military expenditures consumed nearly all the funds allocated for Morocco. Civilian inhibition in Morocco, like civilian inhibition on military reform, provided the political opposition with a vulnerable target; by immunizing the army from criticism, it guaranteed that abuses would continue. By the time the dynastic politicians were able to perceive the link between the abuses and the criticism, it was too late to deny the army what it considered its due. The military rebellion of 1923 was the defensive response of an institution whose power and privileges were under attack.

CHAPTER TWO

The Failure of
Military Reform

The interdependence of the state and the army in Spain grew out of the resistance of traditional society to the onset of modernization: the army protected the ruling oligarchy from the demands of newly mobilized social groups; the politicians in turn respected the desire of the military middle class to avoid professional reforms damaging to vested interests. As a consequence, the Spanish army was only partly professionalized by the turn of the century.[1] The military had been a career open to talents since the Napoleonic wars; by 1900 the officer corps was recruited primarily from the middle class and trained in military academies rather than in the regiments. Yet Spanish officers continued to resist essential aspects of professionalization such as selective promotions and rationalization of the military bureaucracy, because the underdeveloped Spanish economy offered them few other alternatives for employment. In addition, the army's institutional autonomy was limited by the determination of the politicians and the king to use promotions and appointments to reward the politically reliable and the well-connected. Military professionalization was thus sacrificed to the interests of the ruling elites and the middle-class clients who were the support of the Restoration system.

Military professionalization was a function of political modernization; as long as the politicians refused to broaden their base of support in the nation, military reform was impossible. The dilemma facing the politicians was that without military reform, the regime was permanently susceptible to a resurgence of praetorianism. The politicians dared not insist on reform without further antagonizing the already disaffected officer corps. Yet the unreformed army was the weak spot in a regime that was increasingly on the defensive after the turn of the century.

The Structure of the Army

The basic defect of the Spanish army was the excessive number of officers. The problem was decades old: the top-heavy officer corps was a product of pronunciamiento politics, of the amnesty policy that had incorporated defeated Carlist officers into the regular army in 1839, of the civil wars of the 1830s and 1870s and the colonial wars throughout the century. After demobilization in 1899 reduced the standing army to eighty thousand, there was a ratio of one officer to fewer than four enlisted men; eight thousand officers were without assignment.[2] The financial burden these officers represented forestalled the modernization of the army's equipment and training, which were almost completely neglected. As one tough-minded (and unpopular) military reformer put it, "however we look at the problem, we shall see that the first task ought to be and must be one of pruning; and in order to prune, we need energy more than expertise. . . ."[3]

But all proposals for more than a token reduction in personnel encountered the resistance of a bureaucratic middle class that had no other place to go. Rhetoric about the "priesthood of arms" notwithstanding, the average officer's career was his livelihood rather than his vocation. The army, like the state administration, was a haven for the traditional middle classes; to deprive them of the jobs that enabled them to starve to death with dignity was to alienate a sector of the population that, though not large, was essential to the political stability of the regime. Typical of the bureaucratic outlook of most officers was their constant refusal to comply with reductions unless they were duplicated in the civil administration.[4] While generally agreeing that reform was necessary, they invariably resisted cutbacks with the dismayed protest that one generation should not be forced to pay for the folly of previous ones.[5]

Thus, personnel reductions, which required the prolonged implementation of a vigorous policy of academy closures, early retirements, and amortizations, were minimal because of the political risk involved in attacking vested interests. "Amortization" plans involved freezing promotions by eliminating vacancies at a given annual rate. In 1899 the rate had been set at 50 percent: for every two vacancies that occurred at a given rank, only one man was promoted. Because amortizations were designed to eliminate excessive numbers of officers at all ranks but the lowest, they were particularly unpopular among junior officers, who quickly discovered that the freeze had an "exponential" effect that slowed promotions to a snail's pace. (The promotion of one captain required the previous promotion of two majors, four lieutenant colonels, and eight colonels.)

Spanish officers were accustomed to more rapid promotion than their French and German counterparts, at least at the lower ranks. It required only nine to twelve years for promotion from lieutenant to captain in the Spanish army; in the Prussian army, lieutenants spent sixteen to eighteen years in grade.[6] A Spanish Infantry officer usually reached major through seniority between the ages of thirty-eight and forty; a French officer, between forty and forty-nine.[7] At the higher ranks, however, Prussian officers spent less time in grade, since there were proportionately fewer of them. Higher ranking officers in the Spanish army were thus ultimately penalized for their early insistence on rapid promotion. Yet the impulse was understandable, for the large number of officers kept salaries, especially at the junior ranks, very low.[8] Even though amelioration was possible only if the officer corps was radically reduced, the 50 percent freeze of 1899 created so much discontent that General Valeriano Weyler lowered the amortization rate to 25 percent in 1902. At the same time, he prohibited all lieutenants from marrying unless they could demonstrate financial independence.

Significant reduction of the active list was also extremely difficult without a policy of forced retirement. In 1906 the reform-minded General Agustín Luque proposed lowering the retirement age for division generals from sixty-eight to sixty-five and for brigadiers from sixty-five to sixty-two, but he dropped the idea quickly when the senior hierarchy reacted vehemently. With the ¡Cu-Cut! incident still fresh in everyone's memory, confrontation did not seem advisable. Meanwhile, new officers continued to flow into the overcrowded corps from the military academies, which remained open at the insistence of the king and of career officers with eligible sons. In defense of the academies, it was argued that there was a shortage of lieutenants in all the corps. But that shortage, which was real enough, was of the army's own making; the ceaseless demands for rapid promotion continually depleted the lower ranks,[9] while the snobbism and professional insecurity of the academy-trained officers denied regular commissions to noncommissioned officers, who, like the troops they led, were usually of peasant origin. Rankers were promoted into a separate reserve list, which supplied lieutenants when shortages occurred without posing a threat to the career opportunities of the middle-class officers on the active list. By 1912 a surplus of academy-trained lieutenants forced General Luque to end all promotions into the reserve list, thereby eliminating one of the few avenues of social mobility for the lower classes.[10] In any event, this measure did not affect the size of the active list, which included several thousand officers with no assignment at all.

To stave off more vigorous measures, some officers argued that there was not an excess of officers, but a deficit of troops. Indeed, the fourteen divisions, consolidated and reorganized in 1904, were sadly understrength because of budgetary constraints. Many regiments had only five hundred men divided into two battalions, with a third—fully staffed with officers—on paper only. With fourteen divisions and only eighty thousand troops, each division could count at most on fewer than six thousand men. Given the lack of money, the obvious solution was a reorganization of the army into a smaller number of divisions, but of course, this would have also reduced the number of active commands at a time when a large number of officers were already without a post.

Apart from their personal stake in the outcome, the concern of Spanish officers for a large national standing army developed in the context of the arms race in the years before World War I. Dominated by the concept of the "nation in arms," the major powers, led by Germany and France, strove to increase their standing armies through new conscription laws that drafted more young men for longer periods of time. As the expectation of war grew, so did the pressures for even larger armies. In 1914 Germany had 42,000 officers for 820,000 troops; before the passage of the three-year bill in 1913, France had 29,000 officers for 540,000 troops.[11]

In contrast, Spain in 1910 had nearly 16,000 officers on the active and paid reserve lists for slightly more than 80,000 troops. While her officer-troops ratio was two to three times greater than that in France and Germany, her army was only one-third the size, per capita, of theirs. Seized by the same fears and hopes that stimulated military expansion elsewhere, Spanish officers insisted that the standing army be doubled, with a reserve army of 800,000 ready in case of war.

This was the military background for the passage, on February 27, 1912, of the conscription law sponsored by the Liberal prime minister, José Canalejas, and his War Minister, General Luque. A reflection of the European concern for universal conscription, it was also a delayed and partial response to the protests of the Tragic Week of 1909. As a solution to the injustices of the previous system, the law of 1912 was only moderately successful. Nevertheless, it established an ideal definition of the army as the military instrument of a democratic state, and thus represented an official attempt to draw the army out of its moral isolation from the rest of the nation. Its weaknesses, on the other hand, illustrated the ambivalence of the dynastic politicians—even Canalejas—toward the full implementation of democracy in Spain.

The greatest strength of the new law was its requirement that all males, except for physically exempt and hardship cases, receive some military training, after which they would remain eligible for mobilization for eighteen years.[12] But this democratic principle was abridged by a provision for "quota soldiers" released after five or ten months' training upon payment of a fee of two thousand or fifteen hundred *pesetas*. While on active duty, quota soldiers were expected to furnish their own equipment and maintenance. Opposed as undemocratic by Canalejas, the quota system was supported by the army hierarchy, who were fearful of the effect of a rapid influx of well-educated recruits upon troop discipline and military authority.[13] The system also received the support of most Cortes deputies, who argued that middle- and upper-class boys could not endure the rigors of barracks life, which of course remained unsanitary and antiquated as long as only the lower classes were affected. Undeniably, the quota amounted to a new redemption system for the privileged, who did not fail to take advantage of it.[14] Nevertheless, it represented an improvement over the old system, which had provided total immunity from both training and wartime mobilization.

The conscription law did not provide Spain with a large or well-trained instrument of national defense. Once again, the culprit was the top-heavy officer corps, whose salaries continued to devour the military budget. Many conscripts received only a few weeks' training before being sent home; there was, as usual, no money left for new equipment. The principal advantage of the law of 1912 accrued to the officer corps, whose underemployment was partially alleviated by the need for new recruitment and training centers. Furthermore, the compromises in the law of 1912 undermined the basic goals of universal conscription: democratic reform and efficient utilization of the nation's manpower for defense. Spain's army was still composed of the poorest and least fit among the general population.[15] In 1915 there were 6.3 deaths per thousand soldiers, the highest noncombatant death rate in Europe.[16] Fully one-third of the recruits were illiterate, compared to 4 percent in France and less than 1 percent in Germany.[17] In an age in which weaponry and maneuvers had become increasingly complex, the implications were alarming. So were the implications of an undemocratic conscription law in an age in which political equality was increasingly a prerequisite for political strength in the West.

The Military Budget

The military budget measured the extent to which the dynastic politicians were held hostage by the army. Between 1905 and 1915 the military budget expanded, unrestrained, by 110 percent without any noticeable increase in military efficiency; indeed, the army's poor performance in Morocco in 1909 indicated little improvement since the disaster in Cuba at the turn of the century. Burgeoning expenditures provided critics of the regime with an easy target, but apathy, combined with fear of arousing military anger, led most deputies to avoid the entire subject of fiscal reform. Traditionally, the Cortes approved the military budget after little or no discussion.[18]

The intricacies of the budget provided another obstacle to careful parliamentary analysis. Perhaps intentionally, total military expenditures were never consolidated into a global figure, which could be calculated only by adding widely separated line items: the army and navy budgets, the War Ministry totals in the Moroccan section, retirement allocations, the totals for Customs Police in the Development budget and for the Civil Guard in the Interior Ministry. Furthermore, for political reasons, the figures in the "primitive budget" presented for parliamentary approval never accurately reflected anticipated expenditures after 1908; each year the cost overruns, granted as "extraordinary" or "supplementary" credits by royal decree, were submitted to the Accounting Tribunal of the Cortes for post facto approval and funding. Since the overruns usually proved to be for normally foreseeable expenditures on troop maintenance and housing, the Tribunal, defending the appropriations powers of the Congress, often refused to recommend funding. The result was not a reduction of illegal cost overruns, which were simply tacked on to the mounting budgetary deficits, but the institutionalization of a flagrant violation of the constitution and of parliamentary rights.

To confuse critics of the military budget even further, published government statistics employed misleading indexes to mask growing expenditures. For example, the index year chosen for War Ministry budgets was 1911, the year before the creation of the Moroccan Protectorate and the division of the army budget into peninsular and African categories. Using this index, subsequent War Ministry budgets appeared to decline, while actual military expenditures in all categories rose, first gradually, then dramatically after the outbreak of the world war in 1914. In 1915 the War Ministry spent 228 million pesetas, approximately the amount spent in the index year 1911. But expenditures in Morocco in 1915 comprised another 144 million pesetas, for a total of

372 million and a rise in the real index to 161.[19] When the figures for the navy were added in, about 445 million pesetas were spent on national defense and Morocco in 1915, or 18 percent of total government expenditures (nearly half of which were consumed by interest on the skyrocketing national debt).[20] As a percentage of all expenditures except the debt, military costs represented 34 percent of the total, a much larger fraction than any other sector. Understandably, critics patient enough to ferret out the statistics were skeptical of the War Ministry's pleas for more money.

Yet the army was undeniably underequipped, poorly trained, and badly maintained; indeed, Spain was spending less on her army than other European countries in the years immediately preceding the war. If we calculate that the budget represented no more than 10 percent of national income, Spain was spending 3.4 percent of her national income on defense. In contrast, according to A. J. P. Taylor, in 1915 Germany was spending about 4.6 percent of its national income on defense; France, 4.8 percent; Great Britain, 3.4 percent; and Italy, 3.5 percent.[21] Even more significant, the 3.4 percent of Spain's national income totaled only 16 million pounds sterling, while Germany was spending 111 million pounds annually in 1914; Great Britain, 77; France, 57; and Italy, 22 million.

What aroused the critics of Spain's military establishment was not so much the amount spent, particularly in view of the world crisis, but the way in which it was allocated. The army was inefficient and antiquated because officers' salaries comprised 35 percent of the total army budget, over twice the percentage spent in France or Germany.[22] In the "primitive budget" presented by the War Minister, General Luque, in June 1916, salaries and maintenance of military personnel (officers and enlisted men) ate up 63 percent of the proposed budget of 169 million pesetas, a figure that was deliberately underestimated.[23] In Morocco, where the War Ministry consumed 101 million pesetas of the 117 million budgeted, 60 percent went to pay officers and troops. Neither budget included a breakdown of officer and troop allocations in order to disguise the fact that what was left after the officers were paid was not enough to retain most conscripts for more than a few weeks' training. In both budgets only relatively small sums were left over to pay for administrative costs, materiel, barracks, basic rations (bread and fodder), maneuvers, transport, hospitals, and other health services. At the same time, because of the large number of officers, each individual's share was small, and, at the lower ranks, admittedly inadequate under inflationary conditions.

In 1916 the basic annual pay scale for officers was as follows:

Captain general	30,000 pesetas	Captain	3,500
Lieutenant general	25,000	First lieutenant	2,500
Division general	15,000	Second lieutenant	2,115
Brigadier general	10,000	Sergeant	1,300
Colonel	8,000	Subofficial	1,150
Lieutenant colonel	6,500	Brigade	1,080
Major	5,500		

While the privileged senior hierarchy enjoyed a substantial salary, augmented by pay supplements, pensions, and other perquisites,[24] the average officer, a captain in a provincial garrison far from the capital, had to struggle to make ends meet. Although mounted posts, undesirable assignments (like the Canary Islands and the Pyrenean garrisons), and longevity increased one's pay,[25] most officers found it difficult to apply for frequent transfers since the army did not pay moving expenses. Then, too, a change of regiment often meant a change of uniform, particularly in the Cavalry Corps.[26] In some of the older regiments, the trappings of the dress uniform included plumes, gold braid and buttons, expensive epaulets, and fancy swords. Uniforms were expensive enough in any case, since there was no standard fabric or cut, and fashionable tailors vied with one another in developing distinguishing details. Furthermore, without influence in the War Ministry a transfer was difficult to obtain, particularly to the African regiments, where salaries were 50 percent higher.[27] All salaries, whether munificent or not, were subject to the "discount," an income tax on the salaries of all state employees, which ranged from 5 to 18 percent of basic pay.[28] This represented a substantial reduction in the actual salary of officers at both ends of the scale, more than canceling any supplements in most cases and causing serious discontent among lower-ranking officers who found their salaries inadequate to begin with.

One avenue of economic relief was to relinquish one's army salary in order to earn a living in a civil post. As a "supernumerary" an officer could work full time at another career without losing his place on the active list. Often a small municipality would hire an officer as its mayor or police chief; there were other officers serving as civil governors in the provinces.[29] Such an important post was beyond the reach of most officers, however.

In 1916, the average forty-year-old officer was probably still a captain on the edge of promotion to major, earning 3,500 pesetas a year plus 600 pesetas for over ten years of service at the same rank, or 352 pesetas a month. Out of this he was taxed 14 pesetas, leaving 338. This was little enough for a bachelor, especially in Madrid, where rents were high, and nearly impossible for a married officer. And the average officer did marry, usually a young woman from respectable society in his garrison or hometown. But the dashing uniform, so elegant when new, became faded and threadbare with age; so apparently, did the life of an officer's wife. Here is a typical monthly budget for a captain, his wife, and two children in 1917:

Food	120 pesetas	Tobacco	12
Rent	60	Shoes	10
Schools	18	Four meals out	10
Tailor	15	Light	8
Laundry	15	Professional journals	5
Coal	12	Ironing	3

This left about 50 pesetas to cover the cost of family clothing, domestic help, entertainment and holidays, and medical expenses.[30]

This budget is interesting for the light it sheds on the value system of Spanish officers. Most expenditures involved keeping up appearances; officers were expected to live like gentlemen on the income of a lower-middle-class clerk.[31] The eternal obsession of the middle class with appearances was exaggerated even further in the army officer, who felt that the uniform conferred greater social dignity and respect and who worried that military discipline would suffer if officers were forced to live like their social inferiors.[32] In addition, garrison life involved an extraordinary amount of fraternal socializing and gestures of goodwill in the form of testimonial banquets, plaques, and swords, all paid for with contributions from brother officers. In a world in which influence and favor were primary factors in promotion, no officer dared remain aloof from these gatherings.

The economic distress and social insecurity of the average officer do not seem to have been offset by a rich personal life. A glimpse of his preoccupations and amusements can be derived from the three leading military newspapers. Noncommissioned officers read *Ejército y Armada*, the least influential; regular officers divided their loyalties between *El Ejército Español*, the organ of Agustín Luque, the leading Liberal general, and *La Correspondencia Militar*, whose editor, Julio Amado, sympathized with discontented junior officers. By 1917 Amado was publishing five editions a day. In general, neither of the two leading dailies was remarkably informative or analytical, but their editorial pages nevertheless provided a barometer by which to measure the climate of army opinion.

The military dailies were four pages long and cost five *céntimos*. In addition to news on military legislation, assignments, and promotions, they carried a page and a half of national and international news. Editorial comment was restricted to the lead article on the front page; parliamentary debates and social disturbances in Catalonia, usually given regular columns, were generally reported without comment. Entertainment, society, and the palace dominated the rest of the papers, together with the current *crime passionel*, reported in lurid detail. The last page of each paper carried a serialized novel and advertisements for tailors, cobblers, academies, watches, wines, and patent medicines. The professional journals—one for each corps—carried the technical articles that the daily press ignored, along with an occasional uplifting essay by a prestigious general and news about corps members. But to judge from the press, the average officer was interested primarily in his professional status and in social amusements.

Underemployment, limited professional opportunities, and inefficiency fostered boredom, frustration, and hypersensitivity to criticism, especially in the middle and lower ranks. In 1905 this discontent had erupted into open rebellion during the ¡Cu-Cut! affair. In the absence of meaningful professional lives, officers were more likely to turn their attention outward and to fix the blame for military inefficiency on the civilian politicians. Yet their own hostility to personnel reductions made them equally responsible for their plight.

Intercorps Rivalries

Despite the growth of a corporate outlook that isolated the military from the political and social life of the nation, the Spanish army was deeply divided. Military rhetoric stressed the moral cohesion of the armed forces, but corporate solidarity had its limits. The internal unity of the officer corps was diminished by competition and institutional rivalries. Driven by ambition and insufficient salaries, individual officers intrigued for promotion and a larger share of the military budget, while the various branches contended for social and professional pre-eminence. The danger was that these internal conflicts could easily disrupt the political stability of the regime, since officers tended to put the blame for their grievances on the "politicians." Professional satisfaction was therefore the key to the political quiescence of the army.

The greatest gulf in the Spanish army lay between the academy-trained officers on the active list and the noncommissioned officers on the reserve list. The separate promotion lists were jealously guarded by the regular officers, for they successfully reduced the competition for state employment, traditionally the preserve of the Spanish middle class. Poorly paid, with few prospects for advancement, the NCOS tended to see themselves as an exploited subclass whose aspirations for a life of social dignity were thwarted by their superiors.

Equally significant, however, was the spiritual gulf that separated the facultative corps, or technical branches (the Artillery, the Engineers, and the Staff Corps), from the general corps (the Infantry and Cavalry). The privileged position of the technical branches—especially the Artillery Corps—and the ill-disguised resentment of the general branches were serious impediments to the stabilization and professionalization of the officer corps as a whole.[33] The preeminence of the Artillery was primarily a product of its aristocratic composition.[34] Elsewhere in Europe, the technical services had been the first to attract large numbers of middle-class officers. In Spain, however, the aristocratic purity of the Artillery Corps had been maintained by means of compulsory academy training, which had required proof of nobility until 1865, long after the abolition of this requirement in the other branches.[35] This homogeneity was intensified by the small size of the Corps—a little over one-quarter the size of the Infantry.

The social purity of the Corps was further protected by the honor court, an ad hoc system that allowed officers of equal rank to expel their peers for dishonorable conduct—immorality or financial misdeeds—without attracting publicity. It was also useful in reinforcing the solidarity and homogeneity that were the pride of the Corps and the envy of the other branches. The honor court practice was extended to the other corps in 1890. As later events were to show, however, this institution, well adapted to the small, homogeneous Artillery Corps, was difficult to transplant to the larger branches.

The Artillery shared with the other technical branches—the Engineers and the Staff Corps—the distinction that extensive academy training conferred. Although by 1875 academy training was the rule for commissioned officers in all the branches, the extra two years the technical officers devoted to more sophisticated scientific training allowed them to claim a professional superiority that was gained partly at the expense of practice in the field. Staff officers, separately recruited and overly proud of their academy training, had neglected their mission as field advisers in favor of a narrow specialization in cartography. Unlike their counterparts in the rest of Western Europe, they rejected the example of the Prussian General Staff and retained their status as a separate branch of the army.[36]

The most envied privilege of the Artillery Corps was the "closed scale"—promotion on the basis of seniority alone, up through the rank of brigadier general. Until 1889 all the technical branches had maintained the closed scale, which immunized them from the favoritism that governed most promotions in the general branches.[37] At the ranks above colonel, however, officers from the technical branches were represented in numbers far greater than their proportional strength in the officer corps as a whole, owing to the system of "dualism," which allowed them to receive merit promotions in the general corps, where the closed scale was not observed. In this fashion, the Artillery and the Staff Corps had wrested leadership in the army away from the faction-ridden Infantry in mid-century and had retained it throughout the Restoration.[38] When jealous officers in the Infantry and Cavalry pointed out the discrepancy between the small size of the technical branches and the large number of generals drawn from those corps, their protests were dismissed as the "struggle of ignorance against knowledge."[39] In reality, however, the technical branches had been favored for promotion into the senior hierarchy by the dynastic politicians, who liked their corporate spirit and political conservatism.

In 1889, under pressure from the Infantry and Cavalry, some of the privileges of the technical branches had been curtailed.[40] To blunt the effects of favoritism, the seniority principle was extended to all peacetime promotions up through the rank of colonel in all branches. On the other hand, wartime merit promotions were allowed in all the branches, including the technical corps. Dualism was abolished. For promotion to the rank of general, a system of proportional selection was established to eliminate the imbalance between the technical and general corps.[41]

The Artillery Corps was not so easily robbed of its privileges, however. The following year the Central Junta established by the Corps in 1888 to lobby for its interests persuaded the War Minister to allow officers to renounce wartime merit promotions in favor of a pensioned decoration. The closed scale—in both peace and war—thus was secured for any corps that could coerce all its members into refusing wartime merit promotions. In practice, only the Artillery and Engineers—whose members had alternative sources of income—were able to enforce a system of strict seniority promotion.[42] The Infantry and Cavalry were too large and socially heterogeneous to maintain internal controls. In the Staff Corps, the lure of wartime merit promotions, often based on favoritism, proved irresistible, and its morale was soon shattered by a flood of promotions.[43]

Even more demoralizing was the subtle attack on the special status of the Staff Corps by General José López Domínguez, Liberal Minister of War from 1892 to 1895. In 1893 graduates of a new Superior War College (the Escuela Superior de Guerra, or ESG) were given the option of becoming members of the Staff Corps or of returning to their corps of origin as *diplomados*.[44] This might have represented the initial step in the evolution of the Corps into a modern, Prussian-style "service," but López Domínguez compromised his own decree by prohibiting diplomados from occupying Staff positions in the regiments. In other respects, however, the diplomados were a privileged group,[45] and the option attracted officers torn between ambition and corps loyalty.[46] Since the diplomados represented potential replacements in the event of a dissolution of the Corps, Staff officers after 1893 lived in a state of near paranoia that was not totally unjustified.

Attempts to eliminate, or even to moderate, the intense intercorps rivalries were unsuccessful. The General Military Academy (the AGM), founded in 1882 by General Martínez Campos, was destroyed ten years later by General López Domínguez, an Artillerist who shared his Corps's antagonism to the concept of uniform training. A similar proposal in 1904 never left the planning stage.[47] Factional rivalries also undermined long-overdue administrative reforms like the creation of a General Staff, which was not established until 1904. Because it quickly became a sinecure for the friends of the War Minister, the General Staff lacked continuity. Furthermore, it chafed under its subservience to the cabinet and spent much of its time drawing invidious comparisons between the Spanish system and the absolute independence and authority of the German General Staff. This indifference to the distinction between making plans and making policy, and more tragically, to the importance of the principle of civil supremacy in a parliamentary regime, undermined the status of the General Staff, which in any event had neglected both defense plans and the special problems of colonial warfare while expanding its personnel to meet the constant demands for placement in the capital. By 1912 the chorus of denunciations, both civilian and military, was so loud that General Luque abolished it altogether.[48]

Failure in Morocco

Limited professionalization not only increased military discontent, it also discouraged the development of military proficiency. Although there had been a brief surge of interest in technical questions during the 1880s, the majority of officers continued to display little enthusiasm for professional matters. The results were readily apparent in the colonial wars of the 1890s, where the principal cause of the Spanish defeat was administrative incompetence, poor training and equipment, and low morale. The debacle of 1898 should have been a goad to military reform, but the army blamed its poor performance on political neglect rather than professional incompetence. For their part, the politicians were too divided and defensive to risk alienating the army with proposals for reform.

As a consequence, the army was ill-prepared for the outbreak of war in Morocco in 1909. Nonetheless, in contrast to its earlier indifference to colonialism, the army now insisted on monopolizing all activity in the Spanish zone. By the end of 1913, despite the professed intentions of the Liberal prime minister, the Conde de Romanones, to "civilianize" the new Protectorate, the precedents for military domination were set. Although Moroccan expenditures were removed from the War Ministry budget into a section of their own, 101 million pesetas out of a total of 108 million budgeted were delegated to the War Ministry.[49] Furthermore, the implementing orders of 1913 failed to define clearly several cloudy issues that would frustrate plans for a "civil Protectorate." One point of ambiguity was the loosely defined division of authority and responsibility between the Ministries of State and War;[50] another was the vague division of authority within the zone between the High Commissioner in Tetuan and the autonomous commanders general in Melilla, Ceuta, and Larache.[51] Coupled with the irresolute attitude of governments toward the commitment of Spanish forces and resources in Morocco, the ambiguities allowed military authorities to expand their local powers free from guidelines or supervision. In 1913 the Commander General of Larache, Colonel Manuel Fernández-Silvestre, ignored government policy and provoked a tribal leader, the Sharif Mawlay Ahmad al-Raysuni, into rebellion, making military operations unavoidable. The "Campaign of the Tetuan Road" dragged on for two years, unaffected by official government support for a pacification policy or by massive popular opposition to further military action,[52] until military activity halted at the request of the French in August 1914.[53]

Military domination of the Protectorate need not have been unproductive. In fact, the tendency of the politicians to define "political" and "military" policy as mutually exclusive was inconsistent with the realities of colonial occupation, which demanded the judicious application of both, as Marshall Hubert Lyautey was to prove in French Morocco between 1912 and 1925.[54] But unfortunately most Spanish colonial officers saw their own mission as purely military, lacked sympathy with the political aspects of colonial occupation, and regarded "civilianization" efforts as trespasses on their autonomy. The result was a disaster: a civilian policy ineffectively supported and implemented by the Ministry of State in Madrid and resented by the Ministry of War; a military policy inappropriate to tribal warfare in Morocco and unmitigated by political considerations.

Although most of the army defended the Moroccan war, few officers showed an interest in either the theory or the practice of colonial warfare. The academies continued to prepare officers for wars they would never have to fight, while in Africa the tactics and strategy appropriate to classical European warfare were applied, with disastrous results. After the Tragic Week of 1909 vividly demonstrated the reluctance of Spanish conscripts to die in Morocco, the nucleus of a colonial army was created with the organization in 1911 of the Regulars, native shock troops led by Spanish officers.[55] These officers soon became the elite of the colonial army, recognized for their competence, knowledge, and ambition.[56] Generally, however, the quality of the leadership in the African army was low. Desirable assignments in the garrison towns were made on the basis of favoritism, while the unattractive hinterland posts were rotated among junior officers whose only goal was to return to the peninsula as soon as their compulsory two years were completed.[57] The dedicated *africanistas* were overshadowed by an unedifying majority of opportunists and malcontents.

The army was no better prepared for the administration of the Spanish Protectorate, which it dominated at every level, even where civilian entities existed. Except in the largest cities, political action was carried out by unqualified junior officers assigned to the Native Police; the Office of Native Affairs, a civilian bureau, was largely ignored. In Melilla, the military held a majority of seats on the Junta de Arbitrios, or city council; throughout the zone, military courts possessed exclusive jurisdiction. In addition, the army protected and aided the civilian population in its economic exploitation of Morocco. In the eastern zone, the chief beneficiary of this collaboration was the Compañía Española de Colonización, whose secretary and largest shareholder was the son of the Commander General, Francisco Gómez Jordana. After Gómez Jordana became High Commissioner in 1915, the

"Colonizadora" was granted the contract to build the Ceuta-Tetuan rail-way.[58] But corruption flourished at all ranks, especially in the Quartermaster Corps, where the opportunities for fraud and embezzlement were abundant.[59] Indeed, the garrison towns in Morocco attracted a number of sergeants and junior officers who lived comfortably—and often scandalously—on their hardship pay, business ventures, and graft.

Like the costly and ineffective military operations, the endemic corruption provided a convenient target for the opponents of the regime. In 1916 the Catalan Republican deputy, Marcelino Domingo, initiated a humiliating two-front campaign—in the Cortes and the press—that forced the War Ministry to undertake an investigation of improper business dealings among African army officers. While the investigation led to few convictions, the publicity surrounding its findings was damaging to the credibility of the War Ministry and to the integrity of the officer corps.[60]

While such attacks united the army in self-defense, in other ways the Moroccan war divided the officer corps. It also contributed to the growing political alienation of many officers. The privileged position and extra income enjoyed by favorites in the War Ministry and the palace, and the recognition and promotions extended to those in the elite units, were resented and envied by peninsular officers, who were nonetheless unwilling to volunteer for the grueling or risky assignments in the Native Police or the Regulars. Resentment of the African army appeared immediately after the 1909 campaign, when the War Minister, General Luque, dispensed wartime merit promotions with prodigality, particularly among well-connected Staff officers and the sons of prominent generals. In December 1909 *La Correspondencia Militar*, a daily read by middle-ranking officers, carried a series of articles critical of the War Minister and his promotions policy. The articles were signed by "Santiago Vallesoletano," a pseudonym for Gonzalo Queipo de Llano, a Cavalry captain who had played a prominent part in the ¡Cu-Cut! incident of 1905. On January 12, 1910, four hundred young Infantry and Cavalry officers met outside the offices of the newspaper with its editor, Major Julio Amado, to protest wartime promotions. *ABC*, a Conservative daily, summed up their position a few days later: "There are some 2,300 Infantry and Cavalry officers who do not want to be political and who reject any government policy that, along with favoritism, introduces hateful dualisms in the Army, and who consider as an attack on their only property—their respective promotion lists—promotions that are opposed to their vehement desire for promotion on the basis of strict seniority."[61]

The agitation soon subsided, but the same year Major Amado was elected as an "independent monarchist" to the Cortes, where he pressed for the abolition of wartime merit promotions, citing in support his own poll of opinion in the provincial garrisons. In December 1911, for reasons not totally clear, Amado resigned his commission, ostensibly because his previous receipt of a merit promotion compromised his efforts to abolish them.[62] But owing to opposition from General Luque in the War Ministry and from the senior hierarchy, most of whom had been frequent beneficiaries of the existing promotions policy, Amado's dramatic campaign was a failure. The Moroccan war continued to yield a bountiful harvest of merit promotions for the well-connected, the ambitious, and the talented.[63] It also yielded an equally abundant harvest of resentment in the peninsula.[64]

The mounting opposition to wartime merit promotions within the officer corps was another product of the overcrowded lists. The placeholder in any bureaucracy relies on sheer endurance to solve his financial insecurity. Any intervention in the ranks in favor of "merit" only damages his future interests. The only hope for the unambitious career officer lay in the rigid application of the seniority principle; it was this, more than undeniable abuses, that inspired his opposition to the prevailing system of battlefield merit promotions. Proposals to alter the selection procedures and to eliminate the abuses did not modify his opposition. No modern army, of course, promoted officers on the basis of seniority alone, since the policy guaranteed mediocrity in the leadership cadres. If the merit system was open to abuse, it also rewarded a few ambitious and daring officers who saw their only chance for rapid advancement in battlefield heroics. Some officers, particularly those in the technical corps, questioned a system of rewards that neglected less dazzling but more conscientious officers. Yet while this was a justifiable criticism, the application of strict seniority, which rewarded only longevity, was a remedy worse than the disease. The real problem was that for a large number of officers whose military vocation was slight, the principal defect of the seniority system was its major virtue.

By 1914 Spain's military establishment was in shambles, her officer corps divided and resentful, her troops badly equipped and maintained, her morale low. Social and economic change had disturbed the complacency of the dynastic parties, which lacked the cohesion or the vision to respond other than with force. As the army became increasingly identified with unpopular or repressive policies in the peninsula and in North Africa, the gap between it and the rest of the nation widened, and the possibility of effective military reform diminished. Since the abuses, the privileges, and inefficiency of the army were daily visible, the army was the institution most frequently attacked by the critics of the regime. But in fact, the civil-military crisis of the opening decade of the twentieth century was only the most significant example of the general crisis affecting Spain, as her politicians struggled, unsuccessfully, to repair the shattered Restoration settlement.

CHAPTER THREE

The Juntas de Defensa

The disintegration of the Canovite political settlement was accelerated by the impact of the Great War of 1914–18. Rapid economic expansion, class conflict, and ideological bitterness—already discernible in prewar Spain—were intensified by the war; the resulting stresses on an already precarious political structure brought the monarchy first to the brink of revolution and ultimately to its demise in 1923. Although the Spanish army was spared the ordeal of the Western front, it was a protagonist in the political and social struggle that marked the collapse of the parliamentary regime in the postwar period.

The first step in the breakdown of the parliamentary monarchy was the emergence of the military Juntas de Defensa in 1917. Spain's enforced neutrality during the world war drew attention to the professional incapacity of the Spanish army, giving the politicians and the senior hierarchy the determination to pursue military reform that they had hitherto lacked. But by 1916 economic distress had alienated many junior officers from the political system, the policy of merit promotions had opened a gulf between them and their superiors, and professional frustration at Spanish neutrality had made them more sensitive than ever to criticism. In 1917 junior army bureaucrats, organized as in 1905 into "defense committees," once again pressured the government into meeting their demands. Unlike 1905, however, their rebellion was not deflected into traditional channels by their military superiors. Instead, the junior officers asserted themselves as an independent pressure group. Claiming to represent the army as a whole and posing as the instrument of national "renovation," the Juntas de Defensa were in fact created to defend vested military interests, threatened by the novel determination of the dynastic politicians and the senior hierarchy to press for army reform. The effect of their successful rebellion was to dramatize the weakness of the dynastic parties and to widen the support for democratic reform within the nation.

The Perils of Neutrality

The Crown and the dynastic parties clung fiercely to neutrality from the moment the conflict in Central Europe threatened to become a general European war.[1] Given Spain's relative diplomatic isolation and the obvious unpreparedness of the Spanish army, intervention was clearly impossible, although the Conservative prime minister, Eduardo Dato—and much of official Spain—were markedly sympathetic to the Central Powers.[2] The official position of the government did not alter throughout the war. Although the dynastic politicians did not unanimously support Germany and her allies (the Liberal party chief, the Conde de Romanones, was strongly pro-Allied),[3] they did agree that only neutrality could spare Spain a certain military defeat and might possibly win her an influential place as a mediator at an eventual peace commission.[4] The king, too, skilfully maintained an impenetrable neutrality throughout the war, although the early triumphs of the German army seem to have inclined him to anticipate a German victory.[5]

But strict neutrality proved difficult to maintain because the international struggle soon became identified with the bitter domestic quarrel between the "two Spains."[6] The battle was fought among the educated, politically aware upper third of the nation; the other two-thirds, largely rural and illiterate, remained indifferent to the outcome of the war. In general, the right—the aristocracy, the ruling elites, the church, and the army—supported the Central Powers, while the left, with the exception of the Anarchosyndicalists and a minority faction of Socialists who preached proletarian neutrality, desired an Allied victory. The country divided geographically as well, with the industrial periphery pro-Allied and the rural center—and the court in Madrid—pro-German. Barcelona, however, was the focal point of German espionage in Spain, at least partly because of the antiwar convictions of the Anarchosyndicalists and their followers, who considered both sides to be bourgeois reactionaries. For nearly everyone else in political Spain, the outcome of the war was of the greatest significance. The right viewed a German victory as insurance against the extension of liberal and democratic values in Spain; the left yearned for an Allied victory for the same reason. Indeed, as it became clearer that Spanish neutrality could only benefit Germany (and her supporters in Spain), the pro-Allied and progressive left clamored impatiently for Spanish "moral intervention" on the side of the Western powers.

Fully conscious that the army was neither morally nor materially prepared for a full-scale war, the officer corps accepted Spanish neutrality in 1914 with an almost audible sigh of relief. "Moral intervention" on either side would have exposed the incapacity of the army for active belligerency; thus they insisted on adhering to strict neutrality throughout the war. Officers were nevertheless humiliated and frustrated by Spain's isolation from world affairs. Spain had become a "toy in the hands of foreign neighbors, with less freedom of action than a small country like Holland or miniscule Switzerland."[7] Officers vehemently denied their own responsibility for Spain's military impotence, blaming instead the politicians for their neglect of military affairs.

While advocating neutrality, the officer corps was overwhelmingly *germanófilo*, for both positive and negative reasons. Admiration for the Prussian army had been a tradition among Spanish officers since the Prussian victories fifty years earlier, its technical accomplishments only slightly less envied than the discipline and authoritarianism that were a reflection of Prussian society as a whole. The army's enthusiasm for a German victory was also inspired by its hatred of the Allies and of the Allies' supporters within Spain. *Aliadofilismo* was for many officers but another expression of the unpatriotic antimilitarism that had characterized the Spanish left since the 1890s.

The presence of England in the Triple Entente was the biggest obstacle to military aliadofilismo. Unreconciled to the loss of Gibraltar, even after two centuries, Spanish officers eagerly awaited a German victory that would return the lost territory to Spain.[8] In March 1917 the Military Governor of Cadiz, General Miguel Primo de Rivera y Orbaneja, publicly proposed an alternative: the abandonment of the Moroccan Protectorate and the transfer of Ceuta to Britain in exchange for Gibraltar.[9] The suggestion met with little favor, either in the government, which quickly deprived him of his command, or in the rest of the officer corps, which was largely pro-Moroccan and anti-British.

Many officers regarded France with almost equal distaste. Ill feeling over French intrusions into Spanish Morocco in 1911 had not dissipated with the treaty of 1912; the military hiatus in the zone imposed at French request in 1914 only deepened their suspicion. Historical and ideological antipathies also played a role. Like England, France was a traditional enemy whose past sins outweighed present economic and diplomatic interests. Furthermore, the anticlericalism and antimilitarism of the Third French Republic did not recommend continental parliamentary democracy to Spanish officers, who were also inclined to make invidious comparisons between the "degenerate" and "anachronistic" French and the "scientific" Germans.[10] *Aliadófilo* assertions that the war represented the struggle of Western "civilization" against German "barbarism" were vigorously rejected by the military press.

Of course, military attacks on the political and cultural values of the Western powers were also intended for their partisans within Spain, particularly the left-wing intellectuals affiliated with the magazine *España*, edited by the Socialist Luis Araquistáin. Founded in 1915, *España* was aliadófilo, interventionist, and also (somewhat contradictorily) antimilitarist; in the summer of 1916 it contributed to the Republican deputy Marcelino Domingo's exposé of corruption in the African army.[11] Both these campaigns aroused the military press to a fever pitch of denunciation against intellectuals and interventionists in general, and the contributors to *España* in particular.[12]

For the left, Spanish neutrality was an outgrowth, like the war in Morocco, of the corrupt constitutional system that allowed the king, the oligarchy, and the army to rule without regard for popular opinion. Increasingly, they viewed an Allied victory as the precursor to a long-overdue political revolution that would democratize the Spanish regime. On February 1, 1917, the German announcement of renewed submarine warfare against all neutral shipping with England and France exacerbated the tensions between germanófilos and aliadófilos and brought the constitutional issue into focus. The German blockade, which threatened both commercial and agricultural interests in Spain, lent credence to the left's demands for a rupture with Germany, if not intervention on the Allied side.[13] Even the right was shaken by the German announcement. But a rupture without a declaration of active belligerency would have placed the Spanish army in a humiliating position by exposing its inability to fight. When the Romanones government responded to the blockade on February 6 with a note stiff enough to lead to a break in relations with Germany,[14] germanófilos in the officer corps intensified their public and private support for absolute neutrality.[15] On February 16 aliadófilos in the Cortes, including Catalan regionalists and Republicans of various stripes, demanded clarification of the government's foreign and colonial policy, while asserting parliamentary responsibility for the formation of such policy.[16] Caught between the opposition parties in the Cortes and the germanófilo majority in the army and in his own party, Romanones dismissed the claims of parliamentary sovereignty with a call for patriotic unity the following day.[17] Then, mindful that unity was entirely rhetorical, Romanones precluded the possibility of further divisive discussion by closing the Cortes on February 24. In suspending the parliament, Romanones reaffirmed the inviolability of the political settlement of 1876. At the same time, of course, he exposed the principal weakness of the Canovite system: its ambivalent attitude toward popular sovereignty and its dependence on the military.

The Economic Effects of the War

The impact of the European war on Spain was not only ideological but also economic. The nations at war eagerly purchased all the raw materials and manufactures that Spain could send them, regardless of quality. But governments in Madrid proved incapable either of moderating the deleterious effects of excessive demand or of profiting from the economic boom by facilitating industrial expansion. Instead, they clung to their traditional policies of industrial laissez-faire and agricultural protection, thus providing further ammunition for the groups demanding political renovation.

The failure to expand Spain's industrial plant during the war has been blamed alternatively on the lack of entrepreneurial spirit among Catalan businessmen and on the representatives of Castilian agricultural interests who controlled the government in Madrid.[18] Certainly, the hostility of Madrid to Catalan demands for a free port and export subsidies was unrelenting, particularly after the appointment of Santiago Alba, a representative of the Castilian wheat growers, to the Ministry of Finance in December 1915.[19] As a consequence, the party of Catalan big business, the Lliga Regionalista, stepped up its nationalist rhetoric, becoming a vocal segment of the pro-Allied, renovationist opposition to the political status quo in Madrid.

But Spanish industrialists were also partly to blame for the wasted opportunity for industrial expansion. Production of most goods, particularly iron and steel, did not rise nearly as rapidly as prices.[20] The principal beneficiary of the wartime boom was the banking complex that would dominate Spanish finance in the twentieth century. As gold reserves expanded, some prewar foreign investments passed into Spanish hands, and the peseta was strengthened and stabilized on the world market.[21] Otherwise, the only beneficiaries of the war boom were the entrepreneurs and speculators who profited from the Allied demand for Spanish goods. Particularly in Catalonia, a new class of nouveaux riches appeared whose disregard for bourgeois virtue and moderation scandalized both the poor and the well-established rich.

For most Spaniards, however, the war brought scarcity and inflation. As foreign demand for goods and foodstuffs outstripped the ability of Spain's inefficient industries and agriculture to supply them, prices in Spain rose, gradually until 1917, then vertiginously until 1920. Although employers generally acceded to wage demands in order to avoid costly strikes, wages always lagged behind prices, partly because the steady influx of agricultural workers into the industrial centers undercut labor's bargaining power,[22] partly because employers transferred higher wage costs to consumers in the form of higher prices. From 1914 to March 1917, prices rose 23 percent while wages rose only 10 percent. By 1920 the difference would be even greater—a 79 percent increase in wages alongside a price rise of 100 to 120 percent.[23]

Both Conservative and Liberal governments proved incapable of dealing effectively with the economic crisis. Attempts to regulate the export of scarce commodities, especially food and fuel, were timid and ineffectual. Nor were there any successful efforts to equalize the economic burden of wartime inflation. In 1916 Santiago Alba, Minister of Finance in the Romanones government, prepared a program of "national reconstruction" to be financed by new sources of tax revenue and by cutbacks of government employees. On June 3, 1916, he introduced a bill levying a direct tax on "excess" wartime profits,[24] but was forced to withdraw it on July 11 after it was opposed by the already truculent Catalan industrialists, who quite correctly pointed out that no taxes were to be levied against the profits of the Castilian agricultural interests represented by Alba.[25] The result of the confrontation was a further decline in the authority of the Liberal party, balanced by a rise of the political stature of the Catalan Lliga Regionalista and its leader, Francisco Cambó. Meanwhile, the tremendous profits in both the industrial and the agricultural sectors remained untaxed.[26]

Inflation and scarcity, and the absence of vigorous government measures to control them, hit the urban working classes first; their restlessness would spread in 1918, like the inflation itself, to the countryside. During 1916 food shortages, unemployment, and strike activity in the cities increased along with membership in the two major labor federations, the Socialist Unión General de Trabajadores (UGT) and the Anarchosyndicalist CNT. In order to harness popular discontent and to force the government to take action, representatives of the two rival unions established contact in July 1916, thus taking the first step toward healing the debilitating division within the Spanish labor movement.[27] This meeting was immediately followed by a successful strike for union recognition by the Railworkers' Union of the North, and by a joint UGT/CNT pact signed on November 26 in Saragossa that committed the two unions to a twenty-four-hour general strike on December 18 to protest scarcity and high prices. When this strike had no effect, the union leaders agreed on March 27, 1917, to a more radical measure to force the government's hand—a general strike of indefinite duration. Planning for the strike began in April.[28]

Thus, by March 1917 the labor movement, unified for the first time in Spanish history, was demanding government intervention on a scale that would have substantially altered both political and economic power in the nation. The government's response to labor, like its response to the political left and to the Catalan regionalists, was defensive. At each show of labor strength, union leaders were arrested and workers' centers closed. In July 1916 Romanones suspended both the Cortes and the constitutional guarantees, repressive measures he repeated the following spring. While affecting a grim bravura and offering the war as an excuse for these acts of desperation, Romanones exposed the inflexibility of the dynastic parties, who preferred to view the labor problem as one of order rather than as one of social change.[29]

Nevertheless, the threat of an indefinite general strike aroused governmental concern and attracted attention to the plight of the urban working class. The publicity given working-class grievances and the success of the strike tactics were a discernible source of tension in the officer corps. After the UGT/CNT agreement of March 27, *La Correspondencia Militar* editorialized: "There is no governing party or party willing to govern that does not inscribe at the head of its program a series of reforms aimed at the limitless improvement of the working classes. They have attained benefit after benefit, without a hint of declaring themselves satisfied, while another class—unhappy, helpless, and amorphous—the middle class, sees its situation grow daily worse without glimpsing any hope of relief."[30] Salaries in the civil and military bureaucracies, inadequate even before the war, had not been raised, in spite of the accelerating price rise. The military press, especially *La Correspondencia Militar*, complained daily about the export of scarce commodities, profiteering, and the high price of food and lodgings. By early 1917 many officers were impatient both with the government's inactivity and with the legal restraints that prohibited the organized public expression of military grievances.

In the spring of 1917 the political and economic tensions generated by the war appeared to be approaching a climax. In March the abdication of the czar in Russia and the formation of a bourgeois provisional government containing Liberals and Socialists gave hope to the Spanish left, who predicted a similar fate for the Spanish monarchy, once an Allied victory was assured. That victory seemed more plausible in April after the entry of the United States into the war. On April 9 outrage in Spain over the German blockade reached its peak when the Spanish freighter, the *San Fulgencio*, was sunk off the French coast. Romanones, still a convinced aliadófilo, endeavored to persuade the majority of his party to support a severe note to Germany; when he failed, he resigned on April 19. The same day, the king asked the leader of the neutralist faction in the Liberal party, Manuel García Prieto, to form a government.

Alfonso's failure to use his constitutional powers to support an interventionist position further angered the left. Alfonso, however, was worried about the security of his throne, particularly after the sudden collapse of the Russian monarchy in March. Republican and Socialist rhetoric increasingly stressed the extensive power of the monarchy under the Spanish Constitution of 1876; in a well-publicized speech in the Socialist Casa del Pueblo in Madrid on February 27, the Catalan Republican Marcelino Domingo had laid the entire responsibility for the Moroccan war at the foot of the throne.[31] Democratization of the political system might well eliminate the monarchy altogether. Thus Alfonso prepared to use his considerable power and influence to resist political change.

To draw attention to the key role of the monarchy, the pro-Allied left sponsored a meeting in the Madrid bullring on the king's birthday, May 27. Representatives of the bourgeois left, together with some Socialists,[32] assembled to urge "moral intervention" on the Allied side in order to align Spain with the progressive and democratic forces of the West. Comparing the struggle in Europe to the struggle within Spain, a parade of Republican and Radical notables denounced strict neutrality as pro-German, excoriated the Spanish army, and called on the king to initiate the impending transformation of Spanish society. The Radical Republican leader, Alejandro Lerroux, captured the emotions of many in his opening exhortation: "Citizens: left and right, progress and reaction, justice and despotism—that is for me the problem contained in this war."[33] Spain was neutral, but not isolated. The battle had been carried to the very heart of the country.

The Formation of the Barcelona Junta

The formation of the military Juntas de Defensa and their triumph over the Liberal government of Manuel García Prieto on June 1, 1917, can be understood only in the context of the political and economic crisis brought about by the war. By exposing the incapacity of the army, the war forced the dynastic politicians to confront the necessity of serious military reform. The proposed reforms, however, struck at the security of bureaucratic middle-ranking officers, who also suffered most from inflation, shortages, and the antimilitaristic propaganda of the aliadófilo left. When junior officers organized to protect themselves from further reforms damaging to their interests, the government and the Crown were too shaken by the prospect of political and social revolution to offer effective resistance. Civil supremacy was thus sacrificed to secure army loyalty.

Parliamentary consideration of military reform had begun within a year after the outbreak of the war. On November 8, 1915, General Ramón Echagüe, Minister of War in the Conservative government of Eduardo Dato, had introduced a group of reform bills that included earlier retirements, personnel reductions, and the reestablishment of the two chief organs of military planning, the General Staff and the Junta of National Defense, both abolished by General Luque in 1912.[34] Only the last two administrative reforms had been approved, however, when the government fell after a Liberal interpellation on the preparation of a new budget. General Echagüe's reforms were abandoned, and the officer corps seemed once again to have escaped the agony of radical surgery.

The reprieve was a brief one, however, for the new Liberal prime minister, the Conde de Romanones, brought to the War Ministry General Agustín Luque, the reformer who had engineered the conscription law of 1912. During 1916 Luque prepared a comprehensive military reform bill, which was introduced in the Senate immediately after the opening of the Cortes on September 27.[35] At the heart of the plan was an increase of the standing army to 180,000, financed by a substantial, though hardly radical, reduction of officers. Luque proposed a reduction of the first-line army from fourteen divisions to ten, with another eight divisions in cadre; the active divisions were to be strengthened and relocated for strategic defense. Although the eight skeleton divisions provided active posts for more officers than before, Luque calculated that the new organization would require only 13,805 officers, making 3,171 active and paid reserve officers currently with assignments superfluous.[36] Nearly all the excess officers were at the rank of captain or above;[37] in fact, the new organization required 1,067 more lieutenants than were available on the lists in 1916. Although the excess—nearly 25 percent of the names in the *Anuario Militar*—would continue to receive their current salary "as a burden of justice," their numbers were to be gradually reduced by a combination of amortizations, earlier retirements and selective promotions. As a first step, Luque had established a 50 percent freeze on promotions in January 1916. In the long run, Luque predicted his reductions would amount to an annual savings of 11 million pesetas. The savings could be directed toward modernization of equipment and training and to the elevation of salaries for the remaining officers.

The bill also addressed the touchy question of merit promotions.

Out of both habit and conviction, Luque was a die-hard supporter of selective promotions. Nevertheless, he was anxious to placate the advocates of the seniority principle, who still remembered his deluge of battlefield promotions in 1910. As a compromise, Luque suggested a theoretical affirmation of the selection principle at all ranks, with proportional representation for all branches at the ranks above colonel—to be implemented, however, at some unspecified time in the future, when his proposed reforms had made a selection procedure based on aptitude and experience more meaningful. In the meantime, the existing peacetime seniority system would continue, modified only by aptitude tests administered to officers eligible for seniority promotions. In this fashion, the physically or professionally unfit could be prevented from rising above their capabilities.

In another effort to overcome his personal unpopularity, Luque proposed reopening the reserve list, which he had closed to noncommissioned officers in 1912. While this contradicted his goal of reducing the number of officers, it was a gesture aimed at expanding the social base of the officer corps and at opening career opportunities for the lower classes, while at the same time redressing the deficit of subalterns. The bill also proposed lower retirement ages for all ranks in order to speed up promotions and to modify the age structure of the officer corps, which was excessively elderly. In order to soften the blow for the senior hierarchy, Luque advocated a two-tier system to allow generals to retire in stages.

Luque's reform bill was a brilliant exercise in compromise. The number of divisions was reduced, but the number of active commands was reduced very little, thus minimizing the necessary cutbacks. The aptitude tests undermined the cherished principle that an officer's job was his inalienable property, but stopped short of a selection process based solely on merit. Luque opened the reserve list to NCOs, but hesitated to challenge the traditional separation of active and reserve lists. Officers would retire earlier, but in stages. It was the bill's moderate approach to reform, however, that made it a plausible first step after decades of immobility. By December 3, 1916, it had passed the Senate and had been introduced in the Congress. Its success was not entirely due to Luque's skill as a political compromiser, but also to the profound shock of the European war, which had exposed Spain's military disarray to public scrutiny. Even the most tradition-bound military senators, agreeing for once on the need for action, declined to oppose the bill because of its retirement provisions, as they had in the past.

Of course, the sacrifices imposed by the bill would have affected the senior hierarchy least; its major provisions threatened officers in the ranks below colonel, who wanted military efficiency and higher salaries without cost to themselves. Even before the details of the reform bill had become known, *La Correspondencia Militar*, and the middle- and lower-ranking peninsular officers for whom it spoke, began to protest the promotions freeze and the aptitude tests, which were already in effect, pending passage of the law. When the Ministry announced in January 1917 that in one year 272 vacancies had been amortized, at a savings of 1.4 million pesetas, the paper reminded Luque and its readers that "exaggerated virtues degenerate into vices."[38] By that time, however, junior officers in Barcelona had moved beyond complaints into action, forming a defense committee to resist implementation of the reforms.[39]

The incident that touched off their rebellion was the announcement in mid-1916 of the commencement of proficiency tests for officers eligible for seniority promotions. The protest arose in Barcelona, where envy and resentment of the favored Madrid garrison was strongest and where the economic and political tensions created by the war were most concentrated. The Captain General of the Fourth Region, General Felipe Alfau Mendoza, proposed a series of exercises that would have halted the advancement of officers grown fat and lazy after long, inactive careers behind their desks. One general asked to be passed to the reserve immediately rather than submit, and overall resistance was so great that the matter was dropped for several months. When Alfau returned to it, he chose to examine two majors and a lieutenant colonel from the Infantry on a public field before a large audience of not very reverent spectators. Although the officers passed the tests, which were simple enough, their public humiliation aroused much indignation in the Barcelona Infantry regiments, particularly after they learned that the Artillerists and Engineers had refused to submit to the inspections.[40]

After discussing their grievances, junior Infantry officers concluded that the Juntas de Defensa of the technical corps were responsible for their immunity from the detested reform. The Artillery's Central Junta, created in response to the reforms of 1888–89, had successfully lobbied against measures detrimental to the interests of the Corps on several occasions, preserving the Corps's traditional immunity from wartime merit promotions and promotions from the ranks.[41] At the local level, regimental Juntas occasionally acted as ad hoc honor courts to enforce the renunciation of merit promotions and to punish otherwise undesirable conduct. The reforms of the 1890s had inspired the formation of similar Juntas in the Staff Corps and in the Engineers;[42] eventually, impressed by the privileges and solidarity of the Artillerists, the diplomados and the Cavalry had established Central Juntas as well. Although only the Artillerists and the Engineers had been able to enforce the renunciation of battlefield promotions, the various Central Juntas had often been able to act as a pressure group to further the interests of their respective branches or to resist unwanted "reforms."

Now, in the fall of 1916, junior Infantry officers in Barcelona began to organize their own Junta de Defensa.[43] The grievances common to Spanish officers after the turn of the century were felt most keenly in the Infantry; it was they who had suffered most from inadequate salaries, wartime merit promotions, royal and party favoritism, amortizations, and most recently, Luque's reform bill, whose details were made public in August 1916.[44] It was natural that Infantry officers should find a logical connection between their victimization and their lack of a Central Junta, equally natural that the movement should originate not in the favored Madrid garrison, but in Barcelona, where resentful officers were firsthand witnesses to the activities of labor and regionalist groups.

The organizers of the movement harbored both immediate and long-range goals: resistance to further implementation of the Luque reforms, the establishment of a "closed scale" for the Infantry, and the elimination of favoritism. All this was to be achieved by means of a binding and sacred pact among all members of the Corps except the generals, who were considered to be part of the problem. Soon the young officers had persuaded a majority of the field-grade officers in the Barcelona regiments to support the Junta,[45] and leadership of the movement was assumed by the colonel in command of the Vergara regiment, Benito Márquez Martínez. Once they had solidified their support in Barcelona, the *junteros* began to promote the formation of local Infantry Juntas in garrisons throughout Catalonia by petitioning a change of assignment for organizers from the Barcelona units.

In December 1916 the Infantry Junta submitted its proposed statutes to the Captain General of Barcelona, General Felipe Alfau, for approval. The statutes were reflective of the trade-union character of the Junta, whose organization and goals were designed to protect the job security and professional advancement of the military middle class. The document began with an extensive preamble that explained the formation of the "Junta de Defensa of the Active List of the Infantry" in glowing terms: "The ardent desire to make the Fatherland great and powerful by means of the combined effort of all its children; the conviction that this requires a strong, well-endowed, trained, and enthusiastic army; the consequent desire for improvement and progress that the Infantry has felt for many years. . . ."[46] Similar high-minded language described the aims of the Junta in the first article, but beneath the rhetoric the basically bureaucratic orientation of the Junta was clearly visible. The ultimate goal, the "internal satisfaction" of Infantry officers, was defined in the statutes as depending on the exclusion from the Junta of generals and rankers, the enforcement of group solidarity, and the improvement of economic conditions. At one level, these aims reflected a reasonable desire for institutional autonomy from political favoritism; at another, they represented an unhealthy impulse to remove standards of excellence or achievement as criteria for promotions and appointments.

Most of the articles outlined the structure and operating procedures of the Junta de Defensa, a hierarchy of local and regional committees with a Superior Central Junta in Barcelona—not Madrid. Local Juntas composed of representatives from every rank were to act as the link between the individual officer and the Corps as a whole, whose collective opinion was to be established by a two-thirds vote of all Junta members. Once determined, this collective or corporate opinion was to be binding upon all members, who were also sworn to secrecy under threat of expulsion. Initially, members would be recruited individually in the regiments, but in the future, graduating cadets would be asked to sign a pledge as they did in the Artillery. The "act of adhesion" obligated the individual to place the collective good—as defined by the Junta—ahead of his own well-being. In return, his colleagues promised to protect him from ministerial reprisals by supplying any resulting loss of income.[47]

Both the statutes and the pledge were attempts to adapt the envied traditions of the aristocratic Artillery Corps to the much larger and heterogeneous Infantry. Inevitably, this meant the substitution of coercion for natural solidarity and similarity of outlook. The Infantry Junta, as conceived by its founders, was to act as a pressure group not only against the government but also against recalcitrant members who might be tempted to place personal ambition ahead of the collective good. In the Artillery, the "opinion of the Corps" had been a general sentiment shared by gentlemen of independent means; in the Infantry, it was to be determined by majority rule, a "democratic" provision that guaranteed a preponderant voice to the lower ranks and, in effect, stood the chain of command in the regiments on its head.

Somewhat surprisingly, given the insubordinate tone of the statutes, General Alfau received them with approval. One can only speculate about his motives, but it is possible that he may have viewed the Juntas as potential clients on which to build a political power base, much as Luque had done in 1905. Alienated from Romanones and the leading Liberal generals since a brief tenure as High Commissioner in Morocco in 1913, Alfau may have sympathized with the anti-Madrid sentiments of the younger men. He also enjoyed a modest reputation as an intellectual and reformer, which perhaps explains his sensitivity to their grievances. His own explanation of his actions in 1917 focused on the injustice of prohibiting the Infantry Junta when Juntas existed legally in the other corps. In his view, this discriminatory policy might well lead to outright rebellion.[48]

The statutes of the Infantry Junta, however, already contained overtones of rebellion, or at the very least, of insubordination. The pointed exclusion of generals, the rigid hierarchical organization, and the centralization of the Junta in Barcelona indicated that the goals of the Infantry Junta outstripped the limited ones of the other branches. Significantly, Alfau unsuccessfully attempted to persuade Colonel Márquez to delete the provisions excluding the generals. Yet apparently he offered no objections to the other articles. It seems likely, therefore, that Alfau's sponsorship of the Barcelona Junta was at least partly inspired by his own political ambition.

By November 1916 the activity of the Barcelona Junta had come to the attention of the War Minister, General Luque, whose instincts were offended by both the goals and the methods of the Barcelona activists. Resolving to nip the movement in the bud, he instructed all captains general to question their colonels about the existence of Juntas in their regiments. Within a week, he had received reassuring replies from everyone but General Alfau in Barcelona.[49] Alfau did not respond to Luque's November telegram until January 8, when he finally admitted to his contacts with the Junta. Arguing that the best policy was "to use and guide the currents of union and esprit de corps toward legitimate and beneficial objectives," Alfau assured his superior that discipline was not endangered by the existence of the Junta. At the same time, he enclosed a slightly modified version of the statutes for the Ministry's approval.[50]

Luque responded by ordering Alfau to Madrid to discuss the situation. On January 13 Alfau was in the capital, where he conferred with both Luque and the king. Apparently he was instructed to put an end to the Junta, for on January 29 he informed the Ministry that it had been officially dissolved.[51] In reality, the Barcelona Junta de Defensa had been formally dissolved for only twenty-four hours.[52] When it re-formed, Alfau took no further measures, although he seems to have temporarily curbed juntero proselytizing. On February 10 Alfau returned to Madrid, where he again attempted to persuade the king and the government to authorize the Junta in the name of both equity and political expediency. Perhaps to gain time, Romanones and Luque agreed to reconsider if the Infantry Junta adopted a form similar to the older Juntas: they suggested abandoning the elaborate syndical organization in favor of a looser structure entrusted primarily with honor court functions.[53] This gave Alfau and the Junta the loophole they needed. On February 26 Alfau wrote again to Luque, enclosing the statutes of a theoretically new organization, christened the "Union of the Infantry" and supposedly modeled on the other branch Juntas.

This time, Alfau's ace in the hole was the conditional support of the king, who, he assured Luque, "believed that the moment had arrived to organize a junta in harmony with what the other Arms and Corps had done."[54] Aware of the existence of the Infantry Junta since the summer of 1916, Alfonso had initially opposed the idea,[55] since it was partially directed against the circle of royal and ministerial favorites in Madrid. But by the winter of 1917 the king was acutely sensitive to the need to keep army opinion on the side of the throne. After his conversations with Alfau in January and February, he seems to have decided to compromise.

By this time, however, General Luque had reconsidered his agreement with Alfau on February 10. In a letter to Alfau on March 7, he vigorously rejected the statutes of the proposed "Union of the Infantry." Luque saw the Juntas as an institution appropriate to the smaller, more homogeneous branches. In the Infantry, "the branch of the multitudes," they presupposed a formal and rigid organization that posed a threat to military discipline. Luque closed his letter by announcing that he would advise the king to forego his support of the Union of the Infantry.[56] Alfau tried one more time, rather peevishly complaining of the unjust discrimination against the Infantry, when Juntas in the other branches continued to exist.[57] But on March 17 Luque pointedly advised Alfau that he had persuaded the king to support his viewpoint and that he would discuss the matter no further.[58]

The Expansion of the Juntas

As far as Luque was concerned, his letter of March 17 was his final word on the subject, but to placate ruffled tempers, he and Romanones made two important concessions. On March 26 a royal decree reduced the amortization rate on vacancies to 25 percent. Then on April 3 Alfau received a telegram announcing the dissolution of the Central Juntas of

the Artillery and the Engineers.[59] The government expected this measure to put the Juntas to rest for good. Instead, the decree galvanized
the various branch Juntas to act in concert. By May 1917 the Juntas de
Defensa were able to present a united front to the government.

It was intercorps rivalries, not army solidarity, however, that first
reactivated the Juntas of the technical corps in 1917. Artillery units
in the provincial garrisons were alarmed by the organization of local
Infantry Juntas, which, as the La Coruña Artillery Junta put it, "in
trying to achieve their goals, might diminish ours and invade some of
the important functions presently entrusted to the Corps."[60] On the
other hand, the local Artillery units shared the resentment of their
Infantry counterparts against the officers in Madrid, including their
own Central Junta.[61] The friction between the provinces and the capital exploded into open conflict after April 3. The decree dissolving
the Central Artillery Junta was a political maneuver engineered by
its president, Colonel Angel Galarza, who owed the prime minister,
Romanones, a favor. In 1916 the newly created General Staff had
begun to study the elimination of the closed scale, and Galarza, a
senator affiliated with the Liberals, had persuaded Romanones to
cancel the study. In April 1917, when Romanones asked Galarza to
repay the favor by dissolving the Central Junta, Galarza acquiesced.[62]
Thus betrayed by their own leadership, local Artillery units moved to
defend themselves. On May 2 the Barcelona Artillery Junta sent a
circular to all regimental Juntas (except the perfidious Central Junta in
Madrid), lamenting the actual situation of the Corps and urging them
to send delegates to an assembly in Barcelona on May 15 in order to
decide upon a unified course of action.[63]

The emergence of the Infantry Junta also prodded Juntas in the
other corps into action. The solidarity that had eluded the Staff Corps
since the 1890s appeared quickly enough after the formation of the
Infantry Junta, many of whose members resented the privileges and
even the existence of the Staff Corps. In November 1916 the Central
Junta of the Staff Corps drew up statutes similar to those formulated
by the Infantry and asked Staff officers in each captaincy general to
collect signatures to a pledge of solidarity and mutual defense. By
February, 255—more than two-thirds of the Corps—had signed, although the general distrust of the officers stationed in Madrid had
prompted Barcelona Staff officers to insist that their Central Junta contain representatives from each military region.[64] The dissenters who
refused to sign the pledge were mainly colonels and officers in the
Madrid garrison, men with a stake in the status quo.[65] But the desire to

present a united front against any inopportune demands of the new Infantry Junta made them reluctant to oppose actively the organization of a defense junta for their own corps.

By late April 1917 there was an extensive network of Juntas in all branches of the army. The ease and rapidity with which these units were organized measured the degree of professional discontent and economic insecurity within the officer corps. Significantly, the last to join the movement were the Infantry regiments in Madrid and neighboring Guadalajara, and in Melilla, where organization was slowly getting underway under the direction of Colonel Eduardo López de Ochoa.[66] Provincial junteros viewed these holdouts as proof of their contention that officers in the capital and in Africa owed their comfortable posts to intrigue and favoritism,[67] charges angrily denied by the accused, who counterattacked with warnings against "committees that tend to compel or diminish the prerogatives of public power."[68] However accurate these criticisms, they were interpreted as a desperate defense of threatened privilege by the junteros. With opinion in the officer corps overwhelmingly against them, the Infantry regiments in Madrid and Africa would soon fall into line under the pressure of *"compañerismo."*

In the midst of this activity, which had been carefully concealed from the public, Romanones resigned. Caught between mounting interventionist sentiment, with which he sympathized, and the adamant neutrality of the majority of his cabinet, Romanones found himself without support at a moment when confrontation over the Juntas was increasingly likely and, because of the political and social unrest provoked by the war, also increasingly risky. It was probably somewhat with relief that Romanones resigned in favor of García Prieto on April 19, even though the political crisis signaled the end of his undisputed leadership of the Liberal party.

Replacing Luque in the War Ministry was General Francisco Aguilera Egea, the leading general in the *garciaprietista* faction of the Liberal party. Although his appointment marked the eclipse of Luque, the rivalry between the two was personal and political, not ideological; Aguilera had no sympathy for the critics of the system he had just inherited. Therefore, when he discovered the extent of juntero activity in all the branches, he refused to temporize. On May 9 Aguilera ordered the captains general to prohibit all juntero meetings; in recognition of the leadership provided by the Barcelona garrison, he wrote a personal note to Alfau labeling the Juntas "seditious" and urging energetic action.[69] Apparently still determined to protect the Juntas, Alfau's response on May 10 contained little more than verbal assurances from regimental officers that all illegal activity had stopped.[70]

In fact, juntero activity in Barcelona increased after May 10. Delegates to the assembly called by the local Artillery Junta began to arrive during the second week in May; on May 15 they pledged their support to the Infantry Junta, an indication that for the time being, army solidarity would prevail over the usual rivalries.[71] Later in the week, they formally replaced their defunct Central Junta with an organization similar to that in the Infantry. In the meantime, the Infantrymen had resumed their proselytizing, mailing propaganda circulars on May 24, two weeks after they had received Aguilera's order to disband.

The Crisis of June 1

This overt defiance of the War Minister was the opening act in the crisis that culminated a week later in the victory of the Juntas de Defensa. During the last week in May, the government in Madrid, the king, and the military defense committees engaged in a test of wills, a test the king and the politicians failed because of their fear of political and social revolution. The struggle was kept secret from the Spanish public, then transfixed by the war, the impending general strike, and the interventionist demonstration in Madrid on May 27. When the outlines of the confrontation between the army and the state were revealed after June 1, the possibility of revolution seemed nearer than ever.

The crisis began with the Infantry Junta's defiance of their military superiors. When General Aguilera learned of the Junta's noncompliance with his ultimatum, he directed General Alfau to take "more energetic measures," an order to which Alfau finally submitted. Early on the morning of May 25, Alfau asked the Superior Junta to disband within twenty-four hours.[72] The same day, Alfau informed Aguilera of his action and offered two alternatives for dealing with the crisis. The "most military" was to order all officers to resign their membership in the Juntas within forty-eight hours under pain of arrest or even death, extreme measures that would be difficult to conceal from the public. With opinion so bitterly divided over the war, news of division within the officer corps might prove politically dangerous. The other alternative was to order the heads of the local Juntas to dissolve their own organizations, a method that was perhaps less military, but that held "without doubt less danger of violence."[73]

It was indicative of the tense political situation in the nation that the "less military" solution was chosen. On the afternoon of May 25, Aguilera told Alfau to order Márquez to instruct the local Juntas to dissolve and received assurances from Alfau that Márquez would comply.[74] The next day, bolstered by a supportive letter from the Marqués de Estella, the president of the Supreme Military Council,[75] Aguilera repeated his order and added that Alfau should initiate a summary court-martial in the event of a refusal.

But his firmness was matched by the intransigence of the junteros. Márquez and the other members of the Superior Junta refused to comply with Alfau's order to disband, leaving the Captain General no alternative but to arrest them for insubordination.[76] Early on the morning of May 28, the seven officers were imprisoned in Montjuich, the military fortress usually reserved for strikers and terrorists.[77]

The movement was not to be so easily quelled, however. No sooner were Márquez and the others in the Superior Junta imprisoned than a second, "shadow Junta," was formed.[78] More ominously, the rest of the officer corps—except the generals—were lining up behind the arrested officers. All over Spain, Junta leaders presented themselves for arrest in the captaincies general,[79] while officers in the Artillery and Cavalry Juntas in Barcelona awaited orders to act. Furthermore, it appeared that Alfau was still trying to assume the role of mediator between the Barcelona officer corps and the government. Aguilera therefore recalled him to Madrid and relieved him of his command, replacing him with a highly respected member of the senior hierarchy, General José Marina.[80] In Marina's former post as Captain General of Madrid, he placed the Conservative General Echagüe in order to emphasize the united front presented by senior officers in both parties. In conference with the king, the generals agreed upon the execution of Colonel Márquez, the leader of the rebellion. On May 30 Marina left for Barcelona.

The same day, Aguilera responded to one of the principal grievances of junior officers with a decree establishing strict seniority for all appointments through the rank of lieutenant colonel.[81] To eliminate favoritism, all aspirants were to petition the War Ministry "through regular channels" for the post they desired. But the decree excluded the choicest positions, including those in the General Staff, the Military Household, the War Ministry, Aviation, and the academies—in short, in all positions requiring more qualifications than mere seniority. The dilemma was that it was patronage, not merit, that had often ruled these appointments in the past, and the decree provided no guarantee of objectivity for the future. Consequently, it did not appease the insubordinate officers, who were by now in a state of extreme excitement. As Marina's train passed through Saragossa, local junteros wired Barcelona to ask if they should stop it and detain him.[82]

When he arrived in the Catalan capital, Marina found most of the garrison united and unwilling to participate in the execution of Márquez. On the evening of May 31, Artillerists informed Marina that if he did not release the Superior Junta immediately, they would do it themselves. The Cavalry was equally defiant; the Engineers, slightly less so.[83] As the new Captain General prepared for a review of the barracks on June 1, officers braced themselves to refuse him admittance.

Undoubtedly they were encouraged to stand firm by signs that the united front in Madrid was crumbling. Despite his agreement to support a hard line, Alfonso was fearful of alienating the officer corps at a time when he was under attack from the left, whose meeting in the Madrid bullring had just taken place. To hedge his bets, he sent Cavalry Major Mariano Foronda, the director of Barcelona's streetcar system, to negotiate with the imprisoned officers. Foronda, however, was unsuccessful; certain of victory and emboldened by this sign of vacillation, the Infantry Junta remained intransigent.

At eight o'clock on the morning of June 1, before Marina could begin his rounds, the acting Infantry Junta presented him with a manifesto announcing that if the original Junta were not released within twelve hours, "the army" would take matters into its own hands.[84] The author of the manifesto, Captain Isaac Villar Moreno, had two goals in mind: to convince Marina of the determination of the Barcelona garrison to resist the government and to prevent Marina from touring the barracks, where his prestige might be expected to overawe junior officers and undermine their will to resist.[85] At the same time, the regional Juntas were ordered to take possession of local political and military administrative offices on June 2 and to cut off railroad lines leading into Barcelona if the government should send troops.[86] Clearly, the Barcelona Junta was contemplating a full-scale coup d'etat.

The overblown renovationist rhetoric of the manifesto also supported this view. The junteros floridly proclaimed that the crisis had arisen exclusively out of their concern for the welfare of the nation and complained repeatedly of the sacrifices uselessly and unilaterally imposed on the army for the last twenty years. The language was ambiguous, but its general tone suggested that Spain's military problems were part of the larger problem of national regeneration. Thus the junteros appeared to be yet another of the political forces demanding meaningful reform in 1917. Unlike the regionalists, the Republicans, or the Socialists, however, the Juntas had few specific political remedies to propose. On the contrary, the grievances specified in the text were strictly bureaucratic ones. Regenerationist language notwithstanding, "internal satisfaction," or rather, the lack of it, was the sole cause of the military rebellion of June 1. Although willing to borrow the rhetoric of dissent, the Juntas de Defensa did not desire a change of regime. Ironically, the manifesto of June 1 was the first step in its destruction.

Undaunted by threats, Marina refused to release the prisoners, though he did forego his morning inspection, thus averting a violent confrontation in the barracks. As the day wore on and Marina showed no signs of giving way, tension mounted in the city, and word circulated that the junteros would be liberated by force at eight o'clock. Spotting a potentially revolutionary situation, the Radical Republican leader Alejandro Lerroux sent word to Márquez, placing eight hundred men at his disposal.[87] But Lerroux received no reply. The coup contemplated by the Superior Junta was a military one, made by and for junior officers alone.

It was the cabinet, and especially the king, who finally lost their nerve. Foronda, still active in the barracks, could report nothing encouraging; at five o'clock in the afternoon, Marina received orders to release the prisoners the following day. When Foronda returned to Montjuich to inform the Junta that the king had intervened to secure their freedom, Márquez loftily replied, "He does not free us; we free ourselves. He can be thankful that we leave him in Madrid."[88] Further proof of the self-confidence of the junteros was forthcoming an hour later, when they agreed to ignore their ultimatum and spend the night in jail, provided the legitimacy of their organization were immediately recognized.[89] Having given in once, the government found it easy to do so again. On June 2 the Barcelona Superior Junta, now officially sanctioned, emerged from their cells; the next day, Junta leaders in La Coruña, Vitoria, Seville, and Badajoz were set free.[90]

The Junta had triumphed because the king and his government were fearful of losing military support at a moment of political and social crisis. Had the king and his cabinet been as wary of militarism as they were of political change, they might have chosen to meet the rebellion of June 1 head on. Unlike 1905, in 1917 the government had the full support of the senior hierarchy, whose authority in the officer corps had declined but not vanished. Most of the army outside Barcelona could be counted on to follow their military instincts and obey orders. Nor was the Junta leadership, either before or after June 1, genuinely revolutionary. The manifesto of June 1 was a threat that never had to be acted upon; it would be unjustified to assume that the government could not have called the bluff.

But the Spanish state was on the defensive in the spring of 1917, and the dynastic politicians were unwilling to test its—and their—strength in an open confrontation with the army. Fresh in everyone's mind was the March revolution in Russia, which had begun with the defection of the army. The Spanish prime minister, Manuel García Prieto, was a man of mediocre talents and personality, who owed his career to his marriage (to a daughter of Montero Ríos) and to the personal rivalries within the Liberal party. The beneficiary and symbol of a political system in an advanced state of disintegration, he lacked the moral authority and the political imagination to confront the military challenge energetically.

Even more responsible than the cabinet was the king, whose political power had been enhanced since the closure of the Cortes in February. Through Alfau, Alfonso had encouraged the formation of the Infantry Junta; through Foronda, he had guaranteed its victory. From the beginning of his reign, and with greater frequency after 1917, Alfonso would show more concern for the preservation of his throne than for the constitutional regime that legitimated it. Forced to choose between the army and his own government, he chose the army, and the weakened government could not resist. Alfonso and the army triumphed over García Prieto in 1917; they would do so again in 1923.

The Fall of García Prieto

With the release of the junteros, the principle of civil supremacy had been severely compromised. Nevertheless, the government explained the crisis to the country as a minor incident that would have no lasting effect on the stability of the cabinet.[91] It was clear, however, that the government was in imminent danger. The Infantry Junta was determined to bring down García Prieto, who had now belatedly decided to withstand further pressure. As proof of this new resolve, the cabinet refused to accept the resignation General Aguilera submitted on June 1.[92] Aguilera remained in office as a symbol of resistance to further juntero demands.

But resistance was complicated by the absence of effective government representation in Barcelona. In an abrupt about-face, General Marina had become the spokesman for the Infantry Superior Junta, for reasons that are not yet clear. Possibly Marina hoped to heal the breach between the senior hierarchy and the junior officers by assuming leadership of their movement, much as Luque had done in 1905. Whatever his reasons, like Alfau before him, Marina allowed the

Barcelona Captaincy General to become the official channel through which juntero demands reached Madrid.

Above all, the Infantry Junta wanted immediate approval of its statutes; in addition, it demanded the abolition of wartime merit promotions, the breakup of the king's *camarilla* of military favorites, a pay increase, parity of civil and military amortizations, the dismissal of Francisco Gómez Jordana, the High Commissioner in Morocco, whom they accused of favoritism, and the reinstatement of General Alfau as Captain General of Barcelona. Beginning with the recognition of the statutes, the implementation of this program would have inverted the traditional structure of authority within the military and severely limited the power of the government to formulate policy and control appointments. Quite naturally, the cabinet, and especially General Aguilera, were unwilling to meet these demands. García Prieto was willing to approve the first article of the statutes, which gave the Junta formal recognition without sanctioning its proposed methods or organization, but the matter was taken out of the hands of the cabinet on June 9, when Marina, under pressure from the Junta and without prior cabinet approval, authorized with his signature the entire statute.[93]

This was the equivalent of a military coup d'etat, the final blow to the authority of an already discredited government. Upon learning the news, the cabinet resigned, opening a political crisis of transcendent importance for the future of the constitutional monarchy. Wartime stresses had exposed the incapacity of the dynastic politicians for forceful leadership, the turno was defunct, the need for political renovation widely apparent. As in the struggle over neutrality, the Crown's constitutional powers appeared to be the decisive factor in propelling the country out of its immobility. The nation—and the army—waited expectantly for the king to call a cabinet capable of governing, rather than of merely presiding over an unpredictable denouement.

But the king did not rise to the historic occasion. Turning his back on the tentative appeals to use the power of the monarchy to renovate the political system, on June 10 Alfonso appointed the regular Conservative party leader, Eduardo Dato, as prime minister.[94] Alfonso elected to rely on the docility of the turno politicians and the strength of the army rather than on a still problematic national consensus that in 1917 could manifest itself only in negative fashion. In doing so, he mortgaged both himself and the constitutional monarchy to the will of the army.

From the king's perspective, Dato—and the continued suspension of the Liberal Cortes—were the only reliable choices, because they were the only predictable ones.[95] The Juntas had vetoed the return of the Liberals, who were still unwilling in any case to recognize the statutes without reopening the Cortes to share responsibility for it. But Alfonso was even more suspicious of the Cortes than he was of the Juntas, fearing that the national demand for reform might lead to its conversion into Constituent Cortes. New elections under Conservative leadership might produce the same result, particularly if the prime minister were Antonio Maura, the maverick Conservative leader who had, since the turn of the century, advocated political reform directed from above.

Among the Juntas, sentiment was strong for a Maura ministry— rumor reported that he had already been approached by Junta representatives. Although Maura refused to place himself at the head of a military party, he fully recognized the significance of the political moment and of his own potential role, as a relative outsider, in it.[96] But Alfonso, who had always been intimidated by Maura, had no intention of calling on him, in spite of his desire to appease the Juntas. If anyone were going to use the junior officers as a power base, it would be Alfonso himself.

Undoubtedly, both Alfonso and Dato believed that the threat posed by the Juntas de Defensa was only temporary. In a gesture of authority, the government appointed as Minister of War the ancient Marqués de Estella, a Conservative whose association with the Canovite system was as old as the system itself. But venerable generals could not tame the Juntas. Perhaps the most obvious result of the crisis of June 1917 was the eclipse of the political generals who had dominated the army and civil-military relations for nearly a century. The collaboration of civilian and military politicians, traditionally believed to be the key to military reform, had finally coalesced in 1916 under the pressure of the war. But by 1916 the generals could not automatically guarantee the support of the rank and file. Alienated from a system that had primarily benefited the court and party favorites, junior officers now saw the Juntas as a means of insuring that their voices would be heard. Confronted with an alternative power base in the army, the civilian politicians lacked the nerve to challenge it. Their collapse sealed the fate of the political generals, of military reform, and ultimately, of the parliamentary regime itself.

The triumph of the Juntas was complete on June 12, when the new cabinet approved the entire statute of the Infantry Junta de Defensa. In so doing, it legitimated an illegitimate situation; in effect, it institutionalized army indiscipline. The Juntas had emerged from the crisis with unexpected, but certainly not unappreciated, political power. They had toppled one cabinet and influenced the composition of a new one, the king was courting their favor, and public opinion expectantly awaited their next move. For the next three months, during the revolutionary summer of 1917, the Juntas would dominate the political situation and decide the outcome of two attempts to renovate the Restoration settlement.

CHAPTER FOUR

The Revolutionary Summer of 1917

As the Conde de Romanones put it, after June 1, 1917, the Juntas were "the masters of Spain."[1] Yet they owed their power as much to the timidity of the government and to the favorable public reception of their rebellion as to any serious threat of force. The Juntas set the example for two currents of protest in the summer of 1917. One was the syndicalization of civilian bureaucrats and noncommissioned officers, whose economic and professional grievances had grown during the war. The other was the renovationist movement, composed of regionalists, Republicans, and Socialists, who viewed the wartime crisis as a mandate for constitutional change. As in the years of the Isabelline monarchy, the inflexibility of the governing parties encouraged their political opponents to turn to the army as a moderating power; in the aftermath of June 1, the renovationists would hail the Juntas' revolt as the harbinger of a dramatic reorientation of Spanish political life. In response, the Infantry Superior Junta would attempt to claim an active role for the army in the impending revolution.

But the majority of officers were not prepared to follow the lead of the activists in the Superior Junta. Although they employed regenerationist rhetoric, the majority of junteros were, as they so often insisted, essentially "apolitical," indifferent to the details of political organization so long as their professional demands were satisfied. After June 1, the dynastic parties reacted to the slightest shifts in military opinion, leaving the Juntas in the enviable position of dictating policy without being responsible for government in general, a situation they had every reason to wish to preserve. Thus they stood by the government and the monarchy during the revolutionary summer of 1917.

The loose alliance between the regionalists and the Republican and revolutionary left would not last through the summer. Frightened

by the threat of social revolution, the Catalan bourgeoisie would withdraw from the coalition into an alliance with the ruling oligarchy in
Madrid. Alone, the left did not possess the strength to transform the
regime, especially against the will of the army. The revolutionary moment of 1917 slipped away, and the parliamentary monarchy emerged
weakened, defensive, but essentially unchanged.

First Reactions to the Juntas

The Junta manifesto of June 1 appeared at a moment in Spanish
history when most of the politically significant forces in Spain recognized the urgency of reform. War, rapid industrialization, labor unrest,
and inflation presented problems that only strong government could
resolve, while at the same time awakening hopes for social and political
democratization. Yet by 1917 the traditional political leadership was
discredited, divided, and too distracted by intraparty squabbles to deal
effectively with the national crisis. By summer, the usual critics of the
Canovite system had been joined by the more thoughtful members of
the dynastic parties in demanding "renovation" of Spain's political
life.

This politically charged atmosphere explains the enormous impact
of the manifesto of June 1. Its regenerationist language, really a smoke
screen for the professional demands of the military middle class, was
taken at face value by those who wanted to be convinced that the
Juntas' protest against the military oligarchs was indicative of a broader
democratic spirit within the officer corps. Thus, men who in normal circumstances would have unconditionally condemned the Juntas' breach
of civil supremacy hailed the rebellion as the first step toward radical
change: the military crisis that began on June 1 and ended ten days
later with the appointment of Eduardo Dato as prime minister had laid
bare the inadequacy of the dynastic parties, the inflexibility of the
system, and the unreliability of the Crown as an agent of reform. In
general, this was the view of bourgeois liberals who hoped to mod-
ernize the constitutional monarchy without destroying it. It was best
expressed in *El Imparcial* on June 13 by José Ortega y Gasset in an
article entitled "Beneath the Arch in Ruins":

> What has happened is a rupture of the basic legality of Spain; it is
> an act that nullifies the Constitution. Nothing effectively constitu-
> tional, nothing fully authoritative can be born of a Constitution
> slashed from top to bottom. There is only one remedy: to reconsti-

tute the Constitution. For that, a temporary Power broader than those existing on May 31 would be necessary. In a fraternal and renovating embrace, that organ of Spanish life that is outside the law would return to its bosom. In other words: Constituent Cortes.[2]

The same viewpoint was shared by the Lliga Regionalista, the party of the Catalan industrial bourgeoisie, whose resentment at their exclusion from the Canovite system had deepened since the beginning of the war. On June 14 regionalist senators and deputies released a manifesto calling for the constitution of a federal, democratic state reinvigorated by the full participation of the Basque and Catalan provinces. The regionalists condemned the military rebellion as "a manifest transgression of constitutional law, a true peaceful pronunciamiento" that in a normal country would have provoked "a formidable reaction," but that in Spain had been received with "clear sympathy" because of the decadence and injustice of the existing regime. Like Ortega, the Catalans demanded the reopening of the Cortes to begin the process of constitutional revision.[3]

On the left, the military rebellion was viewed with even greater optimism because it seemed to presage the collapse of the parliamentary monarchy. On June 5 Republicans and Socialists under the nominal leadership of the Reformist Melquíades Álvarez formed an alliance to work for a bourgeois democratic republic; on June 16 the Revolutionary Committee, composed of Alejandro Lerroux, Álvarez, and Pablo Iglesias (represented by Julián Besteiro), issued a manifesto calling on "all the left" to work together for the "triumph of popular sovereignty."[4] The Socialists provided the link with the revolutionary general strike being planned for later in the summer. Their alliance with the Anarchosyndicalists had grown out of the economic crisis; the pact with the bourgeois left was a response to the political crisis ushered in by the officers' rebellion of June 1. The Socialists' attitude toward the Juntas was ambivalent. On the one hand, they seem to have feared a military coup, perhaps in support of a Maura ministry. On June 7, and again on June 12, the Madrid Socialist Group published protests against the "seditious" military breach of civil supremacy.[5] On the other hand, the Socialists also seem to have hoped that the Juntas were not only "antioligarchical" but also "democratic" and that the military would support a revolutionary change of regime.[6] On the fourteenth, the Federation of Socialist Youth qualified a warning against military repression by carefully distinguishing between "militarism" and "the army."[7]

The Juntas inspired the most enthusiasm in the state administration, where employees suffered many of the same economic hardships and professional inequities as the military middle class. A "Law of Authorizations" of March 2, 1917, had allowed the government to initiate 25 percent personnel reductions in all ministries except the Post Office and the Ministry of Public Instruction. Although half of the savings thus acquired were eventually to be used to raise salaries, this was of necessity a long-range benefit whose effects were less immediate than slower promotions and inadequate salaries.[8] Civil servants had never been well paid; nearly one-third of the employees were earning between 1,080 and 1,380 pesetas annually.[9] Furthermore, most low-level employees lacked job security, being subject to patronage turnovers and transfers as well as hiring freezes. When the military Juntas emerged as the collective voice of the military bureaucracy, employees in other ministries quickly followed suit. By mid-June, Juntas de Defensa of civil servants had been formed in the Ministries of Finance, Interior, Development, and Public Instruction, in the Corps of Telegraph and Postal Workers, and in the municipal police. Finally, in self-defense, a Defense Junta of Taxpayers was organized.[10] In a movement potentially as revolutionary as those of the regionalists and the left, Spain was witnessing the full-scale syndicalization of its middle class.

The Juntas Enter Politics

The profound political impact of the manifesto of June 1 brought national attention to the Infantry Superior Junta, whose members quickly came to believe that the Juntas had a mission beyond the protection of professional interests. On June 6 *La Correspondencia Militar*, the self-appointed voice of the Juntas, referred to the manifesto of June 1 as "perhaps the most grandiose document of the contemporary age" and suggested that it represented "the death sentence . . . of the rule of caciquismo and oligarchy in every order of national life. . . ."[11] On June 11 the Superior Junta issued a public declaration of its new motto, Morality and Justice, and offered to extend its "protective aegis over all the organisms of the state administration,"[12] an offer readily accepted by the civilian Juntas then being formed. By mid-June, the leaders of the Superior Junta could well imagine themselves the political masters of Spain.

The president, Colonel Benito Márquez, accepted his destiny with relish. At fifty-nine years of age, Márquez was a stout and slightly deaf peninsular officer with a uniformly undistinguished career behind him. In many ways, Márquez seems typical of the officers he represented: a lackluster but self-important military bureaucrat with a limited under- standing of politics and history. An acquaintance later called him "a well-intentioned man, although easygoing and uncultivated," and sug- gested that the real intelligence within the Junta was its secretary, Captain Manuel Álvarez Gilarranz, who manipulated the vanity of Márquez for his own ends.[13] Another source of political ambition was the author of the June 1 manifesto, forty-four-year-old Captain Isaac Villar, whose rhetoric had started the Infantry Junta on its political journey. None of the juntero politicians had a previous history of serious political concern, let alone experience. Instead, they were re- sponding to the heady atmosphere of 1917 and to their even headier taste of personal political power.

Having influenced the formation of the Dato government, which compliantly sanctioned the Junta statutes on June 12, and encouraged by the attention of the political opposition, the Superior Junta imme- diately embarked on a rather indiscriminate search for a civilian leader to form a "regenerationist" government whose first concern would be the redress of army grievances. While Major Rafael Espino made the rounds of the monarchical parties in Madrid, Márquez and Gilarranz made contact with the antidynastic parties through Lerroux. The first choice of the Junta, however, was still Antonio Maura. Through an intermediary in Barcelona, Márquez and the secretary of the Artillery Junta offered to bring down the Dato government in favor of a Maura ministry, an offer that Maura refused diplomatically in a letter of June 23 and denounced more intemperately in a private letter to his son Gabriel a few days later.[14]

Temporarily thwarted in their effort to enlist a civilian leader, the Superior Junta decided to make a public appeal for support. On June 25 *El Noticiero Universal*, a Barcelona daily, published a manifesto ad- dressed to the country at large that explained the formation of the Junta, justified the insubordination of June 1, and outlined its goals, which were now expanded to claim a permanent political role for the military within the Spanish state.[15] The lengthy document first sum- marized the injustices the army had suffered since the War of 1898, culminating in the humiliating proficiency tests that had triggered the formation of the Defense Junta in 1916. This was followed by an analysis of the ills affecting the Spanish army, categorized, in de- scending importance, into moral, technical, and economic questions, and containing the familiar complaints against favoritism and neglect.

Less familiar—and more alarming—were the sections on civil-military relations, which basically denied the principle of civil supremacy. While neither prepared nor willing to govern the state, the Infantry Junta did claim the right to govern the internal affairs of the Corps independently, separate from and marginal to the civil power. This was not merely an appeal for internal institutional control over professional matters; the Junta demanded a "renovation of political concepts" to give the army a greater role in policymaking. To replace the prevailing constitutional system, the Junta proposed a model of the executive branch in which the civil and military coexisted, "harmonized" by the "moderating power"—presumably the monarchy. Arguing that the supremacy of any power was a sign of "abnormality" in the state, the Junta made clear its intention to secure the military reforms it desired with or without the aid of civilians. The manifesto of June 25 was thus simultaneously an ultimatum to the dynastic parties, an appeal to the monarchy, and an invitation to the opposition.

The clearest political notion in the manifesto was the assumption, shared by the civilian opposition, of a connection between military and political reform: the failure of the state to undertake military reform was symptomatic of its impotence. But vague references to "reform" on both sides conveniently masked differences as to what reform entailed. Most of the democratic left envisioned a small but efficient army that would no longer be a drain on the national budget; junteros wanted efficiency, but not at the expense of their own job security. For civilian reformers, military reform was a small part of a greater political or social revolution; for the Junta, reform of the state was the means to an end—the professional autonomy of the army. This confusion of purpose would thwart any concerted effort between the army and the civilians to reform the Spanish state in the summer of 1917.

The Reaction in the Army

Although the Infantry Junta claimed to speak for the army as a whole, in reality the appearance of the Juntas divided the military along its traditional fissure points. The victory of June 1 had overcome the resistance of officers in Madrid and Morocco to the Juntas; by June 6 a majority had signed the "act of adhesion."[16] But the generals had not relaxed their opposition. A few of the more accomplished political maneuverers, however, made small gestures of appeasement during the month of June. While eighty-year-old General Weyler toured the provincial garrisons bearing greetings from the king, the equally ancient War Minister, the Marqués de Estella, made a series of appointments intended to demonstrate the government's good will. Other generals made quiet overtures to the Junta leadership, apparently hoping to use them as a personal power base. The most prominent was the nephew of the War Minister, General Miguel Primo de Rivera, who had initially denounced the Infantry Junta in a letter to a friend as "untimely, illegal, inopportune, and divisive."[17] When this letter was leaked to the press early in June, Primo attempted to mend his fences by praising the Juntas in letters to strategically chosen colleagues. But the Barcelona Junta remained wary of his sincerity.[18] Primo was the epitome of the system of patronage that they had risen to protest. Nevertheless, Primo would continue his courtship of the junteros during the next six years. In 1923 they would provide support for his pronunciamiento against the parliamentary regime.

What the generals failed to recognize in 1917 was the extent to which the officer corps was alienated from the political and military elites that controlled the Restoration system. From the perspective of the military bureaucrats, the senior hierarchy had sacrificed the army's welfare to personal ambition on countless occasions in the past and would undoubtedly do so again in the future. The generals plainly could not countenance the Juntas' major demands, which subverted the normal chain of command in the army. Thus, throughout the summer, the Juntas remained overtly hostile to the senior hierarchy in general and the War Minister in particular.[19]

The formation of the Infantry Junta also provoked an open break between regular and noncommissioned officers. Relations between the NCOs and the academy-trained, middle-class officers on the active list had deteriorated since 1912, when General Luque had prohibited further NCO promotions into the reserve list.[20] Both reserve officers and NCOs resented their second-class status and limited career opportunities, for which they correctly held regular officers responsible. Their suspicion of their superiors hardened into hostility in June when the Infantry Junta forced reserve officers to form separate Juntas and rebuffed the overtures of the newly created Central Defense Junta of Subofficials, Brigades, and Sergeants.

The NCO Junta—also based in Barcelona—had initially hoped to flatter the commissioned officers into supporting its goals. On June 12 the Central Junta directed an appeal to the Infantry Superior Junta sonorously praising the "noble cry and saving rebellion" of June 1 and asking for a sympathetic hearing. "Before all, above all, and on top of all," the NCOs requested greater "social dignity." They resented being treated like common soldiers when in reality they too were professionals in "the august religion of arms." More concretely, the NCOs demanded the abrogation of the 1912 law ending promotions into the reserve list. The manifesto closed with a scarcely veiled threat: "if, contrary to what we hope, facts in time convince us of the sterility of these hopes, the ties of our affection will be broken and the bitter moment will have arrived to think and to *believe* that our superior officers are going to be the first dam we must level when the solemn hour of our longed-for demands sounds in its turn."[21]

Neither the flattery nor the threats moved the Infantry Junta. Despite the "democratic" pretensions of the Superior Junta, regular officers had joined the Junta to protect and extend the exclusivity of the active list. An influx of officers from the ranks could only cut further into already limited funds and appointments. If anything, Infantry junteros would have preferred to imitate the Artillery Corps and abolish the reserve list altogether.

Perhaps not too surprised at their failure with the Superior Junta, the NCOs then turned to the generals, hoping to profit from their antagonism toward the new organization. On June 14 their Central Junta wrote the War Minister, denouncing the "hateful and reckless conduct" of the Infantry.[22] The NCOs explained that the "absolute divorce" separating them from the officers had its origins in their "systematic opposition" to all measures aimed at the improvement of the "moral situation" of noncommissioned officers and repeated their request for the abrogation of the law of 1912. In conclusion, the manifesto guaranteed that NCOs would disobey their superiors in the event of a confrontation between the officers' Juntas and the government.

Unfortunately for the NCOs, their appeal to the War Ministry was not as warmly received as they had expected. In the revolutionary summer of 1917, with officers brandishing swords and revolvers in the streets of Barcelona and soldiers shouting slogans in the cafes, the syndicalization of the NCOs conjured up visions of workers' and soldiers' soviets, and not only for the beleaguered government. The left was conscious of the same possibility. On June 20, as rumors of the conflict between the NCOs and the Superior Junta circulated through the city, the Catalan Republican Marcelino Domingo published an article entitled "¡Soldados!" that was essentially a plea for insubordination when the revolutionary movement planned for later in the summer got underway.[23] In tense Barcelona, its impact was enormous. Copies of the June 20 edition of *La Lucha* were selling for three and four pesetas apiece when the paper was denounced under the Law of Jurisdictions and continued to circulate for many days afterward, especially among soldiers in the Barcelona barracks. Marina asked the government to allow him to arrest Domingo, who as a deputy possessed parliamentary immunity, but his request was refused. Thereafter, Domingo and his paper were special objects of juntero resentment in Barcelona.

In the meantime, rumors of the quarrel between officers and NCOs had reached Madrid. On June 22 *El Socialista* and *El País*, a republican daily, and some of the right-wing press as well, printed the manifesto of the NCOs to the Infantry Superior Junta.[24] Energetically—and vainly—the government tried to stifle the conflict by stifling public knowledge of it; within a few days five more newspapers had been denounced under the Law of Jurisdictions.[25] As news arrived from Africa of Juntas of NCOs, and even of corporals and soldiers,[26] Estella decided to take more vigorous action. On June 23 he wired all captains general to keep the NCOs under surveillance and prepare to suppress their Juntas with force if necessary.[27] Estella was not blind to the difficulty of prohibiting the NCO Junta when those of the regular officers were being condoned and even courted. But the fear of revolution forced him to try. If the antidynastic flirtations of the Infantry Superior Junta were threatening, the revolutionary potential of the working-class NCOs was much more obvious. The government's best hope lay in a policy of divide-and-conquer. For the immediate future, survival demanded the continued cultivation of the officers' Juntas.

The government's fortress mentality was reinforced by the appearance of the manifesto of the Infantry Superior Junta on June 25. In order to suppress the circulation of the manifesto and thus knowledge of the continuing disaffection of the officer corps, on June 26 constitutional guarantees were suspended and prior censorship established.[28] Newspapers were prohibited from discussing the army, the war, political meetings, or the social question—in short, any subject of real interest in 1917. These measures only further infuriated the democratic left. Prudently, the government attempted to buy support in the army for the revolutionary siege that lay ahead. A decree of July 2 raised the daily food allotment for both noncommissioned officers and troops to compensate for inflation, a necessary expedient that nevertheless failed to pacify the NCOs. More successful was another decree the following day that modified the king's Military Household to require the inclusion of officers below the rank of colonel and to limit membership to four-year terms. While the decree displeased the king, who was forced to dismiss six regular members of his camarilla, it answered one of the principal grievances of junior officers and somewhat lessened their hostility toward Madrid.

The Assembly of Parliamentarians

The Assembly movement of July 1917, initiated by the Lliga Regionalista and seconded by Catalan Republicans, the Reformists (the party of the Asturian bourgeoisie), and the Socialists, was an abortive attempt to modify the Restoration settlement of Cánovas, which had concentrated political power in the hands of the agrarian interests of Castile and Andalusia. Economic expansion since the beginning of the war had strengthened the political leverage of the regions of industrial and mercantile power in Spain even as it convinced them that their needs were not understood by the parties of the turno in Madrid. The Assembly of Parliamentarians was designed to alter the constitution, both literally and functionally, to reflect the new balance of forces in Spain. In short, it was an attempt at bourgeois revolution.

The mutiny of June 1 created a revolutionary situation that the political dissidents in Barcelona hoped both to exploit and to control. The leader of the Lliga Regionalista, Francisco Cambó, initially tried to achieve his political revolution legally, through Constituent Cortes under the direction of a "national" government composed of representatives of all significant political groups in Spain.[29] When neither the king nor the Dato government responded to the regionalists' demand for a reopening of the Cortes, the Lliga called a meeting of Catalonia's entire parliamentary delegation on July 5 to work out plans for calling an unofficial session of the Cortes to consider constitutional reform. After the July 5 meeting still produced no positive response from Madrid, an invitation was extended to all Spanish senators and deputies to attend an extralegal parliamentary assembly in Barcelona on July 19.[30]

The Lliga's decision to defy the government brought it the collaboration of the revolutionary committee of Reformists, Republicans, and Socialists that had been formed in early June to establish a bourgeois republic. The alliance was an uneasy one, however. From the beginning, the Catalan bourgeoisie were uncomfortable with their new allies, especially the Socialists, whose goals exceeded the purely political transformation envisioned by the Lliga. Moreover, Cambó's political instincts correctly warned him that if the Assembly were to capture majority sentiment in the country, it would have to counterbalance its leftist orientation and overcome the public tendency (encouraged by the government) to see the movement as nothing more than a separatist attack on the unity of the nation. Accordingly, Cambó took precautions to prevent the calling of the general strike on July 19 and made every effort to enlist the cooperation of Antonio Maura and the Juntas de Defensa.

The absence of Maura from the Assembly movement of 1917 was the key to its failure. Not only would his presence have reassured an essentially conservative middle class, it would have legitimated the Assembly as a reunion of *all* the political forces in Spain alienated from the old oligarchies and excluded from the turno. Yet Maura remained aloof, both out of respect for the legal authority of the government and out of disdain for the industrial and commercial elements represented by the Lliga. Both publicly and privately in the weeks before July 19, Maura indicated his lack of sympathy for the movement, which he alternately referred to as "subversive" and as a "professional souk."[31] Maura's abstention from Cambó's "revolution from above" was his greatest political failure. Spiritually aloof from the changing political and social reality of twentieth-century Spain, he resisted compromise with new political forces that might have transformed the regime, while claiming the role of a disinterested statesman.

The inability of the Assembly movement to attract Maura meant that it would fail to attract the Juntas as well. In addition to his great prestige within the officer corps, Maura offered a guarantee against social revolution and separatism. Fully conscious of this, in the two weeks after July 5, Assembly supporters did their best to compensate for the absence of Maura by flattering the Junta leadership into an alliance. A flurry of circulars, manifestos, and speeches addressed directly or indirectly to the Juntas, appealed to the supposedly "democratic," antioligarchical orientation of the Juntas, while Cambó attempted to reassure them of the movement's moderate goals. In a persuasive and flattering letter on July 10, Cambó assured Márquez that "Catalonia neither is nor can be separatist" and argued that the common enterprise that lay before Catalonia and the army must be to "liberate the whole of Spain from a political system that, if it persisted, would lead Spain to her perdition."[32]

Receptive to the attention and praise and increasingly dissatisfied with the resistance of the War Ministry to their major demands, the Superior Junta did nothing publicly to discourage the idea that they were spiritually a part of the renovationist movement. In an effort to restore the army to its role as the bulwark of the regime, the government nervously sent the Civil Governor of Barcelona, Leopoldo Matos, to negotiate further concessions with Márquez on July 9. But Márquez, now completely infatuated with political power, refused to promise anything, and the official Junta reply to Matos was extremely cool.[33]

Márquez's evident interest in the Assembly movement persuaded Cambó to contemplate abandoning his alliance with the left. A few days before the proposed Assembly, he met with Márquez, two members of the Superior Junta, Captains Arturo Herrero and Isaac Villar, and a military chaplain, Padre Planas, who had previously served as an emissary from the king. After refusing to cancel the Assembly (as the king requested through Planas), Cambó agreed to its peaceful dissolution after the first meeting. The Lliga would thus be assured of a moral victory without risking a social revolution. In exchange, Cambó expected royal and juntero support for an autonomous Catalonia within a federal Spanish state. The Lliga and the army in turn would defend the monarchy against the challenge from the left coalition of Republicans and Socialists. Márquez readily acquiesced in this plan, in the belief that he was securing a tutelary role for the Juntas within the new political order.[34]

As it developed, both Márquez and Cambó had miscalculated. On July 13 a majority in the Infantry Superior Junta censured Márquez and ordered local Juntas to remain loyal to the government on the day of the Assembly.[35] Two days later, a joint note signed by all the branch Juntas in Barcelona declared their "firm intention to remain apart from political struggles and to obey the orders of the legally constituted government."[36] Apart from Márquez and his allies, Villar and Herrero, sentiment in the Infantry Superior Junta and among the juntero rank and file was strongly against an activist role for the army, particularly if it involved support for the Assembly movement. Many officers distrusted even the mild regionalism of the Lliga, making no distinction between Cambó and the separatists who occasionally appealed to the warring European powers for "liberation." Some officers also blamed Catalan industry and the protective tariff for the scarcity of consumer goods and high prices. Moreover, within the Superior Junta, opposition was mounting to the political pretensions of Colonel Márquez, who was thoroughly enjoying his preeminence, his contacts with leading political figures, and his access to the king.[37] The Juntas had arisen to protest the personalist politics of the military turno; they were not eager to exchange political generals for equally political colonels.

Thus, by July the unanimity of June 1, even then illusory, had completely vanished. Officers could unite against real or imagined assaults on their professional interests, but they lacked a consensus on a course of positive action. In the chaotic summer of 1917, the power of the Juntas was real enough, but that power was essentially negative: without army support, none of the contenders for political power could hope to survive.

The abstention of Maura and the Juntas, the reservations of Cambó, and the press campaign directed against the movement by the government, successfully emasculated the Assembly of July 19.[38] Only 71 of the 760 senators and deputies attended, and most of these were Catalans, giving the Assembly the aspect of a separatist meeting, which was not overcome by the collaboration of the Republicans and Socialists. Before the Assembly, the participants had agreed on two points of substance: the necessity of Constituent Cortes and the incorporation of the left—represented by the Reformist Melquíades Álvarez—into the new political settlement.[39] At the meeting itself, the delegates had just enough time to schedule a second meeting for August 16 in Oviedo before the Civil Governor dissolved the Assembly and arrested its members, who were set free as soon as they left the building.

In the weeks that followed, Cambó tried once again to bring the Infantry Junta into open support for the movement, counting on the favorable reception given the Assembly in the press and the absence of popular disturbances in Barcelona to overcome the resistance of the junteros to collaboration. As in July, Cambó turned to Márquez and their intermediary, Padre Planas, to make it clear to the king that the political revolution desired by the Lliga posed no threat to the monarchy. Márquez was still a willing accomplice and still convinced that he could speak for the army as a whole. The first week in August the three political activists in the Infantry Junta—Márquez, Villar, and Herrero—prepared a message for the king after consultation with one of Cambó's colleagues, the Conde de Güell.[40] After the usual renovationist preamble, the message urged the king to undertake directly the reconstruction of the Fatherland in harmony with the national will and the army. Only vigorous action could forestall the resurgence of separatism, the inflammation of social disorder, and possibly, the loss of his throne. Specifically, the message reiterated the demands of the Assembly movement—Constituent Cortes, under the direction of a "national government of concentration" that included Melquíades Álvarez—and proposed an independent Interior Minister—preferably General José Marvá, the social reformer—to supervise free elections.[41] In the improbable event that the Cortes should threaten the Crown, the army promised to dissolve them.

Alfonso, who now held the tactical advantage, paid no attention to the message, which was delivered by Padre Planas. In its first test, the Infantry Junta had stood by the king and the government, not by Márquez or his political allies in Catalonia. Furthermore, the government was by early August confident of its ability to discredit the Assembly movement through the general strike scheduled for later in the summer; quite possibly, plans had already been laid to defuse the strike by provoking it prematurely. In any event, the Minister of the Interior, José Sánchez Guerra, confidently wired the civil governors that the Juntas could be safely ignored.[42]

The General Strike

The second session of the Assembly movement was postponed because of the outbreak of the general strike on August 13.[43] The failure of the strike guaranteed the defeat of the renovationist movement of 1917 by shattering the uneasy alliance between the bourgeoisie and the revolutionary left. It also settled any lingering doubts about the essentially conservative temper of the Juntas de Defensa. Emerging from the strike with their political leverage greater than ever, the Juntas were in a position to press their professional demands on the politicians and the king in Madrid.

The general strike was an attempt by the Socialist UGT to capitalize on the mounting labor unrest created by wartime shortages and inflation. Since 1916 the UGT and its rival, the Anarchosyndicalist CNT, had joined in a series of pacts to direct this discontent against the political system; the failure of the government to respond positively to the workers' distress led to a radicalization of the movement's goals in 1917. On March 25 UGT and CNT leaders agreed to call an "indefinite general strike," hoping to deploy the growing strength of labor to force basic structural changes in the regime: political democratization and state intervention to secure social and economic reforms. In June the Socialist leadership joined the coalition of Republicans that was planning the creation of a bourgeois republic; at the same time, links were established with the Assembly movement through Alejandro Lerroux and Melquíades Álvarez. Thus in early July all the opposition in Spain had been loosely united in a movement aimed at substantive political change.

Plans were not made to call the general strike to coincide with the Assembly, although Socialist party (PSOE) and UGT leaders agreed in mid-July to call a general strike should the Juntas attempt a coup on July 19.[44] Broad support for the strike was not yet assured: Cambó was openly hostile; the Republicans, hesitant; the Juntas, still uncommitted. On the other hand, the CNT and industrial workers throughout Spain had by July worked themselves into a fever pitch of revolutionary excitement. During June there were strikes in Bilbao, Beasáin, Cartagena, Huelva, and San Sebastian, and on July 4 a large strike of metalworkers began in Bilbao.[45] On July 17 the Anarchosyndicalists, impatient with the methodical preparations of the Socialists, outlined their revolutionary program—a mélange of practical trade union demands and utopian social projects—in a widely circulated manifesto.[46]

Despite the caution of the Socialists, on July 19 a strike broke out in Valencia that ultimately—and fatally—led to the premature declaration of the general strike on August 13. The origins of the Valencia railway strike are still obscure: it is possible that it was initiated by agents provocateurs in order to divide the left from their bourgeois allies in the Assembly movement.[47] Events following the Valencia strike, which was over by July 23, tended to confirm this hypothesis. The Compañía del Norte refused to rehire thirty-five members of the local branch of the Railworkers' Union of the North, who retaliated on August 1 by calling a strike on all company lines for August 10. Since this would have blunted the impact of the general strike, the Socialist-dominated National Federation of Railworkers convinced its affiliate to compromise with the Compañía, which was also being pressured into conciliation by the Development Minister, the Vizconde de Eza. On August 9, however, negotiations were abruptly broken off at the insistence of the Interior Minister, Sánchez Guerra, who announced at his press conference that he was "ready to go to the strike."[48] Rising to the bait, the Federation voted by the narrowest of margins to go out on a sympathy strike on August 13.

Having been outmaneuvered by the government, the national committees of the UGT and the PSOE, meeting in Madrid, reluctantly agreed to call their revolutionary general strike to coincide with the railway strike on August 13, even though plans were not yet complete. With the railway strike a fait accompli, they succumbed to their fears and illusions: fears that the revolutionary momentum of 1917 would be dissipated; illusions that the wavering Republicans would provide substantial support and that the army would side with the workers against the regime.[49] In order to reach as wide an audience as possible, the strike manifesto of August 12 contained only political, not social or economic, objectives. The strike was aimed only at the peaceful establishment of a democratic republic.[50]

But as the government had calculated, the broad revolutionary coalition did not materialize. Although the strike, which began in Madrid on August 13, spread quickly to the major urban and industrial areas of Spain, it found no echo in the countryside, where a majority of the Spanish population still lived and worked. Had the general strike begun a year or two later, when inflation and the Bolshevik Revolution had raised the expectations of rural workers, it might have succeeded, although whether the political goals emphasized by the Socialists in 1917 would have aroused much enthusiasm among illiterate peasants and farm laborers is of course open to doubt.[51] Even in urban Spain, the impact of the strike was blunted by the lack of coordinated leadership, especially after the arrest of the strike committee in Madrid on August 15. Some organized labor, including railworkers on the Madrid-Saragossa-Alicante line, abstained from the strike.[52] In spite of the committee's decision to protest peacefully, violence broke out in most cities, including Madrid—where a riot was brutally suppressed in the Model Prison—and in Barcelona, where CNT organizers were prepared from the first for a bloody confrontation. And the Republicans, with the exception of Marcelino Domingo in Barcelona, provided little support once the fragmentary character of the strike became apparent.

As the government had anticipated, the alliance between the Lliga and the left did not withstand the initial outbreak of violence in Barcelona. On August 14 a manifesto signed by the leaders of the Catalan parliamentary delegation made it clear that the Assembly of Parliamentarians would neither support nor accept responsibility for the general strike.[53] Cambó was furious, and with reason. The outbreak of the strike had forced cancellation of the August 16 meeting of the Assembly in Oviedo and, as he noted on August 18, had led to the accusation that the Lliga had "provoked the strike and then abandoned it, frightened by our own handiwork. . . ."[54] Much of the Assembly movement's goodwill had thus been at least temporarily dissipated.

Most significant for the failure of the general strike was the attitude of the army, whose repressive zeal on the whole exceeded the demands of the situation. As a precaution, Infantry regiments in Barcelona were placed under surveillance by more reliable Artillery and Cavalry units, as well as by the Civil Guard and police, but the fears of the government were not realized.[55] On the contrary, in Sabadell, where Colonel Márquez's regiment was posted, clashes between workers and the army produced ten deaths.[56] Noncommissioned officers also ignored appeals for class solidarity and temporarily buried their grievances against their superiors. On August 15 Marcelino Domingo was arrested on the orders of General Marina, in violation of his rights as a deputy, and was nearly shot out of hand by officers resentful of his earlier efforts to subvert the troops. To insure his safety, Marina ordered him transferred to the cruiser *Reina Regente*.[57] In the north, where the militancy and high wages of the Asturian miners kept the strike alive for nearly five weeks, the military response was exceptionally severe.[58] Although for the first four days of the strike the miners employed only peaceful tactics, the Military Governor of Oviedo, General Ricardo

Burguete, insisted on forcing the strike into more violent channels. In two notorious edicts of August 13 and 17, Burguete accused the strikers of *lèse patrie* and treason and promised to hunt them down "like wild beasts," a promise he eventually made good.[59] Subordinates who attempted to negotiate with the rebels, like Major Borbón and Colonel Angel Rodríguez del Barrio, were either dismissed or reprimanded. In time, the implacable repression of the Military Governor and the failure of the strike elsewhere in Spain took their toll. On September 17 the miners returned to work. Official figures after the strike showed 80 dead, 150 wounded, and 2,000 arrested.[60]

In spite of this grim harvest of violence, the days of the August general strike soon became known as the "Comic Week," a bitter parody of the Tragic Week of 1909.[61] The strike and the renovationist movement had raised hopes high; the collapse of the coalition of mid-July inevitably spread cynicism and disillusionment. The failure of the strike and the defection of the bourgeoisie also postponed indefinitely the unification of the Spanish labor movement by confirming the Anarchosyndicalists in their apoliticism and estranging them once again from the Socialists. The Socialist leadership, on the other hand, retreated rapidly from their brief foray into violent revolution into a new preoccupation with electoral politics. In 1918, when inflation, the armistice, and the news of the Bolshevik Revolution raised millennial hopes among both rural and urban workers, there was little enthusiasm among the Socialist leadership for another attempt at revolution.

Their reluctance was understandable. The Spanish regime had showed its resiliency in 1917, when appearances had indicated that its defenses were weak, while the revolutionary forces, seemingly confident and united, had been divided and destroyed, one by one. Most significantly, the army, which had seemed to promise political renovation in June 1917 had, during the course of the summer, repudiated reform and acquired a debt that could be collected only by preserving the political status quo. After 1917, the left had no illusions about the success of an appeal to the army. On the contrary, the army appeared as the first and most essential obstacle to political and social change.

The Aftermath of the Strike

After their enthusiastic repression of the strike, the Juntas were in a position to make almost unlimited demands upon the Dato government; Márquez's new nickname—Benito I—summarized the political moment. As before, the political leverage of the junteros was derived largely from the defensive position of the government. On June 1, July 19, and August 13, the principal weapon of the Juntas had been the threat of *inaction*, of withdrawal of support from a regime that from the first had implicitly relied on the military to secure its existence. To translate this negative gesture into positive action, however, required greater unanimity within the officer corps than in fact existed. Although Colonel Márquez would once again try to establish a reformist political role for the army in the fall of 1917, the bulk of the Juntas would forsake him for the promise of a military reform bill tailored to their interests.

Thoroughly conscious that the loyalty of the army had been decisive during the August strike, the Dato government moved quickly to repay its debt. On August 21 the cabinet voted a 77 million peseta credit for defense expenditures.[62] But the Juntas wanted more: continuation of martial law and the execution of the Socialist strike committee, composed of Julián Besteiro, Francisco Largo Caballero, Daniel Anguiano, and Andrés Saborit. Refusing the latter demand, the government found it convenient to allow the court-martial, which began in Madrid on September 28, to deal as harshly as it chose with the committee. The military prosecutor presented two accusations against the committee: a frustrated attempt at military sedition, punishable under the Code of Military Justice by life imprisonment, and a successful attempt at common rebellion, punishable under the Civil Code by a nine-year prison sentence.[63] Although the committee was enthusiastically defended by two young officers with Masonic connections, Infantry Captains Ramón Arronte Girón and Julio Mangada Rosenorn, the outcome of the trial was never in doubt.[64] On October 4 the court found the four Socialists guilty of common rebellion, but ruled that a frustrated intent to commit military rebellion was not punishable under military law. Nevertheless, the court imposed the maximum military penalty—life imprisonment—to satisfy the Juntas. Captain Mangada received fifteen days' corrective arrest for his excessive zeal in the committee's defense.

The Juntas were equally intransigent about the release of Marcelino Domingo, who was scheduled to be tried for rebellion before a court-martial in Barcelona in violation of his rights as a deputy, which required the submission of a *suplicatorio* to the Cortes requesting permission for the trial.[65] As president of the Congress, the Liberal Miguel Villanueva repeatedly pointed out to Dato that the army's disregard for Domingo's rights implied a disregard for the sovereignty of the Cortes as well, but Dato would respond only with vague public assurances that the law would be observed.[66] In private, he was unable to persuade the Juntas to surrender jurisdiction over the Republican deputy. It was not until the eve of Dato's fall in late October that the civil Supreme Court asserted its jurisdiction over the case, and not until November 5, two days after the formation of a new coalition government, that Domingo was placed in provisional liberty.

As outrage over the strike faded, public opinion turned in favor of the persecuted strike leaders and against the Juntas, whose professed progressivism now seemed rather thin. In order to recoup some of its lost moral authority, the Infantry Superior Junta began to distance itself publicly from the repressive policy it was privately forcing upon the government. In a circular of September 7, it warned local Juntas of the danger of a rift between the army and the people, and for the first time made a distinction between the *general* protest of August and the goals of a tiny, revolutionary minority. While justifying the court-martial of these subversives, the Superior Junta now recommended a more conciliatory policy toward the rest—specifically, the end of martial law, supposedly imposed by Dato in order to discredit the army. Finally, the Junta leadership asked for a prior vote of confidence in the event they were called upon to fulfill their "sacred obligation" to impose on the politicians "morality, justice, and foresight."[67]

At the same time, the activists in the Infantry Junta tried to lead the membership into a more active political role. Since early August delegates from the regional Juntas (representing the eight military districts) had been in session in Barcelona, their deliberations only temporarily interrupted by the general strike.[68] On September 12 the assembly reconvened and agreed to intervene directly in the political process by writing letters to the government, the press, the king, and favored generals, with the vaguely stated purpose of restoring "morality and justice" to government under the benevolent eye of the Junta. On September 25 they dispatched General Marina to Madrid to warn the prime minister of their displeasure at the adverse publicity surrounding their role in the general strike and to advise him of their intention to intervene in the political crisis. Although Dato's official reply could not have been more temporizing,[69] the Junta leadership was now more eager than ever to replace him with Antonio Maura.[70] Márquez and his allies in the Superior Junta still envisioned themselves as the shepherds of the renovationist movement.

The majority of the Infantry Junta, however, was less interested in politics than in the professional grievances that had originally sparked its formation. In August the delegates had vented their anger against the senior hierarchy by compiling a blacklist of generals, some of whom should be immediately retired, others of whom might be rehabilitated after a proper penance. The sessions in September were equally absorbed by the bureaucratic matters that had preoccupied Infantry officers for decades, especially the extension of the seniority principle and the elimination of favoritism. Rejecting General Aguilera's appointments decree of May 31, the delegates proposed that all appointments be made on the basis of strict seniority. On September 25 the Junta moved against the Staff Corps, voting to require candidates for the Superior War College to indicate in advance of their acceptance whether they intended to enter the Staff Corps or return to the Infantry as diplomados after graduation. Officers who chose the Staff Corps and then failed the entrance exam to the War College would not be allowed to return to the Infantry but would find their careers at an end. This measure, which reflected the widespread resentment in the Infantry against the privileges and rapid promotions of Staff officers, demonstrated clearly the general desire to convert the Junta into a professional union.

When the government finally restored constitutional guarantees on October 18, these deliberations were made public. Freed from prior censorship, two Madrid dailies, *El País* and *El Parlamentario*, published several of the supposedly secret Junta circulars and letters, together with the August classifications of offending generals. Outraged by this evidence of insubordination, the Marqués de Estella resigned from the War Ministry the same day. On October 20 both Estella and General Luque, the senior political generals of the turno, publicly condemned the vetoing process and demanded an immediate return to the normal chain of command.[71] But the government and the king had decided that real power in the army now lay with the Juntas. Ignoring the generals, Dato endeavored to placate the irate Superior Junta, which had dispatched two of its members to Madrid to investigate the source of the leaks to the press. To replace Estella in the War Ministry, Dato appointed the general most favorable to the Infantry Junta, General Marina. Even Marina, however, was less sympathetic to the Junta since the revelation of its vendetta against the senior hierarchy.[72]

The Crisis of October 1917

During the last week in October, the renovationist coalition mounted its final assault on the government. Thoroughly discredited by its pusillanimous conduct during the fall, the Dato government was clearly doomed; although the Liberals made haste to add their voices to the rising chorus of criticism, it was equally clear that their own party was too divided to assume office. The Assembly movement, temporarily eclipsed by the strike, now appeared as the only possible solution to the political stalemate. During September and October Cambó had made the rounds of the principal resort cities, mustering support for a coalition government that would dissolve the existing Cortes and proceed toward constitutional reform. It was a measure of Cambó's persuasiveness and of the general disillusionment with Dato that the Liberal president of the Cortes allowed one of the Assembly's study commissions to meet in the Palace of the Cortes itself in mid-October. The program of constitutional reform the commission released to the press on October 18 made a calculated appeal to popular indignation over the conduct of the government since the August strike.[73] Cambó also endeavored to exploit the well-known hostility of the Juntas toward Dato by publicly praising their rebellion against an illegitimate government, although he apparently did not renew his contacts with Márquez.[74] Having thus at least temporarily resuscitated the broad opposition movement of early June, Cambó scheduled a second session of the Assembly for October 30.

On October 23 the Infantry Junta moved against the government. In collaboration with Captains Villar and Leopoldo Pérez Pala, Colonel Márquez wrote another message to the king. This time, however, he submitted it to the assembly of regional Junta representatives for approval, hoping to avoid the disunity of the summer.[75] The assembled colonels not only approved the message but also voted to allow the king only seventy-two hours to take the first steps toward meeting their demands for political renovation. If there were no response, the army would recover its freedom of action to proceed "in the national interest," probably by seconding the decisions of the Assembly of Parliamentarians. On October 24 Márquez presented the message to the presidents of the other branch Juntas, whose reluctance to sanction a flagrant breach of constitutional legality was overcome only with great difficulty. After several false starts, however, all the branch Juntas save the Engineers signed the document, which was entrusted to two separate sets of emissaries for communication to the king.[76] In an interview with *El Heraldo* on October 24, Márquez justified the ultimatum to the Spanish public as necessary to avoid "dangerous temporary incumbencies or long constituent periods." While insisting that the army believed in civil supremacy, he warned that the nine thousand members of the Infantry Junta, and the other corps as well, stood unanimously behind his leadership.[77]

On October 26 two events convinced Alfonso that the hour had arrived to sacrifice Dato. The president of the Congress, Villanueva, once again permitted two study commissions of the Parliamentary Assembly to meet in the Palace of the Cortes, a sign that the Liberals were growing impatient for power. The principal order of business of one commission was an army reform bill—more proof, if any were needed, that the Lliga was still courting the Juntas.[78] In the evening there was a large meeting of junteros in the military casino. When Dato waited on the king the next morning, he was discreetly asked for his opinion of the "Liberal situation." The same afternoon, Dato resigned.

It was clear, however, that a Liberal solution was impossible. Above all, the unrelenting hostility of the Juntas and the Lliga since June had been directed against Dato as a symbol of the old turno; their success in finally bringing him down meant that they had destroyed the turno as well. The political postmortems that followed the news of Dato's resignation recognized this at once, just as they recognized the impossibility of any solution that could not guarantee military discipline, as the faction-ridden Liberals certainly could not.[79] At stake was the principle of civil supremacy, a fact understood by everyone, but articulated most emphatically (if somewhat orotundly) by Antonio Maura, whose reference to the Juntas as "a seditious armed band" made it clear that he was still uninterested in cultivating juntero support. Maura diagnosed the problem of the regime as its failure to lay a secure foundation in national opinion. He then offered a quasi-fatalistic prognostication of military dictatorship that was destined to be repeated incessantly during the next six years: "If this [civil supremacy] is not achieved, then those who do not allow others to govern, should govern themselves, assuming complete responsibility."[80] At issue, of course, was the kind of solution that could generate the broad national support needed to resist military pressure. Maura's star had faded since June. The left was still vociferously opposed, the Juntas had been put off by his cool reception of their overtures, and the Catalans now vetoed a Maura government. But other dynastic party leaders could offer no promise of substantial reform.

The only alternative seemed to be the Assembly of Parliamentarians, who held their second plenary session in Madrid on October 30, in the midst of the crisis, and reiterated their demand for Constituent Cortes and an opening to the left, symbolized by the inclusion of the Reformist Melquíades Álvarez in a new government. The breach in the alliance with the Republicans and Socialists had been mended; chastened by the failure of the revolutionary general strike, the Socialists now aimed only at the making of a bourgeois revolution. Bowing to forces that could no longer be ignored, Alfonso sent a message to Cambó asking him to leave the Assembly to come for a consultation.

As he had in July, Cambó betrayed his alliance with the left. The decision of the Lliga leadership to abandon the Assembly movement had been made on October 25 after an Executive Committee meeting with Lerroux and Iglesias; in the deepening crisis, Cambó was no longer certain he could contain the revolution from the left.[81] Under the circumstances, it seemed necessary to sacrifice the bourgeois revolution in order to save the monarchy and the social order. Cambó had already partially defused the threat from the Juntas by persuading one of the emissaries sent to Madrid to refrain from presenting the ultimatum to the king.[82] At his meeting in the palace with the king and the Liberal leader García Prieto on October 30, Cambó agreed to the formation of a coalition government in which the Catalanists would be given two portfolios. In return, he agreed to drop the Assembly's demands for Constituent Cortes. Although it supposedly represented a break with the past, the new government would be committed primarily to the preservation of the political status quo, slightly expanded to include the Catalan bourgeoisie. García Prieto offered no reform other than free elections guaranteed by an independent Interior Minister.

To neutralize the threat from the Juntas, Cambó and García Prieto agreed on the appointment of Juan de la Cierva as Minister of War.[83] As a civilian, La Cierva represented a break with the traditional military turno that controlled the War Ministry. A Conservative with a strong authoritarian streak, La Cierva had already made contact with the two remaining Junta emissaries, who were distracted from their political mission to the king by the promise of immediate attention to the junteros' professional grievances. The junteros, Major Espino and Captain Miguel García Rodríguez, had never supported the renovationist program advocated by Colonel Márquez. Thus they were easily persuaded to throw their support behind the proposed coalition government. As La Cierva suspected, their indifference toward political reform was characteristic of the majority of the officer corps.[84]

In Cambó's view, the participation of La Cierva was a realistic response to the threat posed by the Juntas, who might otherwise have brought down the throne.[85] The evidence for this is thin, however. As Cambó was aware (he had been insisting on it all summer and fall), the political leverage of the army was less of its own making than of the government's. It was unlikely that the army would overthrow the monarchy in the fall of 1917, because it lacked the unity to do so. The junteros pressing La Cierva's candidacy during the crisis were no more representative of the entire army than was Márquez, who was in Barcelona, unaware of the negotiations underway in Madrid. For one thing, the appointment of La Cierva was a repudiation of the political generals, who had hitherto controlled access to the War Ministry. With the officer corps internally divided, a coup was not likely to be attempted; it would most certainly not succeed. His arguments in favor of "realism" notwithstanding, Cambó's attitude in 1917 smacked heavily of opportunism.

The inclusion of La Cierva in the García Prieto coalition completed Cambó's break with the left, which since 1909 had stood firm against a return of Maura and his former lieutenant, La Cierva, to office. Melquíades Álvarez refused to participate in the new government as a matter of principle, although he was offered a portfolio. The final goal of the renovationist movement—an opening of the regime to the democratic left—was thus abandoned.

The resolution of the crisis undeniably enhanced the political power of the Juntas, particularly of the majority faction concerned with purely professional demands. Few civilian observers made the distinction, of course; it was assumed that "the army" had acted as one. Moreover, the turbulent summer and fall of 1917 had convinced the dynastic parties that government in opposition to "army opinion"— supposedly represented by the Juntas—was impossible. But with the officer corps, and even the Juntas themselves, divided, the army would not be able to respond decisively or constructively to the political responsibilities impressed upon it by civilian government. The Juntas' attempt to exercise their power would therefore be disruptive and demoralizing for both the regime and the army.

Their first victim would be the coalition government that took office on November 3, 1917, a conglomeration of political forces that quickly earned its nickname, "the Horatian monster."[86] Inspired by the patriotic "unity" governments of wartime Europe, the Spanish coalition lacked the continuing presence of a common enemy to give it cohesion once the threat of the Juntas had been removed. Furthermore, the left was completely excluded. A positive program to eliminate the root causes of military power in 1917 by broadening the base of the constitutional monarchy was thus not likely; apart from the commitment to free elections, García Prieto had no other program than to appease the army. Indeed, his very lack of substance made García Prieto the ideal minister for the final years of parliamentary government in Spain, as the dynastic parties revealed their incapacity to rule. Between 1917 and 1923 he would head four cabinets.

Besides the Juntas, the real victor in 1917 was Francisco Cambó, who had negotiated the incorporation of the Catalan bourgeoisie into the governing elite by exploiting the chaos created by the army. At the same time, he had manipulated the Juntas so skilfully that their potential danger had been blunted, or at least deferred. The community of interest between conservative Catalans and the army would endure another six years, overriding the original military distrust of regionalism. That community of interest would disappear and the old hatreds flare up only when the army discovered that it could govern by itself.

CHAPTER FIVE

The Army Reform Law of 1918

The coalition government came into office on November 3, 1917, to restore military discipline and lead the country toward political reform. It did neither, but instead left the constitutional monarchy and the principle of civil supremacy even weaker than it had found them. Nor would the prestige of the so-called National Government of April 1918 achieve more than the momentary salvation of the completely bankrupt dynastic parties. The problem was that neither coalition was truly "national"; instead, each represented only the disparate elements of the fractionated turno parties, fortified by the inclusion of the Catalan Lliga. Instead of restoring the credibility of the traditional parties, the coalitions of 1918 only emphasized their lack of constructive solutions to the problems facing the nation.

Intrinsically weak, the coalition governments of 1918 would not risk a challenge to the army. Instead, they would attempt to neutralize the officer corps by passing a reform law tailored to juntero demands. The law, enacted first by royal decree, then by the Cortes, raised salaries, increased employment opportunities, and established strict seniority promotions in both peace and war. It was thus a "reform" bill that met the complaints of bureaucratic officers against favoritism and stagnant careers. Conversely, it did not attack the real defect of the Spanish army—excessive personnel—for fear of alienating those same officers.

The mistaken assumption underlying the reform law of 1918 was that the interests of the Juntas were those of the army as a whole. In practice, the law further divided the officer corps, since it did not speak to the professional interests of other groups in the army—in particular, the africanistas—and since it limited the discretionary powers of the military elites that had traditionally controlled internal military affairs.

As a result, the bill encouraged, rather than discouraged, the tendency of military factions toward political activism.

Most significant, the government's capitulation to juntero demands was an invitation to continued military intervention in the future. Having given in once, the dynastic parties found themselves open to blackmail by any faction with a grievance. The policy of reliance on the army, originally adopted to secure the stability of the regime, thus came to pose as great a danger to that stability as the opposition groups demanding political change.

The formation of the coalition government under García Prieto on November 3 resolved the political, but not the constitutional, crisis of 1917. The political ferment that had filled the summer and fall continued, heightened, on November 7, by news of the Bolshevik Revolution in Russia. Eventually, the establishment of the first socialist state would preoccupy the entire Spanish labor movement, but in November 1917 its impact was most profound on the wildly enthusiastic Anarchists and the horrified bourgeoisie. Spanish Socialists were slower to react, finding the domestic crisis and the European war of more immediate interest.[1] In Madrid, a press campaign for amnesty for those arrested during the general strike was initiated by *El Socialista* and supported by most of the democratic left press, including the new "renovationist" paper, *El Sol*, founded on December 1. In the municipal elections held on November 11, the four imprisoned Socialists of the strike committee were elected to the city council in Madrid, along with nine other Republicans and Socialists, although the results were later annulled on a technicality. Thus encouraged, the parties in favor of reform hoped to use the government's promise of free elections in February to overwhelm the dynastic parties at the polls and to direct the new Cortes toward constitutional revision.

The role of the Juntas in the resolution of the cabinet crisis, together with the universal recognition that they continued to hold the political advantage, made them the subject of seemingly endless analysis. During December political figures ranging from the Socialist Pablo Iglesias to the Carlist Juan Vázquez de Mella debated the legitimacy of the juntero rebellion of June 1 in *El Liberal*, a "Trust" paper sympathetic to democratic reform. Most of the regime's critics, including Iglesias, Cambó, and Álvarez, agreed that the illegitimacy of the turno justified the breach of military discipline. In a burst of ill-considered enthusiasm, Ortega y Gasset wrote in *El Sol* that the appearance of the Juntas on June 1 was "the most glorious, healthy, original, European act that Spain has presented to the world in the last one hundred years."[2] The dynastic politicians were understandably less enthusiastic, although in print they were reluctant to denounce the Juntas with vigor. The exception was Joaquín Sánchez de Toca, an independent Conservative who plainly labeled the unionization of the armed forces as a "monstrosity" incompatible with constitutional government or public order.[3]

The debate was not over the legitimacy of the Juntas but the legitimacy of the regime. Thus the left thoughtlessly acquiesced in the emergence of the army as a political moderating power, failing to foresee that an army allowed to destroy one "illegitimate" regime might easily take it upon itself to repeat the action. In the crisis of 1917, the right perceived more clearly the threat to civil supremacy. Nevertheless, in the chaotic years that followed, none of the dynastic politicians would find the courage to resist the demands of an army that protected them from political revolution and social disorder.

La Cierva and the Juntas

This public discussion annoyed the new War Minister, Juan de la Cierva, because it complicated his plan for domesticating the Juntas. Unlike many politicians on both the left and the right, La Cierva shrewdly perceived that the minority of activists in the Superior Infantry Junta had led the officer corps farther into civilian politics than most of them cared to go. Because he did not object to military indiscipline on philosophical or constitutional grounds but as a threat to orderly government, La Cierva did not fear the Juntas and was able to manipulate them skilfully. After ingratiating himself with the army as a whole, he used the bureaucratic majority in the Superior Junta to eliminate Benito Márquez and the NCO Juntas. Next, he responded to the professional grievances of the military middle class with his army reform bill, assuming that this would enable him to demand the dissolution of the Juntas. What La Cierva failed to foresee was that the success of the Juntas' insubordinate tactics in 1917 would encourage them to repeat those tactics the next time a new grievance arose. Basically an unreflective instrumentalist, La Cierva overlooked the connection between means and ends and unintentionally hastened the erosion of civil supremacy.

La Cierva's hubris also led him to believe that he could use the Juntas as a political power base. He sympathized with army officers, whose views on order and authority were similar to his own, and they returned his admiration. With the Conservative leadership divided, he hoped to profit from his military clientele, posing as a bulwark against revolution and as the tamer of the army. This, however, was a miscalculation. In the confrontation between the military and the government in March 1918, his own career would be sacrificed. The Juntas would lose their voice in the cabinet, but their real power would remain intact. La Cierva in effect created the force that destroyed him.

From the first, La Cierva made it clear to the officer corps that he was sensitive to their professional problems. To avoid charges of favoritism, his aides were chosen at the recommendation of the various Superior Juntas. On November 28 the government granted an extraordinary bonus to all civil and military employees earning sixty-five hundred pesetas or less, which included all officers below the rank of colonel. Meanwhile, the War Minister flaunted his concern for military honor by authorizing a liberal use of the Law of Jurisdictions[4] and by making personal appearances in the provincial garrisons. In his most publicized speech, delivered at the Cavalry Academy in Valladolid on December 13, he praised the "potent and providential voice" of the Juntas and promised to consider their interests his own.[5] These tactics soon produced their calculated effect. On December 18 *La Correspondencia Militar* praised the War Minister as "one of the most serious, sensible, and prestigious figures in Spanish public life."[6]

At the same time that he built up his own prestige, La Cierva undermined the authority of Benito Márquez, whose political ambitions had not diminished since the resolution of the cabinet crisis (in which he had played no part). Indeed, Márquez now seemed ready to launch a political career on the strength of his following in the military and civilian Juntas. The Junta of the Corps of Postal and Telegraph Workers elected him honorary president in November, and it was rumored that he would stand for election from Madrid in February.[7] Furthermore, Márquez, whose idealism was sincere, if naive, was less enthusiastic than others in the Superior Junta about the new War Minister. Undoubtedly, his jealousy of La Cierva's popularity played a role. In any event, he had resisted sending a letter of support to the Minister when the rest of the Superior Junta had voted to do so. Márquez thus posed a double threat—to the end of military political activism and to the cultivation of a Junta leadership committed exclusively to La Cierva.

Accordingly, La Cierva set about provoking a confrontation with Márquez, correctly calculating that the colonel would be betrayed by the juntero rank and file. On November 30 he wrote directly to the peninsular regiments, asking for their opinions on professional questions, which he promised to consider when preparing his military reform bill.[8] Because this procedure deliberately bypassed the juntero hierarchy, and in particular, the Superior Junta, it infuriated Márquez, who sent three members of the Superior Junta to Madrid to remonstrate with the War Minister.[9] It was a measure of Márquez's political innocence that his chosen emissaries were the three junteros who had intrigued with La Cierva during the recent cabinet crisis—Major Espino and Captains Pérez Pala and García Rodríguez. On December 23 the three returned to Barcelona, where they informed Márquez and his one remaining ally, Captain Herrero, that they had sworn allegiance to La Cierva and were removing Márquez from the Junta presidency. Angry but incredulous, Márquez retorted he would resign first. To his chagrin, the resignation was immediately accepted and announced to the press on December 26. As La Cierva had anticipated, the remaining junteros, except for Herrero, quickly closed ranks against Márquez, whose petition for reinstatement before the assembly of regional representatives was politely and firmly rejected on January 7. A month later, a new Superior Junta oriented toward purely professional objectives was elected in Barcelona.[10]

The Suppression of the Union of Noncommissioned Officers

With Márquez successfully eliminated from the Superior Junta, La Cierva's goal of muting its political proclivities seemed a step closer. His task was made easier still by the reactivation of the NCO Junta, which decided in December to test the receptivity of the new War Minister to its demands. Since the rebuff from the officers' Junta the previous June, leadership of the NCO Junta had passed to Madrid, where organizers, in strictest secrecy, had established a network of provincial Juntas based in Valencia. At the end of December the Madrid Junta drafted a letter to the War Minister, which was transmitted to Valencia for approval.[11] In style and content, this manifesto resembled those of the previous summer: the NCOs wanted "dignity," promotion into the reserve list, and the right to express their grievances collectively. In deference to the influence of the officers' Juntas, the NCOs eliminated the earlier hostile references to their superiors. But the officers were not mollified by the obsequious tone of this document, which was leaked to the War Ministry before it could be officially presented. As quick to recognize the danger of syndicalization among the lower ranks as they were slow to recognize it among themselves, the Infantry Superior Junta insisted that La Cierva dissolve the "Union of Noncommissioned Officers" and cashier the organizers.

Several members of the senior hierarchy, including Generals Luque and Weyler, vigorously opposed the dissolution of the NCO Junta, which they supported as a counterweight to the officers' Juntas.[12] But La Cierva saw his chance to indebt the officers' Juntas to himself; the dissolution of one Junta could be potent leverage to use against the others. Furthermore, he was opposed to the NCO Junta because it was much more likely, in his view, to slide into radical politics.[13] On January 4, 1918, La Cierva acted decisively. With the aid of telegraph workers, who worked all night to code the lengthy instructions to regional military authorities, he ordered the immediate dissolution of the NCO Juntas and cashiered over two hundred sergeants and troops in Madrid, Barcelona, and Valencia who refused to sign a pledge not to organize further.[14] The official note from the War Ministry justified the action to the country by stressing the unauthorized traveling of the NCO organizers, their coded communications, and the intervention of "outside elements" that would have led the movement into military insubordination and political subversion, a line echoed that evening in *La Correspondencia Militar*.[15]

But there was little evidence that the NCOs were pursuing revolutionary political goals; in any case, their procedures were no more revolutionary than those employed by the officers' Juntas the year before. The real motive for the suppression of the NCO Junta was the professional jealousy of their immediate superiors, who had single-handedly carried out La Cierva's orders. All the generals stationed in the capital, including the Captain General, had manufactured official business to keep them elsewhere.[16] As the partisan nature of the re-pression became known, even those who had taken a tolerant view of the officers' Juntas a month earlier now criticized the government for missing an opportunity to dissolve them.[17]

In La Cierva's view, a dissolution was premature. He intended to remind the Juntas of their opposition to the NCO Junta after their griev-ances had been met and they had been reconciled with the senior hierarchy. In the aftermath of the NCO conflict, a solution to the latter problem seemed as urgent as it was difficult. On February 20 La Cierva achieved partial success with an anniversary celebration of the Gen-eral Military Academy (AGM). The younger generals and many of the middle-ranking officers who formed the backbone of the Juntas in 1918 had graduated from the AGM during the ten years of its existence, 1883–93. Moreover, as a temporary antidote to the exclusivity of the technical corps, the AGM was particularly cherished in the Infantry. Thus while Artillery officers were somewhat miffed, the AGM banquet gratified Infantry junteros at the same time that it reunited them with the youngest and most vigorous generals in a fraternal celebration of collegiality from which only the senior Restoration generals were excluded. The AGM banquet also reaffirmed the loyalty of the officer corps to the king, who stressed his own commitment to the military in a speech that provoked great enthusiasm and emotion.[18] The obvious harmony between junteros and young generals received much favorable comment in the press and marked La Cierva as the most effective figure in the García Prieto cabinet.

The Cortes Elections of 1918

After the flurry of interest generated by the banquet, attention reverted to the most absorbing political event of the winter of 1918— the election of deputies on February 24. As the government had promised, the Minister of the Interior provided no guidance to local election boards, giving reformers hope that the electorate would return a majority committed to constitutional revision. The outcome of the first "free" elections of the parliamentary monarchy, however, merely dramatized how deeply rooted were caciquismo and voter apathy.[19] To be sure, in the urban areas, where caciquismo was less effective, the two principal protest movements of 1917 achieved substantial victories. Vast expenditures by the Lliga insured them a large majority in Catalonia, while the Socialists, who had campaigned on a platform of amnesty, won a moral victory against the government and the army by electing the four imprisoned members of the strike committee. With Pablo Iglesias and Indalecio Prieto, a young journalist from Bilbao, the Socialist representation in the Cortes now formed a recognizable voting bloc of six. The only protest parties to be repudiated at the polls were the Reformists and the Republicans, whose vacillating policies the previous August had won them no friends in either camp.

Yet despite these gains, the dynastic parties continued to dominate the elections. The absence of centralized electoral manipulation did not destroy rural caciquismo, which continued to operate effectively at the local level, using its traditional tools of patronage and influence. Instead, it merely destroyed the Canovite mechanism for achieving a workable majority, leaving the Cortes of 1918 divided almost evenly between the Liberals and the Conservatives, who in turn were divided into three rival subgroups each (followers of García Prieto, Romanones, and Alba, for the Liberals, and of Dato, Maura, and La Cierva, for the Conservatives).[20] "Free" elections in a country that was still largely rural, illiterate, and politically apathetic (34 percent of the electorate abstained from voting) produced a parliament with no internal cohesion and no mandate for reform. Although a slight Liberal majority allowed the García Prieto coalition government to stay in office, it seemed unlikely to survive the antagonisms that had been deprived of parliamentary expression for over a year.

La Cierva's Army Reform Bill

In anticipation of this, La Cierva resolved to enact his army reform bill by decree before it could fall victim to political partisanship in the Cortes, scheduled to reopen on March 18. Because the Cortes had been closed since the previous February, there had been no debate on the Juntas de Defensa or on the army's role in the August general strike, making rapid passage of a military reform bill problematic. Yet without the bill, La Cierva doubted he could keep the Juntas under control. His plan was to secure enactment of the bill by decree and then to submit the decree, in toto, to the Cortes for legislative approval. In this manner, the decree would acquire force of law with less risk of alterations in its provisions.

La Cierva's insistence on a decree—essentially a repudiation of the legislative power—completely disrupted the García Prieto government, which was supposedly committed to democratic reform. His announcement of his intentions on February 27 provoked the departure of the two Catalans from the cabinet and opened an ongoing political crisis that the hapless García Prieto was powerless to resolve. In a cabinet meeting on March 6, La Cierva read his bill and insisted on its immediate enactment by decree. García Prieto offered to resign in his favor, but La Cierva refused to assume responsibility for his actions by forming a government himself. Faced with an impasse, the prime minister and the rest of his cabinet, with the exception of the Romanonist, Amalio Gimeno, finally surrendered.[21] The king signed the decree on March 7.

The cabinet was immediately plunged into another crisis when La Cierva released to the press a scathing attack on Joaquín Sánchez de Toca, whose pointed criticism of the War Minister and the Juntas[22] had driven officers in the Madrid garrison to the brink of direct action.[23] García Prieto submitted the resignation of the entire cabinet in protest, but La Cierva refused to comply. Moreover, the Juntas had already made it known that they would not tolerate the replacement of La Cierva in the War Ministry. The public reaction to La Cierva's high-handedness transcended the usual political boundaries. Headlines in the liberal press screamed "dictatorship," Sánchez de Toca labeled La Cierva a "dictated-to dictator,"[24] and the Madrid Socialist Group denounced the breach of parliamentary rights and the threat of military dictatorship in a protest declaration on March 8.[25] La Cierva, however, refused to confirm these predictions by forming a government of his own. Once again, García Prieto ended the stalemate by resuming office with the same cabinet on March 10. How long it would last clearly depended on the benevolence of La Cierva and the Juntas de Defensa.

The same day that García Prieto resumed office, the royal decree on army reform appeared in the *Gaceta*.[26] Coming less than two weeks before the opening of the Cortes, the decree, which carried appropriations provisions, was a slap in the face to parliamentary government, and, together with the recent cabinet crisis, was the clearest proof to date that the army was the most decisive political institution in Spain.

La Cierva's reform bill reformed nothing, but rather reconfirmed the defects that had incapacitated the Spanish army for at least a century. Written to juntero specifications, with benefits for generals and NCOs as well, it sacrificed efficiency and modernization in order to protect and advance the interests of the swollen military bureaucracy that formed the core of the juntero movement. Unlike General Luque's reform bill of 1916, the 1918 decree did not make even a compromising attempt to alleviate the overcrowded lists and, thus, the strain on the budget. On the contrary, by expanding the number of divisions from fourteen to an unnecessary sixteen, tripling the number of Cavalry brigades, and setting the troop strength at 180,000, La Cierva actually increased the number of active posts by 1,714. Even this generous allowance left nearly 4,000 existing personnel without employment, but the decree did not introduce significant measures to reduce their numbers. Although the decree contained inducements to early retirement, only half of the vacancies so obtained were to be amortized, thus perpetuating the excess of officers at the higher ranks. In addition, the 25 percent amortizations at all ranks established by General Luque in 1916 were apparently to be abandoned.[27]

The benefits of the lower retirement ages prescribed by the decree were also vitiated by the creation of a two-year "reserve" situation in which officers would continue to be eligible for active posts at a slightly lower salary, an ingenious scheme borrowed from General Luque that softened the blow for retiring officers while speeding up promotions for those below.[28] With the memory of the NCO Junta still fresh, La Cierva opened the reserve list to noncommissioned officers and even provided for the incorporation of academy-trained NCOs into the active list, a highly unlikely contingency that posed no real threat to regular officers. Since there was currently no deficit of subalterns, these provisions were justifiable only in terms of social justice, or political pragmatism, not economy, efficiency, or need.

This inflated bureaucracy was given a pay increase, as follows:

Division general	20,000 pesetas	Major	6,500
Brigadier	15,000	Captain	4,500
Colonel	10,000	First lieutenant	3,000
Lieutenant colonel	8,000	Second lieutenant	2,500

The pay of corporals and soldiers was raised by 25 céntimos daily, while sergeants and subofficials received a 30 percent increase (the rank of brigade was abolished).

Inflation had made a cost-of-living increase necessary, but the proposed pay scale increased salaries proportionately at all ranks, rewarding the already comfortable senior officers more than the truly impoverished lower ranks. Thus the pressure for rapid promotion would continue, only partly alleviated by the introduction of a five-hundred-peseta annual bonus for each five years in grade. The upshot of all these provisions was to guarantee that the War Ministry budget would continue to be consumed by salaries.

The other major sections of La Cierva's bill dealt with juntero grievances concerning favoritism in promotions and appointments; it was here that the reform bill of 1918 differed most markedly from that proposed by General Luque in 1916. Generally speaking, all promotions in peace *and* war were to be made on the basis of strict seniority. At the ranks of captain and colonel, a "Classifying Junta" composed of five lieutenant generals was to rule on individual eligibility for promotion to the next rank. Promotions to general would be made from the top one-third of the lists, proportional to the percentage of each corps within the army as a whole, in order to combat the traditional favoritism shown officers from the technical branches.[29] Most important, all battlefield decorations would be purely honorific, pensions and merit promotions having been eliminated. For special cases, the bill allowed merit promotions to be voted by law in the Cortes after an investigation and recommendation by the Supreme Military Council.

In general, the decree deprived the War Ministry of many of its discretionary powers in the hope of undermining the patronage system. Unfortunately, by guaranteeing equal rewards to the Moroccan field officer and the mediocre peninsular bureaucrat, it undermined excellence as well. Predictably, the decree would have a disastrous impact on the morale of the African army, particularly after operations were resumed in 1919. For peninsular junteros, however, the establishment of the closed scale was the crowning achievement of the reform bill of 1918.

Other sections of the bill provided for the creation of an Aeronautics service and for the expansion and modernization of the army's equipment on a grand scale. The details of where the 1.3 billion pesetas itemized in the decree were to be found were left to the discretion of the Cortes. Given the limitations of the Spanish treasury, particularly in light of the salary increases, it seemed unlikely that this part of the decree would ever be realized, with or without legislative approval. These sections of the reform bill were largely for display. The goal of the bill was not a strong, well-trained, and well-equipped standing army, but a return to the "neutral" officer corps of the Restoration.

But neither La Cierva nor his reform bill could completely restore the tranquility of the Canovite years, for the political weight of the officer corps had grown in direct proportion to the strength of the forces demanding political and social change. Lower-ranking officers had discovered that they could achieve their goals without the intervention of the political generals, whose ability to maintain military discipline had evaporated. Most significant, the officer corps, always disunited, was divided even further by the promotions provisions in the reform bill. The coincidence of growing military power with growing military disunity would ultimately have fatal consequences for the regime.

The Expulsion of Márquez

With the enactment of the reform bill by decree on March 7, La Cierva was nearing the end of his program. He was now convinced that he could persuade the Juntas to dissolve, on the grounds that all their grievances had been satisfied. He also intended to remind them of his dissolution of the NCO Junta. On March 8, during the cabinet crisis, he quietly but officially requested all the Juntas to disband. Once they were gone and forgotten, he believed he could use his considerable political power to form a government without running the risk, as surely would have been the case at that moment, of being accused of aspiring to a military dictatorship.

But on March 10, as the García Prieto cabinet dutifully returned to office, La Cierva's carefully laid plans were upset by two unforeseen events: the reemergence of Benito Márquez and the refusal of three of the Juntas to dissolve. Since his removal from the presidency of the Infantry Junta in December, Márquez had not fallen into oblivion but had kept the problem of the Juntas alive by taking his case to the country in a letter of denunciation and revelation published in *El Mundo* on January 30. In addition, as honorary president of the Junta de Defensa of postal and telegraph workers, he had supported the slow-down strike they had begun on January 21. The publicity surrounding Márquez had attracted unfavorable attention to the Juntas, making La Cierva's attempts to lull them into quiescence much more difficult. The War Minister had been encouraged, then, when in late February the newly elected Infantry Superior Junta appointed an honor court to try the colonel for violating his oath of secrecy.[30] La Cierva had expected Márquez to be quietly out of the way by March 7.

Instead of resigning gracefully, Márquez once again appealed to the public for justice. In a manifesto published on March 10, he denounced the new Superior Junta and their ally, the War Minister, and warned that the "Juntas, which might have been the leaven that altered the life of the State, may be the shroud of this unfortunate Nation" instead.[31] Coming on top of the cabinet crisis, Márquez's accusations threatened to ruin La Cierva's political prospects. The War Minister immediately ordered the formation of another honor court, which expelled Márquez from the army on March 12. To isolate Márquez further, officers and soldiers were forbidden to associate with him under pain of expulsion.[32] On March 20 La Cierva abrogated Article 34 of the Junta statutes, which provided for an appeal from an honor court to the Supreme Military Council, in order to prevent the antijuntero generals on the Council from striking a blow against La Cierva and the Junta by reinstating Márquez. The ambitious colonel had been totally outmaneuvered.

For a short time, Márquez remained in the public eye, as opposition groups made a halfhearted attempt to turn him into the Spanish Dreyfus. During the next few months, the former colonel was approached by the Socialists, the Republicans, and some of the sergeants expelled from the army on January 4.[33] Márquez returned their interest, but as his notoriety—and his political potential—waned, so did the contacts with the left. Part of the problem was that Márquez, unlike Dreyfus, was not an innocent victim of "militarism," but a military politician who had been bested by others cleverer than himself. As the left recovered more completely from their infatuation with the Juntas, they found Colonel Márquez, and the concept of military insubordination, ever less defensible. After a final attempt at finding an audience among radical Catalan nationalists in early 1919, Márquez accepted an offer of a job in Cuba from the Conde de Romanones in February of that year and devoted the rest of his life to self-justification. By the time he died in exile in 1923, his megalomania was of unlimited proportions.[34]

The Fall of La Cierva

La Cierva had tamed Márquez, but he had not tamed the Juntas. The weakness in his scheme to destroy them was revealed on March 10, when he received their response to the request made two days earlier that they dissolve. The Juntas of the Engineers and the Staff Corps promised to comply, but those of the Infantry, Artillery, and Cavalry firmly refused.[35] The division showed that the occasional unity of the officer corps was superficial; it also demonstrated the futility—and the danger—of trying to bribe the army into obedience. Moreover, the refusal gave the lie to the abundant rumors that La Cierva was plotting a military coup. Had he contemplated such a move, he would never have risked alienating the Juntas by requesting their dissolution.

La Cierva was not to be thwarted. Realizing that he could not use force against the Juntas, he resorted to less direct tactics, seeking to create a situation that would leave them no alternative but to disband. He found it in the slowdown strike in the Post Office, which had begun on January 21 and showed no signs of resolution. The strike was a response, like the Juntas de Defensa themselves, to the economic crisis; poorly paid and professionally frustrated, state employees had eagerly followed the lead of the military bureaucrats in the summer of 1917. But unionization did not automatically produce the anticipated relief. Lacking the threat of force possessed by the military, the civilian Juntas were unable to secure formal approval of their statutes, let alone consideration of a reform bill to ameliorate their professional status. January 1918 brought harsh temperatures and severe scarcities of food and fuel in Madrid and other cities, leading to riots and outbreaks of violence that caused several deaths. On January 21 the Corps of Postal and Telegraph Workers decided to adopt working-class tactics and began their slowdown strike.

The unionization of civil servants was as abhorrent to the dynastic politicians as the unionization of the officer corps, and the civilian Juntas were much more vulnerable. On March 13 La Cierva persuaded the cabinet to authorize militarization of the postal and telegraph workers and to order the dissolution of the extralegal civilian Juntas in all the ministries.[36] As La Cierva had anticipated, the response of the officer corps was ambivalent. While they disapproved of the "seditious" strike tactics of the civil employees,[37] they immediately understood the implications of the government's disciplinary measures for their own organizations. The military press on the evening of March 14 attempted to distinguish between the military and civilian Juntas ("the first forgot its class character, the second based itself exclusively on it"),[38] but it was clear that public opinion would soon demand equal treatment for both.

Thus, when La Cierva again asked the Juntas to dissolve, they felt compelled to compromise. On March 15 the War Ministry announced that henceforth the Juntas would consist of only one Central Junta per branch, modeled on the Artillery Junta prior to 1917 and concerned only with internal matters.[39] The hierarchy of Juntas, and their political pretensions, would be abandoned. La Cierva believed he had successfully rid the officer corps of both its syndicalist and its praetorian tendencies.

Having apparently outmaneuvered the military Juntas, La Cierva now prepared to crush the civil servants, who had not been cowed by the militarization decree of the fourteenth. Fortified by declarations of solidarity from the other ministries, postal and telegraph employees walked off the job on March 16. As temporary head of the postal service, La Cierva was empowered to act unilaterally; with his usual vigor, he mobilized the reserves to replace the absent employees and dissolved the Corps of Postal and Telegraph Workers, while the rest of the government looked on apprehensively. Public opinion was overwhelmingly on the side of the civil servants, the Cortes was scheduled to open on March 18, and the military reform decree made it difficult to justify the harsh tactics being employed by La Cierva against the postal workers. Less confident than La Cierva of his government's right to rule in defiance of popular opinion, García Prieto opened negotiations with the strikers behind the War Minister's back.

Outraged at what he considered to be a betrayal, La Cierva resigned in protest on March 19, and the rest of the cabinet, bereft of its strongest member, followed suit, opening up a crisis as severe as that of the previous autumn. With the state employees still out on strike and the Cortes temporarily suspended, a rapid solution was necessary, but elusive. The divided Cortes offered no obvious solution; the turno, in any event, was dead. The most likely leader of a new coalition, Antonio Maura, was vetoed by the Catalans. Another problem was La Cierva, who refused to accept any ministry but War, but whose presence in any future government seemed to guarantee continuing military pressure. Finally, on the night of March 21, Alfonso summoned the leaders of the principal governing parties and threatened abdication. The result was the so-called National Government of Antonio Maura, which took office on March 22, 1918.[40]

The National Government contained representatives of every principal dynastic faction, including the Lliga, but excluding Juan de la Cierva, who had been denied the War Ministry by Maura. His plan to use his power over the Juntas to make himself indispensable to any political situation had failed because he had been content to settle for the restoration of order at the expense of a truly independent civil power. Others, like Maura, saw more clearly that La Cierva had unintentionally indebted himself and the state to the Juntas. They saw just as clearly that La Cierva must go.

A bitter La Cierva left the War Ministry with his political reputation shattered but his personal standing in the officer corps still intact. During the cabinet crisis, he had refused the king's request to order the total dissolution of the military Juntas, accepting with satisfaction the Juntas' argument that they might be needed to protect the army from a new War Minister less sympathetic than La Cierva to military needs.[41] As he left for Murcia on March 23, a large number of officers gathered at the train station to see him off, a common method for officers to make their political views public.[42]

The National Government of 1918

After nine years at the periphery of Spanish political life, Antonio Maura assumed office on March 22, 1918, with little enthusiasm.[43] The dynastic parties, the army, and much of the normally apathetic middle class nevertheless viewed his return to public office almost messianically. The National Government seemed to be the "renovationist" government hoped for in 1917;[44] when it broke down only eight months later, the country, victimized by its own ill-founded illusions, was more than usually disappointed. Although the government accomplished most of the modest goals set for it by Maura, it contained no representatives of the left and thus could offer no durable solution to the constitutional crisis. Once the political crisis of March had faded, the bond that held the coalition together loosened, and the divergent political and personal tensions represented in the cabinet reemerged. By November internal dissension outweighed external threats, and the cabinet collapsed under the weight of its own contradictions and limitations.

The confidence that the government enjoyed facilitated some early achievements. On March 23 the decrees dissolving and militarizing the Corps of Postal and Telegraph Workers were abrogated, and workers returned to their jobs. Shortly thereafter, a reform bill for the civil administration was introduced in the Cortes. The rules of the Cortes were modified by the introduction of the cloture rule (*guillotina*), and an amnesty law was passed, enabling the four imprisoned members of the strike committee to take their seats in the Congress the second week in May. Meanwhile, two of the most dynamic cabinet members, Francisco Cambó, in Finance, and Santiago Alba, in Public Instruction, were preparing reform legislation for submission to the parliament.

The top priority of the government, however, was the preparation of a bill giving force of law and providing the credits for La Cierva's military reform decree of March 7. Maura, uncomfortable with the excessive military influence tolerated by La Cierva, hoped that legislative approval of the decree would partially erase the memory of the affront to parliamentary rights and shore up the somewhat shaky principle of civil supremacy. At the same time, he hoped that passage of the bill before the beginning of the new fiscal year July 7 would be interpreted by the army as a gesture of goodwill. Preparation of the bill was entrusted to the new War Minister, General Marina, whose good standing among both generals and junteros was supposed to heal further the wounds in the officer corps and to restore military discipline.

The priority given the bill was a sign that the National Government was as dependent on the military as its predecessors. Even before the introduction of the reform bill on May 1, the "military question" dominated the Cortes. Since it had been suspended for a year, this was the first time the Juntas had been discussed in parliamentary debate. The left, represented in early April by Indalecio Prieto and Marcelino Domingo, quickly discovered that the Juntas were a more specific and convenient target than the "militarism" that they had denounced since 1910. The Juntas not only embodied "militarism"—that is, military influence in political decisions of every variety—they had also exerted that pressure publicly and in defiance of the constitution. From April 1918 on, leftist attacks on the army would often take the form of attacks on the Juntas, even though the equation was a specious one.[45]

At the same time, the Juntas gave the left the chance to make an occasional nice distinction between "the army"—a national institution not necessarily incompatible with democracy and social justice—and the bureaucratic, egotistical, and antidemocratic members of the Spanish officer corps, who were perverting "the army's" true function.

Junteros and the Juntas thus allowed the left to attack selectively, in the hope of not alienating the more moderate or progressive officers. This, of course, proved to be a naive miscalculation.

In late April Prieto and Domingo particularly hammered away at the erosion of civil supremacy, a process that had begun with the Law of Jurisdictions in 1906 and had reached its culmination with the capitulation to the Juntas de Defensa the previous June. In tracing this process, the two deputies located its origins in the defensive posture of the dynastic parties, which had neither the will nor the popular support to solve Spain's economic and political problems. Dismissing the euphoria surrounding the formation of the National Government, Domingo accurately described it as "not a national Government, but a Government of monarchical concentration against the forces of the left. . . ."[46] Thus, the debate on the military question became a debate on the legitimacy of the regime.

The introduction of the reform bill and the arrival of the four amnestied Socialists in mid-May only intensified the debate on the army. At first, discussion focused on the military repression of the general strike in August. Once again, the left extended its criticism of the army to include a general critique of the monarchy and the ruling classes.[47] The provisions of the reform bill also illustrated the inherent weaknesses of the regime, especially Article 2, which allowed the War Minister to add credits to his annual budget to pay for the reforms in years when the Cortes refused or neglected to vote funding. As several deputies pointed out, this provision effectively deprived the Cortes of the power of the purse.[48]

Although the Socialists used their platform in the Cortes to denounce the reform bill and the political decadence that it symbolized, the parliamentary sessions of 1918 indicated that the regime was in fact capable of transformation. Whatever the inclinations of the dynastic parties, the economic and social changes effected by the war were leading inexorably, if slowly, toward political change. The outcome of the February elections revealed that caciquismo had lost its effectiveness in the larger cities and indeed could be expected to lose ground wherever the opposition possessed sufficient strength and energy to mobilize the electorate. Furthermore, the debates illustrated the potency of the parliament as an instrument for mobilizing opinion, for it provided the only existing guarantee of free speech, the press being permanently subject to partial censorship through the Law of Jurisdictions.

While the reopening of the Cortes represented a democratic advance for some, it appeared to many officers as a step toward anarchy and national self-destruction. The army reacted angrily to the debates, which seemed little more than subversive rabble-rousing protected by parliamentary immunity.[49] The hero's welcome given the amnestied Socialists upon their return to Madrid also worried a few officers, who feared the consequences of a divorce between the army and the nation.[50] Moreover, the attacks by the left on both the army and the politicians drew them closer together; on May 25 *El Ejército Español* warned "agitators" that they would find the army a "firm and insuperable obstacle."[51] The dynastic politicians received this news gratefully and repaid the favor with rapid consideration of the military reform bill.

Thus, although the left was able to keep the military question alive, they were unable to hinder passage of the bill, which was sponsored, with more obstinacy than enthusiasm, by Niceto Alcalá-Zamora, the Liberal president of the parliamentary committee on military affairs. Alcalá-Zamora conceded that the bill was less than perfect. Acknowledging the defects of the seniority principle, he defended its inclusion in the law on the grounds that a large majority of officers preferred "the certain, inevitable, but mechanical injustice of the law to the lesser, but partial and arbitrary injustice of favoritism." To the critics of the March 7 decree, Alcalá-Zamora replied that it had to be seen as the only solution to an otherwise insoluble conflict between "the zealous custodian of parliamentary rights" and "the yearning for progress in behalf of the armed forces."[52] This unprincipled approach made constructive debate almost impossible; in despair or resignation, the opponents of the bill bowed to the inevitable and allowed the bill to emerge from the Congress on June 24 with only one amendment—a stipulation, clearly aimed at the Juntas, that any "association, group, or collective representation" of employees of the War Ministry obtain the "express approval" of the Minister.

If debate in the Congress had produced few results, it had at least been extensive; in the Senate, the bill was approved in four days. While General Marina watched impassively,[53] a few of the senior generals debated the technical sections, and General Luque criticized the closed scale and the bloated personnel provisions. The other political generals, including Aguilera and the Marqués de Estella, recognized that the bill was detrimental to army interests, but discreetly refrained from criticizing either the bill or the Juntas on the Senate floor. On June 29, 1918, the day La Cierva's reform bill became law, the "disillusioned" General Marina submitted his resignation to Maura because he did not "agree with the essence nor with the structure of the reforms. . . ."[54] Marina insisted that his continuation in the War Ministry would be both "ineffective and prejudicial," but he was ultimately persuaded by

Maura to remain in the cabinet in the interest of national unity. It was clear, however, that the military reform law of 1918 had intensified the serious divisions between junior and senior officers.

Equally serious was the response in the African army, where the law was greeted with resentment and concern.[55] The first great army reform of the twentieth century did not even mention the only area in which that army was engaged in operations—Morocco—because it had been written to meet the interests and grievances of peninsular bureaucrats. While the European war kept colonial operations at a standstill, this defect was relatively easy to ignore. But with the end of the war a few months later, the African theater would become active again under French initiatives, and the African army would be forced to deal with an institution that had not improved with the passage of the reform law. Then the recriminations would begin.

The Revival of the Juntas

The euphoria of the junteros over the new law lasted nearly a week; then it was transformed into rage. The upshot was the reemergence of the Juntas to protest the implementation of the reform law that had been passed to insure their disappearance. This time they did not bother to disguise their professional grievances in regenerationist rhetoric, but frankly began to function as a powerful, if illegal, pressure group.

The problem was that the military bureaucrats were not willing to tolerate *any* governmental efforts to reduce the officer corps. They applauded a decree of July 3, implementing the retirement provisions of the new law, because it meant vacancies at the higher ranks.[56] But they were outraged by other decrees emanating from the War Ministry in the month of July that indicated that Marina and Maura were determined to ignore the more extravagant provisions in the law. On July 4, 20 percent of the troops were released early because of a lack of funds to pay for them, making the goal of a standing army of 180,000 even more remote.[57] The next week Marina announced a new round of 50 percent amortizations to reduce the officer corps to the number prescribed in the reform law.[58] Two other dispositions eliminated a number of pay supplements, including the five-year bonuses, in order to bring the military law into conformance with the reform bill for the civil administration, then being discussed in the Cortes. The civil service reform was a response to the bureaucratic grievances aired so dramatically in March. Like the military reform, it dealt primarily with pay scales and promotions.[59] But peninsular officers were unwilling to admit their similarity to other civil servants and continued to insist on the maintenance of their extra privileges until the two dispositions were rescinded.[60]

Even more exasperating was the continuing authority of the War Minister over top-level appointments and promotions. General Luque, the bête noire of the Infantry Junta, had been appointed to the Classifying Junta, or promotion review board, in April. In promoting colonels and generals to fill the vacancies left by the new retirement provisions in the reform law, the Classifying Junta had not observed the principle of strict seniority, as the Juntas desired, but had exercised its prerogative to select candidates from the top one-third of the promotions lists, as the law allowed.[61] As a final provocation, a protégé of Luque's, General Dámaso Berenguer, was promoted to division general and appointed Undersecretary of the War Ministry in mid-July.[62] On July 12 *La Correspondencia Militar* warned that the return of the old abuses would probably mean a return of the Juntas.[63]

As predicted, the Juntas began to organize during the month of July. Since their capitulation to La Cierva in March, they had been without the official statutes that were mandated by the reform law passed in June. In late August the new proposed statutes of the Infantry Junta were leaked to the press.[64] In conformance with the agreement with La Cierva, the statutes provided for a single Superior Junta located in Madrid, which would speak officially for the collective opinion of the Corps and serve as a permanent honor court. The other corps also reorganized their Central Juntas and put pressure on the government to interpret the reform law in their favor.

The National Government had secured passage of the reform law to lay the Infantry Junta to rest; it was not prepared now to grant it legal status by approving the new statutes. As a result, the Junta reverted to its former complex organization of local and regional Juntas led by a Superior Junta in Madrid, whose members drew handsome salaries paid by membership dues. Although entirely illegal, it continued to act as a pressure group in the War Ministry, its power enhanced by the social crisis that accompanied the end of the world war. By late 1918 the presidents of each of the branch Juntas had developed the habit of meeting in a joint Assembly in order to minimize intercorps conflicts and to coordinate policy. La Cierva's careful scheming the previous winter had not eliminated the Juntas; its only lasting result was the military reform law that would compound the military problem in the years ahead.

.

The Fall of the National Government

The collapse of Maura's National Government on November 6, 1918, marked the failure of the only serious attempt to save the regime with a coalition government representing all the dynastic parties.[65] Its difficulties lay in the inherent contradiction between a coalition government and a parliamentary system dependent on party politics. In April 1918 the political crisis had provided a short-term bond for the disparate interests represented in the cabinet. Once the aura of crisis had dissipated, the consensus disappeared as well. The political urge could not be stifled forever by appeals to patriotism and loyalty.

By common agreement, the responsibility for the fall of the National Government was settled on Santiago Alba, the Minister of Public Instruction.[66] Alba undoubtedly deliberately provoked the crisis over teachers' salaries in an attempt to disengage himself grandiosely from a situation he found increasingly untenable.[67] The subsequent parliamentary debate, in which Alba was routed, made him a convenient scapegoat for the collapse of the government a month later. He was henceforth discredited among all those who had hoped for salvation from the National Government, which was much of the country, including the army.

But Alba's defection was only the precipitant of a collapse that was inevitable. That the fall of the National Government was interpreted as a turning point for the regime was due to the extra burden assigned to it by some of its members, particularly Francisco Cambó, who believed, mistakenly, that a coalition of the dynastic parties could permanently resolve Spain's postwar problems. In his view, only a coalition could take the decisive action necessary to restructure the national economy and to defend the social order against the importunate demands of the working classes. For Cambó, the dynastic parties represented not only a political but also a social class with common interests transcending political differences. For this reason, Alba's refusal to cooperate any longer made him a traitor to the regime and to his class.

Alba, however, interpreted Spain's political dilemma differently from his colleagues, especially Maura and Cambó. For Alba, the future depended on the regime's ability to incorporate the left, which had been boycotting the Cortes since the discussion of the Espionage Law in July. Alba recognized that only a revitalized turno, based on a genuine left and right, could provide the dynamic needed to deal positively with Spain's economic and social problems. Furthermore, unlike Cambó, he realized that without the incorporation of the left, the dynastic parties would be unable to overcome their defensive posture and would allow petty differences to impede constructive action.

The tragedy was that in 1918 there was no simple political solution to Spain's problems. If Cambó refused to recognize that the task of national reconstruction could not be undertaken without the incorporation of the bourgeois left and the working classes, Alba overestimated the potential of a revitalized turno as an efficient response to the national crisis. Like the right, the Spanish left was not monolithic, but composed of three factions—the working-class parties, the bourgeois Republicans, and the dynastic left represented by Alba—all of whom might be expected to disagree on specific economic and social issues. As the elections of February 1918 had portended, truly representative government in Spain could also lead to stalemate and inaction.

Given the political differences that divided the National Government in 1918, the only sort of continuing success open to it was the defense of the status quo, a dismal fate precluded by the political crisis of November. Its failure did not have to mean the failure of parliamentary government. The possibility of a reconstitution of the regime would remain open until 1923, when the army would abruptly halt the slow and agonizing birth of political democracy and civil supremacy in Spain.

CHAPTER SIX

The "Bolshevik Triennium," 1919–1921

As if signaling the end of an era, the fall of the National Government preceded by only five days the end of the world war. During the next three years, Spain, like the rest of Europe, was racked by conflicts that had been both stimulated by and contained during the hostilities. Essentially a revolution of rising expectations, the Spanish postwar effervescence was both political and social. Among the Republicans and the parliamentary Socialists, Wilsonian idealism renewed hopes for a democratic reorientation of Spanish political life; among regionalists in the Basque provinces and especially in Catalonia, it provoked new demands for self-determination. For the working classes, however, the Armistice set off a wave of revolutionary activity and labor militancy whose goals were primarily social and economic. As Gerald Meaker has observed,[1] this postwar enthusiasm owed as much to the example of the Russian Revolution as to economic distress, although accelerating inflation certainly contributed to the intensity of activity, which by 1919 was as apparent in the countryside as in the urban centers.

These rising expectations were met by the intransigence of the established interests, particularly in Barcelona, Spain's most industrialized city. After 1919, optimism gave way to desperation and violence. The drive for Catalan autonomy was resisted by the Castilian centralists and the army, then abandoned by the regionalists themselves when a disciplined and self-confident working class proved its strength in the first postwar confrontation between labor and capital. Animated by the dual specters of world communism and declining profits, the industrialists of the Lliga sacrificed their political alliances—and their political goals—in order to preserve their class interests. Catalanism, henceforth abandoned to the radical left, was once again denied a voice within the system. The revolutionary left, too, was decimated and divided in the postwar struggle: the Republicans from the Socialists over the Third International; left and right Socialists over the same issue; the UGT from the CNT, and the Syndicalists from the Anarchists and Anarchosyndicalists, over objectives and tactics. In contrast, the ruling elites, increasingly committed to an inflexible policy of resistance and repression, closed ranks.

In this period of conflict and confrontation, the army emerged with even greater power than it had previously possessed. On the one hand, the majority of dynastic politicians, viewing the postwar social crisis either as a breakdown of public order or as part of a worldwide "Red" conspiracy, relied completely on the army to solve the conflict, thereby compromising their independence even further. The majority of officers, viewing the crisis in similar terms, although professing to believe that the army was a national institution transcending social class, defended the established order with enthusiasm. In the process, the traditional antipathy between Catalan regionalists and the army was not overcome, but moderated, by a new alliance between the Catalan bourgeoisie and the army garrisons in Catalonia based on their mutual horror of social revolution and labor unrest.

The most significant result of this relationship was the growing autonomy of the army in Catalonia. Less the servant of the state than an independent agent, the army effectively prevented the regime from adjusting its response to the working-class challenge. Although governmental attempts at conciliation and pacification were admittedly few, they soon ceased altogether as it became clear that they would not be honored by the army. Moreover, the army's insistence on repressive tactics undercut the credibility of moderates on both sides of the conflict, making each new effort to find a workable compromise between labor and capital in Barcelona less likely to succeed. By confirming the governmental parties in their intransigence and forcing even the moderate opposition to conclude that only revolution could accomplish significant political or social change in Spain, the army played a critical role in the breakdown of the parliamentary monarchy.

The Campaign for Catalan Autonomy

The failure of the coalition governments of 1917–18 to renovate the parliamentary regime was followed by a four-year period in which the dynastic parties attempted, with an equal lack of success, to reconstitute the turno. This political panacea only wasted valuable energy without affecting the structural imbalances in the system. Although the oligarchs were still strong enough to retain their exclusive control over the state, they were increasingly able to do so only with the aid of force and completely unable to transform their defensive strategy into constructive action. Thus, as the dynastic parties disputed power with one another while doggedly resisting change from without, the pressure of events shattered one cabinet after another.

The first party government to follow the National Government of 1918—the "Liberal concentration" government of García Prieto formed on November 9, 1918—prefigured the postwar pattern by collapsing over the issue of Catalan autonomy after only a month in office.[2] With the signing of the Armistice and the prospect of a Wilsonian peace, the Catalan campaign, dormant since the failure of the Assembly movement the previous autumn, was resurrected by Cambó, who was disillusioned by the failure of the National Government to undertake the program of national reconstruction he had envisioned. Cambó found himself allied with the left, just as he had in 1917. On November 13 Republican deputies presented a Catalan autonomy statute in the Cortes;[3] several days later, a newly created National Federation of Republicans issued a manifesto in favor of a federal republic.[4] The Socialists also lent their support to the movement.

As in 1917, both the regionalists and the left viewed the alliance as a temporary but necessary precondition for the achievement of very different goals. The left was less interested in Catalan autonomy than in exploiting Catalan separatism in order to topple the regime; Cambó overcame his abhorrence of revolutionary politics only to enhance his party's leverage. In a private interview on November 14, Cambó convinced Alfonso XIII to support the autonomy campaign after persuading him that moderate Catalanism could unite the propertied classes and strengthen the regime to withstand the proletarian challenge.[5] On November 25 Cambó's committee in the Mancomunitat made public its proposed statute, which granted regional legislative and executive autonomy to Catalonia.[6]

Instead of unifying the country, the autonomy issue split it in two.[7] Catalan nationalists and Republicans carried their anticentralist convictions into the streets; crowds in Madrid and other Castilian cities, protesting the "dismemberment" of the Spanish nation, responded in like fashion. The first victim was the García Prieto government, which split on the issue on December 3. The prime minister in the new cabinet was the Conde de Romanones, whose long-standing support for the victorious Allied powers and flexibility on the autonomy issue compensated for his scant support in the Cortes.[8] Yet not even the politically dexterous Romanones was able to engineer a compromise. The Castilian party, led by Antonio Maura (a Mallorcan), rejected all concessions to Catalonia, while the Catalan Republicans refused to participate in the extraparliamentary commission appointed by the government to write an autonomy statute acceptable to all parties. Remaining loyal to its current policy of "no enemies on the left," the Lliga also refused to participate in the commission. While the deadlock filled Cambó with pessimism, it exactly suited the revolutionary objectives of the Republican left in Barcelona, who encouraged the frequent clashes between regionalists and centralists. Tension in the city was compounded by the renewed activity of the CNT, although Syndicalist leaders expressly dissociated themselves from Catalan nationalism, which they dismissed as a bourgeois phenomenon. On December 22 CNT organizers initiated an extensive propaganda campaign in the regions of agrarian unrest in Andalusia and Levante.

With neither the government nor the Lliga in control of the situation in Barcelona, it was the army that finally insisted on action. By January military tolerance for even moderate regionalism was wearing thin. The Barcelona garrison bore the full force of anticentralist sentiment; to avoid verbal and even physical abuse, many officers removed their uniforms before walking out in public. In addition to these personal affronts, officers were scandalized by the antipatriotic street demonstrations[9] and disillusioned by Cambó's continuing alliance with the left. The final outrage was the reemergence of Benito Márquez, still searching for a cause and an audience, as a focus of Republican and separatist propaganda.[10] By mid-January officers in the Barcelona garrison, especially the younger ones, were ready "to begin shooting in the street." Their indignation was communicated to the rest of the peninsular officer corps through *La Correspondencia Militar*, whose editor, Julio Amado, was in close contact with Major Espino, a juntero activist in Barcelona.[11]

Alarmed as much by the state of excitement in the barracks as by the rising tide of revolutionary propaganda, Romanones suspended constitutional guarantees in Barcelona on January 16, which enabled the government to crack down on demonstrations and to arrest dozens of Syndicalist leaders. But the prime minister immediately dissipated the goodwill these measures engendered among Barcelona officers by publicly stating that he had acted under military pressure.[12] On January 18 *La Correspondencia Militar* vigorously denied the assertion and stiffly pointed out that, without the suspension of guarantees, the officer corps would have been obliged "to avenge with its exclusive personal effort the outrages of the miserable horde that constitutes the

Catalan separatists. . . ."[13] On January 19 Romanones retracted his statement, but tension continued to mount throughout January. On the twenty-fourth, the Mancomunitat rejected the compromise proposals of the extraparliamentary commission, voting instead for its own statute. On January 26, fearing violence between Catalan separatists and the army, the Captain General, Joaquín Milans del Bosch, confined all officers to quarters.

In a situation of stress, the Juntas reemerged as the mouthpiece of general military discontent. On January 27 the branch Juntas in the Barcelona garrison informed the Captain General that if the Civil Governor did not take action against the separatists, the army would.[14] The next day, after consultation with the Interior Minister, General Milans del Bosch prohibited the display of colored ribbons and flags, a symbolic measure that nonetheless calmed the garrison and avoided a street confrontation. The same day, the local Infantry Junta sent the government a document urging a hard line on separatism in order to avoid a conflict between Catalonia and the army.[15] In an effort to remove an additional source of irritation, Romanones arranged for Benito Márquez to leave Spain immediately for a post in Cuba.

The outrage was not limited to officers in Barcelona. In the Cortes, traditionally antiregionalist senior officers denounced all proposals for Catalan autonomy and urged the government to defend the honor of the army in Barcelona; simultaneously, *La Correspondencia Militar* committed itself to arousing sentiment in the provincial garrisons. The hints of army intervention grew less and less subtle. Catalan separatism seemed about to provoke a new *¡Cu-cut!* affair.

Unwilling to alienate the army with revolutionary tension mounting in the peninsula, Romanones backed away from the autonomy statute, which stood little chance of approval by the Cortes in any case. In response, Cambó began to consider a revolutionary break with the regime: a boycott of the Cortes by the Lliga in conjunction with mass resignations of government officials throughout Catalonia.[16] By late January 1919 the constitutional crisis was as acute as it had been in 1917.

But, just as in 1917, the attack on the regime was deflected by a general strike, initiated this time by the Anarchosyndicalist CNT in Barcelona. Once again the threat of social revolution would divide Cambó from his allies, with fatal consequences for the cause of Catalan autonomy. After 1919 the Lliga would protect its economic interests through an ad hoc alliance with the Barcelona garrison, abandoning the direction of Catalanism to the Republican left and thus insuring that Catalan autonomy would lose its legitimacy as an issue under the parliamentary monarchy. During the next four years, with the aid of the army, the Catalan bourgeoisie would secure a different kind of de facto autonomy that would enable it to carry out a repressive social policy independent of government control.

The Canadiense Strike

The strike in La Canadiense, the Canadian-British company that supplied Barcelona with electric power, dramatized the growing strength of syndicalism in Barcelona, itself a manifestation of the revolutionary mood that overtook the Spanish working classes, both urban and rural, in the postwar period.[17] The causes for this revival, after the slump in enthusiasm that followed the defeat of the general strike in August 1917, were both ideological and economic. News of the Russian land seizures aroused the landless laborers and marginal peasants of Andalusia, who from mid-1918 on organized local syndicates and strikes in preparation for a similar upheaval in Spain. Urban workers, many of them newcomers to industrial occupations, responded with equal enthusiasm to the Bolshevik capture of the Russian state. Economic distress also contributed to the revolutionary ferment. While the postwar economic slump that left thousands unemployed by 1920 was significant only in the Asturian mines in late 1918, other kinds of economic dislocation made life difficult for large numbers of workers. Inflation continued to accelerate, making a serious impact for the first time on smaller provincial towns, where prices by September 1918 were 66 percent higher than in 1914, 84 percent higher a year later.[18] The problem of high prices for basic commodities was compounded by scarcities resulting from unregulated exports, which triggered frequent and often serious street riots and looting in the major urban centers during the winter months.[19] By late 1918 the pressure of heavy emigration from the south and southeast into Barcelona, the ravages of the influenza epidemic, and economic distress had together created a tangible state of revolutionary tension in Barcelona.

A major indicator of the mounting unrest was the rapid expansion of the two Spanish labor federations. The Anarchosyndicalist CNT was the chief beneficiary of this growth, particularly after July 1918, when the Regional Labor Confederation of Catalonia (the CRT) formally committed itself to industrial unionism, thereby expanding its appeal for the thousands of unskilled workers who had arrived in Barcelona during the war boom. By the end of 1918 there were 345,000 members—about 30 percent of the Catalan labor force—in the CRT, many of them organized into the nine major Sindicatos Únicos, or vertical industrial unions.[20] In the entire country, the CNT claimed 700,000 militants, including 25,000 in Andalusia.[21] For the Syndicalist leadership, this massive influx represented the first real possibility of establishing the right of Spanish labor to collective bargaining. For the pure Anarchists within the CNT, the postwar ferment was the foundation on which the coming revolution would be made.

The Socialist UGT, whose membership had declined dramatically after the abortive general strike of 1917, also saw its numbers increase in mid-1918—from 89,600 in June 1918 to 134,356 a year later. But it continued to lag behind its rival, largely because the Socialist leadership's commitment to electoral tactics and trade-union gradualism was less attractive to the mass of workers and peasants who believed the revolutionary hour was at hand.[22]

The Catalan employers, especially the smaller entrepreneurs who had made their fortunes during the war, watched the expansion of organized labor with growing alarm. Foreseeing a postwar decline in foreign demand that might endanger their high profits, the owners mobilized to break the power of the unions, preliminary to cutting wages, which had risen—although not as rapidly as prices—during the years of peak production. In January 1919, in preparation for their coming battle with the CRT, the Catalan bourgeoisie reconvened their Employers' Federation, which had been relatively inactive since its organization in 1914, and resolved to meet the "Bolshevik" threat in Barcelona with force.[23]

In General Milans del Bosch, the Captain General of Catalonia, the employers found a willing ally. Milans was a courtly, formal officer of the old school, "a gentleman to the tip of his fingernails,"[24] but profoundly conservative and jealous of his own and the army's honor to the point of fanaticism. Like most officers, he interpreted the social question as one of public order and was thus a willing instrument of the policy urged upon him by the Catalan employers. Furthermore, Milans himself was a Catalan, a product of the same social milieu as the diehards in the Employers' Federation. An alliance, then, was almost inevitable.

To subdue the CNT, Milans found it expedient to employ the services of the former Police Chief and sometime German agent, Manuel Bravo Portillo. During the last years of the war, Bravo Portillo had engaged a band of *pistoleros* to harass and occasionally to assassinate manufacturers supplying materiel to the Allies; in 1918 he had been fired and briefly imprisoned after the CNT paper, *Solidaridad Obrera*, published documents implicating him in espionage activities.[25] Shortly after Bravo's release from prison, Milans had taken him on as an under-cover "attaché" of the police department, where he acted as an agent provocateur, a role for which Milans, as a gentleman and an officer, felt personally unsuited. Milans had thus resisted suggestions from the War Ministry to dispense with Bravo's services. In February 1919 this antilabor coalition was strengthened by the appointment of General Severiano Martínez Anido as Military Governor of Barcelona. Together, Milans, Bravo Portillo, and Martínez Anido—and behind them, the army garrison in Catalonia—would feel confident enough to defy not only the CNT, but the government in Madrid as well.

In January 1919 General Milans del Bosch had been momentarily distracted from his impending battle with syndicalism by the confron-tation between Catalan nationalists and the Barcelona garrison. On January 16 he had pressured Romanones to suspend constitutional guarantees in the city, using the opportunity not only to suppress separatist demonstrations but also to arrest the leaders of the CNT and to close workers' centers and newspapers.[26] At the same time, he lifted the prohibition on urban militias, which led to the rapid formation, under the auspices of the Lliga, of neighborhood Somatenes modeled on the rural militias active during the Carlist wars.[27] Even at the height of the Catalan crisis, Milans del Bosch perceived syndicalism to be the greater danger.

On February 5 the CRT responded to these measures with a strike aimed at demonstrating the legitimacy and strength of organized labor in Barcelona. Although the dispute arose out of an economic issue, it became a strike with essentially political goals when the management of La Canadiense dismissed eight workers for appealing to the Sindi-cato Único of Water, Gas, and Electricity for support. To establish both its right and its ability to represent the working class in Barcelona, the CRT called on all its affiliates to show their solidarity with the fired workers. Although nearly all the CNT leaders were still in prison, the strike was a spectacular success. By March 7, 70 percent of Barcelona's industries were closed down, her transportation system was paralyzed, and army Engineers and troops were providing the manpower to keep the city supplied with gas, water, and light.

As soon as the strike became generalized, Romanones was under heavy pressure from Milans del Bosch, the Civil Governor, and the Employers' Federation to respond with force. As early as February 17, the Captain General recommended the mobilization of strikers, many of whom he insisted would welcome the excuse to return to work.[28] The government resisted, not least because a total mobilization re-quired a vote of the Cortes, then in session. As the strike spread, however, the cabinet's resolve weakened, while pressure from Barcelona intensified. On February 27 Romanones recessed the Cortes, just as he had at a moment of stress in February 1917. Then on March 9 he ordered a partial mobilization of workers in all public service industries in Barcelona. As a conciliatory gesture, workers were allowed to substitute service in other peninsular regiments for service in the utility plants.[29]

Contrary to the Captain General's predictions, however, these drastic measures only stiffened the resolve of the strikers. Under instructions from the strike leaders,[30] workers resisted mobilization, disobeyed orders, terrorized the city with bombs, and jeopardized discipline among the regular conscripts.[31] To prevent a further breakdown of authority and to pacify his own officers, who were outraged at this defiance of military discipline, the Captain General now demanded a declaration of martial law. Although he told Milans that he considered him partially responsible for the deteriorating situation, Romanones agreed that order had to be established before the unrest spread to the rest of the peninsula. Food riots had broken out in Madrid the first week in March and there were frequent outbreaks of violence in Andalusia, where the syndicalist fever was rising. On March 13 he reluctantly granted Milans's request; immediately, nearly three thousand insubordinate workers were imprisoned in Montjuich.[32]

To his credit, Romanones understood that only compromise would restore lasting peace to Barcelona, and he simultaneously began to prepare for negotiations by replacing the intransigent Police Chief and Civil Governor of Barcelona with two more liberal appointees, Gerardo Doval and Carlos E. Montañés. On March 14 they arrived, along with the prime minister's personal secretary, José Morote, to work out a settlement. Despite warnings from Milans about army opposition, by March 17 Morote, Doval, and Montañés had hammered out an agreement between the company and the strikers that included the immediate release of political prisoners, the rehiring of all strikers, wage increases, an eight-hour day, and half a month's indemnization for time lost during the strike.[33] The next day martial law was lifted, and on March 19 twenty-five thousand strikers assembled in the bullring of Las Arenas were convinced by the moderate head of the CRT, Salvador Seguí, to accept the settlement and return to work.

Up to this point, the Canadiense strike was the most successful strike in Spanish labor history. Not only had it demonstrated the strength of the Syndicalist movement in Barcelona, it had obtained substantial gains for the working class—in particular, the eight-hour day. In a sense, the conclusion of the strike also represented a victory for the Romanones government, which, overcoming its initial impulse to rely exclusively on force, had discovered the benefits of compromise. Had the Canadiense strike ended on March 19 with the peaceful return of the strikers to work, the result might have been a gradual reorientation of the traditional Spanish response to labor problems that might ultimately have freed the dynastic politicians from their dependence on the army.

The Army and the Social Question

Instead, the strike was pushed into a second, less successful, phase by the army's refusal to honor the government's commitments, and the opportunity for moderates on both sides was lost. The independent course followed by the army in Barcelona nullified the government's efforts to work out a new policy more attuned to postwar realities, just as it allowed the Anarchist extremists in the CNT to repudiate the cautious tactics of the Syndicalist leadership. All at once, the implications of their repeated capitulations to military insubordination were clarified for the dynastic politicians, who had created the beast they could no longer control. After the spring of 1919, the more flexible of the politicians would find it hopeless to try to govern in opposition to the army, leaving the way clear for a suicidal continuation of the old policies of repression by the civilian and military intransigents.

From the army's point of view, the government's negotiations with the strikers were nothing less than a betrayal of a loyal servant. The army had restored vital services and reestablished order, exposing military discipline to great risk in the process; they resented the negotiations that allowed the "rebels" to return to work without penalty. Furthermore, the Captain General, whose authority was absolute in a region under martial law, was furious that the settlement had been worked out without his participation or consent. Forgetting that they had insisted upon a repressive policy from the beginning of the strike, officers in Barcelona now saw only that the reversal of that policy by the government made it appear that the army was solely responsible for the mobilization and arrests. For two months Catalan separatists and strikers had vilified the army in slogans, on posters, and in the press. It now seemed as if the army—and with it, the nation—was to be sacrificed to the forces of anarchy and disunion.

Officers elsewhere in the peninsula agreed with them. During February the venerable Marqués de Estella, the president of the Supreme Military Council, told the press that the only solution to the social problem was the formation of a patriotic volunteer army led by career officers, regular conscripts being increasingly unreliable in confrontations with members of their own social class. Estella pointed out that he was not opposed to social justice, "but justice is one thing, and another is imposition, violence, and threats to property, home, faith, and all that is lawful or represents authority or hierarchy."[34] Other officers shared the ancient lieutenant general's fear of subversion in the ranks. In March the Assembly of Junta Presidents in Madrid approved a plan for a "supplementary military organization," led by officers and composed of "elements of order."[35] The project was also favored by the War Minister and, with some reservations, by Milans del Bosch, who had authorized the formation of urban Somatenes in January.

The peaceful resolution of the Canadiense strike, then, was interpreted by the army as both an affront and a dangerous concession to bolshevism. To register his displeasure, General Milans del Bosch submitted his resignation the day after martial law was lifted in Barcelona, on the grounds that he could not be expected to implement the government's new policy of conciliation.[36] If the government was seriously committed to such a policy, the only possible response to this threat of insubordination was, indeed, immediate acceptance of the resignation. But Romanones, lacking parliamentary or public support, dared not risk a confrontation with the Barcelona garrison. Milans remained at his post. Within a week he had provoked a second strike by refusing to implement the government's agreement to release all imprisoned strikers, including those subject to military law. Although the Syndicalist leadership advised further compromise, extremist "action groups" within the CNT pushed the CNT masses into a revolutionary general strike on March 24.

During the second strike, the army made it clear that it would settle the conflict on its own terms. On March 27 Romanones received a joint declaration from the Assembly of Junta Presidents entitled "The Intervention of the Army in Social Conflicts," which outlined the conditions under which the army would break strikes and restore order.[37] A declaration of the army's policymaking prerogatives, it represented as grave a challenge to civil supremacy as the manifesto of June 1. It also revealed the contradictory and ambivalent attitude of the military toward "the social question."

The first section of the document indicated that the Juntas were concerned about the army's public image, much as they had been after the August 1917 strike. In their view, the army, an impartial *national* institution, was being unfairly employed as an instrument of repression in behalf of a single social class, the capitalists. Furthermore, the army was asked to take responsibility for the functioning of public services, a complex task for which it was naturally unprepared. In the interest of restoring the army to its original function, the Juntas proposed new guidelines for military intervention in social disturbances: henceforth, the army would support mobilization to secure national services, but not regional or local class interests. To avoid class conflict, the Juntas suggested that national and local authorities pass appropriate legislation to resolve the social problem.

Having expressed their reluctance to intervene in social conflicts, the Juntas then insisted that the army should be allowed to resolve such conflicts without outside interference. Once the army had been summoned into service, it would not tolerate any diminution of its authority or any instructions to "parley, compromise, or temporize." Defiance of mobilization orders by strikers seriously threatened military discipline, particularly when the rebels were subsequently treated by the government with "considerations, indulgences, respect, and forgetfulness, when not with flattery and praise." In the future, the Juntas demanded equal and unbending application of the military Code for conscripts and mobilized workers alike.

What angered the Juntas was the ambivalent government policy that relied on the army to maintain social order while refusing it permission to employ the tactics that would restore discipline at once. Events during the past year had accustomed the Junta leaders to think of the army as an institution independent of and even superior to the state, which they viewed as corrupt and irresolute. The Juntas now complained that the army was being victimized by the weakness and inconsistency of civilian authority; they lacked the objectivity to see that military insubordination—most recently exemplified by Milans's refusal to release the strikers—had contributed greatly to that weakness.

The document of March 1919, written largely by the Infantry Junta, also revealed vestiges of the antioligarchical impulses of 1917. The middle-class origins of most Infantrymen made them wary of great wealth and power, whether in Madrid or Barcelona; as consumers and wage earners, they were not totally out of sympathy with the plight of workers. Furthermore, their concept of the army as a national institution transcending class made them reluctant to admit that it was a tool of the oligarchy.[38] But these conscious sentiments were in conflict with other unconscious, but deeply held, military prejudices against disorder and in favor of discipline and hierarchy. In practice, the authoritarian instinct usually prevailed, and the psychological tension between conscious and unconscious disposition made officers even more prickly and resentful of government authority.

Above all, the document was clearly another challenge to the principle of civil supremacy and was interpreted as such by Romanones, who nevertheless postponed his resignation until order should be reestablished in Barcelona. In the meantime, the king managed to salvage some of the government's authority, as well as to enhance his own standing with the officer corps, by agreeing to receive the document in place of the War Minister.[39] To keep news of this latest ultimatum from reaching the public, the government established prior censorship on March 29.[40] The fall of the government, however, was obviously only a matter of time. Real authority in the country belonged to the army.

Events in Barcelona made this evident, as the general strike was quickly brought to a halt by the vigorous measures of Milans del Bosch. Martial law had once again been declared in Barcelona, followed by the suspension of guarantees throughout the peninsula on March 25. The whole country appeared to be in a state of siege. In Madrid, troops sorted and delivered the mail in the absence of striking postal workers; in Barcelona, they once again operated the city's utilities. Nearly all the CNT organizers were in jail, Syndicalist centers and newspapers in Barcelona were closed, and workers themselves were harassed by the Somatenes, whose membership had risen to eight thousand. Young men in suits and fedoras patrolled the streets with rifles and on the twenty-sixth forced the opening of shops. Among the marching militia could be found most of the Lliga, including Cambó, who abandoned the autonomy campaign and his left alliance to meet the challenge to the social order.[41] The only conciliatory gesture came from Madrid on April 3, when a royal decree officially established the eight-hour day.[42]

By April 3 the strike had been broken, and the power acquired by the CRT during the Canadiense strike had been lost. Many commentators have criticized the CRT for initiating the general strike, arguing that as a quixotic protest it was doomed to failure and only served to harden the Catalan bourgeoisie against the labor movement. Furthermore, the subsequent repression of Syndicalist activity left the field open to the terrorists and pistoleros who did so much to discredit the movement. While this is true enough, it minimizes the responsibility of General Milans del Bosch and the Barcelona garrison for the strike. Even if the militants had overreacted, the provocation came from the military. The real tragedy was that extremists in the CNT would now have a strong reason for opposing negotiations sponsored by the government, which could speak for itself, but not for its supposed servant, the army.

The final proof of this—at least for the Conde de Romanones—
came on April 14, when the Captain General forcibly ejected the government's representatives, Doval and Montañés, from Barcelona.[43]
Once again, the issue was negotiation, now more unpopular than ever
with the army and the Employers' Federation. When Milans del Bosch
imprisoned two Syndicalist leaders to prevent further contacts between
them and the civil authorities, Doval and Montañés submitted their
resignations to the government, taking the opportunity to suggest to
Romanones that labor relations in Barcelona might be improved by the
dismissal of Bravo Portillo. The Captain General not only refused to
countenance such a possibility, he decided to anticipate Romanones's
acceptance of the resignations by placing the two officials on the next
train to Madrid. In effect, this represented a military veto over government appointees, and Romanones had little choice but demand
Milans's resignation or submit his own. Unwilling to alienate the army,
Alfonso accepted the resignation of Romanones, who vowed never to
return to office while the Juntas existed. At issue, however, was not
the existence of the Juntas, but the inability of civilian government to
free itself from its dependence on the military.

As the principal victim of the army's pressure tactics, Romanones
received a certain amount of sympathy; yet his own behavior was not
above reproach. Like other dynastic politicians, Romanones deplored
"militarism" directed against his own government, but yielded to the
temptation to suspend the constitution and govern through the army
when confronted with social disorder. His tentative search for a modus
vivendi with organized labor was thus compromised from the beginning by his earlier concessions to the army. Behind those concessions
stood the regime's years of dependency on military power. In any
event, Romanones's attempt at negotiation had been made from a
position of weakness. While the Canadiense strike had proven the
strength of syndicalism, the will of the army had ultimately proven
even stronger, not least because the government lacked significant
political support for its policy of pacification. The greatest cost of the
failure to broaden the base of the parliamentary monarchy in 1917 was
that it denied the government a national consensus that could be used
to support a program of economic and social reform. Trapped by their
own weakness into immobility, the dynastic parties could only persist
in their fortress mentality and lend credence to those who argued that
the only route to progress lay through frontal assault.

With the battle lines drawn, the power of the army grew corre-
spondingly. Calls for military dictatorship to replace the weakened
civil power could be heard as early as the spring of 1919.[44] The most

spectacular appeared on May 7, when General Aguilera, the Captain General of Madrid and the leading general in the garciaprietista wing of the Liberal party, renounced his affiliation after a slight from the party leadership.[45] In a public letter, Aguilera called for the recon- struction of the turno to "place a dike against the revolutionary and anarchistic wave that may otherwise crush us all. . . ." As if certain of the failure of this remedy, the general went on to predict the emergence of another "self-sacrificing and altruistic organ" that would save the Fatherland from destruction.[46] Yet references to military dictatorship did not all emanate from the military, but from civilians more attached to property than legality. The inevitable consequence was the further degradation of civil supremacy and the heightened improbability of a peaceful resolution of the social and political crisis.

Repression and Conciliation, 1919–1921

As he had been in 1918, Antonio Maura was again summoned to form a government prestigious enough to withstand military pres- sure without alienating the army. Yet Maura's government of 1919— essentially a party government rather than a coalition[47]—lacked the sense of mission that had characterized the National Government of the previous year. The National Government, an optimistic, if ulti- mately unsuccessful attempt at "renovation," closed one era; the Maura government of 1919, a cynical, uninspired attempt at preservation, opened another. For the next three years, Conservative governments would struggle vainly to restore the old turno; the Spanish electorate, frightened by the rising tide of revolution in Europe, would return comfortable Conservative majorities in the elections of 1919 and 1921. Nevertheless, the Conservative leaders were too divided among them- selves to undertake constructive political reform or a consistent social policy. Alternating instead between brief experiments with conciliation and longer periods of repression, the Conservatives pursued a vacil- lating course that undermined the position of the moderates in the labor movement, favored the rise of terrorism, and reduced the regime to even greater dependence on the army.

Ever the enemy of revolution from below, Maura came into office on April 15, 1919, prepared to adopt a hard-line policy. He had never been inclined toward participatory democracy; now he was resolved to govern alone, with the aid of the army and with minimal regard for the constitution. In Barcelona, Milans del Bosch continued to employ the draconian measures that he believed obligatory under martial law without significantly deterring the growth of the CNT or establishing order. On the contrary, the repression only allowed extremists on both sides to emerge as the most convincing spokesmen for their causes; it was from this period that clandestine groups of Anarchist pistoleros began to prevail over the more moderate Syndicalist leaders in the CNT.[48] In addition, the obvious failure of the repression threatened to discredit the use of martial law as a method of social control, an outcome that worried officers and led Milans to request the government to lift it as soon as possible. Maura, however, lacked confidence in the ability of civil authorities to keep order.[49]

For the same reason, Maura ignored the advice of the Captain General of Seville, who had been following a policy of leniency with regard to the mounting agrarian unrest in Andalusia. Maura sent the army into Cordova province to crush the general strike that broke out in late May, and on May 29 declared martial law in the region. By June 6 the War Minister, General Luis Santiago, reported with disapproval that there were fourteen Infantry and six Cavalry companies, in addition to the Civil Guard, in the area.[50] While this temporarily halted the agrarian syndicalist movement, which had been gathering force since mid-1918, it did not destroy it, but only provided further proof, if any were needed, of the charge that the army was the major prop of the capitalist order.

The politics of repression yielded none of the anticipated results and only destroyed the mystique of moral superiority that Maura had cultivated since the beginning of his career. In the elections of June 1919, the majority of Conservative votes went to followers of his rivals for party leadership, even though Maura (aided by La Cierva) had conducted the elections without restoring constitutional guarantees.[51] On July 21 a cabinet of "Conservative concentration" took office under the leadership of Joaquín Sánchez de Toca.[52]

An intelligent and fiercely independent Conservative, Sánchez de Toca rejected Maura's simpleminded approach to the social question and the excessive reliance on military power that it implied; he was determined to restore stable, constitutional government with a policy of compromise in all areas of dissent. He soon discovered, however, that compromise was elusive in the Spain of 1919. Within four months, Sánchez de Toca had fallen, the victim of two of the most uncompromising groups in Spain—the Employers' Federation and the Juntas de Defensa. Following his resignation, another cycle of violent repression followed by timid conciliation would begin.

The Minister of the Interior in the new cabinet was Manuel Burgos y Mazo, a Dato supporter and a man of strong Christian Democratic principles. Although a firm advocate of "social discipline," Burgos y Mazo agreed with the prime minister that the road to order lay through the satisfaction of moderate labor demands.[53] Furthermore, he considered the Catalan bourgeoisie to be largely responsible for the chaos in Barcelona, a conclusion reinforced by his centralist prejudices. To reverse the trend toward anarchy in Barcelona, he appointed Julio Amado, the editor of *La Correspondencia Militar*, as Civil Governor of Barcelona on August 15.

At first glance, this was a startling appointment. Since 1917 Amado had been intimately connected with the Juntas; his paper was a reliable barometer of opinion among middle-ranking officers, who had largely supported Milans del Bosch in his battle against syndicalism and government negotiators during 1919. As recently as early July, Amado had referred to syndicalism as "leprosy and misery" and had denied any relationship between the "conscious" syndicalism of Western Europe and syndicalism in Spain: "I cannot compare Briand with 'el Noy del Sucre' [Seguí]."[54] Yet Amado suffered from the same contradictory ideas as many officers about the domestic role of the army. Like the juntero authors of the March document on the social question, he believed that using the army to break strikes jeopardized military prestige and probably national security as well. Thus, although he sympathized with the martial attitudes of Milans del Bosch, he was willing to experiment with the conciliatory alternatives proposed by Burgos y Mazo, in the hope of rescuing the army from an uncomfortable situation. From the government's point of view, of course, Amado was the ideal appointment, for his standing with the officers in Barcelona would make it difficult for them to oppose the new policy.

A preliminary reconnaissance in Barcelona soon after his appointment quickly persuaded Amado that the current policies of Milans del Bosch only increased social disorder. Amado found fifteen thousand workers in jail or deported, another fifty thousand locked out of work by the Employers' Federation, and a band of criminals at the service of Bravo Portillo and the employers engaged in bloody street warfare with the gunmen of the action groups. Despite the repression, syndicalism continued to flourish in Barcelona.[55] General Milans del Bosch, however, rejected Amado's proposal to negotiate and charged that the new Civil Governor's frequent contacts with CNT leaders diminished his authority as Captain General of a region under martial law. The government responded by lifting martial law on September 2, a policy that suited both Amado and Milans, who was thereby relieved of responsibility for implementing a conciliatory policy that he knew would be unpopular with the Employers' Federation and much of the army.

For observers of the military, the interesting aspect of the quarrel between Amado and Milans del Bosch was its impact on the rest of the officer corps. Significantly, the Barcelona garrison split over the issue of conciliation along lines that reflected the old intercorps rivalries as well as the conflicting military attitudes toward labor unrest: the Infantry, following its stated policy of "neutrality" in class conflicts, sided with its old ally, Amado; the other corps, instinctively concerned with law and order, unanimously aligned themselves with Milans del Bosch.[56] Clearly, with the officer corps divided, the most prudent policy was one that minimized the role of the army. Milans withdrew his opposition to negotiation, convinced that Amado's policy would discredit itself while his own prestige remained intact.

Far from discrediting itself, the government's policy of compromise initially showed promise of ending the stalemate between the employers and the CNT. By bringing moderates on both sides together to negotiate, Amado was able to achieve rapid results. On September 9 a general amnesty was issued and the lockout ended, enabling thousands of workers to return to work. On October 1 the eight-hour day decreed by Romanones on April 3 went into effect. And on October 11 another decree created the Mixed Commission, an arbitration board composed of workers, employers, and government mediators, to resolve the remaining differences between the parties.

But conciliation was never given a chance to prove its worth, for just as it was beginning to show results, extremists on both sides sabotaged it. In the CNT, the Anarchist purists, who argued that compromise was a betrayal of the class struggle, continued to operate clandestinely; on September 17 CNT pistoleros assassinated Bravo Portillo. At the Second Congress of the Spanish Employers' Federation held on October 20–26, the delegates voted to renew the lockout on November 3 after declaring that they found "guarantees of order and tranquility" only in the army.[57] Although the new arbitration board managed to negotiate the reopening of factories,[58] *ultras* in the Employers' Federation refused to rehire Syndicalist leaders when workers reported to their jobs on November 14. This final betrayal by the employers destroyed the credibility of the moderates within the CNT. The Anarchists now successfully insisted on a break with the arbitration board, which made the workers technically responsible for ending negotiations. The blame for the rupture, however, belonged entirely to the employers, who in the deepening postwar economic crisis, were determined to destroy the labor movement altogether. On November 25 a new lockout threw nearly two hundred thousand out of work until January 26, 1920.

Henceforth, extremists on both sides would prevail. Its confidence shaken by the failure of its social policy, the Sánchez de Toca government resigned on December 5, after the Infantry Junta threatened a sit-down strike over an unrelated issue.[59] Amado returned, disillusioned, from Barcelona on December 10 and was replaced as Civil Governor by José Maestre Laborde, the Conde de Salvatierra, who resumed the hard-line policy temporarily abandoned the previous August. In the CNT, the new lockout discredited the moderate Syndicalists and cleared the path for the extremists, who returned with zest to their violent war with the employers' police, now led by a shady foreign adventurer named Baron de Koenig, a protégé of the chief of the Barcelona General Staff, General Manuel Tourné Esbry.[60] The moderate Syndicalists, while conscious of the counterproductive effects of the terror, nevertheless tolerated the action groups, whom they were in any event powerless to control. The predictable result was the decline of the CNT as a powerful bargaining agent for organized labor in Catalonia. In late 1919 a rival union, the Sindicato Libre, was organized. Initially composed of moderate workers alienated by the tactics of the CNT extremists, it rapidly became a tool of the Employers' Federation, as adept at assassination and terrorism as the underground Anarchist groups.[61] By the spring of 1920 gunmen from the two syndicates had converted the streets of Barcelona into a battlefield.

The events of 1919 had demonstrated to the government in Madrid the difficulty of pursuing a policy independently of the Employers' Federation and the army. Lacking popular support, and themselves fearful of social revolution, the dynastic politicians were unable to resist the constant pressure from Barcelona for a hard-line policy, even when such policies clearly aggravated, rather than ameliorated, the endemic violence. At the same time, they found themselves under attack in the Cortes, where both Republicans and Socialists accused them of abandoning the principle of civil supremacy. For the Liberals, the dilemma was especially acute. Their only hope of returning to office was as a truly "liberal" party committed to civil supremacy and political reform. But their own inclinations and interests, not to mention personal rivalries, were a permanent obstacle to the revitalization of the party. Under siege from both the left and the right, the dynastic politicians were not able to adhere to a consistent policy; the resulting cycle of repression followed by conciliation made it even harder for moderates in the labor movement to make themselves heard. The ultimate beneficiaries were the Catalan employers and the army, who felt vindicated in insisting on even more vigorous repressive measures.

The government of Manuel Allendesalazar, which took office after the resignation of Sánchez de Toca on December 5, 1919, was a coalition of Conservatives and Liberals formed to assert the authority of the government over both the Juntas de Defensa and the intransigents in Barcelona.[62] Its task was made more difficult by new outbreaks of revolutionary violence. The most shocking was a mutiny in the Carmen barracks in Saragossa, where a solitary Anarchist zealot named Angel Chueca, accompanied by several corporals, sergeants, and soldiers, killed a second lieutenant and a sergeant before being subdued.[63] Chueca died during the revolt; in the aftermath, a court-martial sentenced two corporals and five soldiers to death. In the Cortes, Alejandro Lerroux warned that "bolshevism has knocked heavily at the doors of the barracks" and urged social reform.[64] But others saw the Carmen mutiny as justification for sterner measures of social control.

One of those was General Milans del Bosch, who took the opportunity to reassert his autonomy from the government. After two attempts on the lives of the Syndicalist leader, Salvador Seguí, and the president of the Employers' Federation, Felix Graupera, in early January, the Captain General declared martial law and issued a threatening edict that was followed by mass arrests and the wholesale closure of unions and newspapers. This was too great a provocation for the Liberals in the cabinet, who demanded that the Captain General retract his edict. Milans, however, refused, and as telegrams of support for the Captain General poured in from the Somatenes, the Employers' Federation, and the leading military figures in Barcelona, the cabinet backed down, lacking sufficient political support to impose its will. To emphasize his disapproval of the Liberals, Milans next released his correspondence with the government during the Canadiense strike the previous year to a Conservative senator, who read it aloud in the Cortes in order to prove that the Romanonist Liberals, both in the past and at present, had favored a policy of compromise with syndicalism.[65] Outraged, Romanones threatened to withdraw his representative, Amalio Gimeno, from the cabinet unless Milans were removed from his post for insubordination, a challenge Milans accepted by submitting his resignation. This time, however, the cabinet refused to capitulate. Although telegrams of support once again poured in from Barcelona, the government accepted the resignation in order to keep the governing coalition together.

Its firmness was short-lived, however. Protests were immediately heard in the Cortes, where one Catalan leader labeled Milans's dismissal an "anarchising" act.[66] More ominously, the Barcelona garrison was in a mutinous mood. The new Captain General, the ancient but still loyal General Weyler, was snubbed by officers when he arrived in the Catalan capital. The same week, the chief of the Barcelona General Staff, General Tourné, and the president of the Infantry Junta, Colonel Silverio Martínez Raposo, were received by the king in Madrid, which was by now buzzing with rumors of an ultimatum from the Juntas de Defensa. To protest the ongoing military indiscipline, the Liberal Gimeno resigned from the cabinet on February 14, a resignation that was accepted by the Conservatives with little regret, since it enabled them to distance themselves from the policy of conciliation associated with the Conde de Romanones. Although General Milans del Bosch was not reinstated, he was made head of the king's Military Household in May. Once again at peace with the army, the cabinet remained in office until passage of the new budget.

In spite of the army's united stand behind the former Captain General, by 1920 a few officers were beginning to advocate a more subtle approach to the problem of social conflict. Literature in the military press echoed that of the 1890s, when social unrest had first begun to trouble the calm of the Restoration. Middle-class in outlook and authoritarian by training, military authors offered advice aimed not so much at comprehension as at catechization. Most advised individual officers, especially at the lower ranks, to utilize their opportunities for close contact with the troops to lead them out of error. Once an officer had communicated his concern to the common soldier, he would find him receptive to little lessons on patriotism, religion, and social discipline.[67] Thus, the "social mission" of the army, a national institution, was that of reconciling and harmonizing class interests. Only occasionally did an author suggest attacking the social problem by attacking the social conditions that gave rise to it.[68] In general, it was assumed that to restore class harmony one had only to deny the reality of class conflict.

The Conservatives briefly returned to a policy of conciliation in May 1920, when Eduardo Dato replaced Allendesalazar as prime minister.[69] On May 8 a royal decree creating a Ministry of Labor finally elevated the "social question" to cabinet status. In Barcelona, the intransigent Conde de Salvatierra was replaced as Civil Governor by Federico Carlos Bas, who quickly released hundreds of imprisoned

Syndicalists, ended prior censorship, reopened workers' centers, and turned a deaf ear to the demands of the Employers' Federation to "give battle."[70] But the tactics that had worked for Amado in 1919 were slower to produce results in 1920. Worker enthusiasm for the CNT had been blunted by the long lockout the previous winter and by the still-growing influence of the underground terrorist groups within the organization; many workers thus failed to pay dues, while others joined the rival Sindicatos Libres. During the spring and summer of 1920, street warfare between the two labor federations was added to the usual violence between bands of Anarchist and secret police gunmen. As tension mounted, the demands of the Employers' Federation and the army for a return to an energetic policy of repression appeared increasingly justified.

The international situation did not portend a peaceful resolution of the social crisis, either. The foundation of the Comintern, or Third International, in March 1919 had had profound repercussions for left-wing parties all over Europe, raising the enthusiasm of the masses while frequently dividing the traditional leadership. The Spanish left, too, had been divided; the issue of Comintern membership had split the National Committee of the PSOE and had separated the party from the Socialist labor federation, the UGT, while the CNT approached the Comintern with serious reservations. To the oligarchy that ruled Spain, however, these schisms and doubts were of much less significance than the provisional adhesion of the CNT (in December 1919) and of the PSOE (in June 1920) to the revolutionary Communist International and the formation of a small Communist party in Madrid in April 1920.[71] During the summer, three separate Spanish delegations made pilgrimages to Moscow, while the Spanish right trembled.

By late summer Dato was ready to abandon his pacification policy and allow the "elements of order" to regain control over Barcelona. On July 5 he had removed General Weyler from the Captaincy General, rewarding his loyalty with a new title, the Duque de Rubí. Weyler's replacement was the colorless General Carlos Palanca y Cañas, who was completely overshadowed by the Military Governor of the city, General Severiano Martínez Anido. By September, Martínez Anido and the Employers' Federation had convinced Dato to replace the liberal Minister of the Interior, Francisco Bergamín, with the more reactionary Conde de Bugallal, an ominous sign that hastened the achievement of a defensive alliance between the UGT and the CNT on September 3. Using this pact as further proof of the need for a harsh policy, on November 5 the Catalan bourgeoisie drafted a stern note to the government demanding the resignation of the moderate Civil

Governor, Carlos Bas.[72] On November 8, amidst new rumors of a coup, the Dato government removed Bas and replaced him with General Martínez Anido.

The appointment of Martínez Anido as Civil Governor of Barcelona marked the beginning of a reign of terror in the city and the almost total disappearance of the rule of law. A thoroughgoing military martinet, Martínez Anido was the least likely officer to fill a civil post; while he served as Civil Governor, Barcelona was effectively under martial law. Like General Milans del Bosch, under whom he had served in Barcelona from February 1919 to February 1920, he was deeply committed to the preservation of military prestige and public order, but he lacked his superior's breeding and sensitivity. Brusque and stubborn, neurotically jealous of his own authority, and insensitive to both public opinion and the long-range consequences of his acts, Martínez Anido would rule Barcelona for two years, with disastrous results, but with complete self-confidence as to the effectiveness of his policies. Like Milans del Bosch, he would be the principal ally and hero of the Barcelona bourgeoisie.[73]

While the government in Madrid discreetly looked the other way, Martínez Anido undertook the "definitive pacification" of Barcelona through a policy of police terrorism aimed at the total eradication of the labor movement in the city.[74] The new Civil Governor wasted little time in implementing his program. On November 19 he issued an edict declaring war against the "tyrannical dominion of those few who forgot they were men" and inviting moderate workers to collaborate with him, an offer accepted by the Sindicatos Libres the same day.[75] On November 20 he initiated his attack against the CNT, imprisoning and later deporting sixty-four leading Syndicalists, including all the moderates. The continuing assassinations by underground CNT gunmen were answered by the Sindicato Libre, now protected and financed by the Civil Governor. Within twenty-one days, there were twenty-two political murders, including the pro-syndicalist Republican lawyer and deputy, Francisco Layret, on November 30. In January 1921 Martínez Anido revived the notorious "Ley de Fugas" that institutionalized the assassination of workers "trying to escape."

Despite the energy and conviction with which it was carried out, Martínez Anido's policy did not produce the anticipated results. It merely stimulated the action groups to greater extremes of murder, robbery, and terror, which were matched, crime for crime, by the Sindicatos Libres and the police, whose chief, General Miguel Arlegui, was a faithful servant of the Civil Governor. In 1921 there were 254 crimes of violence committed in Barcelona.[76] Since most of the victims were workers, however, Martínez Anido and the Employers' Federation considered his program to be an unqualified success. By 1922 the Civil Governor could claim victory of a sort; after the imprisonment of thousands of militants, the assassination of dozens of terrorists, and the depletion of CNT rolls by workers defecting to the Sindicatos Libres or relapsing into apathy, the CNT had ceased to make its presence felt in Barcelona.

On February 10, 1921, the parliamentary Socialists, led by Julián Besteiro, condemned the Dato government for tolerating the counter-terrorism that Martínez Anido himself did not deny.[77] The government had no intention of dismissing the general, whose relentless persecution of the labor movement coincided with the heightened reactionary mood in the country evidenced by the Conservative victory in the elections the previous December.[78] On the other hand, it was not true that the government dictated policy to General Martínez Anido, who governed Barcelona on his own terms, as he freely admitted in a press interview in 1921: "The characteristic of my command . . . is that I scarcely speak with the Government. All the responsibility is mine. The Government has not tried to give me instructions, as it has been doing with former Governors."[79] It was ironic, then, that Eduardo Dato was assassinated on March 8, 1921, by an Anarchist who announced that he had not fired against Dato, but against the ruler who authorized the Ley de Fugas.[80] Still, if Dato had not directly ordered the use of political assassination, he had appointed Martínez Anido and had refrained from moderating his excesses in order to save the interests of the ruling elites. His successor, Allendesalazar, continued to allow the Civil Governor a free hand.[81] In a perverse way, the employers of Catalonia had won their autonomy with the aid of the army.

The reign of Martínez Anido in Barcelona was an extreme example of the anarchy and disregard for law that increasingly characterized the resolution of political and social problems in Spain. Martínez Anido and the Employers' Federation may have been the worst offenders, but they were tolerated by the shortsighted oligarchy that ruled in Madrid, applauded by the military,[82] and imitated by other would-be lawbreakers. With the constitution still suspended, the press muzzled by the Law of Jurisdictions and occasionally, by prior censorship as well, the parliament an ineffective repository of fear and obstructionism, the dynastic politicians found it increasingly difficult to invoke the principle of civic obedience or to defend the regime on its own terms. Inspiring no enthusiasm on the right, which found them pusil-lanimous, or on the left, which thought them beyond redemption, the ruling parties were left to defend their right to rule with the only force available to them—the army. As a consequence, the "military question" became a topic of concern for all those preoccupied with the fate of the parliamentary monarchy in Spain.

CHAPTER SEVEN

The Debate on the Army, 1919–1921

The question of military power in Spain, introduced by the constitutional crisis of 1917 and prolonged by the passage of the army reform law in 1918, was debated with even greater intensity between 1919 and 1921 because of the intensification of two conflicts in which the army was intimately involved: the postwar struggle with the revolutionary left and the colonial war in Morocco. Because both conflicts exposed the function of the Spanish army as the major guarantor of the political and social status quo, the "military question" led logically into a debate on the future of the regime. For the left, imperialism, capitalism, and monarchism endured only because of their alliance with militarism; for the right, the army was the last defense against bolshevism at home and barbarism in Africa. The undeniable influence of the Spanish army, then, owed as much to the obsessive preoccupation of civilians at both ends of the political spectrum with military affairs as to the aggression of a united and belligerent officer corps.

By 1921 the immobility of the dynastic parties suggested that the resolution of the national crisis would depend in some way on the army. Yet a consensus within the army did not exist; like the rest of the nation, the Spanish officer corps was badly divided by the conflicts that attacked the parliamentary monarchy from 1917 on. The superficial unity achieved in June 1917 had quickly dissipated, eroded by the usual intercorps rivalries, the absence of widely acknowledged leadership in the senior hierarchy, the controversial provisions of the 1918 reform law, and the understanding by officers themselves of the army's crucial role. In the absence of strong civilian government this disarray acquired a new resonance that contributed further to political instability. Military disunity invited exploitation by both the left and the right, which politicized the officer corps by drawing the various factions closer to the center of the national crisis. By 1921 military reform and political vitality—however defined—were so intimately interconnected that no one could think of one without considering the other. The debate on the army had become a debate on the future of Spain itself.

The ESG Affair

The incident involving the Infantry Junta de Defensa and twenty-five students from the Superior War College (the ESG) in December 1919 brought home to the country the centrality of the army in Spanish political life: a petty squabble between military bureaucrats became a major political incident because the Sánchez de Toca government dared not risk a confrontation with the army at a moment of extreme tension in Barcelona. The ESG affair dramatized the significance of military professionalization for the neutralization of the officer corps; more important, it clarified the connection between military reform and political modernization. Critics of the regime used the ESG affair to illustrate their contention that the government had abandoned control over military policy to the Juntas, to the detriment of both popular sovereignty and stable government. Because it crystallized many of the issues surrounding civil-military relations in postwar Spain, the ESG affair is worth examining in some detail.

As we have seen, one of the principal animosities that moved the clientele of the Infantry Junta was directed against the Staff Corps. This resentment, which dated back to the mid-nineteenth century, was not wholly unjustified. Staff officers had traditionally been favored for promotion by the dynastic parties; like the other technical corps, they presumed to great professional superiority over the Infantry and Cavalry. In practice, they had neglected both regimental service and strategic planning for more arcane pursuits—chiefly mapmaking. After the French abolished their Staff Corps in 1886, Spanish military reformers had aspired to do the same thing. Ever since the creation of the "diplomados" by General López Domínguez in 1893, Staff officers had lived in fear of seeing their beloved Corps—and its privileges—replaced by a "service" open to certified individuals from all corps. When the Infantry Junta began to organize in the winter of 1916–17, Staff officers had organized their own Junta in self-defense.

On the other hand, juntero criticism of the Staff Corps was not based on purely professional grounds; it grew largely out of their general resentment of selective promotions of any kind. In their haste to equate all nonseniority promotions with favoritism, junteros lost sight of the institutional need to reward competence and develop effective leadership, favoring instead a leveling process that would have represented no improvement over the existing system. It was this bureaucratic outlook—not a disinterested desire for military reform—that animated the Infantry Junta's attack on the Staff Corps in 1917. Delegates to the Assembly of Regional Juntas in September 1917 had voted to require War College candidates to declare, prior to acceptance, whether they would ultimately become Staff officers or remain in the Infantry as diplomados.[1] Those choosing the former but subsequently failing the entrance examinations were to pledge to resign immediately from the Infantry.[2] The incentive was thus strong for officers to reject the Staff Corps option from the outset. In time, the Corps might be expected to wither away from lack of new personnel.

The first test of this strategy in May 1918 indicated that aspiring Staff officers would not be easily intimidated. Several Infantry lieutenants refused to sign the pledge before obtaining the examination results; moreover, local Juntas proved reluctant to prosecute these recalcitrants.[3] Despite exhortations from the Superior Junta, no action was taken anywhere except in Burgos, where the local Junta ordered garrison lieutenants to form an honor court against Lieutenant Ramón Martínez de Aragón, who was acquitted of dishonorable conduct by his peers and entered the ESG in the fall of 1918. Undaunted by this verdict of innocence, the Burgos Infantry Junta, with the cooperation of the Superior Junta in Madrid, utilized the "democratic" provisions of the original Junta statutes to solicit the nationwide "opinion of the Corps" on the question of the lieutenant's "honor." Shielded by the anonymity of the ballot, juntero officers approved a vindictive policy that they were unwilling to implement at a personal level. The Superior Junta then ordered the first-year Infantry lieutenants in the ESG to form a new honor court against their colleague, Martínez de Aragón.[4] An impasse was reached, however, when the thirty-five Infantry lieutenants in the War College refused to form the honor court, even when threatened with expulsion from the army by the Superior Junta.

The Junta's vendetta against the Staff Corps was frustrated again in July 1919, when a diplomado Cavalry captain, Arsenio Martínez Campos (the grandson of the Restoration general), introduced a proposal in the Cortes to replace the Corps with a General Staff composed of diplomados "on service" from the various corps. In the words of its sponsors, who included Reformists, Radical Republicans, and the Romanonist Liberals, the bill was to rid the General Staff of "bureaucratism and irresponsibility" and to reorganize it along the lines established in other nations.[5] While this was a legitimate, and indeed, overdue reform, the sponsors were motivated largely by a desire to embarrass the new Conservative government of Sánchez de Toca. By bringing the proposal before the Cortes, they hoped to assert the constitutional prerogatives of the parliament as well as to construct a "liberal" voting block in the Cortes on the issue of military reform.

Although the proposal coincided with its own goals, the Infantry Junta was understandably wary of legislative debate that might easily be diverted to a discussion of the Juntas. Within a few days, it opened a two-front campaign against the Staff Corps and the government to achieve the dissolution of the Corps by decree before the opening of the autumn sessions of the Cortes. The first step was to intimidate the Staff Corps. In early August the Assembly of Junta Presidents in Madrid expressed support for the principle behind the legislative proposal (with the dissenting vote of the Staff Corps president, of course); on August 21 they demanded that the Staff Corps Junta present a reorganization plan by September 1, or face an Assembly vote on the dissolution of the Corps. Hoping to save some of its prerogatives, the Staff Junta submitted a plan for "limited service" that would have transferred part of the privileges and responsibilities of the Corps to the other branches. The Assembly did not want compliance, however, but the destruction of its enemy. On September 11 it issued a pamphlet stating the reasons why the Staff Corps should be abolished.[6]

At this point, the Corps recognized it must fight for its life. First it circulated a pamphlet among the officer corps justifying its existence and accusing the Assembly of Junta Presidents of betraying the principle of mutual protection that had characterized its past deliberations.[7] Then on October 17, 1919, twenty-five of the thirty-five lieutenants in the ESG resigned from their Junta, explaining their actions to the officer corps in another pamphlet that described the pressures put on them by the Superior Junta in connection with the case of Martínez de Aragón.[8]

But the Infantry Junta was just as quick to retaliate. On October 21 this pamphlet was leaked to the press, quite probably, as the students suspected, by the Superior Junta, which took advantage of the publicity given the resignations by *El Sol* and other papers to order the formation of an honor court against the students on the grounds that they had violated the Junta code of secrecy. At the same time, the president of the Superior Junta stepped up the campaign to secure the dissolution of the Corps by decree, contacting the king, the War Minister, and an old ally, Juan de la Cierva, whose animosity toward the prime minister, Sánchez de Toca, dated back to 1918. On October 27 an honor court composed of the remaining ten Infantry lieutenants in the ESG found sixteen of the twenty-five guilty of dishonorable conduct and recommended their expulsion from the army. The validity of the sentence was doubtful, however, because the Code of Military Justice stipulated that a minimum of four-fifths of the officers at a given rank was necessary to form an honor court against a colleague. In the present case, ten lieutenants had tried twenty-five of their peers.

The dubious legality of the sentence allowed the government and the senior hierarchy to move against the Junta. Presented with an order separating the sixteen lieutenants from the Infantry, the War Minister, General Antonio Tovar, refused to sign it and instead referred the verdict of the honor court to the Supreme Military Council. On November 28 the senior generals on the Council ruled fourteen to two that the verdict was invalid. In the meantime, Sánchez de Toca had appointed an ad hoc committee of generals to study the reorganization of the Staff Corps; its chairman was the reliable General Weyler, himself a Staff officer and currently chief of the General Staff.[9]

By early November the conflict in the officer corps had been brought to the attention of the nation by the opponents of the government. Both the Liberals and the left exploited the scandal created by the Juntas to comment unfavorably on the government's tolerance for military insubordination.[10] But Sánchez de Toca, a longtime enemy of the Juntas, was not to be robbed so easily of the issue of military reform: on November 18 he borrowed the Liberals' old stratagem of introducing a bill abrogating the Law of Jurisdictions while incorporating its main provisions into the civil and military codes.[11] Rightly viewing this as a red herring, Republicans and Socialists responded on November 26 with a proposal declaring the illegality of the Juntas, whose statutes had never received the official approval required by the Law of 1918.[12]

The debates illustrated the extent to which Spaniards now associated the power of the military with the weakness of the regime. But they also demonstrated that the will to proceed beyond verbal attacks on the Juntas was lacking among all groups except the far left. Crucial to the outcome of the debates was the rising tide of revolution in the peninsula. During the last week of November 1919, the Employers' Federation declared a lockout in Barcelona, and food riots erupted in Malaga, Valencia, and Saragossa, where martial law was briefly declared. For most deputies, the distinction between "the army" and "the Juntas" was not clear enough to risk alienating the military at a moment of extreme tension. Even Santiago Alba, who prided himself on his openness to the left, felt compelled to refer to the threat of "bolshevism and dissolution" while cautioning against a rash assault on the Juntas.[13] When the final vote was taken on November 28, the proposition outlawing the Juntas was defeated seventy-two to twelve.

Astutely exploiting the fear of revolution, the Infantry Superior Junta next announced that "the army" would begin a sit-down strike unless a new honor court were formed to expel the twenty-five ESG students from the army. This was a hollow threat. The officer corps was, as usual, divided over the ESG affair: the War Minister and the Supreme Military Council were resolutely antijuntero, and the technical corps were less willing than the Infantry to provoke a confrontation with the government during the social crisis.[14] Two of the younger Infantry generals—the Captain General of Madrid, Aguilera, and General Primo de Rivera, of the First Division—were sympathetic to the Infantry Junta and had represented their cause to the government and the king. They had also made clear their refusal, however, to lead a coup with the officer corps badly divided.[15]

Yet, faced with the collapse of its policy in Barcelona, the government lacked the self-confidence to act decisively. On December 1 General Tovar resigned, fearful of a showdown, and the government, worn out by its four turbulent months in office, agreed after some debate to follow suit.[16] With the officers' strike scheduled to begin the following day, however, Alfonso was unwilling to allow them this avenue of escape. Forced, at the king's insistence, to remain in office, the government devised an ingenious plan to allow the Infantry Junta the appearance but not the substance of victory. On December 3 General Tovar signed an order establishing special conditions for honor courts composed of fewer than four-fifths of the officers' peers, which enabled a new honor court to find twenty-three of the twenty-five ESG students guilty the same day. According to the government's strategy, Tovar was then supposed to defer the verdict to the Supreme Military Council, which was expected to rule once again in the students' favor. Instead, the War Minister, without consulting his colleagues, signed the separation order and resigned on December 5. The cabinet, too weary to insist on judicial review, yet unwilling to accept the capitulation to the Junta, resigned with him.[17] For the fourth time in thirty months, the Juntas de Defensa had brought down a government.

The significance of the ESG affair was that it clarified civilian responsibility for military power—power conferred by a combination of political weakness, fear of revolution, and military aggressiveness. The incident also exposed the consequences of earlier failures to eliminate the structural defects in the officer corps. By avoiding military reform for forty years, governments had nurtured professional rivalries and incompetence; by 1920 military affairs had acquired such political significance that these internal quarrels transcended the petty world of the War Ministry and destroyed a government supposedly committed to the principle of civil supremacy.

The Advisory Commissions

The ESG affair represented the high point of juntero power, or to put it another way, civilian government was at its weakest in December 1919. The government formed by Manuel Allendesalazar on December 12, 1919, basically a Conservative coalition fortified by the Romanonist Liberals, was not prepossessing, but it would surprisingly survive its internal upheavals and achieve its basic mission—the approval of a new budget in May 1920. In addition, it would tentatively assert its authority by replacing the Juntas de Defensa with the "Advisory Commissions," a symbolic gesture whose chief significance lay in the inability of the Juntas to resist it. From 1920 on, weakened governments and the chastened Advisory Commissions struck an uneasy balance, while real military power took shape in Barcelona and across the Straits in Morocco.

The decree creating the Advisory Commissions was signed on December 30, 1919, after the government had been in office less than three weeks, because the military question for the moment eclipsed all others. Opinion against the Juntas was at an all-time high; somewhat histrionically, the Ateneo de Madrid had voted honorary membership for all twenty-three of the lieutenants expelled from the army.[18] The government did not wish to expose the Juntas to its enemies in the Cortes, however, because of the precarious situation in Barcelona. Bypassing the parliament, the government chose the more expedient method of royal decree.[19] On the surface, the decree appeared to abolish the old, extralegal Juntas, which were to be replaced by new commissions installed in the War Ministry under the direct supervision of the Undersecretary and the section heads. In fact, the government lacked the power to enforce its decree, which in the end changed nothing except the name of the Central Junta of each corps, which now became known officially as the "Advisory Commission," or, in the case of the Infantry, as the "Directory." Not even the personnel changed; the same officers remained in Madrid, collected dues (although at a lower rate of one peseta a month),[20] and generally ignored the nominal authority of the War Minister. Furthermore, the Infantry Junta retained its organization at the regional and local levels, in violation both of the new decree and of La Cierva's decree of March 18, 1918. As it was obvious to everyone that there had been no real change in the structure or autonomy of the Juntas, only official government spokesmen—and the junteros themselves—took the trouble to refer to them by their new name.

All the same, the Juntas did not possess the power or the self-confidence to protest the decree as they might have done a few months earlier. They too had been damaged by the controversy over the ESG students. The affair had exposed the pettiness of the Infantry Junta and dramatized the extent to which political stability depended upon military tranquility. Furthermore, the incident had revealed a disturbing lack of solidarity within the officer corps, not only between the senior hierarchy and the lower echelons, but among the corps. Forced to acknowledge a real erosion of support, the Superior Junta was reluctant to protest the decree creating the Advisory Commissions, particularly since it figured to lose none of its real power. The Anarchist uprising in the Carmen barracks in Saragossa on January 9, 1920, further convinced them that their power to protest was limited.

During early 1920, then, as tension continued to mount in Barcelona, both the government and the Juntas followed a policy of exquisite discretion. Further discussion of the ESG incident in the Cortes was quashed by the government, while for its part, the Infantry temporarily dropped its campaign against the Staff Corps, which had ironically benefited from the well-publicized attack against it. During January the generals appointed to study the reorganization of the Corps recommended that it be retained unaltered, and the War Minister, General José Villalba, privately informed the Staff Corps's Central Junta that the bill introduced by Captain Martínez Campos the previous July would be allowed "to sleep the sleep of the just."[21] Thus a needed reform was once again postponed, the victim of intercorps rivalries and political expediency. A month later the Infantry Junta was still maintaining a low profile when the resignation of General Milans del Bosch as Captain General of Barcelona provoked a storm of protest in the garrisons there. Although rumors of a coup circulated, in fact the Juntas did not act. For the next year and a half, the "Advisory Commissions" would tend to internal matters, unmolested by Conservative governments, each of them unwilling to revive the "military question" for fear of provoking further attacks from the left.

The 1920 Budget

Although the Juntas and the Conservatives did their best to discourage debate, national concern over the army remained high. By 1920 social revolution and colonial warfare had demonstrated the importance of military efficiency as well as military loyalty. With the future of the regime clearly in the balance, the specific character of Spain's military organization, as well as its pervasive political influence, attracted serious attention for the first time since the outbreak of the world war in 1914. In particular, the passage of the government's budget—the first since 1914—which allocated one-third of total state expenditures to the army, stimulated considerable discussion before the government ended debate with the cloture rule five days later.[22]

The staggering size of the War Ministry budget, which was 150 percent higher than that of 1917, was due to two recent developments —the reform law of 1918 and the renewal of the Moroccan war—whose costs had been obscured by previous failures to pass a budget. The new budget made it clear that these costs would well exceed available revenues, draining resources from other vital areas. Repeated challenges from the left also made it clear that in determining the military and foreign policy reflected by the budget, the government preferred to recognize the will of the army rather than the will of the parliament.

The War Ministry budget was tailored primarily to the needs of the peninsular military bureaucracy, somewhat less to the necessities of the African army. It was immediately apparent that the reform law of 1918 had not repaired the imbalances within the budget; on the contrary, it had exacerbated the financial burden imposed by the excess of officers. Personnel expenditures comprised 50 percent of the total permanent budget of 426.5 million pesetas, nearly double the absolute amount spent for this purpose in 1917, before salaries had been raised by 20 to 25 percent. Moreover, because prices had risen by at least 40 percent since passage of the law, the new budget contained recommended increases of another 20 to 33 percent for all ranks, raising the prospect of an even larger budget in years to come.[23] Little headway had been made since 1918 in reducing the number of officers. Only a few generals had retired to the second reserve, and the amortization rate for all vacancies had been lowered to 25 percent in August 1919. Although General Villalba promised that the money for the new raises would be derived from further amortizations, he refused to agree to more drastic and rapid reductions.[24]

The other side of the personnel problem was the increase in troop strength, which was set at 216,000 men, an increase of nearly 88,000 from 1917. Since higher call-up levels implied national priorities that properly fell within the jurisdiction of the parliament, the subcommittee reported in a lower figure in protest. But the government ignored the report. The larger standing army reflected the demands imposed by the creation of two new divisions in the Law of 1918 and by the escalating conflict in Morocco. Rather than arouse either the junteros or the africanistas by agreeing to a reduction in troops, the government withdrew this portion of the budget and called up the 216,000 conscripts by decree the following fall. In both the peninsular and the Moroccan budgets, large increases over the minimal sums spent in 1917 for housing, provisioning, and hospital care reflected the inflation and the growing class consciousness of conscript troops that were part of the new social and economic reality of postwar Spain.

A major item in the 1920 army budget was the provision for "temporary" or once-only expenditures totaling 80 million pesetas, another legacy of the Law of 1918. Like the law itself, this section provided only for the peninsular army; the Moroccan budget included separate, although much smaller, line items for new equipment and materiel. Significantly, however, the principal objection to these expenditures came not from the left but from a right-wing military deputy, Lieutenant Colonel Joaquín Fanjul, who complained that the new equipment would undoubtedly be transferred to Africa, leaving the peninsula defenseless.[25] As peninsular officers like Fanjul were aware, the African army was beginning to overshadow its peninsular counterpart, its success providing a welcome contrast to the bumptious troublemaking of the peninsular bureaucrats. While the War Ministry budget drew attacks from across the political spectrum, the Moroccan budget of 154 million pesetas was approved after little debate.

In spite of the unusual amount of discussion—and the enormous sums involved—the entire budget was approved by both houses of the Cortes by April 21. Only the left had tried to raise philosophical questions about the kind of army Spain wanted or could afford.[26] The government had refused to recognize the legitimacy of their concern for parliamentary discussion of policy alternatives. Nevertheless, the dynastic parties were also acutely aware of the economic and political burden posed by the unreformed army. When Allendesalazar resigned on May 5, his successor, Eduardo Dato, appointed a civilian, the Vizconde de Eza, as Minister of War. Unlike Juan de la Cierva in 1917, Eza did not enter the War Ministry to placate the army but to put its house in order.

The Juntas in Disarray

The appointment of the Vizconde de Eza was a continuation of the antijuntero policy inaugurated by the Allendesalazar government the previous December. A technician who had performed competently in the Development Ministry under Dato in 1917, Eza had no contacts or clientele within the officer corps and thus seemed a suitable choice for a government aiming to maintain its independence from military pressure. While the attention of the government was primarily focused on Barcelona, where a new attempt at conciliation was inaugurated, it was hoped that Eza could redress some of the imbalances perpetuated by the Law of 1918 without unduly alienating any faction in the army.

The moment seemed ripe for a beginning. Public opinion, alerted to the expense of the military bureaucracy by the budget discussions and captivated by the heroic advance of the army in Morocco, was unanimously against the Juntas, which had not recovered from the ESG affair of six months earlier. Furthermore, within the officer corps, support for the Advisory Commissions continued to erode. In June colonels in the Fourth Military Region, under the leadership of the Commander General of the Artillery, formed a Regional Catalan Delegation to petition for the disappearance of the Advisory Commissions.[27] There were also signs of alienation in the Staff Corps, which still carried the scars from its struggle against the other Juntas the previous winter.[28] Even within the Infantry Junta, the self-aggrandizing policies of the Directory had created dissension; especially provoking were the attempts by the Junta leadership to acquire special privileges at the expense of the bureaucratic norms they had been elected to defend.[29] Membership in the Infantry Junta had fallen from a high of nine thousand in October 1917 to five thousand in late 1919. It seemed at least possible that the Juntas might disintegrate of their own accord because of the apathy or disillusionment of the rank and file.

Yet the Juntas would not disappear while the juntero mentality prevailed in the officer corps. As long as the technical corps had privileges to protect, they would not deprive themselves of their means of self-defense; as long as Infantry officers imagined themselves abused, they would continue to support the Directory. The Juntas were the symptom, not the cause, of the malaise affecting the Spanish army. The only way to eliminate the army's praetorian tendencies was to professionalize it, eliminating both the structural defects that robbed it of efficiency and the political interference that deprived it of institutional autonomy. By mid-1920 the regime was too precarious to undertake a vigorous military reform policy. But the Dato government did instruct the new War Minister to initiate an indirect and piecemeal approach to the army's problems.

The top priority seemed to be the reinstatement of merit promotions for combat officers in Morocco, a justifiable measure on which there was no consensus within the Infantry Corps. Initially, the juntero aversion to battlefield merit promotions was rooted in the obvious favoritism shown the military elites and in the conviction that most promotions awarded during the halt in operations were unearned. With the renewal of operations in early 1919, however, these abuses had become less significant, while the need to reward the hardship and risk of a difficult campaign had increased. Commanding officers in Africa found morale low and urged repeal of the 1918 ban on all merit promotions. But successive governments had turned a deaf ear, fearing to alienate the Juntas, who had not relaxed their opposition to merit promotions in any form. On the contrary, as the Moroccan campaign began to attract national attention to the Africa army, their intransigence hardened. In early 1920 junteros in the Wad-Ras regiment in Madrid suggested eliminating the exception clauses in the Law of 1918 on the grounds that they damaged "personal and collective decorum."[30]

In July 1920 the new War Minister made his obligatory inspection tour of Morocco, where a protest demonstration by officers impressed him even further with the need "to open the hand in the concession of rewards and favors to those fighting in Africa," a decision he announced to the press after his return on July 22. The reaction of the Juntas was immediate. The same day, *La Correspondencia Militar* warned against favoritism and prodigality and ominously closed with an exhortation to "Remember June 1, 1917!"[31] Even the threat of military rebellion was enough to frighten the Dato government in the summer of 1920. Eza was forced to back away from his proposal at once. In his official report to the cabinet, he opposed the reinstatement of wartime merit promotions, suggesting instead a triple salary increase for those stationed in hardship posts in the interior of the Protectorate.[32] Henceforth, he would not take the initiative in formulating military policy either in the peninsula or in Africa, preferring to avoid controversy by deferring to the pressure group nearest at hand.

The opportunity to enact a needed reform at the expense of the disunited Juntas was thus lost. As usual, the government believed itself even weaker than its adversaries. Appointment of a civilian War Minister was not enough to assert the authority of civilian government; it required popular support and a sense of purpose. By August 1920 both were evaporating for the Dato government, particularly in Barcelona. With the specter of communism threatening Europe, Dato abandoned his policy of conciliation, while Eza in the War Ministry, fearful of alienating the peninsular army at a moment of crisis, had little choice but to let events drift. The result during the next year was continued military squabbling in the peninsula and, in Africa, the disaster at Anual.

While Eza deferred to the Directory in Madrid, in Africa the Infantry Junta became increasingly unpopular. In late 1920 officers in the elite Regular units in Larache resigned from the Junta to protest the prohibition on merit promotions, and the Directory was unable to cajole the rebels back into the fold or to coerce the rest of the Larache garrison to form an honor court against them.[33] Discontent spread to the rest of the Protectorate in 1921, particularly in the shock units, whose young officers chafed under the bureaucratic rule of the Juntas in the major garrisons. The tension finally erupted when the membership of the Infantry Junta as a whole voted on April 30, 1921, to require all officers to renounce any merit promotions voted by the parliament under the exception clauses in the Law of 1918.[34] In protest, officers from the African shock units deluged the War Ministry with transfer petitions,[35] a gesture with serious implications for the outcome of the African campaign. But the Allendesalazar government, caught between two military factions and preoccupied with the leadership crisis posed by the assassination of Eduardo Dato two months before, could offer no redress. It would take the military debacle of July 1921 to dramatize the deleterious effect of juntero dominance on africanista morale.

The Debate on the Army

Perhaps the most significant result of the noticeably declining power and prestige of the Juntas was that it clarified for some observers the distinction between the Juntas and the army. This enabled critics to discuss the army as a problem in itself, complicated by, but not limited to the problem of the Juntas, which, it was increasingly clear, had not seized their power, but had received it from civilians in 1917. For thoughtful observers interested in political change, the Juntas were only symptomatic of two larger ailments—the failure of military reform and the instability of the parliamentary regime. The most serious writing on civil-military relations in Spain, which appeared between 1918 and 1921, focused on one or both of these problems.

The best known of the new critics was the Conde de Romanones, an archetypical dynastic politician who had atypically shown signs of flexibility since the beginning of the national crisis in 1917. Perhaps for this reason, by the spring of 1920 Romanones was at the periphery of Spanish political life, isolated from the mainstream of the Liberal party by the combined efforts of his rivals, García Prieto and Alba, and also estranged from a large part of the army because of his interest in military reform, his opposition to the Juntas, and his efforts to reach an accommodation with organized labor in 1919. Since his last ministry, which had been destroyed by the Juntas de Defensa and General Milans del Bosch in April 1919, Romanones had sought to build a new "liberal" coalition on an issue with wide appeal: civil supremacy. Presenting himself as the victim of "militarism," Romanones had urged the necessity of military reform, which he correctly linked to the future of the parliamentary monarchy. On the other hand, Romanones knew that no one could govern Spain in opposition to the army. The publication of *El ejército y la política* in 1920 was designed to fortify his credentials as a military reformer and to establish a clientele in the faction-ridden officer corps as well.

Written after the budget debates in the spring of 1920 (from which he had been conspicuously absent), the book represented the author as a democrat and a knowledgeable technician. A loyal monarchist, Romanones evaded an extended *theoretical* analysis of the function of an army in a democracy. On the other hand, he argued forcibly for the democratization of the "transitional" conscription law of 1912 as the only means of reconciling the working classes to military service. For the most part, however, the book was a technical discussion of the role of the army as the instrument of national defense. The bulk of the essay was an indictment of the Spanish army measured by this standard.

Romanones leveled his criticism against the peninsular army and the politicians who had permitted it to grow top-heavy, expensive, and inefficient. With considerable skill, he identified the army's major defects: the anachronistic privileges of the technical branches, the moral isolation of the officer corps, and above all, the bureaucratic mentality exemplified by the closed scale. Although he did not mention the Juntas, he was bluntly critical of the Law of 1918. If fully implemented, Romanones's reform package would have eliminated many of the professional sources of instability in the Spanish officer corps. The beneficiary would ultimately be the civil state.

At one level, then, the book was written for civilians concerned about the excessive power of the military. At another level, however, it made a calculated appeal to the one group untouched by the count's wide-ranging criticism—the colonial army. Since his initial investments in Morocco in 1907 (which he no longer held), Romanones had been an enthusiastic colonialist; he now apparently hoped to build a Moroccan party composed of colonial-minded officers and civilians under the leadership of the king, who would then see Romanones as a logical choice to head a government. The military reorganization proposed in the book was designed to make the Spanish army effective in pacifying Spain's North African empire. Truly democratic conscription would take the edge off the unpopularity of African service, the reduction of the officer corps would free funds for modernization, and the reinstatement of battlefield promotions would encourage the ambitious young officers naturally attracted to the African campaign. Above all, a successful colonial war would restore vitality to the decaying political system, popular support to the monarchy, and political recognition to the statesman who made it all possible—the Conde de Romanones.

In fact, the book was a personal triumph for the Liberal politician. Its proposals were sound, the pages of statistical data reinforced his image as a practical military reformer, and the timeliness of the subject singled out Romanones as one of the most capable and perceptive of the dynastic politicians. If the theoretical framework was sketchy and the subject somewhat narrowly defined, this was due more to Romanones's political discretion—and to his authentic political conservatism—than to a lack of intelligence. Although his motives were not wholly disinterested—and no one who knew Romanones was deceived on this point—his book was a significant contribution to the national debate on military reform.

One of the few adverse responses came from Manuel Azaña, a young litterateur and Reformist party regular who had made an unsuccessful run for parliament in 1918. Reviewing the book for the left-wing journal *España* in November 1920, Azaña dismissed Romanones's proposals as "not what he is going to do in the Government, but what he believes it convenient to say and to propose in order to return to the Government." In addition, he argued that Romanones's Moroccan interests and his fear of social disorder would override any abstract interest he might have in military reform.[36] This ad hominem attack obscured Azaña's substantive objections to Romanones's proposals for military reform, objections that were based on the count's philosophical assumptions about the nature of civil-military relations, a subject to which Azaña himself had given a great deal of thought. In 1919 he had published a lengthy essay in book form entitled *La política militar*, the first in a projected series of three *Estudios de política francesa*.[37] The other two volumes, which never appeared, were to deal with laicism and the suffrage. In other words, Azaña had undertaken a theoretical investigation of the three basic institutions of the state—concretely, the French state, by implication, the Spanish state.

Unlike Romanones, Azaña was not concerned with military organization as an end in itself and still less with its relevance to a successful colonial policy. Instead, he was interested in the subject that Romanones had skirted: the army as a reflection of society and the state. The intimate connection between civil and military organization made it imperative for political reformers to think with equal seriousness about military reform in order to avoid an incompatibility that would inevitably lead to a constitutional crisis. As an illustration, Azaña reviewed the Dreyfus case, which had arisen out of a conflict between a republican state and a monarchist army and had been resolved in 1905 by the "republicanization" of the officer corps. What Azaña proposed was a reversal of the process—the transformation of Spain's old-regime army as a necessary prelude to the establishment of a republic: "The actual regime, in which the Crown is only that, a crown, is supported . . . exclusively by the army. Thus one may say that the suppression of the permanent army would bring freedom to Spain."[38]

Azaña acknowledged the possibility of a just war, particularly in the national defense, and thus, the necessity of a national army. But however necessary, a conscript army was tolerable only when it demanded equal obligations from all citizens and when it was integrated spiritually with the state. In a democracy, the army—like the state—must reflect the national will. Both colonial warfare and domestic peacekeeping—which for Romanones had justified the existence of a modern and efficient army—for Azaña fell outside the permissible activities of a democratic army organized for national defense.

A similar, if somewhat more radical, analysis of civil-military relations by the Socialist Luis Araquistáin appeared in 1921.[39] An essayist and journalist who had initially applauded the Juntas de Defensa as "democratic and antioligarchical,"[40] Araquistáin had later concluded that they represented a tendency toward military syndicalization that could not be halted by appeals to older concepts of military discipline. Instead, he argued that both historical circumstances and the lessons of the world war mandated the abolition of the military profession in favor of a "citizen's army." Araquistáin advocated the replacement of unnecessary and unproductive career officers by reserve officers drawn from the universities and the professions. In this way, the army would cease to be a threat to social modernization and political stability.

Dissimilar as were their analyses, Azaña, Araquistáin, and Romanones shared a crucial perception of the political reality in which they lived: military reform was the key to the past and the future of the regime. Romanones hoped to save the monarchy and the dominance of his social class by eliminating the structural defects that made the army a disruptive political force and by giving it and the country a common goal—a Spanish empire in North Africa. In a sense, his program was designed to make real the political neutrality and professional autonomy that had existed as a fictional ideal since the days of Cánovas. Azaña and Araquistáin, on the other hand, envisioned a reformed army that would be at once the symbol of and the support for a reformed state—the Republic. It was a reversal of the Canovite scheme—an unprofessional army made safe by a high degree of politicization and integration with society as a whole. In 1931 Azaña would be given the chance to implement his theory.

Another pundit who perceived the fundamental relationship between the army and the Spanish state was José Ortega y Gasset, who published his insights in an extended essay entitled *España invertebrada* in May 1921.[41] Like Azaña, Ortega detected a unity between a nation and its army, "which measures with awesome exactitude the carats of national morality and vitality." But for Ortega, the Spanish army's "decadence"—and especially, its "particularism"—was not the principal cause, but merely a symptom of a larger national decadence attributable to "social inelasticity." Like other social classes and groups, the army had ceased to see itself as part of an organic whole and had lost faith in the capacity of public institutions to resolve conflict, preferring direct action instead. The insubordination of the Juntas de Defensa was a striking example of the modern "moral subversion of the masses against the select minority" that made resolution of the national crisis so difficult. But the army's selfishness was not unique; its resonance derived from its monopoly of the instruments of force. In conclusion, Ortega called for the revitalization of the state through the selection of minorities capable of imposing their greater talents and vision upon the rest of the nation, including the army.

The Drift toward Dictatorship

Ortega's call for a natural aristocracy of leaders to restore order and stability was a sophisticated version of a growing national conviction that only a dictatorship could solve the postwar political and social crisis. The hope of a democratic solution was now only a bitter memory for the parties of the left, which alternated between debate on the dictatorship of the proletariat and denunciation of the military dictatorship that they believed imminent. On the right, cries for military dictatorship had accompanied every intensification of the social crisis, particularly after the quasi-dictatorial rule of General Martínez Anido began to erode the strength of the underground action groups in Barcelona. Parliamentary stagnation and obstructionism, simultaneously more chronic and less tolerable since 1918, aggravated the growing national impatience with the political system, producing repeated allusions to General Pavía, who had overthrown the "ungovernable" Cortes of 1874.[42] Even Ortega himself, although denying the political capacity of the military, had allowed himself in 1920 to entertain the notion that a military dictatorship might be a salutary destructive prelude to an era of national reconstruction.[43] If the army did not produce an obliging dictator, it was not for lack of agreement with the critics of the parliamentary regime, but because there was neither a charismatic figure nor a consensus in the officer corps on the nature of and remedy for the national crisis.

Symbolic of the pervasive disillusionment with parliamentary government was the king himself, who hinted in a speech in Cordova in May 1921 that he would welcome a popular mandate to bypass the Cortes and govern directly.[44] Alfonso's regard for the parliamentary system had never been high. From the beginning of his reign, he had expressed his resentment of the constitutional limitations on the authority of the Crown, occasionally circumventing or ignoring constitutional channels in order to exercise personal power.[45] Furthermore, since 1918 the Cortes had included a relatively greater number of the enemies of the throne, making it a less reliable ally than the army. Alfonso's feel for the national mood told him that his impatience with parliamentary government was shared by a large number of Spaniards. Therefore, in Cordova he suggested that "the provinces should begin a movement of support for the King and for legislation that would be beneficial," in order to remind the parliament "that it is the agent of the people. . . ." He also washed his hands of responsibility for the current political impasse.

The king's speech was a reproach to, if not an implicit repudiation of parliamentary government; significantly, it was cheered enthusiastically in Cordova. Although the government was able to arrange for an altered version of the speech to appear in the press,[46] it could not manage a national consensus in support of the parliamentary regime, whose structural deficiencies had been magnified by the postwar crisis. What Alfonso chose to label "political trivialities" were really the labor pains of a political system forcibly becoming more representative against the will of the vested political interests of the nation. To compound the difficulty, there was no national consensus on social and economic issues in Spain; even had the Cortes been a representative forum, no clear-cut mandate for decisive action would have emerged. The mounting calls for military or royal dictatorship merely measured the frustration of a developing nation overwhelmed by the complexity of modern social and economic problems and tempted to rely on highly visible and authoritarian institutions to solve them.

Astonishingly, the dynastic politicians seemed unable to comprehend the source of their isolation from the nation. Shattered by the death of Dato the previous March, the Conservative party was unable to put forward plausible leadership to move the country out of its stagnation. On June 20, having failed to secure passage of a badly needed railway reorganization bill, the government recessed the Cortes that had been made to order for Dato the previous December. It was the sixth time since 1917 that the Cortes had been suspended or closed in a time of stress.[47] On July 6 the cabinet split over the bill and its sponsor, Juan de la Cierva, only to re-form two days later with no significant reorientation of personnel.[48] Indeed, the government seemed almost perversely determined to justify the alienation of the king, the army, and its many critics on the left and the right. Quite possibly, the parliamentary regime might have collapsed of its own weight in 1921, unlamented by anyone, had not the military disaster at Anual and the ensuing campaign for responsibilities revived hopes once again for a democratic transformation of the system.

CHAPTER EIGHT

The Road to Anual, 1919–1921

The end of the world war enabled France to turn her attention once again to North Africa. As a result, Spain was also obliged to abandon the passive policy she had followed since 1915. But the new policy, devised and implemented by a competent africanista, General Dámaso Berenguer, suffered from the same ambiguities and internal contradictions as the old—in particular, from the failure to clarify the lines of authority in Madrid and in the Protectorate.[1] Without a clear commitment to colonialism, successive governments neglected their obligation to integrate and control civil and military policy; beleaguered by domestic problems and conscious of widespread anticolonialist sentiment, the dynastic politicians demanded only easy victories at minimum expense. Ultimately, the attempt to win a colonial war on the cheap—behind the back, as it were, of the anticolonialist majority of the nation—was the greatest political error of the parliamentary monarchy. For failure left the regime caught between an angry people and an equally angry military establishment.

If Berenguer's assignment in Morocco was complicated by the equivocal support he received from civilians inside and outside the government, so too did it suffer from the poor quality of the military instrument at hand. The African army shared many of the defects of the peninsular army: an excess of officers, outmoded equipment, poorly trained and maintained conscripts, and low morale. Moreover, it had to operate in the face of the indifference or hostility of most of the peninsular army. Even among officers eager to serve in Africa there was often little enthusiasm for the slow, methodical warfare advocated by Berenguer or little comprehension of the Protectorate policy supported by him and the Spanish government. Furthermore, both the Juntas and the older Restoration generals used their leverage in the

War Ministry to resist government attempts to provide greater financial or professional rewards for the African army.

Despite these obstacles, with patience, meticulous care, and strong leadership, Berenguer succeeded in forging an efficient colonial army that made steady progress toward the subjugation of the western half of the Protectorate without provoking much criticism. Unfortunately, in the eastern zone, the combination of a headstrong commander, encouraged by a headstrong king, a demoralized army that had imbibed none of the spirit of *africanismo* typical of the western sector, a weak government that had supported but not guided Moroccan policy, and Berenguer's own excessive tact, would undo the labor of twelve years.

The Renewal of the War

Since September 1915 there had been little fighting in Morocco. Although the African army had chafed, the dynastic parties had welcomed the French request for a military hiatus, since it provided them with an excuse to avoid the unpleasant responsibilities of imperialism without sacrificing the status that colonies conferred. To maintain calm in the Protectorate, the High Commissioner, General Francisco Gómez Jordana, had been instructed to sign a pact with the de facto political authority in the western sector, a tribal leader named al-Raysuni, who received a generous subsidy in return for a promise of nonaggression. A similar policy of bribes was followed in the east. By 1917 this policy had permitted the repatriation of 20,563 conscript troops[2] and the submission of a Moroccan budget that was 33 million pesetas less than in 1915.[3] Given the lack of colonial enthusiasm in the country, the policy was admirably suited to both the nation's mood and its pocketbook.

The African army, however, was less satisfied with the enforced inaction. Al-Raysuni proved an unreliable ally, collaborating openly with German agents and provoking the Spanish garrisons with minor acts of aggression. But the government had repeatedly denied the High Commissioner's requests to issue a military rebuke, not least because labor unrest and the Juntas de Defensa made opening a third area of conflict highly unpalatable. Gómez Jordana obediently carried out government policy and was therefore retained at his post in spite of heavy pressure from the Juntas to dismiss him. When he died at his desk on November 18, 1918, he was writing the government to complain of the absence of merit promotions and pensions and its effect on the morale and performance of his officers.[4]

Gómez Jordana's death coincided with the end of the world war and the return to office of the Conde de Romanones, who had long believed that "Morocco comprised the last chance offered for Spain to occupy a place worthy of her history in the European concert."[5] A political realist, Romanones was aware that few Spaniards shared his colonial enthusiasm; on the other hand, he believed that apart from the Socialists, whose hostility to imperialism was ideological and absolute, equally few were in favor of total abandonment. In Spain, doctrinaire anticolonialism was basically antimilitarism: the working classes hated military service; the parties of the left repudiated military administration of the Protectorate. Even the Republicans, newly united in a National Republican Federation, supported colonialism when it involved a "civilizing mission" rather than conquest.[6]

This was a goal shared by Romanones himself, although he had been unable to achieve it as prime minister in 1913. Upon returning to office in 1918, he once again made plans to "civilianize" the administration of the Protectorate. On December 11 a royal decree deprived the High Commissioner of the title of General-in-Chief, a designation made in 1915 to overcome the decentralization of military authority in the Protectorate. If the new High Commissioner was to be a civilian, primarily concerned with "political and administrative work," this was a logical measure; its unfortunate corollary was the return of the ambiguity surrounding the lines of authority within the Protectorate. According to the decree, the commanders general would assume "the jurisdiction and the full complement of attributions . . . consequent to said commands, in local and military matters," while the High Commissioner would retain the ultimate authority in the Protectorate, "both in the political and administrative order and in the execution of military operations and the maintenance of security in the region." It was impossible to determine from the decree which operations required the approval of the High Commissioner and which might be considered purely "local and military."

The decree clearly postulated a civilian High Commissioner, but none could be found. As in so many cases, civilian abdication contributed to military power. Romanones first asked Miguel Villanueva, a garciaprietista Liberal who had long been critical of military influence in Morocco, to serve as High Commissioner, but Villanueva, just as he had in 1913, refused. Another refusal came from Manuel González Hontoria, a Liberal career diplomat who had participated in the Moroccan negotiations of 1906 and 1912.[7] Since then, González Hontoria had been critical of the debilitating rivalry between the Ministries of State and War, a rivalry certainly not overcome by the decree of December 18.

For whatever reason, the two most prominent Liberal critics of the military domination of Spanish colonialism were unwilling to undertake the "civilianization" they demanded.

Romanones still had not made an appointment when he journeyed to the Paris Peace Conference on December 18 hoping to secure Spanish rights to the international city of Tangier. His talks with Clemenceau and Lyautey made it clear that Spain would not get Tangier; on the contrary, the French were eager to absorb the entire Spanish zone and would find the absence of military pacification a convenient excuse for intervention.[8] Determined to prove Spain's worth as a colonial power, Romanones was forced to reconsider his plans for a civil Protectorate. Foreseeing the need for military operations to establish an effective Spanish presence, he asked his War Minister, General Dámaso Berenguer y Fuste, to take the post of High Commissioner. On January 25, 1919, the appointment was announced, followed by a royal decree making the High Commissioner the Inspector of all the "civil, military, and naval authorities and services" within the Protectorate, thus partially rescinding the compartmentalization of political and military authority implied in the decree of December 11. At least in the short run, the High Commissioner would continue to preside over military action in Morocco.

General Berenguer

Dámaso Berenguer was a large man, ponderous in appearance, but subtle and precise in taste and expression.[9] As an officer, his strength lay in his careful preparation and judicious leadership, unusual qualities in a Spanish Cavalry officer. If his rather reserved personality could not elicit wild enthusiasm in his colleagues or subordinates, his intelligence and authority did win him their respect and loyalty. At the same time, his discretion and sense of the possible—probably the two qualities valued most highly by the dynastic parties—earned him the support of civilian politicians. This combination of qualities made him in some ways an ideal choice for High Commissioner; in other ways, his political discretion made him overly tolerant of professional jealousies, civilian indecision, and royal interference. As a result, he failed to impose his authority on the chaos of conflicting interests in Morocco that eventually destroyed his campaign and his career.

As a *politique* and an *africanista*, Berenguer was unpopular with the Juntas, who viewed his brilliant career as a by-product of the patronage of General Luque and the king. Undoubtedly, he had profited from these connections and from his intimacy with General Manuel Fernández-Silvestre, who had served as head of the king's Military Household since his involuntary resignation as Commander General of Larache in 1915. Nevertheless, Berenguer's preeminence was well earned. A rarity among Spanish officers, he had taken a serious interest in Morocco and in colonial problems. In 1911, after a tour of Tunisia and Algeria, he had organized the first native shock units in the Spanish zone, the Regulares de Melilla, of which he was the first commander. Under the influence of the French colonialists, Joseph Gallieni and Hubert Lyautey, he had written his own treatise, *La guerra en Marruecos*, published in 1918. Rejecting the prevailing cult of unthinking machismo, along with the Nietzschean exaltation of the will advocated by his contemporary, Ricardo Burguete, Berenguer argued that successful colonial warfare depended on flexibility, professionalism, and experience. "Political action"—good roads and schools, respect for Muslim culture, strategic alliances, and judicious bribes— was essential if military advances were to be consolidated; in the words of Gallieni, "All forward movement must receive, as a sanction, the effective occupation of the conquered territory. . . . It is the method of the oil stain."[10] Once the native population was truly reconciled to the Spanish presence, only skeleton forces were required for security, as Lyautey had proved in neighboring French Morocco during the war.[11]

Romanones appointed Berenguer in January 1919 not because he was a reliable political general, but because he was a thoughtful technician of proven leadership abilities whose colonialist views coincided with his own. Mindful as he was of the unpopularity of military operations, however, he instructed Berenguer to assess the possibility of an effective occupation of the zone through exclusively political action, especially through a renegotiated pact with al-Raysuni that would insure his submission to the authority of the sultan. With revolution threatening in Catalonia, Romanones did not wish to risk another Tragic Week.

The Conquest of the Jibala[12]

After a month's inspection tour of the Protectorate, Berenguer reported, predictably, that effective control of the zone would require military as well as political action. Although he might have been accused of fitting the situation to the theory outlined in his treatise on colonial warfare, in fact his appraisal was a realistic one. The alliance with al-Raysuni was logical only so long as the Spanish were content to maintain a limited presence in the zone. Under French pressure, Spanish objectives had changed; so, too, must their means of occupation. Thus confronted with the implications of their decision to forestall a French takeover, the cabinet divided over a renewal of operations. With the Canadiense strike at its height, it was a difficult decision to make. Yet probably because the cabinet's attention was distracted by events in Barcelona, Romanones and Berenguer—with the decisive aid of the king—prevailed.[13] When the High Commissioner returned to Tetuan on March 14, Spain was committed to a more aggressive policy in Morocco. The transition had been made without attracting much notice; the nation's attention was focused on the more dramatic problems of food shortages and high prices, the Catalan question, the Juntas, and the Canadiense strike. As usual, Morocco was abandoned to those who were interested in it—the king, a few politicians, and the army. Only reverses and heavy casualties could stimulate national interest in colonial policy.

Since he was well aware of this, Romanones insisted that the occupation be carried out with the minimum expenditure of lives and money, a political consideration that Berenguer understood and accepted. His three-stage plan for the occupation of the Spanish zone consisted of first linking the two western commands of Larache and Ceuta by pacifying the rebellious tribes loyal to al-Raysuni, which separated their commands; next, dominating the interior of the western sector, the Jibala; and only later undertaking the conquest of the eastern sector, the Rif, which was, for the present, relatively quiescent if not submissive. By relying heavily on political preparation, Berenguer hoped to limit military action; by conducting his campaign in stages, he would require fewer troops and less equipment. The operations initiated near Ceuta on the day after Berenguer's return from Madrid, March 16, 1919, were so successful that they set a pattern for subsequent operations against al-Raysuni in the Jibala. First, Native Police and Moroccan agents "prepared" the advance by convincing as many *qa'ids* (tribal notables) as possible of the advantages (both economic and political) of cooperation with the Spanish; next, strong mobile columns moved in to occupy the area, only to withdraw immediately to the base camps, leaving behind a temporary front of small outposts known as *blocaos*, manned by either European or native troops. Nearly one-third of the available forces in the zone were occupied in these defensive positions. Behind the line, Native Police continued their political activity, generally disarming the tribes except where their loyalty was unquestionable. To minimize European casualties, minor offensive and defensive operations at the front were undertaken by contingents of Regulars or Police.

Essentially, the system took advantage of the Moroccan respect for the power nearest at hand. Once the line was established and the threat of force real and immediate, the tribes submitted willingly enough and the administration of the new area could be entrusted to the Police. Berenguer proudly pointed out that "the transition from the state of rebellion to that of submission is scarcely perceptible."[14] But this virtue had the defect of making the system of advance appear easier than it was. Its success depended on two fundamental ingredients: skilful political preparation and a careful deployment of available forces that guaranteed friendly tribes protection from al-Raysuni. Berenguer never advanced until convinced he could hold a territory, preferring to allow some areas, like the Ghumara, to remain neutral until he could insure effective occupation. Unfortunately, the system would not be understood so well by General Silvestre, whose rapid advance in the Rif in 1920–21 would result in the defeat at Anual.

Berenguer was well aware—and was incessantly reminded by successive governments in Madrid—that excessive casualties might trigger the latent popular hostility toward the Moroccan war. Indeed, his cautious, piecemeal advance was dictated as much by these political considerations as by strategic necessity; its flexibility and limited objectives made it possible to adjust operations to the rhythm of events in the peninsula, and the moderate expenditures of lives and funds made no significant impact on public opinion. Above all, Berenguer's system guaranteed success—little glory, perhaps, and much tedious preparation—but success that kept widespread criticism from emerging. It was a colonial strategy admirably suited to a nation where there was no popular colonialist sentiment.

As the campaign progressed, political preparation in the peninsular press became as important as it was in the field. Gradually in 1919, and more regularly in 1920 and 1921, the press turned its attention toward Morocco. The illustrated weeklies carried photographs of the barren hills, mysteriously labeled as "military objectives," and introduced their readers to the camps, plazas, airfields, and personalities in the western sector under a perspective that exaggerated the glamour, bravery, and efficiency of the Moroccan enterprise. As the major dailies began to establish permanent correspondents in Morocco, Berenguer took pains to cultivate them, extending interviews and invitations to observe field operations. The gratified journalists responded with welcome propaganda in favor of Spain's mission in North Africa. Weary of justifying the domestic failures of the governmental parties, the dynastic press turned with relief to the "triumphs" in Morocco. The renovationist *El Sol*, under the leadership of its editor, Manuel Aznar, also became an enthusiastic supporter of the Moroccan enterprise, not only because it seemed to qualify Spain as a modern "European" power, but also because the African army provided a useful contrast to the peninsular bureaucrats in the Juntas.[15] Thus, both the supporters and the moderate opponents of the regime came to have a political stake in the continuing success of the African army.

The extreme left, however, could not be seduced. For the Socialists, opposition to imperialism was a matter of principle; opposition to the war, a matter of political tactics based primarily on the injustice of the conscription system. At the Ninth International Congress of Trade Unions held in Amsterdam in August 1919, UGT representatives attempted to arouse international opinion against the war in northern Morocco; shortly thereafter, the Madrid Socialist Group agreed to continue its propaganda campaign in favor of abandonment.[16] The Republicans, too (with the exception of Alejandro Lerroux), rejoined the opposition, after the renewal of operations in early 1919 made it clear that military action would continue to take precedence over Spain's "civilizing mission." After the capture of Fondak in early October 1919, Socialists and Republicans staged a joint protest in Madrid.[17] As it had been after 1909, Morocco once again became a symbol of the undemocratic character of the regime.

The antiwar propaganda of the left could be neutralized by a successful campaign, as the general clamor of approval for the occupation of Fondak showed. Casualties or defeats, on the other hand, provided a national audience for what was otherwise a sectarian protest. In July 1919, in the early stages of the campaign, an incident at Cudia Rauda, just west of Tetuan, showed how easily an error could be exploited by the political opposition. Berenguer, who was quietly organizing for the assault on Fondak, had informed *El Sol* on July 13 that "the military effort is already done" and had promised few casualties in the future.[18] Thus, when the Commander General of Ceuta, General Domingo Arraiz, requested permission the next day to establish a position at the edge of the Wad Ras territory, Berenguer consented only on the condition that it be limited to a police operation by native troops.[19] The officer in charge of the operation, Colonel Angel Rodríguez del Barrio, decided, however, that such limitations were "more appropriate for Hebrews than for a nation that comes to impose its civilization and its force,"[20] and undertook the maneuver with two columns of inexperienced European conscripts, suffering two hundred casualties when the retreat back to the base was ambushed. To make matters worse, through two days of combat, the colonel and his superior, Arraiz, refused to respond to Berenguer's frantic demands for accurate information, making it impossible for him to relay the details of the incident to the press.[21] Predictably, the leftist press accused Berenguer of a cover-up and repeated its traditional denunciations of Spanish imperialism,[22] while in the Cortes, the Republican deputy, Augusto Barcia, questioned the Maura government on the incident, triggering a debate that culminated in a vote of no confidence. Cudia Rauda shocked the nation, alarmed the politicians, and delighted the opposition. In the long run, however, it may have contributed to the success of the war against al-Raysuni, for it alerted Berenguer to the organizational defects that had contributed to the setback.

The Organization of a Colonial Army

Cudia Rauda and Berenguer's subsequent decision to strengthen the African army coincided with the designation of Joaquín Sánchez de Toca as prime minister. Sánchez de Toca had presided over the Spanish League of Africanistas from 1912 until February 1919, when he had resigned to protest the renewal of military operations. An advocate of a civil Protectorate, he might have opposed Berenguer's military plans, but the circumstances of his four months in office left him little time to devote to Moroccan affairs. As the prime minister grappled with General Milans del Bosch, the Juntas, the CNT, and the Employers' Federation, the War Minister, General Tovar, seconded by the Minister of State, the Marqués de Lema, generally approved Berenguer's efforts to reform his army. These efforts were vindicated by the successful capture of Fondak in October 1919. Thereafter, the War Ministry dominated Moroccan policymaking. After the fall of Sánchez de Toca in December, no Conservative prime minister took much interest in Morocco. The Marqués de Lema, who remained in the Foreign Ministry until July 1921, allowed his ministry to be superseded without protest, undoubtedly because the military overshadowed every civilian entity in Morocco.

Badly in need of reform, the African army suffered from divided lines of authority, limited funding, and a lack of professionalism. With major operations planned for 1920, all of these problems were pressing, but none more so, in Berenguer's view, than the first. His system of advance was designed to compensate for meager material support, the creation of professional units was a matter of time and experience, but the incident at Cudia Rauda had dramatized the dangers of an ambiguous command structure. The difficult situation was exacerbated by the prickly sensitivity of the commanders general to any infringement of their autonomy, particularly by a relatively young and only recently promoted division general whose conservative approach to conquest was not in Spanish tradition. The Commander General of Ceuta, General Arraiz, had been uncooperative since Berenguer's arrival. The situation became even more delicate in July 1919, when General Silvestre was appointed to replace him. Silvestre and Berenguer were old friends, graduates of the AGM who were commissioned together as lieutenants in the Cavalry Corps in 1893. Silvestre, however, was two years older than Berenguer, and one place ahead of him in the active list; in addition, as an intimate of the king and head of his Military Household, he had been in a position to promote Berenguer's political career.[23] Finally, Silvestre was a Cavalry officer of the old school—brave, but also rash, impatient of detail, and unfamiliar with Berenguer's brand of colonial warfare. Shortly after his arrival he advised Berenguer that he could not undertake operations with the existing forces—some 11,800 troops—without the addition of a complete regiment from the peninsula.[24] With the government already fearful of alarming popular opinion, this ultimatum jeopardized the proposed assault on Fondak. It was only with difficulty that Berenguer was able to convince Silvestre—and the government—that his methods did not require the same number of forces as conventional warfare.[25]

In January 1920 Berenguer arranged for Silvestre's transfer to the General Command of Melilla, "a command of greater responsibilities and with an independence more compatible with his distinguished personality. . . ."[26] From Berenguer's point of view, the transfer was politically astute and militarily harmless so long as no major operations were contemplated in the Rif. But Silvestre had fretted on his short leash in Ceuta. Once relieved of Berenguer's restraining presence, he began a precipitous, unprepared—and, for the moment—unopposed advance into the heart of the Rif. Somewhat nervously, Berenguer warned Silvestre of the need for caution.[27] But, conscious of Silvestre's support in the palace and unwilling to damage a friendship, he stopped short of ordering Silvestre to halt his advance. Indeed, Silvestre's easy conquests won new friends for the campaign in the peninsula and gratified the king, who shared Silvestre's contempt for Berenguer's caution.

Berenguer was aware of the source—and the danger—of his inhibition with regard to Silvestre. Therefore, after a visit to the eastern sector in May 1920, he requested the title of General-in-Chief of the

African Army in order to "subordinate to a common goal personal initiatives, which when repressed, consider the autonomy officially granted them to be infringed upon. . . ."[28] A response from Madrid was not immediately forthcoming, however. Berenguer's elevation to General-in-Chief was sure to cause resentment among senior generals in Africa and in the peninsula. More important, the title would officially confirm the steady erosion of the concept of the civil Protectorate, and consequently, of the policymaking authority of the Ministry of State. Perhaps most decisively, the measure might alarm the nation, which had been lulled into passivity by the steady advances and low casualties of the first stage of the campaign. The decree, issued September 1, 1920, was therefore a compromise: it gave the High Commissioner, as long as he was a general, the nominal "command in chief" of the African army without designating his office as a *necessary* communications link between the general commands and the War Ministry. Furthermore, where major operations were not anticipated, the High Commissioner might delegate his military functions to the commanders general. Since none were scheduled in Melilla, Berenguer did not insist on exercising his new authority in that sector, out of deference to Silvestre's notorious pride.[29] He apparently hoped, naively, that his new title would by itself curb Silvestre's headlong rush into enemy territory. Instead, the decree merely legitimated Silvestre's continued direct contacts with his partisans in the War Ministry. By delegating his military authority to Silvestre, Berenguer saved himself a confrontation with his friend and, possibly, with the king. He also made himself ultimately responsible for the disaster at Anual.

The other problems facing the African army—specifically its insufficient funding and the absence of professional colonial units—became more urgent as Berenguer moved into the second stage of the campaign in early 1920. Fortunately, the parliamentary deadlock over a new budget was broken in April 1920, allowing Berenguer to plan for an autumn assault on Xauen (Chaouen), a pilgrimage city that lay between the Jibala and the Ghumara. The War Ministry's share of the 169 million pesetas budgeted for Morocco was 154 million, a 50 percent increase from 1917.[30] Nearly 60 percent of this total, however, was consumed by personnel expenditures. As in the peninsula, the garrisons were top-heavy with unnecessary officers, who enjoyed a 50 percent pay supplement for African service.[31] Troop expenditures were greater, too, for conscripts served their full three years to keep the regiments at full strength. Still, the 1920 budget provided more funds for artillery, transportation, aviation, and hospitals, which would be supplemented later in the year by credits totaling 2 million pesetas.

Another 20 million in credits would be forthcoming the following summer.[32] On the whole, the budget represented a vote of confidence in Berenguer and the African army; most criticism centered on the much larger War Ministry budget, which was itself an obstacle to further spending in Morocco. Only the left and a few die-hard supporters of the peninsular army expressed discontent with either the policies or the priorities of the Moroccan campaign, even though the enormous imbalance between military and civil expenditures in the Protectorate was an obvious point of attack.[33] The relative lack of discussion was a measure of the general indifference toward anything but prestige considerations in Morocco.

The increases in military expenditures were not large enough to alter radically the material circumstances of the Moroccan campaign. Until a significant reduction could be made in the colonial officer corps, salaries—raised again in the 1920 budget because of inflation—would continue to stand in the way of modernization. There were two solutions: military reform or substantially higher funding. But military reform would surely have resuscitated the Juntas, and a larger Moroccan budget might have aroused public opposition to the war, whose costs were at present proportional to its rewards. Both a general and a politician, Berenguer thus adopted a middle course, privately urging the government to increase expenditures, while assuring both the government and the public that his army was adequately supported.[34] By concentrating the available equipment in the western sector, he was able to take maximum advantage of his resources, while sparing the nation the burden of a two-front war.[35] When al-Raysuni had been defeated, equipment and funds could be diverted to the eastern sector for the final stages of the campaign. With this in mind, he ignored General Silvestre's repeated requests in 1920 and early 1921 for reinforcements and more credits.

A more intractable, and yet more urgent, problem was the condition of the Spanish troops. The class basis of the conscription system made the war—and of course the regime itself—vulnerable to attacks from the left. An inspection tour of the Protectorate in July 1920 appalled the new War Minister, the Vizconde de Eza, whose official report described at length the physical condition of the troops, the degrading and unsanitary quarters in which they lived, the lack of proper clothing and equipment, and the scarcity of hospitals and medical supplies.[36] African service represented three years of painful servitude and often illness or death, even for troops largely spared the risks of combat. For Eza, as for Berenguer, it was clear that the Moroccan enterprise would remain vulnerable until conscripts could be replaced by professional volunteers, a long-range—and extremely costly—goal.

On August 31, 1920, Eza authorized recruitment for the Spanish Foreign Legion, or Tercio de Extranjeros, which Berenguer had been advocating for nearly a year. Officially created on January 28, 1920, the project had remained on paper because of the opposition of the Juntas, who were suspicious of "elite" units, and of General Silvestre in Melilla, who continued to believe, against all the evidence, that the war ought to be fought with Spanish conscripts led by regular officers. Eza, however, now believed otherwise, and recruitment for the first *bandera* (battalion) was immediately undertaken by Lieutenant Colonel José Millán-Astray, who had observed the French Foreign Legion in Algeria. High salaries and enlistment bonuses, excellent rations and quarters, and an exotic uniform designed by the first training officer, Major Francisco Franco, made recruitment relatively easy; funds were made available by discharging two third-year conscripts for every new legionnaire.[37] By emphasizing fanatical courage, iron discipline, and personal stoicism, Millán-Astray and Franco quickly forged a combat unit whose romantic view of life and death made it remarkably effective in combat.[38] The Tercio was in the vanguard at the capture of Xauen in October 1920 and in all major operations in the Jibala thereafter. In the Rif, however, Silvestre refused to authorize the formation of comparable units.

Expansion of the previously existing combat units—the Regulars and the Native Police—proved more difficult. Inadequate pay had kept recruitment low, despite a small increase in June 1919, when Moroccans had totaled only 10,570 out of 64,666 troops in the zone;[39] even unskilled day laborers could earn more than the three pesetas a day offered to native soldiers. But even had more funds been available, Berenguer was reluctant to expand the native troops much beyond one-third of his total forces because of their potential unreliability.[40] Although France had a much higher percentage in her colonial armies, the size and ethnic diversity of her empire had made it unnecessary to rely on Moroccans to suppress other Moroccans.

Officer recruitment for these units was no easier. Assignment to the shock units involved much greater risks and sacrifices than assignment to the garrisons in the principal cities, without offering compensatory rewards. Although the Regulars had always attracted the most dedicated africanistas, there were too few of these in the Spanish officer corps to fill all the available places, especially in the Rif; the Native Police, less prestigious and also less exciting, suffered even more. Since 1914 it had been necessary to fill these posts by rotation, compelling the most junior peninsular officers to serve two years in the Moroccan hinterland, an unsatisfactory solution that placed demoralized and inexperienced officers in the most sensitive positions. After the advent of the Juntas and the abolition of merit promotions in 1918, the situation had deteriorated.[41] Morale was low—in the west because officers exposed themselves to hardship and danger for no reward, in the east because the boredom of front-line service was rarely alleviated by periods of combat. Alarmed by a protest demonstration by officers in the Jibala during his tour in July 1920, the Vizconde de Eza had spoken publicly of the need to ease the existing restrictions on merit promotions, but the outcry from the Juntas had quickly changed his mind. Instead, salaries were raised in both the Regulars and the Police.[42] While this satisfied some, other young officers with professional ambitions transferred into the Tercio, which offered high risks, but also glamour, prestige and esprit de corps.

The difficulties of forging a professional colonial army exacerbated the tension between peninsular and African officers. The latter blamed the Juntas for the general lack of zeal for the campaign within the officer corps; the former saw only that merit promotions—earned or unearned—would slow down their own promotions. Furthermore, the success of the African army and its isolation from the political tensions in the peninsula had given the left another avenue through which to attack the Juntas. The potential of this approach, which permitted distinctions between the Juntas and "the army," was realized almost immediately by *El Sol*, which began making invidious comparisons between the "sterile, counterproductive, and harmful" Juntas and their "brave victim," the Moroccan army, as early as 1919.[43]

The Juntas angrily defended themselves, but even the most stubborn juntero could not fail to be impressed by the mounting insurrection in the Jibalan garrisons. Although no mention of this friction appeared in the military press, it was indirectly visible in the new line adopted by *La Correspondencia Militar*, which first proposed purely honorific decorations, and then more radically, an autonomous colonial army with a separate promotions list.[44] Not surprisingly, this suggestion aroused little enthusiasm among africanistas, most of whom harbored professional ambitions that transcended the boundaries of the Protectorate. In rebuttal, africanistas argued that distinguished performance in combat was the best criterion for selecting the leadership of the peninsular as well as the colonial army; by isolating African officers from the rest of the officer corps, the Spanish army would condemn itself to mediocrity. In the spring of 1921 the training commander of the Tercio, Major Franco, submitted an article to the *Memorial de*

Infantería that was rejected by its Junta-dominated editorial board. Franco insisted that Africa provided the only reliable training ground for the leadership cadres of the future and urged the immediate restoration of merit promotions. Otherwise, he warned, military vocation would soon be "suffocated by the weight of the list in the lazy life of the garrisons."[45]

Clearly, there was emerging in the western sector of the Protectorate a group of young officers of strong military vocation and equally strong ambition, whose impatience with the political favoritism of the older generation was surpassed only by their contempt for the incompetence and sloth of the peninsular junteros. It was these same officers whose steady advance against al-Raysuni between 1919 and 1921 provided the only victories for the dynastic parties, who were otherwise mired in repression and obstructionism. As both the Conde de Romanones and the king perceived, the African army offered the regime an opportunity to identify with a competent faction of the officer corps and with a successful campaign. To a certain extent, the Conservative governments of 1920 and 1921 took advantage of this, claiming credit for the military advance in the west and co-opting the formerly Liberal General Berenguer, whom they made a life senator in 1921. Yet these same governments did not actively promote the Moroccan campaign; they merely exploited its victories. Underfunded and unrewarded, the African army saw its interests sacrificed to those of the Juntas, whose leverage derived from their proximity to the social crisis in the peninsula. As a consequence, the africanistas withdrew into a moral isolation that was rooted in the conviction that they alone were responsible for the conquest of the Jibala and that was nourished by both pride and resentment.

While the African army advanced, the nation—the "political nation"—applauded. Although the working classes and the working-class parties remained opposed to colonialism, the middle and upper classes, protected from service by the quota system, traded their earlier indifference for enthusiasm. Even *La Correspondencia Militar*, hostile to the africanistas, was committed to Spanish imperialism in North Africa, not least because it perceived that in large measure, anticolonialism in Spain was merely antimilitarism in disguise. In the military press, *abandonistas* now received the venom earlier reserved for aliadófilos.[46] Public support for the campaign picked up after the capture of Xauen in October 1920, a well-executed (and well-publicized) operation that provided exoticism, intrigue, and few casualties. During the coming spring, Berenguer continued to tighten his net around the rebellious al-Raysuni. By mid-July 1921 he had encircled him in his mountain refuge at Tazrut. National attention had shifted during the spring of 1921, however, toward the General Command at Melilla and its colorful commander, General Silvestre.

Silvestre in the Rif

Shortly after his transfer to Melilla in January 1920, Silvestre had initiated an unauthorized but successful advance into the Rif, occupying the Tafersit territory in August. At this point, Berenguer had instructed him to subdue the hostile tribes on his right flank that lay between Melilla and Alhucemas Bay, the access point to the central Rif. For the High Commissioner, this implied many months of preparatory action by the Native Police. Only two months later, however, Silvestre startled Berenguer by requesting permission to operate immediately in order to forestall the spread of a rebellion that had developed in the Beni Waryaghil tribe near Alhucemas.[47]

The leader of the rebellion was a former client and employee of the Spanish, Muhammed ʿAbd al-Karim (or Abd el-Krim, as he was known to the Spanish).[48] Born in 1882, educated in both Muslim and Spanish schools, Abd el-Krim had been closely identified with the Spanish since 1906; by 1914 he was a *qadi*, or judge, specializing in mining rights in the Office of Native Affairs in Melilla and an editor of *El Telegrama del Rif*. During the war, however, he and his family had been punished for their pro-German activities. At the end of the war, Abd el-Krim briefly resumed his duties at the newspaper. Then, fearful of extradition to the French for punishment, he had returned to his home at Ajdir in January 1919. The following year, Abd el-Krim, his father, and his brother began a war of rebellion against the Spanish.

The Abd el-Krims were guided by a mixture of idealism and self-interest. Alarmed by the appearance of Spanish agents in Beni Waryaghil territory, they were determined to retain their tribal independence, which they experienced as a kind of ethnic nationalism. More immediate provocations were the loss of their pensions and their exclusion from an informal mining consortium that included the correspondent for *El Sol*, the Republican mining engineer who also owned *El Liberal* of Bilbao, Horacio Echevarrieta, and his agent, Idris bin Said.[49] By the winter of 1920–21, the brothers' charisma and organizational abilities had enabled them to assemble a *haraka*, or militia, of several thousand Beni Waryaghil tribesmen, who were motivated by xenophobia, religious hatred, economic distress, and the passion for independence that had characterized the region long before the arrival of the Spanish.

Still unwilling to cross his strong-minded colleague, Berenguer reluctantly accepted Silvestre's reasoning and gave him permission to operate, even though the second stage of the campaign in the west was not yet complete. He was reassured when Silvestre's advance was unopposed, then alarmed again by a pessimistic report from Colonel Gabriel Morales, the head of the Office of Native Affairs in Melilla, on February 16, 1921.[50] A protégé of Berenguer's, Morales was a conscientious Staff officer familiar with the system of advance in the Jibala. In his view, Silvestre had abused that system, whose success depended entirely on political preparation before and after military operations. Having advanced 120 kilometers with a minimum of political action, Silvestre's forces were now overextended, tied down in a string of strategically indefensible blocaos that stretched from the capital to the position at Anual on the forward line. Now Morales suggested that after extending the front from Anual to Sidi Dris on the coast, operations should cease until more troops were available to deal with the hostile Beni Waryaghil near Alhucemas Bay. After a personal inspection of the eastern command on March 28, Berenguer agreed and instructed Silvestre to halt his march toward Alhucemas until troops and equipment could be transferred from the Jibala. At the same time, however, Berenguer did nothing to discourage the popular enthusiasm in the peninsula for Silvestre's rapid advance, even announcing to the press in early April that Alhucemas Bay was "mature fruit."[51]

After seventeen months of inhibition, Berenguer had finally dared to restrain his friend Silvestre. But by March 1921 it was too late. For one thing, the halt left Silvestre's forces dispersed and immobilized in a position system designed to be shifting and temporary. For another, the security of the entire line depended on the highly problematic quiescence of the tribes both beyond and behind it. Finally and most important, Silvestre was too volatile and too self-confident to accept for long a policy of inaction. Within a few months he would upset the uneasy equilibrium in the Rif and trigger an attack by Abd el-Krim's haraka that would obliterate the achievements of twelve years of Spanish occupation.

Silvestre's decision to ignore Berenguer's orders seems to have been made in Madrid, where he spent several weeks on leave in late April and early May 1921. Hailed in the press and honored at testimonial banquets, Silvestre's vanity grew along with his sense of personal injury.[52] With public opinion expecting an immediate assault on

Alhucemas Bay, he was undoubtedly depressed by the knowledge that his day of glory must wait until Berenguer had completed the campaign against al-Raysuni. Most decisively, Silvestre's frustration was shared by Alfonso XIII, whose support for the Moroccan war had been unflagging since the beginning of Spanish involvement and whose colonialist enthusiasm had compensated for the indifference of the governmental parties. Like his former aide, Alfonso was impatient of Berenguer's cautious brand of colonial warfare and resentful of the financial constraints that held up military operations in the Rif. More generous support for the Moroccan campaign was partially behind his antiparliamentary speech in Cordova on May 23, 1921, as he revealed during an interview in exile in 1933:

> The real responsibility for that disaster [Anual] may be appropriated to those who refused to vote the military credits indispensable in those circumstances.
>
> Perhaps the only thing I have to repent is having scrupulously observed the articles of the Constitution in those years. If I had ceased being constitutional King in order to be simply King, it is possible that the disaster at Anual might have been avoided and subsequently the Dictatorship that circumstances imposed.[53]

Above all, the king was anticipating an early conquest of Alhucemas, where a new "Ciudad Alfonsina" was to be built.[54] It was reported that during a banquet at the Cavalry Academy in Valladolid, Silvestre promised the king he would be in Alhucemas on July 25, the day of Santiago.[55] By the time he returned to Melilla in mid-May, Silvestre's resentment against Berenguer had grown into a conviction that he should trust in his judgment and his proverbial good luck to achieve the great victory nearly within his grasp.

There were few to dissuade him in the Melilla garrison.[56] Most of the young officers in Melilla worshiped Silvestre, whose virile self-confidence inspired one impressionable writer in *El Telegrama del Rif* to compare him to Alexander the Great and Charlemagne.[57] In return, the Commander General allowed his subordinates to call him "Manolo" and address him with the familiar "tu"; the young officers closest to him were known generally in Melilla as the *"manolos."* This lapse of discipline spread easily into all other areas. Melilla was riddled with brothels, taverns, and gaming houses, where the money obtained through endemic graft and illegal business activities was spent freely. Because the zone was relatively peaceful and service in the outlying positions tedious and uncomfortable, Silvestre allowed most officers to return to Melilla every night, leaving only a junior officer in the field.

In contrast to Ceuta, positions in the Regulars and Police carried little prestige and had to be assigned in rotation, the work of the Staff officers and of the minority of dedicated africanistas in the Native Office was laughed at and ignored, and the General Staff—labeled the "estorbo mayor" by Silvestre—was as resented in Melilla as it was in the peninsula. The atmosphere was, in short, very different from that prevailing in the western sector, where two years of combat and careful supervision by Berenguer had produced a cult of discipline and africanismo. The army of Africa in Melilla, in fact, closely resembled the peninsular army in its inefficiency and bureaucratic laxity, if not in its morals.

Spurred on by the king, a contact in the War Ministry, and his camarilla in Melilla, Silvestre resumed his forward march during the last week in May. Over the objections of his chief of staff and of Colonel Morales,[58] he ordered one of the manolos, Major Villar of the Police, to occupy Abarrán, a mountainous position northwest of Anual. Shortly after Villar's return, the outpost at Abarrán was betrayed by the 50 native Regulars, who joined an attack by Timsaman tribesmen that left 179 of the 200 Spanish troops and officers dead. Three days later, Beni Waryaghil and Timsaman tribesmen began a full-scale attack on the coastal position of Sidi Dris that left another 100 dead. Undeterred by this setback, on June 5 Silvestre informed Berenguer of his intention to occupy new positions along the front once he had been granted more men and equipment.[59]

For the last time, the ambiguous command structure and the lack of informed authority in the War Ministry became critical. Berenguer sailed to Sidi Dris for a meeting with Silvestre the same day. Once again his sense of delicacy, reinforced by his desire to return quickly to the operations in the Jibala, led him to accept Silvestre's assurances that his line was secure. After denying Silvestre's request for permission to retake Abarrán, he informed the agitated Vizconde de Eza and the national press that there was no cause for alarm.[60] Then he returned to his pursuit of al-Raysuni at Tazrut, confident that he could rely on Silvestre to maintain the status quo a few months longer.

In fact, the situation in the Rif veered wildly out of control after Abarrán. Having exposed the vulnerability of the Spanish, Abd el-Krim convinced tribes all along the front to join his haraka, which now numbered between 3,000 and 4,000. Silvestre, ignoring the warnings of Gabriel Morales in the Office of Native Affairs,[61] ordered the construction of an outpost at Igueriben, near Anual, the day after his interview with Berenguer, and bombarded his superiors with requests for reinforcements throughout June and early July. Distracted by events in the west and lulled by Silvestre's erroneous reports of absolute quiescence in the zone, Berenguer and Eza ignored these demands for more troops. According to Silvestre, there were 25,790 troops in the Melilla Command, including 5,000 Moroccans in the Regulars and Police, an adequate force for defense, especially if there were no danger of rebellion. Reinforcements would have to come from the peninsula, an option rejected firmly by both Eza and Berenguer.[62] Even though Silvestre grumbled publicly and privately about the economies imposed on him, he consistently denied the possibility of an attack, complaining instead of the "morbid inaction" and its effects on morale.[63] Accustomed by now to Silvestre's displays of temperament, neither Berenguer nor Eza took him very seriously. On July 20 a column led by General José Sanjurjo was only six kilometers from al-Raysuni's hideout in Tazrut. Berenguer was sure his forces would have taken the position by July 25, the day of Santiago, making it possible to attend to the Rif within a few months.

Anual

Silvestre's assurances notwithstanding, the signs of an impending attack at Anual were visible from the middle of June, and unmistakable after July 7 when the new outpost at Igueriben was occupied. By the fourteenth, supply convoys from Anual were being harassed; by the nineteenth, Igueriben was cut off and under siege. Yet Silvestre's reports to Berenguer still conveyed no sense of urgency; on July 20 he requested "the quantity of men and elements that you deem sufficient" and then more specifically on the twenty-first, five hundred horses, an Infantry regiment, two Artillery batteries, three Quartermaster companies, and a credit of four million pesetas for road construction.[64] Puzzled, Berenguer asked for clarification, while reminding Silvestre that no troops could be spared from the west at that moment. It appears that Silvestre himself did not appreciate the gravity of the situation until he arrived at Anual with all the reinforcements he could muster in Melilla late in the day of the twenty-first. Shortly thereafter, the besieged troops at Igueriben were given the order to retreat. The Moroccan troops mutinied and joined the assault on the three hundred Spaniards, killing all but twenty-five. Next Abd el-Krim began to organize his haraka for an attack on the forty-five hundred defenders of Anual. Only then did Silvestre communicate the urgent need for reinforcements to Berenguer and the War Ministry.

The morning of July 22 Berenguer rushed reinforcements to Melilla, thus losing the opportunity to capture al-Raysuni, whom he had patiently stalked for two years. But Silvestre, suddenly fatalistic, now refused to wait for rescue. Ignoring the advice of Colonel Morales one last time, he ordered an immediate retreat to Ben Tieb, a supply base eighteen kilometers behind Anual. With his characteristic disregard for organization, Silvestre left the operation to his subordinates, preferring to die a hero's death (along with Colonel Morales) at Anual. Consequently, the retreat progressed "without order, orientation, or control, without any guiding principle except to get away from Anual, with complete disregard for the most elemental rules of retreat."[65] If the panic of the Spanish conscripts was excusable, it was not inevitable, the responsibility of officers too demoralized by years of corruption and idleness to retore order and assert their leadership at a crucial moment. As Morales had predicted, most of the native units mutinied and joined their compatriots in the slaughter of the terrified troops, who reached Ben Tieb and continued in a wave toward Melilla, their panic infecting positions all along the route. As word of the retreat spread throughout the territory, the supposedly pacified tribes in the rear, still armed, joined the rebellion, as did all of the Police units and many of the Regulars guarding them. A few blocaos resisted bravely; the majority abandoned their posts without a fight and joined the mob struggling to escape. There were moving cases of heroism. General Felipe Navarro, the second in command at Melilla, left the city, rounded up all the stray troops he could find at Dar Drius, and herded them back toward Melilla, stopping finally at Monte Arruit with thirteen hundred men on July 29. His retreat was courageously covered by the Cavalry regiment of Alcántara, led by Lieutenant Colonel Fernando Primo de Rivera (a cousin of the general), who died of a gangrenous wound several days later. But the few exceptions only provided a contrast with the majority of officers, whose dishonorable conduct would cast a shadow over the Spanish army for many years after.

Berenguer had arrived in Melilla on July 23 with 2,000 men, including two banderas of Tercios, two *tabores* of Regulars, and four battalions led by General Sanjurjo. In Melilla, the High Commissioner was only able to locate 1,800 demoralized and unfit Spanish troops out of the 25,790 that supposedly had existed before the disaster. Between 8,000 and 10,000 Europeans were dead or missing; an unknown number were trapped in Nador, Zeluan, and Monte Arruit south of the city, or were still wandering in the Rif. Still others—perhaps as many as 1,500—had existed only on paper or were illegally on leave in the peninsula.[66] Nearly all of the 5,000 Moroccan troops had defected, with the exception of a few Regulars, who had been disarmed and turned away, leaving them no alternative but to join the rebels.[67] Furthermore, there was almost no equipment in the city. During the retreat, 129 field guns, 292 machine guns, 29,500 rifles, and several hundred head of livestock had been seized or abandoned, and the 6 aircraft at Zeluan had been lost because their pilots had been asleep in Melilla at the time of the disaster.[68]

By July 28 reinforcements from the peninsula brought the number of troops in Melilla to forty-five hundred men, a force sufficient to defend the city, which was highly vulnerable to attack. But, as Berenguer informed Eza on July 29, the quality and morale of the new forces was too low to permit a rescue sortie to the three outposts to the south.[69] The reasons for this inadequacy were political, not military. Fearful of triggering a protest similar to the Tragic Week of 1909, Eza ignored the mobilization plans of the General Staff, which would have required the call-up of complete regiments, including all of the recently discharged third-year conscripts.[70] Instead, he called up isolated battalions composed largely of quota soldiers, who were presumably politically reliable, if not well trained or psychologically prepared to see combat.[71] As a consequence, the only experienced troops at Berenguer's disposal were the Tercios and Regulars from Ceuta. As he watched helplessly in Melilla, the outposts collapsed one by one and the survivors, overcome by lack of water and supplies, surrendered and were slaughtered by their besiegers. Nador fell on August 2; Zeluan, two days later. On August 6, with nearly seventeen thousand expeditionary forces in Melilla, Berenguer and four other generals, including the newly appointed Commander General, José Cavalcanti, agreed to order a surrender at Monte Arruit. On August 9, as the troops emerged from the fort, the Moroccans killed all but General Navarro and about six hundred officers and civilians, who were taken prisoner and held for ransom.

The fall of Monte Arruit was the final stage of the collapse that had begun July 22 and that had wiped out all the gains made in twelve years of military occupation. The cause of the disaster would be debated endlessly for the next two years, until the answer to the question became less important than the political use that could be made of the question itself. In any event, the responsibility lay diffused among nearly all those who would eventually be accused. The disaster at Anual was the consequence of years of inefficiency and waste in the Spanish army, of corruption and indifference in the Melilla Command, of the passivity of successive cabinets and of the unconstitutional intervention of the king, of the impulsiveness and ambition of General Silvestre, and of the excessive discretion of General Berenguer. Above all, Anual was a tragic symbol of the political irresponsibility of the dynastic parties, whose pursuit of cheap glory abroad and political stability at home had led them to abdicate control of the Moroccan enterprise to a defective but ambitious army.

CHAPTER NINE

The Impact of Anual

There was no reason to suspect, in the beginning, that Anual would be any more fatal for Spain than Adowa had been for Italy, or Fashoda, for France. Indeed, in the immediate aftermath of the disaster, most of the country rallied behind the government and the army in their effort to regain the territory and prestige lost at Anual. Nevertheless, Anual would ultimately destroy the parliamentary regime. Even before the initial shock had dissipated, the defeat became the occasion for bitter debate between the antagonists whose conflicts had dominated Spanish political life since 1917: between dynastics and antidynastics, between junteros and africanistas, and most ominously, between the civil state and the military.

Had the dynastic parties been able to provide strong leadership during the months when public opinion was still inflamed over the "betrayal" of Abd el-Krim, the struggle might not have taken on its apocalyptic character. Instead, they contributed to the polarization of the country by following the same vacillating and secretive policies that had always characterized the Spanish presence in Morocco, neither supporting the army's demand for a rapid conquest of the entire zone nor responding to the extensive abandonista sentiment in the nation. By trying to maintain a middle course, the Maura coalition government satisfied none of its critics and guaranteed the prolongation of the war.

The middle course embraced by Maura represented not a consensus but a compromise between the unresolved conflicts over Moroccan policy within the government and the nation. In order to preserve the fiction of a united front, Maura felt obliged to discourage parliamentary debate on military policy and on responsibility for the disaster. This disregard for public opinion, so congenial to Maura himself, only added another source of tension within the coalition, however. Weakened by its internal contradictions and lacking strong support either in the country or in the army, the last coalition government of the parliamentary monarchy disintegrated in March 1922, laying bare the isolation of the dynastic parties from much of the country. The following eighteen months would find those parties making a belated and feeble attempt to adjust to the altered reality of Spanish political life, an attempt cut short by the military pronunciamiento of September 1923.

The Reaction to Anual

As soon as the magnitude of the Anual debacle became clear, the quest for "responsibilities" began. Like "regeneration" in 1898 and "renovation" in 1917, "responsibilities" became a code word for political and social reform. By providing a single focus for the welter of political conflicts that had emerged since 1917, the disaster gave them a new intensity. After Anual, the Moroccan campaign finally became the center of public debate. Ironically, however, policy issues continued to take second place to the political capital that could be made out of the arguments they generated.

Once it had overcome its initial surprise and confusion, the Allendesalazar government responded to the news of the disaster with more resignation than remorse. Like nearly all its predecessors, the cabinet had provided unenthusiastic but unquestioning support for the military campaign in the Protectorate.[1] Faced now with the collapse of the entire eastern sector, the government did not pause to reevaluate the extent or character of Spanish colonial policy; instead, the setback was officially interpreted as an unfortunate personal error on the part of General Silvestre, to be made right by a renewed effort by the army and the nation.[2] To control rumor-mongering, the government established prior censorship on July 26, authorizing only the publication of official notes from Morocco.[3]

The government's fears of antiwar protests duplicating those of 1909 did not materialize, however, because the left had been seriously weakened by internal schism in the summer of 1921. Although miners and metalworkers in Bilbao responded to the Communists' call for a national general strike on July 27 to protest the call-up of troops, the recent split in the Socialist party localized the strike. In Barcelona, Martínez Anido's iron control over the city kept the CNT in check. The fragmented Republican forces, deprived of their best-known national leader by the defection of Alejandro Lerroux, an ardent supporter of the Moroccan Protectorate, lacked the organizational strength to mobilize a mass protest.[4] In the absence of leadership, the working class responded with resignation and, in some cases, with enthusiasm, to the mobilization; Tercio recruiters in Barcelona, for example, reported an increase in volunteers.[5]

The middle and upper classes met the challenge with patriotic fervor, even though the mobilization orders included all trained recruits from 1918, 1919, and 1920, including the quota soldiers. Huge crowds turned out to cheer the first battalions from Madrid as they boarded trains for the coast clutching the religious medals bestowed on them by aristocratic socialites. In large and small provincial cities, young ladies of "good family" sponsored benefits and swamped seamstresses with orders for Red Cross uniforms, in imitation of Queen Victoria Eugenia, who became honorary president of the organization. In a belated attempt to redress the lack of essential supplies so long denied the African army, voluntary funds were established for hospitals, linens, cigarettes, and even airplanes. The Marqués de Comillas's Compañía Transmediterránea offered free transportation for packages sent to the troops; the Sociedad El Seguro Tarrasense pledged to care for the wounded who returned to the peninsula. After years of indifference, Spain's upper classes suddenly found Morocco worthy of their attention. The war was the cause of the year.[6]

Once it became clear that the nation would support the war effort, the government relaxed its control over the press, retaining censorship only over military reports from the front. Within a few weeks, several identifiable groups of critics had emerged to challenge the government's view that responsibility for the disaster lay wholly with Silvestre: the Liberals, still supportive of General Berenguer and his policies, but eager to cast blame on the Conservatives; the anti-Berenguer forces, which included many senior generals in the peninsula; the junteros, who blamed both the African army and the senior hierarchy; the africanistas, who blamed the Juntas; and the extreme left, whose indictment encompassed the entire regime, and in particular, the king and the army.

Because they had no vested interests to defend, the Socialists and the Republican left continued to be the most effective critics of the Moroccan fiasco. Too divided to organize a mass protest, they were able to mount an impressive publicity campaign against the war and in favor of "responsibilities." Their chief strength lay in their freedom to criticize the system, and especially the king, whom they considered personally responsible for the disaster. While the dynastic parties were hobbled by the necessity of defending the regime, the antidynastic left were able to interpret the failure in Morocco as merely the most tragic example of the general incapacity of the Spanish state.[7] Insulated from responsibility for the disaster by their past exclusion from the system, the left monopolized the cloak of morality and emerged as the most effective bloc in the Cortes after it opened in October 1921. Thus, while the overall strength of the left was diminished by schism and repression in 1921 and 1922, the moral authority and political leverage of the parliamentary delegations was enhanced. Indeed, the responsibilities campaign represented the final attempt of the democratic left to broaden the political base of the parliamentary monarchy.[8]

The regime proved easiest to attack through the army, whose failure at Anual, in spite of the "reform" law of 1918, was patent. As the Socialist deputy Indalecio Prieto observed on August 7, Anual was the price for dependency on the army—by the right and occasionally by the left—a dependency that had made real military reform impossible.[9] Both the Juntas de Defensa and the never-ending Moroccan war were merely symbolic of a more general structural weakness in the Restoration system, the inevitable by-products of an overprotected army in an undemocratic regime. By identifying its interests with those of the army instead of those of the nation, the regime had lost its justification for being.

If the left chose to attack the army and its various factions indiscriminately, for other interest groups the split between junteros and africanistas within the officer corps offered the possibility of selective attack and defense. Predictably, the Juntas received the most criticism, particularly from the liberal africanista press (*El Sol*, *El Heraldo*, and *Diario Universal*) and from the elderly lieutenant generals who had been pushed aside by the Juntas in 1917. The Juntas were blamed for the demoralization, disorganization, and fragmentation of the officer corps, for the budgetary neglect of the African army, and for the abolition of merit promotions that had removed the incentives for valor and sacrifice. The disaster at Anual gave substance to the charges that had been leveled against the Juntas for the past four years, and their opponents luxuriated in their role as vindicated prophets.[10]

The appearance of a selective offense, of course, immediately divided the officer corps, whose first response had been to close ranks and to attribute the defeat to governmental neglect and "Moorish cowardice and treachery."[11] Almost unanimously, the officer corps regarded a renewal of the war effort as essential to avenge the honor of the army. As the Juntas began to draw fire, however, *La Correspondencia Militar* began to temper its enthusiasm for the Moroccan campaign with criticism of General Berenguer, a strategy that diverted attention to theories of colonial warfare while winning the Juntas some badly needed allies.

Berenguer was already under attack by the left for his conduct of the war in general and for his relationship with Silvestre in particular.[12] *La Correspondencia Militar* focused its attack on his policy of political attraction and on his dependence on native troops, thus resuscitating the conflict between the partisans of Silvestre and those of Gabriel Morales in the Melilla Command before Anual.[13] Juntero opinion supported those who had advocated military action "a la tremenda" over the scientific approach to warfare, a position advocated even more strenuously after the surrender of Monte Arruit and the slaughter of most of its defenders on August 12. Although Berenguer had excellent reasons for refusing to send a rescue column—his troops were raw and the route to Monte Arruit was dominated by the tribesmen on Monte Gurugú—his decision was widely resented in the officer corps, whose members feared it cast an unfavorable reflection on their manhood. Within the Melilla Command, the dissidents kept their views to themselves, voting unanimously with Berenguer to order a surrender. In the peninsula, officers who had never given a moment's thought to theories of colonial warfare now demonstrated the keenest interest in explaining their considered views to the press. The fate of Monte Arruit gave the senior generals who had resented the elevation of a mere division general to the post of High Commissioner their first opportunity to criticize Berenguer on a policy matter. Even Berenguer's patron, General Luque, felt obliged to condemn his caution as unworthy of "virile nations."[14] Also joining the critics was General Weyler. The General Staff had been denied competence over Morocco since January 1918, an exclusion that Weyler, as its chief, felt as a personal affront. Events had now presented him with an opportunity for revenge.

Berenguer's severest critics, however, were not the elderly Restoration generals, but his rivals among the division generals, Ricardo Burguete and Miguel Primo de Rivera. The three were contemporaries, graduates of the AGM, veterans of the colonial wars in America and Africa, each professionally ambitious and successful. Since 1919, however, Berenguer had won admiration, prestige, and respect as High Commissioner in Africa, while Burguete and Primo de Rivera had been reduced to intriguing with the Juntas in the peninsula. After the collapse of the Melilla Command, each saw an opportunity to improve his own position at Berenguer's expense by appealing to the peninsular resentment of the africanistas.

Burguete moved immediately. As a military theorist with well-known views on the inferiority of "science" to courage and will, Burguete saw the Anual debacle as a personal vindication and had expected to be appointed Commander General of Melilla following the

death of Silvestre.[15] Instead, the government had appointed General
José Cavalcanti, a Cavalry officer known for his courage and impetu-
osity. Thus thwarted, Burguete initiated a critical campaign against
Berenguer in the pages of *El Debate*, the organ of the Catholic right,
which was traditionally opposed to temporizing of any sort, whether
with Moorish rebels or Spanish leftists.[16] Although the new Minister
of War, La Cierva, attempted to placate Burguete by appointing him
Military Governor of Madrid in October, the volatile general continued
to act as a gadfly in the press and among the Junta leadership in
Madrid.[17]

General Primo de Rivera, more tactful and less frustrated than
Burguete, at first refrained from criticizing the government or the campaign. As Captain General of Madrid, he was close to the center of
power; in September his cooperation in the mobilization effort was
rewarded by the grant of a tax-free *grandeza* on the title of Marqués de
Estella, which he had recently inherited from his uncle. Although he
continued to intrigue with the Juntas,[18] his *abandonista* sentiments,
which had cost him his job in February 1917, did not surface until late
November, when during the course of a speech in the Senate (he was
an elected senator from Cadiz), he announced that "to have one soldier
on the other bank of the Straits is strategically a weakness for Spain."[19]
Immediately deprived of his command, he remained idle in Madrid
until his appointment as Captain General of Barcelona by the new
prime minister, Sánchez Guerra, in March 1922.

The attack initiated by the antiafricanista and anti-Berenguer forces
within the officer corps was viewed providentially by the Allendesalazar government, whose members—especially the War Minister, the
Vizconde de Eza—were anxious to absolve themselves of responsibility
for the disaster. At the end of July, Eza asked Berenguer's approval for
an investigation of military responsibilities, a proposal immediately
embraced by the High Commissioner.[20] On August 4 Eza appointed
General Juan Picasso, a member of the Supreme Military Council, to
head a commission to "clarify . . . the antecedents and circumstances
that contributed to the abandonment of the positions. . . ."[21] A highly
decorated Staff officer who had served with Berenguer as Undersecretary in the War Ministry in 1918, Picasso was expected to limit his
investigation to the obvious cases of dishonorable conduct during the
panicky retreat from Anual. By offering a few junior officers as sacri-
ficial lambs, the government hoped to meet the widespread demand
for responsibilities without endangering Berenguer's prestige or the
ultimate success of the African campaign.

Both the Allendesalazar government and the Maura government

that succeeded it were convinced that Spain's international reputation, as well as the prestige of the monarchy itself, depended on a rapid recuperation of the lost territory. Accordingly, they refused General Berenguer's resignation, tendered the same day as Picasso's appointment. Berenguer had proven his competence as a colonial officer in the campaign against al-Raysuni, and his departure would have demoralized the elite units that were to spearhead the recuperation campaign. But by retaining Berenguer, the Conservatives were forced to deny the existence of higher responsibilities for the disaster at Anual, a congenial but indefensible position. In December 1922 the party would succumb to the national clamor for a political accounting.

Junteros and Africanistas

Having decided to spare Berenguer to save the war and thus, the regime, the Allendesalazar government sacrificed itself, resigning on August 12 after the fall of Monte Arruit. The new cabinet, headed by Antonio Maura, was a dynastic coalition like the National Government of 1918, a crisis solution that tacitly recognized the joint responsibility of Liberals and Conservatives for Moroccan policy since 1909. Precisely for this reason, the Reformists, invited for the first time to participate in a cabinet, refused to collaborate. As Melquíades Álvarez pointed out in a letter of August 15 to Maura, "the only ones who could legitimately avoid this responsibility were ourselves and all those in our situation, for the very reason that we had not participated in the Government at any time."[22] Instead, the Reformists strengthened their ties with Santiago Alba, forming a left-Liberal bloc that remained outside the coalition. Of the Liberals, only Romanones—who in any case had been excluded from the Alba-Álvarez consortium—contributed representatives to the cabinet.[23]

The heterogeneous cabinet united around the limited platform outlined by Maura: the recuperation of the territory and prestige lost at Anual.[24] But once this initial objective had been attained, the coalition of 1921, like the National Government of 1918, would be torn apart by irreconcilable internal differences over domestic and foreign policy. The Maura government of 1921–22 was thus the final attempt to restore the old union of Liberals and Conservatives that had once kept the turno running smoothly. A new realignment of forces in Spanish society had pulled apart the center that had anchored the Restoration system; the Anual disaster could provide no more than a temporary cement. As the imminent danger receded, the disaster that had briefly united the nation would begin to divide it, and a new arrangement of political forces and interest groups would tentatively emerge. Unable or unwilling to countenance such a restructuring, Maura would fall.

The new "Reconquest" catapulted the War Minister, Juan de la Cierva, back into national prominence. Once called upon to deal with the Juntas, La Cierva now had to restore the morale and the fighting capacity of the African army. In the process, he also became an opponent of the Juntas, a champion of total military occupation of the Protectorate, the government's bulwark against the clamor for responsibilities, and an adversary of any redefinition of the Restoration system. In fact, La Cierva, not the increasingly cynical and fatalistic Maura, was the soul of the 1921 cabinet.

La Cierva's first goal was to restore the shattered morale of the remnants of the Melilla garrison, whose performance at Anual was the target of both civilian and military critics. Most demoralizing was the ostentatious contempt of the officers in the expeditionary forces arriving daily in Melilla from the peninsula, many of whom were active junteros only too willing to vaunt their presumed moral superiority over their traditional rivals.[25] Although Maura and the king proposed a dissolution of the Juntas (technically, the Advisory Commissions), La Cierva—probably correctly—insisted that a frontal attack would only compound the problem. Instead, he attempted to localize the conflict. After prohibiting officers from publishing comments on current military operations,[26] he allowed two members of the Infantry Directory to go to Melilla, where they spent their energies disputing with General Picasso and the local honor courts the right to prosecute cases of dishonorable conduct.[27]

La Cierva also had to restrain General Picasso, who was displaying more zeal for his task than either the War Minister or the High Commissioner thought appropriate. After receiving a long questionnaire on August 15, Berenguer refused to cooperate, arguing that an investigation of his policies would undermine his credibility as Commander-in-Chief. In response, La Cierva issued an order, dated August 24, prohibiting Picasso from examining "the accords, plans, and orders of the High Commissioner . . . ," an order he repeated, with only slight modifications, on September 1. To impress even further the limits of his jurisdiction on the disgruntled Picasso, La Cierva subsumed the entire investigation under Berenguer's authority as General-in-Chief of the African army on September 6.[28] Berenguer was thus apparently freed, by executive order, from responsibility for the disaster in the Rif.

La Cierva showed the same decisiveness in rebuilding the African army. Cautious as ever, Berenguer refused to begin operations until he could be confident of success. Since the disaster, the situation in the entire Protectorate had deteriorated: al-Raysuni, saved from capture by the opportune victory of Abd el-Krim, had recovered his ascendancy over the tribes around Xauen; in the Ghumara, Abd el-Krim's brother was preaching a *jihad* against the Spanish. Even to return to the status quo prior to Anual required a significant increase in military forces. To give Berenguer the resources he needed, La Cierva resorted to executive decrees; by the end of the year, there were 160,000 Spanish soldiers in Morocco, and extraordinary credits amounted to 419 million pesetas.[29] Because peninsular officers continued to exhibit their traditional lack of enthusiasm for colonial campaigning, all officers were prohibited from returning to the peninsula upon completion of their two-year tours and from going off the active list without pay.[30]

Although most of his new troops were poorly trained, Berenguer began operations in the Rif on September 8 with an army of thirty-six thousand men in order to placate La Cierva and the revanchists in the Spanish press. Because Abd el-Krim's haraka had retired inland to the mountains, where they fortified their line and concentrated on propaganda among the Rif tribes,[31] the Spanish advanced rapidly, almost without opposition. By September 17 they were once again in Nador; from there, battalions of Regulars and the Tercio fanned out, retaking the strategically significant Monte Gurugú on October 10.

The rapidity of the reconquest gratified the nation, which eagerly embraced the opportunity to dwell on heroism rather than disgrace. The colorful leaders of the vanguard units were lionized in the africanista press: General José Sanjurjo, who wore a striped pajama top and Moorish slippers during operations; Lieutenant Colonel Millán-Astray, the founder of the Tercio, wounded during the capture of Nador; his dashing young subordinates, Majors Santiago González-Tablas and Francisco Franco, who were present at every new advance into the Rif. Major Franco acquired even greater prominence after the publication of his book, *Marruecos: Diario de una bandera*, in which praise for the African army was intermingled with scathing criticism of the peninsular bureaucrats in the Juntas:

> what improves the quality [of the troops] is the selection of cadres, the ability to bring them an enthusiastic and valorous officer corps that will educate them in a creed of ideals, that does not need to be sustained with some fistful of pesetas. It is necessary to have a stimulus, that officers specialize in warfare, that they know the enemy, that they not dream of the moment they can return to the Peninsula, having completed their enforced term. Only a just re-

ward can, in this age of positivism, conserve in Africa the cadres of officers appropriate for shock units.[32]

As usual, the king and the government hastened to assure themselves of the support of the strongest military faction. On October 21 the king symbolically aligned himself with the africanistas by appointing González-Tablas and Millán-Astray as gentlemen of the chamber.[33] La Cierva also used his authority in the War Ministry to demonstrate his goodwill toward the africanistas. The result of this favoritism was to restore to the Juntas de Defensa some of the moral authority they had lost since the July disaster. Their partial victory over La Cierva in late October illustrated the pitfalls of relying on a divided army for support.

The Juntas had not been able to turn the defeat at Anual to their own advantage. On the contrary, they had been blamed for most of the army's material and moral defects. In September the Infantry Junta had been forced to elect a new president after it was revealed that the old president, Colonel Silverio Araujo, had surrendered without a fight to the Moroccan rebels during the disaster and was being held for ransom by Abd el-Krim.[34] Later that month, the new president, Colonel Lacanal, was humiliated when he and two other officers failed to secure transit for a supply convoy to the base at Tizza. The Spanish forces incurred fifteen hundred casualties before the Commander General of Melilla, General Cavalcanti, personally led a group of Regulars and Engineers through the line.[35] Back in Melilla, Cavalcanti sharply criticized the conduct of Colonel Lacanal. To avoid another public disgrace, the Infantry Advisory Commission counterattacked by accusing Cavalcanti of rash conduct inappropriate in a commanding officer.

Cavalcanti's conduct probably deserved a reprimand, although it was consistent with his past record. Like many small, proud men, Cavalcanti had made a career of his bravery. As a young lieutenant colonel, he had led a glorious charge at Taxdirt during the 1909 campaign and had been rewarded with a Laurel Wreath, his first title of nobility, and the admiration and friendship of the king, who gave him his second title in 1919. Like Silvestre, his great friend, he had been somewhat unenthusiastic about the careful campaign of political preparation waged by Berenguer, and like Silvestre, he acted impulsively when courage was required. Since his gallantry at Tizza had undoubtedly saved many lives, it was vigorously applauded in the africanista press. This was enough to convince La Cierva. On October 20, after a firsthand consultation with General Berenguer in Melilla, La Cierva recommended Cavalcanti for a second Laurel Wreath and removed Colonel Lacanal, together with the two other officers, General Carlos Tuero and Colonel Juan Sirvent, from their commands.

Stimulated by the apparent success of his African policy, La Cierva did not hesitate to antagonize juntero opinion even further. In early October he used his patronage power to place the son of a political client in a comfortable medical post in Melilla, a blatant example of favoritism that drew a protest from the Medical Corps Advisory Commission. Having secured the support of the other Commissions, the Medical Junta threatened to try the young officer, Captain Fontes, in an honor court.[36] About the same time, La Cierva revealed his intention to secure merit promotions for a number of prominent africanistas from the western sector once the Cortes had reopened. Disregarding the fact that he had sponsored the reform law that had abolished most merit promotions in 1918, La Cierva now insisted that success in Africa depended on a fair system of rewards for the officer corps. For the Juntas, however, merit promotions still connoted favoritism and injustice.

Prior censorship had been reestablished at the commencement of operations on September 8. When the government restored freedom of the press on October 20, the day the Cortes opened, the mounting tension between La Cierva and the Advisory Commissions exploded into open hostility. On the twenty-first, four Madrid dailies published rumors of a twenty-four-hour ultimatum imposed on La Cierva by the Juntas.[37] Responding with characteristic vigor, La Cierva firmly denied the reports and ordered two of the editors indicted for violation of the Law of Jurisdictions. But although the bearers of the message might be punished, the news was still bad. The next day, the Advisory Commissions issued a joint statement of solidarity, and the Captain General of Madrid, Primo de Rivera, seized the opportunity to sympathize publicly with their grievances.[38] At the same time, the smoldering conflict between the junteros and the africanistas was ignited by a letter from General Miguel Cabanellas, the commander of a Cavalry brigade in Melilla, whose forces had just recaptured the fortress of Zeluan. Overcome by the sight of five hundred mutilated Spanish cadavers, victims of the abortive surrender the previous August, Cabanellas had dashed off an indignant letter of reproach to the presidents of the Advisory Commissions, blaming them for the poor quality of the Spanish army, and thus, for the disaster at Anual.[39] Released for publication, the letter produced an enormous sensation, particularly because photographs of the massacred Spaniards were beginning to appear in the illustrated weeklies.

The Juntas' public quarrel with La Cierva and the letter from Cabanellas revived the issue of military interference in politics. Demands for decisive action against the Advisory Commissions appeared in the africanista press and in the Cortes. The other side of the argument, however, was civilian political interference in purely military matters. The continuing vitality of the Juntas, in the face of overwhelming civilian and military opposition, was due to the persistence of the abuses that they had been formed to combat—in particular, favoritism and personalism in the War Ministry and the palace. The official note of the Advisory Commissions, in which they claimed to have redeemed the army from "the caciquismo of the camarillas, from injustice, from adulation . . . and from a despotic, tyrannical, and ignorant command," suggested that they were also aware of this basic strength.[40] Coupled with the endemic weakness of civilian government, this shred of legitimacy continued to provide the Juntas with enough leverage within the officer corps to impose their will, or at the very least, to limit the freedom of action of the government. Civilian government would be strong enough to challenge the Juntas when it could confront them with a clear conscience.

Such was not the case in October 1921. Both La Cierva and the king had ostentatiously favored the africanistas in ways that had little to do with military efficiency or victory in Morocco. Accordingly, against all his instincts, La Cierva was forced to compromise. Captain Fontes was transferred back to his original post; Lacanal, Tuero, and Sirvent were reinstated pending further investigation of the Tizza incident.[41] The case of General Cabanellas, however, was less easy to resolve because of the widespread sympathy for his outburst. Clearly, his letter had violated La Cierva's order against military commentaries on the war; other formal charges against the general were quickly filed by the Advisory Commissions.[42] On November 14 La Cierva finally relieved Cabanellas of his command, softening the blow by dissolving his brigade on the pretext it was not needed.[43] On Berenguer's recommendation, Cabanellas remained in Melilla in order to avoid drawing attention to his case.[44] But although he was later given a new command, Cabanellas appeared to be an innocent lamb sacrificed on the altar of the Juntas de Defensa. Throughout the fall, the battle between junteros and africanistas continued to distract attention from and distort the outlines of the more urgent problems of Moroccan policy and responsibilities.

The Cortes of 1921

The first session of the Cortes after Anual was alternately awaited with impatience or with dread, but nearly everyone shared the assumption that the Cortes would deal effectively with the responsibilities question. The outcome, however, was far different. The autumn session of the Cortes of 1921 proved to be the legislative counterpart of Maura's coalition government—a final attempt to preserve the gentlemen's agreement between the dynastic parties. The still-recent disaster and the ongoing recuperation campaign provided a temporary adhesive for the centrifugal tendencies that would emerge once the crisis had lost its immediacy. But although the dynastic politicians closed ranks to avoid discussion of the divisive Moroccan problem, critics of the army and the regime made it impossible for the evasion to escape unnoticed. The left was still limited to a negative role, but growing middle-class alienation from the war made it possible for them to establish the principle of popular consent more firmly than ever before.

The Cortes opened as scheduled on October 20, 1921. Maura was under some pressure from La Cierva to suspend the sessions in order to protect the African army from potentially demoralizing criticism, a sentiment shared by the extreme right. *El Debate* editorialized on September 28: "The present [hour] is the hour of action; the hour of the military and not of the orators. . . . All that about the democratic opinion that clamors, and the spirit of liberty that revives, and the liberal Spain that comes out of its lethargy is pure folly, and vulgar to boot."[45] For the right, the Moroccan war, like the social crisis, was a national emergency that was beyond the limited capacity of parliamentary institutions to resolve.

For Maura, however, there had been little choice. For one thing, in spite of the contempt expressed by *El Debate*, public opinion—and not just on the left—was overwhelmingly in favor of parliamentary scrutiny of the causes of the disaster. For another, the left, absent from the cabinet, could not be denied access to the parliament as well. Finally, his cabinet lacked the internal cohesion necessary to govern without legislative support. Like the country itself, the government was divided over the future course of action in the Protectorate. In August all had been agreed that the "honor of the armed forces and national prestige" required the reconquest of the territory around Melilla.[46] But as the African army rapidly advanced toward the Kert River, the cabinet had split. One group, led by La Cierva, argued that the expeditionary forces must be allowed to carry the forward line to its former position preparatory to a total military occupation of the

Protectorate. Anything less would mean loss of the zone, first to Abd el-Krim, then to the French. The other group favored a more limited Spanish presence in Morocco: military occupation of the coast accompanied by a policy of "political attraction" in the interior. This faction included Maura, the Minister of Finance, Francisco Cambó, who was alarmed by the mounting military expenditures in Africa,[47] and the Minister of State, Manuel González Hontoria, a career diplomat long convinced of the necessity of a civil reorientation in the Protectorate. Unable to resolve their differences, the cabinet agreed to postpone their decision until the army reached Dar Drius, Silvestre's starting point in 1920.

Maura's position was difficult. Forced to open the Cortes to deal with the national crisis, he was uncertain of his ability to mobilize a majority to support a concrete plan of action in the Protectorate because of the lack of a consensus within his own cabinet. As a consequence, his inaugural statement on October 20 was deliberately vague, his refusal to specify the government's intentions, absolute.[48] The public, however, was eager for meaningful debate, a mood exploited skilfully by both the extreme left and the left Liberals, who saw an opportunity to build a new parliamentary majority on the "liberal" issue of popular sovereignty. On November 15 Santiago Alba and the Reformist leader Melquíades Álvarez introduced a motion demanding military reform, a "civil" Protectorate, and "responsibilities," a maneuver designed to prove their own liberal credentials as well as to discredit the Conde de Romanones, who had contributed two members to the Maura cabinet.[49] Romanones, who had staked his own claim on these issues since 1919, was forced to endorse the motion to retain his credibility as a liberal. A cabinet crisis was averted only by Maura's refusal to interpret a vote in favor of the motion as a vote of no confidence. The cabinet thus survived, but the incident indicated the extent to which public opinion could be mobilized by the left to drive a wedge between the dynastic parties.

The responsibilities question proved a more reliable cement for the "dynastic interests" than the Moroccan war. From the outset, it was clear that no one in a position of authority would be held to account for the disaster at Anual. Because both Liberals and Conservatives had governed since the appointment of General Berenguer as High Commissioner in 1919, neither party was eager to charge him—and by implication, themselves—with negligence. From this perspective, Berenguer's continuing appointment as Commander-in-Chief of an "army in operations" was providential, for it enabled the dynastic politicians to label adverse comments on his past policies as "seditious." Berenguer's utility to the regime was thus grounded in more than his competence as a colonial officer.

To deflect attention from Berenguer, the government tolerated criticism of the Melilla garrison and of the Juntas de Defensa, one of the few targets that inspired general condemnation.[50] Everyone agreed that the Juntas were the source of the financial and professional constraints that had hampered the effectiveness of the African army, just as they agreed that their political meddling had made efficient government more difficult since 1917. But the majority premise was that the Juntas were an exotic aberration in an otherwise sound system. Only the Socialists and the Republican left argued that the Juntas—and the Moroccan war—were the logical products of a weak and cowardly parliamentary system bullied by an army in league with the king.[51] The left's attempts to attribute the ultimate responsibility to Alfonso were received with exceptional hostility by both Liberals and Conservatives; under the Constitution of 1876, the monarchy was beyond discussion or criticism.

The outstanding figure in these debates was La Cierva, whose antipathy to the responsibilities campaign was both ideological and personal. (Minister of Development in the Allendesalazar government of 1921, La Cierva was a potential defendant in any investigation.) As Minister of War in the fall of 1921, his unwavering policy was to deny all accusations (including those aimed at the Juntas), to admit no criticism, and above all, to protect General Berenguer from the Cortes just as he had protected him from General Picasso. At a time when recognition of past errors might have satisfied much of the nation, La Cierva encouraged the Conservative majority to imitate his belligerent impenitence. As a consequence, they forfeited the responsibilities issue to the Liberals and the left and, somewhat deservedly, acquired a reputation as opponents of parliamentary sovereignty.

The frustration induced by the Conservative evasion of responsibilities turned to outrage when La Cierva read his military promotions bill in the Congress on October 25.[52] Undoubtedly, he would have preferred an executive order, but his own reform law of 1918 had curbed ministerial discretion by requiring legislative approval for all merit promotions. Ironically, La Cierva now found himself the first victim of the law. Undeterred by ironies, however, La Cierva forged ahead, anxious to assure the africanistas in the officer corps of his support. The bill promoted fifteen officers, including General Berenguer, to the next highest rank for merits earned in the western sector prior to the disaster at Anual. In November 1921 most of those recommended were in the expeditionary forces spearheading the advance into the Rif.

At least some of these officers deserved promotion. If the African campaign was to be successful, rewards for outstanding performance in the field were mandatory. But the government found it impossible to overcome the public association of merit promotions with political favoritism, an association the Juntas made haste to encourage. In addition, the Socialists mobilized opinion against the bill by arguing that awarding promotions before assigning responsibilities, particularly in the case of General Berenguer, was an affront to the country and its armed forces.[53] Above all, the promotions represented contempt for the responsibilities investigation then underway in the Cortes.

At La Cierva's insistence, debate on the promotions bill opened in the Cortes on November 30. He had secured the acquiescence of the principal Liberal leaders after he threatened to make it a vote of no confidence.[54] Nevertheless, many Liberal deputies were sensitive to the issues raised by the Socialists. After two days of devastating criticism directed against some of the names on the promotions list by Indalecio Prieto, La Cierva was forced to table the bill.[55] Under some pressure from the africanistas to grant the promotions by decree,[56] La Cierva apparently broached the subject with the cabinet, for on December 20 there were rumors of a crisis over the issue.[57] But La Cierva was unable to defy the nation and the constitution with a decree, as he had in March 1918. Anual had aroused a large segment of the country out of its traditional apathy toward the parliamentary prerogative. On the whole, his efforts to enhance the prestige of the africanistas had backfired. The chances for a restoration of merit promotions in the near future were minimal.

The Ransom of the Prisoners

The failure of the promotions bill was not the only indication that the government was isolated from national opinion. Two other issues—the ransom of the prisoners held by Abd el-Krim and the quota soldiers—acquired increasing importance as the recuperation campaign continued into the winter of 1921–22. On these issues, the government found itself caught between the African army and much of the nation, including the hitherto apathetic middle classes. As the Socialists had been predicting since the 1890s, the middle class developed an interest in military and colonial policy as soon as its own sons were forced to serve. By 1921, however, the army had grown too accustomed to its autonomy to countenance civilian interference readily. Throughout 1922 the growing polarization of the army and the middle class added resonance to the traditional antimilitarism of the left. The beneficiaries of this antagonism were the Liberals and center-left, who from the opposition were able to capitalize on the growing middle-class weariness with the Moroccan campaign.

The ransom issue acquired prominence during the first week in December, immediately after the defeat of the promotions bill. Encouraged by this victory, the left-Liberal coalition seized the opportunity to exploit a highly emotional situation; on December 2 the Reformists introduced a motion in the Cortes to give highest governmental priority to the ransom of the prisoners.[58] La Cierva was able to forestall debate on the grounds that a solution was in progress.[59] But in reality the government was unable to find a way out of its dilemma. Negotiations for the release of the seven hundred men and four hundred women and children at Ajdir had been initiated with Abd el-Krim in August, but the Riffian leader had deliberately set his terms impossibly high: four million pesetas, plus the release of all Moroccan prisoners of war. Quite rightly fearing that the money would buy more arms for the rebellion they were trying to suppress, the government had rejected Abd el-Krim's terms. Another stumbling block was the attitude of the African army, unalterably opposed to any solution but a military one. For this reason, La Cierva had discouraged a number of private initiatives to secure the release of the captives.[60] The difficulty was that there was no realistic hope of mounting a military offensive against the rebels' stronghold at Ajdir. Berenguer, always a realist, thus recommended paying the ransom. In this instance, he was unrepresentative of majority opinion in the African army.[61]

The best the government could hope for was delay, but the well-organized pro-ransom propaganda campaign made temporizing difficult. Passions in the Melilla garrison were running high; on December 1 General Cavalcanti witnessed a pathetic and unnerving demonstration by the wives of the prisoners that made him more impatient than ever with the cautious tactics of Berenguer. In the peninsula, the Reformists and Republicans organized mass meetings in which they stressed that the government's failure to pay the ransom was owing to its bondage to the army.[62] As the political pressure mounted, Abd el-Krim raised his terms to include recognition of the "belligerency" of the Riffian state.[63] Anticolonialist forces on both sides of the Straits were discovering that they might mutually defeat a common enemy.

Unpleasant as the publicity campaign organized by the left might be, paying the ransom represented an even more dangerous alternative for the Maura government. Recognition of Abd el-Krim's belligerency was tantamount to admission of the illegitimacy of the Spanish presence in Morocco; furthermore, the government could not afford to alienate the African army, which was already impatient to avenge its honor by storming Ajdir. On December 15 the government was compelled to remove General Cavalcanti from his post as Commander General of Melilla after he criticized the government's inaction in an interview with *La Correspondencia de España*.[64] In late December La Cierva and Berenguer agreed to utilize the good offices of the Red Cross to reopen negotiations, but Abd el-Krim was too clever to relinquish easily such a useful tool. The ransom of the prisoners continued to nettle the army, outrage the public, and frustrate the government for another year.

The Quota Soldiers

Because it directly affected the middle class, the discharge of the quota soldiers was the issue that did most to inflame Spanish public opinion. By the fall of 1921, newspaper articles, books, and Liberal deputies were providing the Spanish public with lurid descriptions of the wretched life of the Spanish conscript in Africa. Conditions, of course, were no worse than they had ever been; on the contrary, many millions of pesetas had already been spent to improve them. But raising the appallingly low standards was slow work. In the meantime, literate young men were unwilling to suffer in silence.[65] Also attracting unfavorable publicity were the inequalities that had developed as some quota soldiers spent their parents' money on better food, clean sheets and underwear, baths, automobiles, and in a few cases, on wine and entertainment for their officers. Many had used their connections to be placed in safe positions in the garrison towns. As might have been expected, their presence demoralized the other troops and their self-assurance bordering on insolence was bad for discipline.[66] By January 1922 Berenguer looked forward to their release as soon as there were experienced conscripts to replace them.[67] Since these were not available, however, the quota soldiers remained in Africa.

Berenguer was not alone in desiring their discharge. The patriotic fervor that had sent the troops off in August to save their country had drained away by late December when the army crossed the Kert River, marking the end of the first stage of the campaign. Many middle-class

Spaniards who had supported the reconquest now believed it was time to halt operations and send the quota soldiers home. This sentiment was skilfully exploited by the bourgeois left, who pointed out the "injustice" of retaining the quota soldiers of 1919, who had paid for their redemption in good faith, long after regular and quota conscripts of later call-ups in the peninsula had been discharged. The leader of this campaign was *El Liberal*, which had lost its enthusiasm for the Moroccan war during the fall of 1921. Increasingly radical in its demands for a democratization of Spanish public life, including the abandonment of the Protectorate, *El Liberal* used the quota soldiers to turn middle-class opinion against the war and the civilian and military oligarchies that sustained it. By April 1922 the issue was so popular that even the conservative *ABC* had joined the chorus demanding repatriation.[68]

The release of the quota soldiers was a purely middle-class demand, as the government quickly perceived. Since it could not repatriate the soldiers, it took refuge behind the argument that democracy and social justice required that all classes serve equally, without regard for quota payments, a position that for once earned it the applause of the Socialists. In addition, La Cierva continued to appropriate funds to improve conditions in the eastern sector, especially in the hospitals. But so long as the quota soldiers remained in Africa, the government could not restore the middle-class indifference that had made possible the prosecution of the Moroccan war in the past.

The Constitutional Crisis of January 1922

The growing gulf between the Maura government and public opinion did not necessarily imply a strengthening of its ties with the army. On the contrary, the factionalism in the officer corps, aggravated since the disaster, made it impossible for the government to devise policies satisfactory to all parties, with the result that military quarrels never entirely receded from public view. Moreover, after an autumn of continuous criticism in the Cortes, military tempers were short-fused. In January 1922 these tensions erupted during a confrontation between La Cierva and the Juntas. The episode soon became a constitutional crisis, a contest of wills between the cosovereigns of the Spanish state, the king and the parliament. Although Alfonso was ultimately forced to capitulate, it was the intervention of the africanistas, rather than the inherent strength of the government, that decided the outcome. The resolution of the crisis was thus not a victory for the principle of civil supremacy, but an illustration of the way in which military disunity could easily be translated into praetorianism.

The crisis grew out of the quarrel between La Cierva, Berenguer, and the Advisory Commissions, which had intensified after the dismissal of General Cavalcanti as Commander General of Melilla in mid-December. Cavalcanti's replacement, Brigadier General José Sanjurjo, was chosen because of his close identification with Berenguer and his colonial policies. But as Berenguer had feared,[69] the appointment of a brigadier offended the senior officers in the garrison.[70] When the Infantry Directory sent a reconnaissance committee to Melilla, it found considerable resentment against La Cierva and against the elitism of the shock units imported from the Jibala by Berenguer.[71] There was also evidence of disaffection in the Madrid garrison. During the first week in January, General Weyler resigned as chief of the General Staff with a flourish, citing as the reasons for his decision Berenguer's incompetence and La Cierva's disregard for his own advice. Enjoying the limelight enormously, the eighty-three-year-old veteran of the Carlist and Cuban wars assured the public that he could have saved the men at Monte Arruit "at the head of four or six thousand horses."[72] Weyler's military tactics had been out-of-date for fifty years, but the resignation gave the many enemies of La Cierva and General Berenguer an opportunity to parade their discontent. For two days officers expressed their solidarity by the traditional presentation of calling cards at Weyler's residence, while La Cierva searched fruitlessly for a general willing to replace him. Just as rumors of a crisis began to circulate, Lieutenant General Luis Aizpuru was persuaded by the king to accept the post.

The Infantry Directory seized the moment to attack, its confidence bolstered by contacts with the Military Governor, General Burguete, and with an aide of the king, who was undoubtedly worried by the extensive political alienation in the officer corps. On January 6 the Directory demanded the resignation of the War Minister through official channels.[73] La Cierva responded by threatening the Infantry Junta with dissolution in the presence of all the Advisory Commission presidents and the principal military officials in the Madrid garrison. Somewhat intimidated, the Junta leaders returned to the Ministry three days later with promises to refrain from political intrigue.[74] But by now, La Cierva was determined to pursue his advantage. Quite unexpectedly, he produced an order depriving the Advisory Commissions of their autonomy by integrating them officially into the War Ministry. Henceforth, their offices would be located in the Palace of Buenavista, their presidents selected by the War Minister, and their expenses met out of government funds. Presidents of the regimental Juntas would be selected by local commanding officers.[75] When the Junta presidents stormed out of La Cierva's office in protest, the War Minister put the order in the form of a decree and took it to the palace for the king's signature on January 11.

The king refused to sign the decree, thus opening a constitutional crisis that exposed the fragile underpinnings of the parliamentary regime. Alfonso's concern was for his throne. Since the opening of the Cortes in October, the parliament had become a forum for the opponents of the monarchy. The dynastic parties seemed unable to quell the criticism or to convince the nation to support a forward policy in Morocco. The best defense seemed to lie with the army; the army, however, was badly divided. Throughout the fall and winter, Alfonso had openly courted the africanistas, while trying to assign the blame for Anual to the politicians. Now, in an effort to appease the enraged junteros, he decided to defy La Cierva.[76] Maura presented the resignation of the government the same day.[77]

Both Liberals and Conservatives agreed that the formation of a new government should be contingent upon the signing of the decree, in order to give the country, as José Sánchez Guerra put it, "the impression of the dignity of the public Power."[78] Since no government was formed, it was clear that the king was still unwilling to sign the decree, although the dynastic parties did their best to minimize the king's role in the crisis in their interviews with the press. Almost overnight, public hostility shifted from La Cierva to the Juntas and the king. On the evening of January 12, Young Maurists were heard shouting "frankly antidynastic" slogans in front of the military casino.

The intensity of the crisis shattered the military unity that had been forged by Weyler's resignation and La Cierva's bravado performance on January 10. As in 1917, the technical corps proved more attached to military discipline than the Infantry Corps; by the evening of the eleventh, they had decided to avoid a confrontation. Two days later, the Advisory Commissions of the Artillery, Engineers, Staff, and Quartermaster Corps all signed formal notes of submission to the War Minister.[79] The Advisory Commissions of the Infantry, Cavalry, and Medical Corps, however, refused to back down, continuing their campaign against La Cierva from the pages of La Correspondencia Militar. Accused in the liberal and left press of interference in civilian politics, they replied unblushingly that "the Fatherland ought to be grateful to the Juntas" for having rid it of bad government in the past.[80] Apparently, they were still receiving encouragement from Alfonso. As the other Juntas announced their submission, the Infantry Junta proclaimed its intention to resist the government while awaiting justice from the king.[81] Unmistakably, both Alfonso and the Infantry Junta were convinced that they, and not the government or the parliamentary regime, represented the national will.

The stalemate was resolved when it became clear that Alfonso and the Juntas could not count on unanimous support in the officer corps. Generals Burguete and Primo de Rivera, no friends of La Cierva, had nonetheless prudently pledged their support to the government.[82] More decisive, however, was a telegram of support for the Maura government signed by all the units in the Melilla garrison, which appeared in the conservative daily, *ABC*, on January 14. Juntero-africanista rivalries had proven more intense than monarchical loyalty and had deprived Alfonso of the support of the most prestigious part of the Spanish army.

Although the telegram suggested unanimous support for Maura and La Cierva, in fact, the Melilla garrison was as divided as the army as a whole between junteros—the former clientele of General Silvestre—and africanistas—the officers in the elite units from the Jibala. The animosity between the two factions was dramatized during the January crisis by a personal confrontation between the Commander General, Sanjurjo, and Colonel José Riquelme, the head of the Office of Native Affairs and, as the ranking colonel in the garrison, the president of the local Infantry Junta. At the height of the government crisis, africanistas in the vanguard column stationed across the Kert at Dar Drius agreed to send the telegram of solidarity to the Maura government signed with the names of their battalions. The dissident junteros among them sent word to Colonel Riquelme, who as president of the Infantry Junta refused to approve transmission of the telegram without the unanimous agreement of all the Infantry officers in the garrison, many of whom were still loyal to the Junta. After a bitter confrontation between Riquelme and Sanjurjo, whose professional sympathies lay with the africanistas and La Cierva, the Commander General asserted his authority and approved transmission of the telegram.[83]

The telegram, by exposing the divisions within the officer corps, also exposed the difficulty of building a political base in "the army"; on the fifteenth, Alfonso was forced to retreat. With as little grace as possible, the three recalcitrant Juntas submitted as well, "so as not to appear . . . as the only rebellious and seditious element . . . in opposition to the public Power. . . ."[84] On January 16 the king signed La Cierva's decree limiting the autonomy of the Advisory Commissions, and Maura returned to office. Although the constitutional crisis had been resolved in favor of the principle of civil supremacy, it was obvious that this had been owing not to the government's strength but rather to the lack of unanimity in the officer corps. Indeed, it was the political frailty of the cabinet that encouraged factionalism in the army. When in 1923 a new cabinet would begin to govern with purpose and authority, the officer corps would close ranks in self-defense.

The Fall of the Government

Although the January crisis enabled the Maura government to display its solidarity, in reality it was near collapse. The unity of the cabinet had always depended on the existence of an external threat—Abd el-Krim, the responsibilities campaign, the Juntas—and on the opportunity to avoid the issues that would pull it apart. On January 10, 1922, the vanguard units of the expeditionary army had reached Dar Drius across the Kert, forcing the cabinet to formulate the long-range Protectorate policy it had postponed for so many months. Within a month the cabinet had fallen.

If anything, disagreement within the government was even more severe in January than it had been in August. Since then the War Ministry had spent nearly half a billion pesetas on the Moroccan campaign; 160,000 troops, including several thousand quota soldiers, were indefinitely stationed in the zone. Although most of the fighting had been entrusted to the Regulars and the Tercio, public opinion was increasingly anxious for repatriation and an end to the military operations, a view shared by Cambó, González Hontoria, and Maura himself. In their opinion, total military occupation of the Protectorate was beyond the financial resources of the nation and of dubious value as a mode of pacification and control. La Cierva, on the other hand, still supported Berenguer's contention that a Spanish retreat to the coast would create a vacuum that would quickly be filled by the French. With the army back at Dar Drius, it should now retrace the route of General Silvestre in 1920–21 toward Alhucemas Bay in the heart of the Protectorate.[85]

The conflict grew out of opposing perceptions of the political significance of the Moroccan Protectorate, both internationally and domestically. The dilemma for Maura and his allies lay in their ambivalent attitude toward the Protectorate, since they wished neither to relinquish it nor to bear the burdens of its expense. For Maura and González Hontoria, Spain's interest in Morocco was largely strategic; a massive military commitment was not only unnecessary, but potentially dangerous for the stability of the regime. Cambó was even less enthusiastic, viewing the Protectorate as little more than a "counter" in international diplomacy. If the funds wasted on military expenditures could not be diverted to meet domestic needs, Spain would forfeit the chance for peaceful economic and political modernization. All three understood that by allowing the army to have its way in Morocco, they were alienating the regime further from the country and increasing its dependence on the military. Yet a radical alteration of colonial policy was possible only if the government made an appeal for popular support, in defiance of the army, a measure that neither Maura nor Cambó was willing to contemplate. For La Cierva, at least there was no ambivalence: anything short of total military victory in Morocco represented dishonor abroad and a fatal concession to the forces of subversion at home.

Still hoping to reconcile the differences, Maura summoned Berenguer to a meeting with La Cierva, González Hontoria, and high-ranking military officials during the first week in February.[86] The conference was held at a private estate in Pizarra, in the province of Malaga, out of the glare of publicity. But the cabinet's differences could not be resolved. In order to present a united front to the nation, a temporary compromise was reached: at Berenguer's insistence, both the Jibala and the eastern half of the Rif would be pacified militarily, but the army would not continue its overland march to Alhucemas Bay. Instead, the government agreed on an amphibious assault to be undertaken at an unspecified date in the future.[87]

The compromise solution satisfied few in the country, which by now was polarizing between those who favored abandonment of the Protectorate and the repatriation of troops and those who supported complete occupation by the army. It is arguable that the compromise desperately adopted by the government was the least desirable of the available alternatives. Because the army was badly divided, it probably could not have offered an effective protest if military operations were discontinued, a measure that would have been extremely popular among large sections of the middle and lower classes. On the other hand, extensive financial and moral support for the campaign would probably have insured its success, a fait accompli that a majority of the nation would have accepted. The hesitant, halfway solution chosen by Maura satisfied no one, the Protectorate was neither relinquished nor controlled, and the opportunity to restore some vitality to the moribund Conservative party was lost.

Exactly a month separated the Pizarra Conference from the cabinet crisis of March 7, 1922, a month characterized by the rapid degeneration of the unity so carefully preserved for the previous six months.

Once it became clear that the left and center-left would not accept the compromise on Moroccan policy proposed by the government, the coalition was doomed. Deprived of the popular support that had made possible the cooperative effort since August, the members of the cabinet followed the polarizing nation in search of clients. Henceforth, the Conservatives would claim as their natural constituency all those—including the army—who favored continuation of the war and, by extension, who opposed any significant alteration of the political status quo. The Liberals, on the other hand, were obliged to court the left in order to broaden the base of their party. For this reason, the cabinet did not fall over the issue of Morocco but over the restoration of constitutional guarantees, which had been suspended since March 24, 1919.

Other tensions had already weakened the cabinet. The constitutional crisis provoked by the king and the army in January, although resolved in the government's favor, had nonetheless exposed the limitations on parliamentary sovereignty in the Constitution of 1876. For the Liberals and Cambó, close identification with the discredited political system was the equivalent of political suicide. After the signing of a tariff highly protective of Catalonia's failing textile industry on February 13, Cambó had begun to disengage from the government. At the same time, the tariff aroused the indignation of agrarian and mercantile interests, as well as of the working-class parties, against the cabinet as a whole. Added to the continuing hostility of the Infantry Junta toward La Cierva and the mounting tension over the war, these issues made it unlikely that the cabinet could withstand any concerted assault on its integrity.

The suspended constitutional guarantees provided the issue around which all the political enemies of the cabinet could unite. On February 19 Socialists in the Casa del Pueblo and Reformists in the increasingly radical Ateneo inaugurated a propaganda campaign that elicited a wider response than would have been possible before the disaster at Anual.[88] In the past, the suspension of civil liberties had affected primarily the working classes; Martínez Anido had used his freedom from constitutional restraints very effectively in the past year, with the approval of much of the Catalan middle class. But as the quota soldiers continued in Africa, the middle class found itself victimized by what it considered arbitrary government power and overnight discovered a passion for democracy and the rule of law.

The leftward shift in the nation complicated the power struggle for leadership within the Liberal party. The need for an opening to the left had been foreseen not only by Santiago Alba, who had negotiated an alliance with the Reformists, but also by Romanones, who still entertained hopes of reestablishing his control over the party. Two days after the Cortes opened on March 1, 1922, Romanones interpellated the government on the issue of constitutional guarantees.[89] If he had hoped for a positive response from Maura, he was soon disabused; Maura insisted that guarantees could not be restored unless the government were provided with extraordinary powers to deal with the enemies of social order. True to his traditional belief in the moral superiority of authoritarian rule by a government of elites, Maura argued that the real danger to freedom came not from the government but from the "excesses" of private citizens, and accused Romanones of duplicating the Liberal betrayal of 1909.[90] With the Socialists demanding that the Liberals prove their "liberalism,"[91] Romanones's representatives in the cabinet had no choice but to resign. Departing the chamber, Romanones remarked, "There is no doubt that the question proves to be most decorous for all."[92] The debate on the guarantees had allowed his faction to withdraw from the Maura coalition on a question of principle while he posed as the champion of civil liberties. At the same time, the crisis had forestalled an airing of the incompatibilities within the cabinet on the Moroccan war, which he still supported. The fall of the Maura coalition meant that the fictional consensus on the war might possibly be preserved a little longer.

What could no longer be preserved was the fiction of an elite consensus superior to party interests. Maura, Romanones, and even Cambó had cherished this idea since the collapse of the turno in 1917; the failure of the Maura government of 1921 put an end to their illusion that the common interests and values that had given strength to the old turno still endured. The defeat at Anual had exposed the weakness in the old system; public opinion now demanded an accounting for past errors and political reform to prevent their recurrence. Perhaps for the first time, meaningful parliamentary government was a possibility. To make it a reality, the dynastic parties had to abandon their reliance on the army in favor of a party system that reflected the political and social evolution of postwar Spain.

CHAPTER TEN

Junteros, Africanistas, and Responsibilities

The Restoration system had functioned so long as there was little need for strong government in Spain. Popular apathy, an elite consensus, and military quiescence had enabled the turno parties to define their differences in purely personalistic terms, frequently without regard for public opinion or the national interest. But economic expansion and social mobilization since 1914, together with the failure of the Spanish army in Morocco, had transformed the Spanish political environment. As the fall of the Maura government in March 1922 made clear, a growing number of Spaniards now found the traditional immobility of the dynastic parties intolerable. If those parties—and the parliamentary monarchy—were to survive, they must meet the challenge of the parliamentary Socialists, who viewed the Moroccan war as the occasion to build a new majority in favor of political and social reform. Until the experiment was cut short by the pronunciamiento of September 1923, first the Conservatives and then the Liberals would attempt to render the regime more responsive to public opinion.

Although Romanones had defected from the Maura coalition in hopes of returning to power at the head of a reunited Liberal party, his ambitions quickly proved to be unrealistic. Not only was Santiago Alba bent on excluding him from the Liberal coalition, but the king was also unwilling to transfer power to the Liberals, whose alliance with the Reformists he distrusted as a potential threat to the military campaign in Morocco and possibly, to the Crown itself. Moreover, with his well-publicized defiance of the Maura government only two months behind him, Alfonso was unwilling to risk new elections to the Cortes. Accordingly, he appointed José Sánchez Guerra, the leader of the Conservative majority in the Cortes since January 1922, who formed a cabinet on March 8 that included Maurist and Lliga representatives.[1]

For the Conservatives in 1922 there were two alternatives: they could emphasize their conservatism by adopting an intransigent posture on the issues of the war and "responsibilities," or they could attempt to expand their power base at the expense of the Liberals by responding more positively to the leftward shift in national opinion. Sánchez Guerra chose the second alternative, a choice signaled by his unilateral decision on March 30 to restore constitutional guarantees throughout Spain. Significantly, this decision immediately destroyed the Conservative coalition. On March 31 the Maurist César Silió and the regionalist José Bertrán y Musitú resigned to protest both the decree and its implications for the future. Undaunted, Sánchez Guerra persevered in his search for a new political equilibrium for the regime. During his nine-month tenure of office, he endeavored to make the Cortes, the administration, and the dynastic parties more responsive to public opinion and less dependent on the army. By late 1922 his success had alarmed the Liberals, who querulously demanded that "if we are to be governed liberally, let the Liberals govern."[2]

Nevertheless, by December 1922 Sánchez Guerra had to admit defeat. His attempt to make the system more responsive without altering its fundamental structure was a failure: it had split his party, alienated a segment of the army, and forced the regime into a discussion of responsibilities that it ultimately could not master. The problem was that in a rapidly polarizing political environment, the center could not hold. Sánchez Guerra was unwilling to give in to the inflexible Conservatives on his right, but unable to foresee or accept all the consequences of his tentative steps toward the left. In the end, the Conservatives reverted to defense of the old system, a decision that brought the Liberals to power.

During 1922 the political influence of the military continued to grow. More factionalized than ever by Sánchez Guerra's sporadic attempts to provide a new orientation for civil-military relations in Africa and in the peninsula, the army still lacked the unity to impose specific programs on the government. But because of their precarious situation, the Conservatives succumbed to the pressures imposed first by one military faction, then by another. The vulnerability of the government was exacerbated by the tendency of civilians on both the left and the right to transform the professional quarrels of junteros and africanistas into symbols of the political debate within the country as a whole. As military issues became even more politicized, it was impossible to conduct a discussion of military reform or Moroccan policy without introducing larger questions involving the basic foundations of the regime. At the same time, the resolution of minor military disputes became the chief preoccupation of the government, distracting it from more urgent political reform. This confounding of political and military issues—the inheritance of the long years of political reliance on the army—made the army the key to the political situation, despite a growing realization on the part of civilian politicians that civil supremacy was the necessary first step toward political and military reform. The confusion was not limited to civilians. In 1923 the army, acting to preserve its professional interests, would believe itself compelled to assume control over the political affairs of the nation.

The Moroccan Campaign

The ambiguities of the path chosen by Sánchez Guerra in 1922 were best illustrated by his approach to the most critical issue facing the government—the Moroccan war. Although the homogeneity of his cabinet spared him the fate of his predecessor Maura, it could not help him close the unbridgeable gap between his desire to respond to public opinion and his party's commitment to military intervention in North Africa. The traditional policy of compromise and vacillation, useful while public opinion remained indifferent to Moroccan affairs, was inadequate to neutralize the rapidly polarizing forces in the peninsula and the Protectorate. On the one hand, an energetic policy seemed necessary to offset Abd el-Krim's escalating offensive; on February 1 the rebel leader had declared the independence of his "Emirate of the Rif" and a month later had initiated heavy shelling of Spanish fortresses in the central Rif. On the other hand, public opinion was eager for a halt in operations. Freed from the self-imposed restraints of the early months of the reconquest, the Liberals freely exploited the extensive middle-class disaffection over the war, demanding the repatriation of the quota soldiers and somewhat hypocritically urging a rapid resolution of the campaign.[3]

As the enormous cost of effective pacification became apparent, public alienation increased. In response, Sánchez Guerra decided to modify the policy formulated at the Pizarra Conference by Maura and summoned General Berenguer to Madrid in late March. During their talks, Berenguer and the government agreed to return to the three-stage plan of operations devised by Berenguer before Anual in order to facilitate budget cuts and a partial reduction in troop strength.[4] Somewhat naively, they hoped that this would also restore the pre-Anual apathy in the nation. But a return to the past was impossible. The staggered plan of operations was feasible only if the Rif were quiescent, as it had been in 1919–20. In the month following his conference with Sánchez Guerra, Berenguer was able to mount a successful campaign in the west by concentrating his forces and utilizing his best officers— Sanjurjo, González-Tablas, Emilio Mola, and Alberto Casto Girona— against al-Raysuni's mountain stronghold at Tazrut, forcing the sharif to flee to the Ghumara for safety in mid-May. But in the east, the line—dangerously exposed and immobile in violation of Berenguer's own theories—was harassed mercilessly by the haraka of Abd el-Krim. The frequent casualty reports alarmed the public and infuriated the army, both of whom thus remained unsatisfied by Sánchez Guerra's attempt at compromise. Furthermore, the prolongation of the campaign made it impossible for the government or Berenguer to promise an early end to the war. For everyone with a son or husband in Africa, total abandonment of the Protectorate became the only guarantee of early repatriation.

Furthermore, public opinion in 1922 would no longer accept the secrecy that had characterized the conduct of the war prior to Anual. Understandably, neither Berenguer nor Sánchez Guerra was eager to publicize the details of their policy discussions for fear of alerting the enemy. Nor were they accustomed to the incessant public debate on Morocco. On April 22 Berenguer threatened journalists who dared to criticize the conduct of operations with the Law of Jurisdictions.[5] Neither the Conservatives nor the army could appreciate the left's increasingly successful efforts to present the war as a violation of popular sovereignty.

Junteros and Africanistas

Throughout 1922 public opinion continued to be distracted by the ongoing quarrel between junteros and africanistas. The problem facing the government was the same as it had been since 1918: how to reward service in Africa without alienating the large bureaucratic faction in the officer corps. The dilemma was complicated by the tendency of nearly all groups in Spain to make political capital out of purely professional disputes. Public controversy over military factionalism usually resulted in political opponents' choosing sides. Consequently, the political leverage of both military factions increased even further.

Upon assuming office on March 8, Sánchez Guerra had inherited a difficult situation. Since January there had been two Infantry Juntas: the domesticated Advisory Commission in Madrid created by the decree of January 16, whose president—Colonel Godofredo Nouvilas Aldaz—

had served in Barcelona prior to his appointment, and the old organization, which continued to operate independently in Barcelona in clear defiance of the decree, under the leadership of Colonel Fernando Berenguer, a brother of the High Commissioner who did not share his africanismo. As usual, Barcelona remained the focus of juntero activity, not least because most appointments in the Madrid garrison were given, at the king's insistence, to africanistas. To alleviate the tension, Sánchez Guerra had chosen the Captain General of Barcelona, General José Olaguer-Feliú, as Minister of War, and had appointed General Primo de Rivera to fill the vacancy in Catalonia. Both were markedly pro-juntero and antiafricanista.

Two days after taking office, Olaguer had to deal with a confrontation between the new, official Infantry Commission and the old one, both of which had called general assemblies in Madrid on March 10. To avoid a public quarrel, Olaguer engineered a joint session between the two antagonists, a tactic that achieved the result he desired—the fusion of the two organizations under the leadership of Colonel Nouvilas. With this maneuver, a potentially fatal breach in the juntero movement was averted, and the intent of the January 16 decree was subverted.

Having overcome their jurisdictional dispute, the delegates at the assembly were able to focus their energies on a common enemy—the africanistas. The accords adopted at the end of the twelve-day session reaffirmed their opposition to all merit promotions—earned or unearned. To enforce this principle, the junteros also reaffirmed its corollary—compulsory unionization. Refusal to renounce any merit promotion awarded after April 30, 1921, meant violation of the juntero oath, punishable by expulsion from the Corps. In compensation, the Junta proposed the concession of nonremunerative decorations for those performing "extraordinary services" for the nation. In addition, the assembly urged the prosecution in honor courts of all military responsibilities, even though "such a severe criterion is not applied in other social sectors or in more elevated ranks of the military hierarchy." Finally, the delegates claimed a more active supervisory role for the Advisory Commission, especially with regard to academy training and the professional journal.[6]

The accords revealed that the grievances that had given rise to the Juntas de Defensa in 1917 still festered. Alfonso's vigorous exercise of his constitutional prerogatives as head of the armed forces was the catalyst for the juntero protest, although africanistas had partially replaced the old military elites as objects of royal and ministerial favoritism. But the root causes of professional syndicalism in the officer corps lay in the structure of the Spanish army and in its relationship to the political system. So long as the officer corps remained top-heavy and underemployed, opposition to selective promotions, however impartial or professionally justifiable, would continue. And so long as the civilian politicians and the king continued to rely on the army instead of on public opinion, the sizable bureaucratic faction represented by the Infantry Junta would be an effective pressure group.

Predictably, the africanistas retaliated shortly afterwards by publicly resigning from the Infantry Junta. On April 15 officers in the vanguard shock units stationed at Dar Drius collectively resigned from the local Infantry Junta, rejecting "any intervention of the Advisory Commissions that is not authorized by the royal decree of last January 16." The decision was communicated to the president of the local Junta by the head of the Tercio units, Lieutenant Colonel Franco, in a letter charged with indignation.[7] Similar letters from two longtime adversaries of the Junta, Colonels Millán-Astray of the Tercio and Manuel González Carrasco of the Regulars, appeared the second week in May, followed by one from the Regulars stationed at Xauen, whose leader, the brilliant young diplomado González-Tablas, had died in the assault on Tazrut May 13. Simultaneously, the Regulars circulated a letter in the Infantry Corps urging unity, professional renovation, and the elimination of the Junta, "whose baneful action uselessly disrupts the life of the nation."[8] The most striking characteristic of all these letters, which were widely reproduced in the press, was their tone, combining the self-pity of the martyr with the outrage and moral condescension of the crusader. Like their rivals the junteros, the africanistas were beginning to see themselves as both symbols and saviors of the nation.

Although the three hundred africanistas who resigned from the Infantry Junta in 1922 represented only a small fraction of the ninety-three hundred officers in the Corps, their political leverage was disproportionately large because they commanded extensive popular support. The africanistas profited from their role as victims of juntero vindictiveness; they had also previously earned the nation's respect by devoting themselves to professional rather than political goals. In appreciation of this, Sánchez Guerra had already decided to resuscitate La Cierva's ill-fated promotions bill even before the latest juntero-africanista conflict became public. By eliminating the controversial promotions of Generals Berenguer and Barrera, two officers who had held high commands both before and after Anual, Sánchez Guerra hoped to separate the promotions bill from the still-unresolved issue of responsibilities. In a private meeting with the Socialist and Reformist leaders, Indalecio Prieto and Augusto Barcia, on April 4,[9] Sánchez Guerra obtained a promise of their cooperation.

Prieto and Barcia were forced to reconsider their promise when General Picasso submitted his completed report on military responsibilities to the government on April 18. Although Sánchez Guerra agreed to submit the Picasso report to a parliamentary committee once it had been reviewed by the Supreme Military Council,[10] the left decided to try to block the promotions bill until after the arrival of the Picasso report in the Cortes in order to drive home the principle of popular sovereignty.[11]

The promotions bill passed easily on May 12, however, both because of the current furor over the africanista resignations and because of the rapid advance by Berenguer's forces in the Jibala.[12] The deputies even added an extra name to the list—Colonel Alberto Castro Girona, a talented africanista who had played a leading role in the capture of Xauen in 1920. Fired by a desire to rebuke the Infantry Junta, both the Congress and the Senate ignored Prieto's arguments in favor of placing responsibilities before rewards, even though the same arguments had been persuasive six months before. No time was spent establishing a set of criteria for promotions; Prieto's efforts to evaluate the merits of each case were dismissed as sectarian protest. On June 6, 1922, the bill became law.

This was the first time the Cortes had exercised its promotion powers since the passage of the Law of 1918. The conduct of both left and right seemed to vindicate the critics, like General Luque, who had always argued that legislative approval was no guarantee of objectivity. During the debates in the Senate, Luque had once again insisted on returning the power to award merit promotions to the War Ministry, meeting the objections against favoritism with the contention that the seniority principle was worse. In Luque's view of the world, patronage was normal, even divinely sanctioned—as he observed in the Senate, did not men pray for favors to the Virgin and the Saints?[13] Even those who did not embrace Luque's somewhat cynical view of the prerogatives of power were tempted to agree that promotions were technical matters best determined within the War Ministry. On June 21 the government presented a bill restoring merit promotions to the executive branch.[14] Although the Socialists opposed the bill in order "to exalt the parliamentary function,"[15] the Conservative majority saw only that parliamentary debate had put meritorious africanistas at the mercy of left-wing politicians. On July 20, 1922, the bill passed the Congress and was signed into law.

Taking advantage of the sympathy for the africanistas, Indalecio Prieto introduced a motion in the Congress on June 14 to reinstate the ESG students expelled from the army by the Infantry Junta in December

1919.[16] Three hundred africanistas had recently committed the same "crime" as the students by publicly resigning from the Junta, without suffering the same consequences. As a result, the government could not oppose the motion without mortally offending the africanistas and public opinion as well. Bowing to the inevitable, Sánchez Guerra agreed to reopen the case of the students if the left would settle for a judicial, rather than a parliamentary, solution to the conflict. After Prieto withdrew the motion, the prime minister ordered the civil Supreme Court to consider the appeals of the students, whose number had been reduced to twenty-two by the untimely death of the source of the whole conflict, Ramón Martínez de Aragón. On July 9, 1922, the court declared its competence over the case, and arguments began.[17] Foreseeing the outcome of the trial, the Infantry Directory and General Olaguer asked Sánchez Guerra to seek a delay while the Junta polled its members on reinstatement. But the prime minister refused, conscious of the interest the case had aroused in the press. On July 11 the Supreme Court reached its verdict in favor of the students. The next day, the Infantry Junta predictably announced that its poll was also favorable to the students. Nearly one-third of the junteros, clustered in Barcelona, Saragossa, and La Coruña, had voted against reinstatement, however, a sign that the strongholds of juntero opinion were still unrepentant.[18] To placate them, Sánchez Guerra denied the reinstated students their rightful seniority in the War College, thereby implicitly sanctioning the juntero vendetta against the Staff Corps. On August 1 one of the former students, José Luis Coello de Portugal, resigned from the army in disgust.[19]

The resolution of the ESG affair was typical of Sánchez Guerra's general military policy in the spring and summer of 1922. By joining the assault on the Juntas, he earned a small measure of popularity for the government. But the prime minister's assertion of civil supremacy owed less to conviction than to pressure from the left; he acted only because he could count on support among the africanista faction of the officer corps. Furthermore, the attack on the Juntas, like the promotion of the africanistas, did not grow out of a conscientious analysis of military policy. Both Sánchez Guerra and his critics were motivated exclusively by political considerations. As a result, the structural causes of praetorianism remained. Throughout 1922 the military factions continued to quarrel publicly, creating issues around which public opinion could coalesce.

The most serious consequence of these small, and generally fruitless, confrontations with the Infantry Junta was that they distracted national attention from the government's indisposition to encourage parliamentary debate on public policy, particularly with regard to Morocco. In June 1922 Sánchez Guerra took advantage of the smoke screen provided by the Juntas to push the new budget through the Cortes. The Maura coalition had collapsed during the budget discussions on Morocco the previous winter. As Santiago Alba argued, the budget was "the numerical expression of a criterion that must be previously established by the Parliament";[20] no funds should be appropriated before the government's domestic and foreign policy had been discussed and ratified. But neither the dissidents in the dynastic parties, like Alba, González Hontoria, and Cambó, nor the deputies on the left were able to arouse the Congress into a serious debate on the proposed figures, which included War Ministry expenditures in the peninsula and Africa totaling nearly eight hundred million pesetas.[21] Instead, most political energy was expended on rejecting the tax reforms that were to provide the revenue to pay for the inflated expenditures. By July 5 the entire budget had been approved after minimal debate in the Congress and even less in the country at large. Until the public could be persuaded that fiscal reform and legislative responsibility were the foundations of democratic government, the Spanish political system would remain defective.

The Indictment of General Berenguer

Although Sánchez Guerra profited from popular apathy over the budget, he would not be so lucky on the issue of military and political responsibilities for Anual. The link between the budget and the unpopular Moroccan war was difficult for a nation unfamiliar with responsible government to perceive; the link between the responsibilities question and the war was unmistakable. The government's attempt to steer a middle course between the two poles of public opinion was a dramatic failure that exacerbated the military situation in Morocco and discredited parliamentary government even further. After five months of reacting thoughtlessly to the divisions in the country and the army, the government would collapse.

The responsibilities issue, carefully left dormant by Sánchez Guerra, was brusquely resuscitated on July 6, 1922, when the Supreme Military Council, after a three-month review of the Picasso report, handed down thirty-nine indictments for negligence or dereliction of duty at Anual, including an indictment of General Berenguer, the High Commissioner and Commander-in-Chief of the African army. A condemnation of Berenguer's policies was implicit in the report submitted by General Picasso on April 18, notwithstanding the circumscription of his investigation by La Cierva in August 1921; indeed, an ill-disguised resentment against La Cierva and the obstacles Picasso had encountered during the investigation permeated the entire document.[22] Without directly accusing Berenguer or his civilian supporters, Picasso condemned the war of positions, the halfhearted governmental support for the war, and the low morale and careless disregard for the security of the zone that had characterized the Melilla Command under General Silvestre. Picasso leveled no specific charges against Silvestre, in part because Silvestre's personal papers had apparently disappeared immediately after his death. For this reason, none of the telegrams the king had supposedly sent to Silvestre before the disaster was ever discovered. The only specific indictments in Picasso's report were against thirty-seven lower-ranking officers for dereliction of duty during the retreat.

The Supreme Military Council, however, acted on the unstated implications of Picasso's report. Denying the legality of La Cierva's efforts to protect Berenguer from Picasso's investigation, the military prosecutor concluded that Berenguer was primarily responsible for Silvestre's mismanagement of the Melilla sector in 1920–21, an accusation of negligence that was in some measure justifiable.[23] But the prosecutor went on to charge Berenguer with responsibility for every defect in the African army, including those that were the result of long-standing government policy, such as the limited use of European troops or the absence of uniform academy training for officers. Significantly, the prosecutor rejected as a "new and lamentable error" the testimony of Lieutenant Colonel Miguel Núñez de Prado of the Regulars, who had blamed the absence of merit promotions for the decline in morale in the zone. For "emitting an opinion contrary to the Legislation on merit promotions,"[24] the Supreme Military Council had added Núñez de Prado's name to the list of thirty-nine accused officers, which also included Generals Silvestre (whose body had never been recovered) and Navarro (still a prisoner at Ajdir).[25] The prosecutor had reportedly also wanted to indict the Vizconde de Eza and La Cierva, the War Ministers who had supported General Berenguer as High Commissioner in 1921–22, but the Council had reluctantly voted against asserting its jurisdiction over civilians.[26]

The Supreme Military Council's list of charges was vindictive and unjust. The public had expected the military to close ranks in the face of civilian demands for high-ranking military responsibilities. Instead, the highest military tribunal had taken the initiative against the General-in-Chief who had been protected from the consequences of the Anual disaster by the civilian politicians in the dynastic parties. The answer to this paradox lay in the incalculable depths of the military factionalism that had paralyzed both civilian government and military reform for decades. The nine-member Council was almost unanimously out of sympathy with Berenguer and his policies; it included several mediocre senior generals isolated from the Moroccan campaign and resentful of Berenguer's meteoric career; a former War Minister, General Santiago, who was doubtless eager to divert attention from ministerial responsibilities; a former rival in Africa, General Domingo Arraiz; Picasso himself; and most important, the head of the Council, General Francisco Aguilera, an ambitious political general whose notorious desire for national prominence had been thwarted since the rise of the Juntas and the renewal of the Moroccan war. Picasso's investigation, influenced largely by the testimony of two juntero colonels from the Melilla Command, Riquelme and Fernández Tamarit, had provided Berenguer's enemies with the ammunition they needed, while furnishing Aguilera with a platform from which to catapult back into the public eye.

His hitherto brilliant career abruptly interrupted by the rise of the Juntas in 1917 and by his break with García Prieto in 1919, Aguilera now found an outlet for his frustrated ambition as the leader of a third military party composed of senior generals isolated like himself from the centers of power. More important, he overnight became the darling of the political opposition, who were discouraged by the government's evasion of the responsibilities question. As in 1917, the left optimistically turned to the army as a source of political regeneration; on July 17 Aguilera received a letter signed by twenty-six well-known writers and journalists—among them, Miguel de Unamuno, Julio Camba, Ramón del Valle-Inclán, Marcelino Domingo, Manuel Ciges Aparicio, Ramón Pérez de Ayala, Roberto Castrovido, and Luis Araquistáin—that hailed the indictments as the gesture "that can be the dignification before History of this infamous hour in Spanish life."[27] A few days later Aguilera thanked the intellectuals for their "historic" letter, and the alliance between Aguilera and the left was sealed.[28] Once again the army owed its political leverage to its civilian supporters.

The Council's decision caught Sánchez Guerra by surprise because his War Minister, the pro-juntero General Olaguer, had not bothered to warn him. As a consequence, his first response was to minimize the implications of the indictment by suggesting that the Council did not intend to ask the Senate to release Berenguer—a life senator since January 1921—for trial.[29] Quickly informed by Aguilera that such indeed was his intention, Sánchez Guerra had no choice but to accept

Berenguer's resignation as High Commissioner, proffered in person on July 9.

On the fourteenth, Berenguer rose in the Senate to defend himself. As he perceived it, the primary charges against him were based on events both before and after the retreat from Anual: he had failed to curb the rash advance of General Silvestre, and he had refused to rescue Monte Arruit in the days immediately after the disaster. The former charge he answered by explaining the relative autonomy of the Melilla Command; the latter, by recalling the lamentable state of the expeditionary forces upon their arrival in Melilla. In conclusion, he turned on the government, accusing it of engineering his indictment in order to remove him from his post.[30] Although this was not true, the War Minister's juntero sympathies made it difficult for him to present a convincing rebuttal. In order to make clear that he had supported Berenguer in good faith, Sánchez Guerra accepted General Olaguer's resignation on July 15 and took over the War portfolio himself.

All the same, the indictment of Berenguer produced a shift in Sánchez Guerra's attitude toward the army. During his first four months in office, he had favored the africanistas in order to combat the Juntas. Henceforth, he would strive to maintain a balance between the two factions in order to avoid a dangerous identification with either of them. It was apparent that continued support for the ex-High Commissioner would be politically disastrous. In the peninsular army, officers with a grievance were delighted to discharge their venom against the africanistas and the governments that had favored them. According to *La Correspondencia Militar* and the elderly lieutenant generals who volunteered their opinions to the press, Berenguer and the Maura government of 1921 shared the blame for not rescuing Monte Arruit and for not taking advantage of the initial popular support for the war to achieve a rapid conquest of the entire Protectorate.[31] By implication, the Conservatives were also guilty for retaining Berenguer and for failing to prosecute the war with vigor. The virtue of this position was that it allowed peninsular officers to attack the africanista faction that had risen to national prominence and royal favor under Berenguer without attacking the Moroccan war itself.

The indictment of Berenguer also reinvigorated the left's languishing campaign in favor of abandonment and the prosecution of responsibilities.[32] The government's initial response was to repress the antiwar demonstrations that broke out in several cities and to arrest the organizers.[33] It was readily apparent, however, that the clamor for a change in policy was not limited to the extreme left, but was widely seconded among the Spanish middle class. Anxious to retain support for his government, Sánchez Guerra made two gestures calculated to appease the critics: he delivered the Picasso report to the Cortes and appointed Berenguer's old rival, Ricardo Burguete, as High Commissioner in Morocco. Unfortunately, these decisions implied a policy reversal that the Conservatives could not entertain. By December the contradictions in its policy would bring down the government.

Although he had agreed under duress in March to submit the Picasso report to the Cortes, it is not clear that the prime minister had thoroughly considered the implications of this concession. Parliamentary examination of the report was sure to disclose the organizational defects that the Supreme Military Council had attributed to Berenguer but that were more correctly attributable to government indifference and neglect. More important, the report's vivid portrayal of the disarray and demoralization in Melilla was bound to resuscitate the debate on the relationship between weak government and the absence of military reform. By July his Conservative colleagues had called the prime minister's attention to these undesirable consequences. But in the wake of Berenguer's resignation, he believed he could not defy the parliament. In order to put pressure on the government to submit the report, all factions but the Conservatives had formed a "Minority Commission" on July 18. On July 23, the last day of the summer session, Sánchez Guerra agreed to the creation of a parliamentary committee reflecting the total political composition of the Cortes, which was to examine the report during the summer recess and prepare its own recommendations for presentation at the autumn session.[34]

Replacing Berenguer was more difficult than countenancing the fait accompli of his indictment. The time seemed ripe for a change of policy. Since June the Liberals had been demanding the creation of a "civil Protectorate" to replace the predominantly military regime in Morocco,[35] a proposal Berenguer had opposed as unrealistic. With Berenguer gone, Sánchez Guerra might now respond to the popular desire for a halt in operations, while at the same time satisfying the anti-Berenguer faction in the army. On July 16 Sánchez Guerra chose General Burguete as High Commissioner. The appointment, gratifying to the Juntas if not to the lieutenant generals who were once again passed over for the position, was initially confusing to knowledgeable africanistas. Burguete was well known for the Nietzschean bellicosity of his earlier writings, but his first pronouncement on his intended policy was ingratiatingly pacifistic.[36] His subsequent statements rejecting a "military solution" to the Moroccan problem made it clear that whatever his past philosophy had been, Burguete was no man to sacrifice ambition to consistency. What he shared with Sánchez Guerra was a desire to avoid controversy and to stay in power. Public opinion demanded an end to operations, and the new High Commissioner was ready to comply, at least verbally.

Burguete's accession thus represented a return to the static policy followed by Spanish governments prior to 1919. Quite predictably, the inherent contradictions in that policy quickly reproduced the conditions that had frustrated colonial officers in Morocco throughout the world war. Having promised an end to operations, Burguete opened negotiations with al-Raysuni shortly after his arrival in Tetuan on July 20, a foolish decision that saved al-Raysuni once again from imminent defeat and converted the Spanish position in the Jibala from one of strength into one of weakness. In the Rif, where the Spanish position was already weak, Abd el-Krim could not be persuaded to negotiate. The tribes near the Spanish line remained hostile, even though General Castro Girona, an officer noted for his skill in dealing with the Moroccans, was appointed head of the Office of Native Affairs in Melilla.[37] There, the middle course favored by the government was impossible; the only logical alternatives continued to be abandonment or a convincing show of military superiority. Abandonment was, of course, not contemplated, and within a month Burguete, infected by the impatience of the vanguard units at the front near Dar Drius, was contemplating a renewal of operations and a future landing at Alhucemas Bay. On August 24, prior to a small security operation near the forward line, Burguete delivered a rousing exhortation to the troops that suggested he had already forgotten his commitment to "peaceful penetration" and was ready to launch an offensive against the rebel stronghold at Ajdir.[38]

The government's dismissal of Burguete's harangue as "wartime literature"[39] did not dispel the public apprehension of renewed military operations, which were indeed inevitable if the government intended to retain control over the Rif. Preoccupied with his political survival, however, Sánchez Guerra did not want to recognize this inevitability, at least not publicly, and possibly not even to himself. Burguete was called to Madrid, where he was reminded once again of his commitment to a policy of peaceful penetration, a commitment Burguete publicly acknowledged on September 1 in *La Correspondencia Militar*. At the same time, he promised the public he would be in Alhucemas by January, "without it having cost us combats to go there. . . ."[40]

To provide institutional support for this policy, on September 16, 1922, Sánchez Guerra signed a decree establishing the "civil Protectorate" demanded by the Liberals and the left. In essence, the decree restored to the Ministry of State most of the functions that had been gradually delegated to the War Ministry or to the High Commissioner as General-in-Chief since 1919. The virtue of the decree, in the government's eyes, was that it made the civilian Minister of State the ultimate authority over the Protectorate while simultaneously bolstering the fiction that the Protectorate was being administered in the name of the sultan by creating a Riffian ʿamil subordinate to the khalif. In addition, the decree facilitated a transfer of credits that appeared as a reduction in the budget of the War Ministry. Despite the reorganization and transfer of the Office of Native Police to the jurisdiction of the Minister of State, however,[41] the decree did not necessarily insure an end to military operations in Morocco. The High Commissioner, who retained the title of General-in-Chief, was given explicit authority to utilize the Native Police (relabeled "Khalifal Forces") as he chose.

Given the reality of the situation in Morocco, the decree in fact affected the practical administration of the zone very little. So long as the Rif remained unpacified, the military would continue to dominate the administration—and consume the budget—of the Protectorate. Furthermore, neither Sánchez Guerra nor Burguete was truly interested in altering the fundamental structure of the Protectorate; their main concern was to rob the Liberals of their best issue. Nevertheless, the decree did contain substantial implications for the formulation of Moroccan policy in Madrid. With the appointment of a strong Minister of State, Santiago Alba, in December 1922, the implications of the decree would be realized.

The decree was less politically profitable than the government had anticipated because its promulgation coincided with the exposure of more corruption in the African army. On September 6 it was discovered that 1,050,000 pesetas from the monthly Quartermaster Corps budget in Larache had been embezzled by a captain in the Corps, Manuel Jordán.[42] Further investigation revealed that nearly 3,000,000 pesetas a year had been stolen in the General Command at Larache alone.[43] Through a system of fraudulent bids and orders, a consortium of Quartermaster Corps officers had received monthly dividends ranging from 60,000 to 30,000 pesetas, according to rank, a comfortable arrangement that might have continued indefinitely had not greed intervened. After a two-month leave in the peninsula, Captain Jordán had returned to Larache to find that he had been eliminated from the cut during his absence. Seeking revenge, he stole the rake-off for the entire month of August 1922—1,050,000 pesetas—and then threatened to report the consortium unless he were allowed to keep the money. His superior officer demanded Jordán's court-martial, thus exposing the entire operation. Word quickly leaked to the peninsula, sparking a public out-cry that forced the government to order a full judicial investigation.[44] Ultimately, the case of the "Larache Millions" would lead to General Pedro Bazán's investigation of military "administrative responsibilities" in 1923.

To offset the scandal, Burguete redoubled his efforts to ingratiate himself with news of a negotiated peace throughout the zone. On September 22 he triumphantly—and prematurely—announced that through the good offices of the ex-sultan, Mawlay ᶜAbd al-Hafiz, Abd el-Krim was about to submit to Spain.[45] But the French had exiled ᶜAbd al-Hafiz in 1913 for disloyalty. The government quickly disavowed the announcement and forced the ex-sultan to disengage publicly from Moroccan politics.[46] Stung by this failure, Burguete compensated by rapidly concluding his negotiations with al-Raysuni, who formally recognized the sultan's sovereignty and returned to a new house and comfortable pension at Tazrut.[47] On October 6 Burguete journeyed to Madrid in order to announce personally the repatriation of twenty thousand troops. To all outward appearances, the "civilianization" of the Protectorate was well underway.

In the Rif, however, the reality was less sanguine. Abd el-Krim's haraka continued to harass the forward positions, and tempers in the Melilla garrison were badly frayed by the demoralizing halt in opera-tions.[48] Thus, even as he trumpeted the success of his pacification plan, Burguete privately requested—and received—permission to re-sume forward progress toward Alhucemas Bay, which he promised to take without casualties.[49] At the end of the month, a column of 30,000 men marched in the direction once taken by General Silvestre, only to be ambushed at Tizi Azza on October 28 by rebel tribesmen. There were 121 casualties, and the skittish government ordered an immediate halt in operations.[50] For the next three years, the Spanish army would be stymied at Tizi Azza, which was difficult to defend and equally difficult to supply. Although there were almost daily casualties, the government was too weak, and the army too proud, to order a retreat. Morocco thus continued to be the weak spot of the parliamentary regime.

The Demise of the Juntas

Critical as it was, the ambiguity in the government's Moroccan policy was again obscured during the fall of 1922 by the resurgence of the factional quarrels that had dominated military affairs in the peninsula since 1917. The crisis was triggered by the king, who wanted to bolster africanista morale—somewhat battered by the discovery of the Larache Millions, the creation of the civil Protectorate, and the halt in operations—with a special homage in Seville featuring the king, the Regulars of Larache, and Major José Varela, a Regular officer who had won two Laurel Wreaths and a merit promotion for his exceptional bravery in the Jibalan campaign of 1919–21. Never averse to exploiting the national popularity of the young officers in the elite units, the Conservative government had unwisely consented to the ceremony, which quickly became the vehicle for a public display of solidarity between Alfonso and the africanistas. Although only the Regulars were invited to Seville, the leader of the Tercio, Millán-Astray, drew attention to his own unit by collecting money from his men to buy the queen a jewel. The preparations for the ceremony, scheduled for October 14, were followed enthusiastically in the africanista press.

In the Infantry Junta, however, the ceremony had aroused much less enthusiasm. For one thing, the homage to Varela, who had been promoted by the Cortes the previous June, was an obvious manifestation of official support for merit promotions. For another, the visibility of Millán-Astray lent an antijuntero cast to the entire proceedings; ever since the africanista resignations the previous spring, Millán had been the target of discreet but constant hostilities by junteros in the peninsula.[51] Most important, however, the personal attention being lavished on the Regulars underscored the potential inequities of a return to battlefield promotions. To emphasize their continuing support for the seniority principle, Infantry officers in the Seville garrison boycotted both the royal presentation on October 14 and a testimonial banquet offered by the government to the head of the Regulars, González Carrasco, three days later.[52] Then, in a press interview on the eighteenth, the president of the Infantry Junta, Colonel Nouvilas, pointed out that the favoritism that had provoked the formation of the Juntas de Defensa in 1917 had not disappeared. Indeed, since merit promotions had been restored to the discretion of the War Ministry on July 30, nearly 250 names had been submitted, including two recommendations for the aide of one of the generals. Nouvilas also criticized the presentation of jewels, which might easily degenerate into "pugilism between the Corps to display their dynasticism."[53]

The conflict sent shock waves through the officer corps, which was still bitterly divided over the issue of selective promotions. Predictably, the junteros were attacked most vociferously by those who had profited under the old system. Luque's *El Ejército Español* urged the Advisory Commissions to "leave the Army in peace" in editorials on

October 18 and 19, and on October 20 the Staff Corps voted against the closed scale with only forty dissenting votes. The same day, officers from the Infantry regiments in Madrid (composed largely of former africanistas and favorites of the king) saw Millán-Astray off at the station as he left for Melilla.[54]

Ironically, the Junta's protest was received most sympathetically by the antidynastic left, whose attitude toward the military Juntas had now come full circle since 1917. Once again, the left found it convenient to view the junteros as the victims rather than the agents of political decay and the Juntas as the only institution strong enough to resist the Crown's tendencies toward absolutism. Alfonso's blatant courting of the africanistas bolstered the left's contention that military indiscipline was only a symptom of the general indiscipline that permeated the Spanish state at every level. Military reform was only a necessary first step toward a more sweeping political renovation that included the subjugation of the Crown to the rule of law.[55]

The government's support for the fete in Seville thus proved to be a political liability—particularly since the issue of military reform was no longer confined to the extreme left but was being exploited by the Liberals as well. Sánchez Guerra was looking for an opportunity to demonstrate his own devotion to the principle of civil supremacy when one was unwittingly presented by General Martínez Anido in late October. The general's resignation as Civil Governor of Barcelona climaxed several months of mounting tension that had begun shortly after the restoration of constitutional guarantees on March 31, 1922. Although the CNT remained an illegal organization, the leaders released from prison had begun to reorganize and the underground action groups had resumed their street warfare with the gunmen of the Sindicato Libre. Fearing a return to the anarchy of 1919–20, the urban middle classes had complained strenuously both to the Diputation and to the Civil Governor himself. Another source of tension in Barcelona was Martínez Anido's aggressive anti-Catalanism. The Lliga's collaboration with Conservative governments in Madrid since 1919 had served the interests of the Catalan bourgeoisie, but the prolonged suspension of constitutional guarantees and, more especially, Cambó's highly protective tariff of February 1922, had alienated a large sector of the lower-middle class. In June 1922 a newly formed left Catalan party, Acció Catalana, was making serious inroads in Barcelona. By continuing to support the resolutely anti-Catalan Civil Governor, the Lliga was once again caught between its class and regional interests.[56] On August 7 Martínez Anido had petulantly resigned, only to be persuaded to return to office by massive displays of civic solidarity and repentance.[57]

To consolidate this support, Martínez Anido and his agent, Police Chief Arlegui, had encouraged the assassins in the Libre, who shot and severely wounded the moderate Syndicalist leader Angel Pestaña on August 25. In a brazen show of his contempt for civil rights, Arlegui then stationed pistoleros outside Pestaña's hospital room to await his release.

For both the government and its critics on the left, the alternatives were clear: the regime of Martínez Anido was incompatible with a normalization of civic life in Barcelona. In an effort to recover his credibility, Martínez Anido staged an attempt on his own life that left four Anarchosyndicalists and a policeman dead. When this ruse was exposed, Sánchez Guerra reacted decisively, firing Arlegui and receiving, as he had expected, the resignation of Martínez Anido as well. If the general had foreseen the usual capitulation by the government, he was soon disappointed. Sánchez Guerra quickly replaced him with a mild-mannered Staff officer, General Julio Ardanaz, who was instructed to follow a more conciliatory policy with regard to the CNT. Nor was Martínez Anido's support in Barcelona sufficient to restore him to his post. The protests registered by the Employers' Federation and the extreme right were perfunctory, and while rumors circulated about rebellion in the garrison, only two of Martínez Anido's closest collaborators in the Infantry Junta actually resigned their posts.[58] In a few months the former adherents of Martínez Anido would find a new hero in the Captain General of Catalonia, General Primo de Rivera.

With the dismissal of Martínez Anido, Sánchez Guerra had once again co-opted the Liberals, whose desire to return to power increased in direct proportion to the remoteness of their opportunity to do so. In June the Liberal-Reformist alliance headed by Alba, García Prieto, Álvarez, and Alcalá-Zamora had been sealed with the announcement of a program that included constitutional reform and the civilianization of the Protectorate.[59] The new coalition had deliberately excluded the Conde de Romanones, who still aspired to sole leadership of the party. Complete unification might have remained elusive if Sánchez Guerra had not shown such success in stealing planks from the left-Liberal platform: during the summer and fall of 1922 the indictment of Berenguer, the delivery of the Picasso report to the Cortes, the decree creating the civil Protectorate, and the halt in military operations had revitalized the image of the Conservative party, without apparently damaging its fundamental political interests. Romanones, in particular, was alarmed, for the Conservatives had captured the africanista clientele that he had aimed to make his own, leaving him isolated from both the throne and the bulk of his own party. Thus in September 1922 his rapprochement with the Liberal coalition had been achieved,[60] and in late October, in a widely publicized speech delivered at the Liberal Circle in Madrid, Romanones cataloged the new Liberal program. Significantly, this program of national reform focused on civil-military relations: dissolution of the Juntas, restoration of merit promotions, and prosecution of responsibilities.[61] Romanones betrayed his party's anxiety over the future when he proclaimed on November 5, "If we are to be governed liberally, let the Liberals govern."[62] The Liberal offensive against the government was expected to begin when the Cortes reopened for the fall session on November 14.

The interdependence of political and military reform was dramatized by yet another outbreak of the juntero-africanista conflict just four days before the opening of the Cortes. On November 10 Lieutenant Colonel Millán-Astray submitted his resignation, and in a theatrical manifesto directed "to the nation" appealed to "mayors, deputies, senators, generals, and officers" for support in his battle against the Juntas.[63] Since their confrontation in October, Millán-Astray had sent several letters to Sánchez Guerra complaining of the continuing harassment of the junteros, only to be put off with vague assurances that "justice would be done."[64] It was clear to him that the government would avoid taking sides unless its hand were forced. Confident of the support of the king and the prestigious africanista wing of the army, Millán felt no qualms in taking his case directly to the nation. Implicit in his manifesto was the assumption that the government's policy of nonintervention thwarted the expression of the national will.

At first the response was gratifying. Opposition parties on both the left and the right delightedly echoed his demand for the dissolution of the Juntas, Young Maurists and other students took to the streets, and antijunteros in the Madrid garrison deposited calling cards at Millán's residence.[65] Within two days, however, the bourgeois left had recovered from its initial enthusiasm for Millán's challenge to the government. As *El Liberal* observed on November 12, one need not support "the partisans of all-out war and of an orgy of promotions" in order to oppose the Juntas. Indeed, the bureaucratic egotism represented in the Infantry Junta was at present less an obstacle to constitutional reform than the unholy alliance between the africanistas and Alfonso XIII.[66] Eagerly awaiting the opening of the Cortes, the Liberal coalition intended to make the principle of civil supremacy a question of confidence for the government.

But once again Sánchez Guerra stole a march on the Liberals. Shortly after the formal opening of the legislative sessions on November 14, the prime minister introduced a bill dissolving the Juntas de

Defensa.[67] Unlike previous attempts at curbing their power, Sánchez Guerra's bill took notice of the grievance that had given them their leverage within the peninsular army: favoritism in the promotions process. Sánchez Guerra proposed a compromise that would enable the state to reward excellence without unduly offending the bureaucratic mentality of the majority of officers. The Law of 1918 was modified to permit merit promotions within a rank, in percentages varying between 5 and 20 percent. In no case could such promotions be refused. Not only would the much-envied closed scale of the Artillery disappear, but also the meteoric careers of royal and ministerial favorites would be held in check. The major significance of the bill was that it mandated the establishment of bureaucratic norms for promotion that, by diminishing the effect of privilege and connections, promised a greater democratization of opportunity for career officers. Thus it satisfied the long-standing aspirations of the military middle class without sacrificing the state's right to select military leaders on the basis of their expertise and accomplishment.

The bill, which was immediately approved, was both politically and legally sound. Not only had it robbed the Liberals of one of their best issues, it represented a long-overdue gesture of independence for the civil state. Sánchez Guerra had not allowed himself to be blackmailed by the africanistas or Millán-Astray, who was replaced as head of the Tercio by Lieutenant Colonel Rafael Valenzuela. He thus began to rescue his party from its uncomfortably close identification with the advocates of military conquest in the Protectorate without falling into the embrace of the rival faction in the officer corps. It was an important first step toward the elimination of military influence in the political process.

Unfortunately, the bill also enhanced the political power of the officer corps by eliminating the principal grievance dividing it. Although the antagonisms between junteros and africanistas were too real to disappear entirely, the dissolution of the Advisory Commissions and the compromise on merit promotions did make it easier for the rival factions to submerge their differences temporarily when it appeared that the autonomy and interests of the army might be seriously threatened by the civil state. Thus the army, encouraged and aided by the king, would not oppose the pronunciamiento of General Primo de Rivera in September 1923.

"Responsibilities" and the Fall of the Government

In spite of Sánchez Guerra's resounding success on November 14, within a month his government would fall, a victim of the responsibilities debates that occupied both the Congress and the Senate as soon as the stir created by the dissolution of the Juntas had abated. Although the government tried to turn the issue to its own political advantage by taking the initiative, it was unable to confine the debate to the military responsibility of General Berenguer and the other officers named in the Picasso report. From the moment Sánchez Guerra had agreed to a parliamentary discussion of the Picasso report, his government, which contained three former members of the 1921 Allendesalazar cabinet, was doomed. The opposition would not be denied a discussion of Conservative responsibilities for the disaster.

The major issue in the Senate was the *suplicatorio,* or release for trial, of General Berenguer, who had been formally accused of negligence by the Supreme Military Council on October 28.[68] Hoping to focus public attention on the military failure in Morocco, the government had agreed to sponsor the suplicatorio, even though it had kept General Berenguer at his post for four months before his indictment. Berenguer had received the news with some bitterness; as he pointed out, he was being asked to serve as a scapegoat for political and military responsibilities that were diffused throughout the system.[69] Nevertheless, on November 15 Berenguer urged his colleagues in the Senate to concede the suplicatorio so that he might defend—and vindicate—himself before the court.

The president of the Senate, Joaquín Sánchez de Toca, and most of the Conservative majority in the Senate, however, were not eager to comply. Less convinced than their leader Sánchez Guerra of the need for a revision of past policies, they had deplored his delivery of the Picasso report to the Cortes in July and were now determined to use every means at their disposal to protect Berenguer and, by extension, the Conservative politicians who had supported him as High Commissioner both before and after Anual. By December 1 the *impunistas,* as they were called by their political opponents, had exhausted most of their parliamentary options and were arguing that a vote on the suplicatorio should be delayed until it was clear that Berenguer would not be coming up for trial in the Senate itself along with others "politically responsible" for the disaster at Anual. By suggesting a trial in the Senate, the unreconstructed Conservative majority clearly anticipated acquittal for everyone, including Berenguer.[70]

These dilatory tactics alarmed all those who considered both civil and military responsibilities to be inseparable from political reform. Already there was evidence that accountability for the Anual disaster would be kept at a minimum. Only a few days before, the first courts-martial in Melilla of junior officers indicted by the Supreme Military Council had resulted in the acquittal of all three defendants.[71] Now it appeared that General Berenguer and his allies would escape as well. This prospect was disturbing to Berenguer's enemies within the army. On November 29 *La Correspondencia Militar* had hinted not too subtly that "the Army" would "watch over the dignity and the intangible prestige of the Fatherland."[72] Just as in 1917, officers perceived and presented their professional grievances to the nation as part of the popular movement for national renovation.

Stung by the accusations of *impunismo*, Berenguer once again requested approval of the suplicatorio on December 5.[73] But he was temporarily rescued from deliverance to his military judges by the fall of the government. The government had foreseen the danger of discussing the Picasso report in the Cortes but had not been able to avoid it. Faced with a belligerent "Minority Commission" formed to examine the report in mid-July, Sánchez Guerra had endeavored to minimize the damage to his party that serious debate must inevitably entail by including majority representatives in the Commission. Having thus sanctioned the concept of parliamentary scrutiny, Sánchez Guerra had hoped that public opinion would be satisfied. Unfortunately, the ten Conservatives on the Commission had been unable to control its deliberations. When the Cortes opened on November 14, the Commission submitted not one report, but three. The Conservatives' majority report predictably denied the existence of political responsibilities that could be "linked to a single government" and hinted at disagreement with Picasso's findings against Berenguer and other high-ranking officers.[74] Ten of the eleven minority members found this whitewash inadmissible, however, and signed one of the two other reports submitted for parliamentary action; only Alejandro Lerroux had refused to express any opinion at all. Given his anomalous position as a Republican supporter of the Moroccan war, it was perhaps his only alternative.

Paradoxically, the responsibilities issue was both the basis for a new national consensus and an obstacle to its translation into a concrete political configuration. Unlike social or fiscal reform, the Moroccan war was an issue that transcended class boundaries, making a broad center-left parliamentary coalition possible for the first time. But the minority members of the Commission were unable to unite around a single recommendation to the Congress. The Socialist deputy, Indalecio Prieto, saw the parliamentary investigation as a way to discredit completely the old system, preparatory to an era of political and social democratization. The Liberals, however, were too deeply implicated in the regime to tolerate its wholesale destruction. For them, the responsibilities campaign provided an opportunity to discredit the Conservatives and to reconstruct the Liberal party on the basis of a new commitment to political reform.

In his report, submitted on November 16, Prieto repudiated the Conservative interpretation of the Anual disaster as a regrettable but intranscendental military setback. On the contrary, the disaster at Anual was the logical result of a greater political failure: specifically, the toleration of an expensive, inefficient, and insubordinate army.[75] Recognizing that "all the Governments since 1900" were responsible for the Moroccan fiasco, Prieto nevertheless imputed direct responsibility to the Allendesalazar and Maura governments and formally accused them of "prevarication" and thus, of violation of Article 45 of the Constitution of 1876. In addition, Prieto demanded the separation from the army of Generals Berenguer and Navarro, the former Junta president, Colonel Araujo, and all of the colonels with a command in Melilla at the time of the disaster. More generally, he suggested abolishing the Quartermaster Corps, the honor courts, and the Law of Jurisdictions. Taken together, Prieto's charges comprised an indictment of a politico-military system in which the state had complacently subordinated the popular will to the interests of an arrogant and incompetent military establishment.

The figure whom the Socialists considered chiefly responsible for the ills of the regime in general and for the failure of the army in Morocco in particular went unnamed in their list of charges, since in constitutional law, the monarchy was above criticism. In his report, Prieto paused to point out that because of the constitution, revolution was the only way to rid the nation of the institutions that had pushed it to the "brink of humiliation and ruin." But this verbal aggression did not disguise the fact that the Socialists were playing by the established rules. Anual, by providing them with an issue with broad middle-class appeal, had introduced the real possibility of a democratic transformation of the regime without the necessity of violent revolution.

This indirect route toward ministerial responsibility—and thus toward constitutional revision—was tentatively seconded by the Liberals, who submitted their minority report on November 24.[76] But the Liberal proposition was neither as bold nor as consistent as the blanket condemnation of the Socialists. As the self-proclaimed champions of popular sovereignty, the Liberals believed the nation could not be denied an accounting for Anual; on the other hand, their own identification with the parliamentary monarchy was too close to suffer prolonged or serious scrutiny. The Liberal report asked the Congress to "censure" Manuel Allendesalazar and his Ministers of State and War (the Marqués de Lema and the Vizconde de Eza) but denied the existence of a specific legal or constitutional violation that would require a trial in the Senate under the provisions of Article 45. This opportunistic compromise, which demanded reform without risking revolution, was endorsed by all the Liberals, the Reformists, and the Lliga.

Quite predictably, the lack of consensus within the Picasso Commission was duplicated in the Cortes, each proposition receiving support or criticism according to the political affiliation of the speaker. Since the Conservatives held a majority, it seemed likely that no charges of political responsibility would ever be formulated, much to the dismay of *responsabilistas* in the Cortes and in the country. On November 27 a general meeting of the Madrid Ateneo voted overwhelmingly in favor of a massive public demonstration to force the Cortes to determine ministerial responsibilities. Yet as Álvaro de Albornoz perceptively pointed out in *El Liberal*, "The disaster at Anual was not due to the negligence of a minister or of various ministers: it was due to a system. That system is an entire political policy. And that policy is the regime . . . and in the trial of a regime, the Parliament of that regime cannot serve as an adequate, efficacious instrument."[77] In effect, the dynastic parties could not *formally* acknowledge the political responsibility of the regime they had created without destroying it and themselves. If the parliamentary monarchy were to continue, Anual could serve only as a stimulus to contrition and gradual reform.

It was probably this realization that provoked the decisive intervention of Antonio Maura on November 30. In a typically erudite, yet elusive, speech, Maura defined the issues before the Congress: whether ministerial responsibility was provided for in the Constitution of 1876, and if so, whether a "censure" by the Congress was an appropriate and adequate response. Answering his own questions, Maura demolished the Liberal position by insisting that ministerial responsibility existed even in the absence of specific legislation defining its parameters; the exercise of power always implied obligations and responsibilities. Under the Constitution of 1876, failure to govern responsibly required not censure, but a formal accusation in the Congress and a trial in the Senate.

Having justified the *legality* of a formal accusation to the satisfaction of everyone but the Liberals, Maura refused to formulate an accusation against one or two individuals on the grounds that responsibility for Anual was diffused through a succession of ministries. Political responsibilities undoubtedly existed, but they could not be pinpointed. Further discussion of the responsibilities issue was therefore useless. Because this argument was much more decorous than the outright denial of responsibility expressed in the majority report, the Conservatives, including Sánchez Guerra himself,[78] eagerly embraced it as their own, much to the outrage of the entire opposition. Maura's thesis allowed the Conservatives to acknowledge the existence of political responsibilities without running any serious risk of a formal accusation, since the Liberals were clearly unwilling to go beyond a political censure. Yet Maura's own impunismo was probably not so self-serving. Unlike Sánchez Guerra and the Liberals, Maura had no doubts about the continuing viability of the regime; the turmoil of the past six years had left his basically authoritarian outlook unscathed. Denying the legitimacy of popular rule, he had no difficulty in refusing to accede to the demands for accountability. From his point of view, all that was needed to weather the current crisis was consistency and confidence in the traditional right of the dynastic parties to rule.

Maura's solution to the responsibilities issue was in fact anachronistic in 1922. But it might well have defused the Liberal attack—which was crippled by the ambiguous Liberal attitude toward political change —had it not been unexpectedly sabotaged by Francisco Cambó, who withdrew his support from the Liberal report on December 1 in order to present a formal accusation against the entire Allendesalazar government of 1921.[79] In answer to Maura's contention that responsibility was too diffuse to locate precisely, Cambó retorted that "the way to do no justice at all is to desire to do perfect justice." The reasons for Cambó's desertion of the regime at this critical moment are unclear. Surely crucial was an interview with the king held earlier that day, in which Alfonso had untactfully offered Cambó power in exchange for his "hispanization." Already under severe pressure from left-wing Catalan nationalists in Barcelona, Cambó received this offer as an insult to his political integrity and refused to abandon his regionalist loyalties. But Cambó's alienation from the system antedated his unfortunate encounter with the king; it stemmed from the regime's failure to respond positively to his own vision of a modern, economically integrated Spain. In any event, Cambó's disillusionment made him, for the moment, the most effective responsabilista in the nation.[80] Immediately after his accusation, three members of Sánchez Guerra's government and the president of the Congress, Gabino Bugallal, all of whom had formed part of the 1921 government, resigned their posts. The Conservatives' thoughtless embrace of the Maura doctrine had exploded in their faces.

After a hasty cabinet reorganization, Sánchez Guerra girded himself to save his government—and the Conservative party—from collapse. On December 5 the prime minister attempted to rally the Conservative majority behind the government by introducing a motion to reject the resignation of Bugallal, a maneuver that might have succeeded had not Juan de la Cierva intervened. Minister of Development in the Allendesalazar government formally accused by Cambó, La Cierva's vehemence was understandable, but the violence of the language he directed against the Catalan leader (whom he came close to accusing of dishonesty during the Bank of Barcelona bankruptcy in 1921) reduced the Congress to anarchy. Unable to restore order or to force a vote, Sánchez Guerra resigned, abruptly terminating—at least temporarily—the responsibilities debate in the Congress and the concession of Berenguer's *suplicatorio* in the Senate.[81]

The sudden collapse of the government represented the end of the Conservatives as a functional political alternative within the parliamentary monarchy. For nine months Sánchez Guerra had endeavored to renew the party's image by responding to popular opinion; satisfied of support in the nation, he had been able to loosen his party's ties to the army and to make several long-overdue decisions, including the halt in military operations, the dismissal of General Martínez Anido, and the abolition of the Advisory Commissions. The responsibilities issue, however, had proven impossible to master because it implied a radical transformation of the regime that neither of the dynastic parties was prepared to countenance. So long as the system remained essentially intact, there could be no resolution of the responsibilities campaign completely satisfactory to the left; its place in a nonrevolutionary reconstruction of the regime could be only as an irresistible goad to reform. This was the path the Liberal government of 1923 would prepare to take, once it had realistically assessed the implications of the responsibilities question. Unfortunately, in seeking the peaceful transformation of the political system, the Liberals would encounter the opposition of the army and the king.

CHAPTER ELEVEN

The Clenched Fist

> Morocco made the fragmented soul of our
> Army into a clenched fist, morally ready to attack.
> —José Ortega y Gasset   España invertebrada

Having endured the Conservative monopoly of power for nearly four years, the Liberal coalition government of 1923 was eager to govern. Vowing to chart a new course for the nation by freeing the state from its bondage to the army, the Liberals pledged to assert civilian control over two areas that the dynastic parties had traditionally entrusted to the military: social policy in Barcelona and colonial policy in Morocco. But the Liberal coalition soon discovered that the symbiotic relationship between the regime and the army was too well established to be easily abandoned. In September 1923 their attempt at constitutional reform was cut short by the king and the army, whose political power and autonomy were threatened by the effort to base the regime on the broader foundation of popular sovereignty.

If the army had not attempted to seize direct control of the state before 1923, it was because it had not been necessary. The political sterility of the dynastic parties, their resistance to social change, and their determination to pursue an unpopular colonial war in North Africa had effectively quelled any enthusiasm for policies—such as military reform—that might find disfavor in the officer corps. Not until the disaster at Anual deprived the dynastic politicians of their traditional political support among the middle classes did they begin to find a reorientation of civil-military relations politically compelling. Furthermore, disunity within the army had loomed as an apparently insuperable obstacle to direct military intervention in politics. The divergence of interests between junteros and africanistas had made it impossible for governments to formulate a coherent military policy; their quarrels had contributed to the ministerial instability that further discredited the parliamentary regime in the postwar period. But the professional divisions had also suggested that the army would not—because it could not—defend itself against a determined assertion of civil supremacy.

In fact, this was a false perception. Like the ability to avoid military reform, military disunity had been a luxury permitted by the absence of strong civilian government. Once the Liberal coalition of 1923 made clear the sincerity of its intention to restructure civil-military relations, the elusive military unity quickly became a reality. While the issues that divided the officer corps were too serious to disappear altogether, they could be temporarily submerged when the privileges and power of the army as a whole appeared to be at stake.

Military unity coincided with the growing popular disillusionment with a parliamentary system that found reform much easier to promise than to practice. The Liberal coalition of 1923 represented a futile attempt to retain a formal two-party system despite the naturally pluralistic bent of Spanish parliamentarism; like its predecessors, the coalition fell apart when put to the test of positive action. In order to survive, the government had to act cautiously, particularly as it became clear that the army was at the brink of revolt. But the government's hesitancy increased the impatience of a public eager for decisive action. Furthermore, a national consensus on issues other than the Moroccan war was lacking. As social disorder once again prevailed in Barcelona, middle-class support for the government wavered. The alienation and frustration that developed during 1923 revived the Spanish propensity to look for an "iron surgeon" to save the nation and deprived the regime of civilian as well as military defenders when Primo's manifesto appeared.

A shrewd political observer, Alfonso perceived the rapidly disintegrating situation and acted decisively to save his throne. The source of many of the army's pretensions as well as many of its discontents, he encouraged the military assault on the constitutional regime that had never allowed him the power he coveted and that now seemed to offer him scant protection against the enemies of the throne. His benevolence toward the military coup assured the cooperation of most of the officer corps—still overwhelmingly monarchist—by giving it a veneer of legitimacy. But Alfonso's own legitimacy rested on the Constitution of 1876; its destruction would ultimately leave him defenseless. The Crown would have as few loyal supporters in April 1931 as the parliamentary regime had in September 1923.

The Liberal Coalition of 1923

High expectations accompanied the installation of the Liberal coalition government on December 5, 1922.[1] One source of the enthusiasm was the composition of the cabinet, which not only reconstituted
the long-fragmented Liberal party but also included for the first time a
representative of the nondynastic left—the Reformist José Pedregal,
Minister of Finance.[2] By returning to their traditional role as the party
of "attraction," the Liberals appeared to be restoring to the political
system some of its former flexibility.

But the virtues of the cabinet were also its defects. As the coalition's lowest common denominator, the prime minister, García Prieto,
was acceptable to all factions, but he offered no counterweight to the
talented, but provocative and controversial Santiago Alba. More important, the fragile unity broke down when it came time to implement
the reforms so easily promised in December. The most damaging frac-
ture point was not between the Liberals and the Reformists—whose
inflexibility on the clerical issue forced their withdrawal from the cabinet in April—but between the left-Liberals led by Alba and the bulk of
the party, who were more deeply committed to the traditional system
of civil-military relations. Vulnerable on the responsibilities issue, instinctively cautious on the social question, the majority Liberals would
tarnish the image of the cabinet, hamper its effectiveness, and dilute its
determination and ability to resist military pressure. Thus, the effort to
revitalize the two-party system in the face of the fundamental pluralism
of the political system ultimately proved to be counterproductive.

But in the hour of its creation the glitter of the cabinet was un-
dimmed. The platform announced on December 7 was a catalog of
reforms that, taken together, amounted to a radical democratization
of the Constitution of 1876; among them were religious toleration (a
plank insisted on by the Reformists as the price for their participation);
democratization of the Senate; reform of the suffrage to a system of
proportional representation; obligatory convocation of the Cortes for
at least four months of every fiscal year; social, fiscal, agrarian, and
military reforms, including cutbacks in personnel; the establishment of
a civil Protectorate in Morocco; and the prosecution of responsibilities.
A Cortes elected to implement these proposals would, in effect, be a
Constituent Cortes.

The reform program reflected the disproportionate influence of
the Alba-Álvarez axis within the cabinet; just how far its specific proposals coincided with national aspirations was open to question. To
judge from the popular press, the Liberal government's primary man-

date was to pursue the "responsibilities" issue, a more immediately and widely acceptable goal that masked the lack of a broad consensus in favor of social and economic modernization. On December 10 an estimated two hundred thousand people participated in the "responsibilities" march sponsored by the Madrid Ateneo. The organizers' sympathies lay with the left, but the marchers included disaffected groups across the political spectrum, ranging from the Socialists, the Republicans, and the Spanish Grand Orient to the Carlists and the Social Catholic Youth of Covadonga.³ Similar demonstrations in provincial cities and towns all over Spain reflected the national perception that the first step toward political renovation must be a reckoning with the past. The wave of protest contrasted vividly with the similar mass support for the campaign of "reconquest" just sixteen months earlier.

The government billed itself as the champion of "responsibilities," but in reality it discreetly avoided the issue as much as possible. While the Reformists were unblemished by past involvement in the regime, the Liberals—particularly Romanones—were deeply implicated in the colonial failure in North Africa. In order to survive, the coalition would have to postpone the responsibilities question as long as possible— at least until after the election of the new Cortes—and in the meantime, display its capacity for leadership in other areas. The steady pursuit of political reform might render a brutal confrontation over the responsibilities issue unnecessary.

Civil-Military Relations

Two decisions in December indicated that the new government perceived its primary obligation to be the establishment of the principle of civil supremacy, a task initiated but not completed by Sánchez Guerra during the previous year. For the first time since 1920, a civilian, Salvador Raventós, was appointed to the post of Civil Governor of Barcelona. Himself a wealthy Catalan, Raventós was acceptable to the Catalan bourgeoisie, who were otherwise skeptical of the return to a policy of pacification, especially when street terrorism was escalating. Next, the government announced that the Basque Republican financier Horacio Echevarrieta (whose mining deals, ironically, had initially provoked Abd el-Krim's rebellion) would shortly reopen negotiations for the ransom of the prisoners at Ajdir.⁴ But formulation of a new Moroccan policy proved more difficult, because the cabinet, like its predecessors, lacked the courage—or the conviction—to abandon North Africa. Caught between the abandonistas in the country and the africanistas in the army, the cabinet was obliged to devise a compromise that would enable Spain to remain in Morocco at no expense. As the Spanish experience in North Africa since 1909 had amply demonstrated, no such compromise existed: colonialism demanded a high price. Nevertheless, the Liberals were determined to succeed where others had failed.

Resolution of the dilemma was complicated by lack of consensus within the cabinet. One point of view, represented by the new War Minister, Niceto Alcalá-Zamora, and the High Commissioner, General Burguete, proposed completion of the previous policy: military operations in the Rif, including an assault on Alhucemas Bay, to eliminate Abd el-Krim before entrusting the Protectorate to civilian administration.[5] The Reformists, on the other hand, insisted on immediate implementation of the "civil Protectorate" outlined in the decree of September 16, 1922. Given the balance of forces in the Rif, maintenance of the status quo without resort to force was a chimera, but the Reformists' moral leverage, as the representatives of the left, gave them the victory. On December 25, after three arduous days of internal debate, the government announced its official policy to the country: "the Government believes that it should flee from halfway solutions and from more or less flexible transitions to a fully civilian Protectorate." Alba assured the public that there would be no further military operations beyond those necessary to secure existing positions.[6] But the new policy was itself a halfway solution that could not stabilize the Spanish position in North Africa.

The driving force in the cabinet was the Minister of State, Santiago Alba. Once converted to the Reformist position, Alba committed himself "with firmness, straightforwardly, without insane alternatives,"[7] to the civilianization of the Protectorate. The Minister of War, Alcalá-Zamora, remained unenthusiastic. The former president of the parliamentary commission that had sponsored the military reform law of 1918, Alcalá-Zamora had a sympathy for the military point of view that was unique in the cabinet. Nevertheless, he grudgingly issued the decrees that made the civil Protectorate a reality. In early January the Commander General of Melilla, General Carlos de Lossada, was replaced by a Liberal officer more sympathetic to the government's policy; at the same time, a somewhat disgruntled General Burguete resigned as High Commissioner and was sent on an inspection tour of Poland. After Miguel Villanueva declined—for the third time—to become the first civilian High Commissioner, the Minister of the Navy, Luis Silvela, agreed to accept the post, despite his previous lack of interest in or knowledge of Moroccan affairs.

The shake-up in the Protectorate administration was accompanied by a major reorganization decree on January 17 that was intended to strengthen the authority of the Ministry of State by depriving the High Commissioner of the title of General-in-Chief. Theoretically, the decree restored the autonomy of the general commands at Ceuta and Melilla with regard to military operations. But since no operations were contemplated, in practice Alba ignored all his military advisers, whether in the War Ministry or in Morocco. Other decrees laid the groundwork for the formation of a professional colonial army independent of the national standing army in the peninsula: all Spanish volunteers for the Tercio were channeled into regular army regiments in Morocco, while conscripts were reserved for garrison duty in the large towns. At the same time, officers were authorized to transfer back to peninsular regiments. By creating a civilian Protectorate defended by a purely voluntary military force, the government hoped to generate enthusiasm for Spain's "colonial mission."[8]

The administrative decrees, which transferred power from military to civilian entities, represented a repudiation of the military domination of the Protectorate. A much more spectacular affront to military pride was the ransom and release of the 326 surviving prisoners of war from Ajdir. Immediately after his appointment, Echevarrieta had contacted Abd el-Krim through the good offices of a mutual friend, Idris bin Said. A clever propagandist, Abd el-Krim had agreed to parley only if the Spanish army were totally excluded from the negotiations. Echevarrieta himself served as a hostage while the final arrangements were made, and on January 27, in exchange for 4,270,000 pesetas, the Moroccans delivered the surviving prisoners, including General Navarro. Contrary to expectations, the hostages could provide no new explanations for the Anual disaster. They did, however, provide the left with ammunition with which to deride the army: a Liberal government and a Basque Republican had been successful where "militarism and bureaucracy" had failed.[9] The right and the army, on the other hand, demanded a punitive attack against Abd el-Krim for his criminal treatment of prisoners of war.

Discontent in the Army

All the initial decisions of the Liberal coalition aimed at reclaiming for civilian government the functions usurped by or abandoned to the army for decades. Although the government had anticipated military discontent, it felt confident enough of its popular support to ignore military pressure and paid little heed to the rumors of military unrest that circulated almost incessantly from the moment it announced that it would ransom the prisoners and civilianize the Protectorate. Yet among the public the rumors gradually created the impression that a military pronunciamiento was not only possible but inevitable.

As early as December 29, *El Heraldo* printed reports of a conspiracy led by General Luque and seconded by three brigadiers with active commands in the capital—Antonio Dabán, Federico Berenguer (Dámaso's brother), and Miguel Cabanellas.[10] No action was anticipated, however, because the head of the fourth brigade, General Leopoldo Saro, had refused to join the movement, which was tainted by the republican sympathies of Luque and Cabanellas. For observers of the military, the significance of the rumor lay in the alleged disaffection of the three young brigadiers, africanistas who owed their prestigious assignments to the influence of Alfonso XIII. *El Heraldo* reported "an atrophy of enthusiasm" for the monarchy among officers alienated by the king's toleration of the governmental assault on military pride and prerogatives. This claim was apparently corroborated when the king's adviser, the Conde del Grove, had to cancel a promonarchist demonstration because of the refusal of one Madrid regiment to participate. Evidence of similar alienation appeared in Barcelona, still a center of juntero feeling, where officers were reportedly dismayed by a government proposal for cutbacks in the officer corps as well as by the reorientation of the Protectorate.[11]

The ransom of the prisoners provided a focus for the vague uneasiness in the military. Outraged both by the pathetic condition of the hostages and by the propaganda value they represented for the left, officers unanimously interpreted the ransom as an affront to military honor that must be avenged by an assault on Ajdir; for the moment, the usual professional rivalries were submerged in a general sense of injured pride. In Madrid, junior Artillery officers circulated a petition demanding an immediate rupture with Abd el-Krim, General Weyler offered to lead a Cavalry assault against the rebels, and sixty-six general and field-grade officers met to discuss their grievances with the Captain General.[12] In Barcelona, a similar meeting took place under the leadership of Captain General Primo de Rivera (who nevertheless congratulated Alba on the ransom in a private letter).[13] Led by *El Debate* and *La Acción*, the right-wing press also sprang to the defense of national honor. When Abd el-Krim declared himself sultan of the Rif on February 8, they intensified their campaign for a renewal of operations.

Publicly, the government acted as if there were no cause for alarm, but the tension in the country was palpable. The army's denunciations of the government were matched by equally violent antimilitaristic attacks in the abandonista press, which only heightened the army's sense of injury. In Catalonia, the friction between officers and Catalan separatists (who often cheered the Riffian nationalists) was so intense that General Primo de Rivera found it prudent to authorize use of the Law of Jurisdictions against the editor of *L'Estat Català*. The Radical *El Diluvio* was another victim of post facto military censorship.[14] The climate in Melilla was even more threatening. On February 4 the outgoing Commander General, Lossada, warned García Prieto that officers in the expeditionary forces were considering "the most rash and perhaps illegal undertakings" and blamed the antimilitaristic press and the government for the almost hysterical state of the African officer corps.[15]

The military indignation was partially justified. First Sánchez Guerra, and then the Liberals, had ordered the army to remain in Africa but had refused to authorize the military operations that would pacify the zone. The government wanted the army to pay—in casualties and prestige—the price for its own political cowardice, and officers, not unjustly, felt victimized and frustrated. But even more crucial to the creation of military unrest was the army's perception that the Liberal government was indifferent, and even hostile, to military opinion. If civilian government could not be relied upon to defend the army from its critics, it lost its legitimacy in the eyes of many officers, who confused the army's interests with those of the nation. To resist the government thus became a patriotic duty.

Rumors of Dictatorship

In 1923 the antidynastic left temporarily moderated its hostility to the regime in order to give it another chance to reform itself from within. The right, refusing from the first to act as a loyal opposition to the government, contributed to the collapse of the system by calling continuously for dictatorship. It was not only the government's military policy that angered the right. The reform program announced by the Liberal coalition in December attacked many of the institutions the right considered essential to the continuity of traditional Spain; oligarchical rule, Catholic uniformity, fiscal and social conservatism, and colonial conquest were as sacred in their eyes as military honor and autonomy. Thus, the extreme right—the Maurists and Catholic Integrists above all—viewed the new government from the beginning as not only iniquitous, but illegitimate.

What was lacking for the moment was a dictator, although in the winter and spring of 1923 several possible candidates emerged. The most prominent was the king, a view Alfonso cultivated by attempting to dissociate himself from the government's policies. Disturbed by the unsettling rumors of an antimonarchical conspiracy in the Madrid garrison and frustrated by the policy reversal in Morocco, Alfonso had little faith in the ability or determination of the Liberal-Reformist coalition to defend the throne. In late February *La Acción* reported that the king was considering abdication and blamed the politicians and the constitution for his silence on issues of critical national importance.[16] A few days later Alfonso stilled the rumors by patriotically proclaiming his determination to stand by the nation in its hour of crisis, thus publicly conveying his own skepticism concerning the Liberals' ability to govern.[17]

Calls for authoritarian government were not restricted to Madrid and Melilla, but could also be heard in Barcelona, where social disorder was beginning to overshadow the Moroccan war as an issue of middle-class concern. Labor stoppages and terrorism in Barcelona had escalated rapidly since the beginning of the year, as had bank robberies, which theoretically provided funds for "the revolution," but which more often went into the pockets of the underworld characters who took refuge behind the facade of the CNT. The moderate Anarcho-syndicalist leaders, Seguí and Pestaña, condemned but were unable to control the extremists,[18] and on March 10 Seguí was shot down in the street, clearing the way for the unrestrained activities of the Anarchist action groups. Accepting the challenge, the Sindicato Libre advised its followers to shoot troublesome members of the Sindicato Único in the forehead.[19] Violence continued to mount throughout the spring and summer, reducing much of the Barcelona population to alternate states of terror and rage.

In this atmosphere the moderate policies of the Liberal Civil Governor Raventós were useless, but the government adamantly refused to declare martial law. Faced with chaos (for which they were of course partly responsible), the middle classes, led by the Employers' Federation and the Lliga, spoke with increasing stridency of the necessity of an authoritarian solution to the anarchy in the streets and factories. In March captains in the Barcelona garrison formed a small proto-fascist group called "La Traza" (The Design), whose initial manifesto proclaimed their intent to "do away with existing confusion and political scandal. . . ." Later, an unverified rumor indicated that the *tracistas* had found a leader in General Martínez Anido.[20] The leading military figure in Barcelona was not Martínez Anido, however, but the Captain General of Barcelona, Primo de Rivera, who had very capably filled the vacuum left by the dismissal of Martínez Anido the previous October. Furthermore, unlike his predecessor, Primo sympathized openly with the moderate regionalism of the Catalan bourgeoisie, praising the language, attending festivities, and deferring especially to Francisco Cambó.[21]

The figure that dominated most talk of dictatorship during the spring of 1923 was General Francisco Aguilera, the president of the Supreme Military Council. The senior lieutenant general on the active list at age sixty-six, Aguilera was the darling of responsabilistas and abandonistas, to whom he presented an image of severity, impartiality, and justice. Not content to stop with the indictment of General Berenguer, in March 1923 the Supreme Military Council voted to indict General Cavalcanti for his rashness during the attack on the convoy to Tizza, disregarding completely the recommendation for a Laurel Wreath that he had received for the same action from Berenguer and La Cierva in 1921. On the twenty-first, another indictment was brought in against the recently liberated General Navarro for his failure to take Monte Arruit during the retreat from Anual. Then on April 8 Aguilera ordered the disciplinary arrest of the three generals who had voted to acquit the first officers tried in Melilla for dereliction of duty during the disaster.[22] In contrast to the evasion and dilatory tactics of the dynastic parties, Aguilera's implacable pursuit of military responsibilities once again raised hopes on the left that the army might be the instrument of national regeneration. To encourage this view, Aguilera had joined the growing ranks of government critics, suggesting that the army would prove a loyal ally to "the people" in defense of the Fatherland.[23]

However prominent, Aguilera was a divisive figure and thus was an unlikely candidate to lead a military dictatorship. Needless to say, he was not popular among the africanistas, who saw themselves as scapegoats blamed for losing a war that the politicians had not allowed them to win. With three of its leading generals—Berenguer, Navarro, and Cavalcanti—under indictment, the Cavalry Corps also harbored a martyr complex and publicized their resentment by abstaining ostentatiously from the tribute to Aguilera that marked his advance to the top of the list of lieutenant generals.[24] Within the officer corps, Aguilera's principal supporters were junteros so delighted by his prosecution of the africanistas that they were willing to forget his opposition to the Juntas de Defensa in 1917.

Indeed, the most striking characteristic of the growing sentiment in favor of dictatorship was the lack of agreement about who should intervene and for what purpose. The political confusion, social disorder, and economic dislocation of the postwar years had exposed the incapacity of the ruling elites and mobilized sectors of the population that had previously been indifferent to political issues. But the general desire for reform masked the lack of consensus about the degree and nature of political change. The political instability frequently inherent to the process of modernization frustrated Spaniards at every point on the political spectrum, making them susceptible to the appeal of authoritarian solutions. The lure of dictatorship united groups whose goals were otherwise incompatible, as Ortega y Gasset pointed out in *El Sol* in early January:

> The craving or enthusiasm for dictatorship is, in Spain, a case of the belief in miracles, or faith in fate, in the prize of a political lottery. Dictatorship, like revolution, either is an effort *pro iure contra lege*, which tramples on positive law in search of a superior juridical state more in conformance with the public conscience, or it is an act of popularity, of confidence in a man that delegates power to him by means of a tacit plebiscite. The dictator must always precede the Dictatorship; here, the Dictatorship is supposed to create the dictator.[25]

The Breakdown of the Liberal Coalition

Only a strong government would have been able to meet the challenge from the army, the right, and the throne with confidence; the fragile Liberal coalition broke down under the strain. For three months the cabinet had preserved its unity by avoiding all controversial issues. Except for the civilianization of the Protectorate and the prohibition of gambling,[26] implementation of the reform program was postponed until after the elections scheduled for April 29. For all those who had expected dramatic action, this immobility was disillusioning, and as the election period approached, the coalition felt compelled to prove its commitment to reform.

For the Reformists, the most pressing issue was the reduction of church privilege. Like the army, the church was one of the institutional bulwarks of the monarchy; like civil-military relations, church-state relations had to be redefined if a real democratization of the regime was to occur. The Reformists had made revision of Article 11 of the constitution a condition of their support for the government. Therefore, in early spring the Minister of Justice, the Conde de Romanones, began to test public support for an anticlerical program.

His initiative soon collapsed, partly because of the hostile response of the king and the church hierarchy, partly because middle-class sentiment was not united on the subject, as it was on the war. A proposal to prohibit the sale of artistic treasures by churches and monastic houses had to be modified after the king personally intervened.[27] Then on March 30 Romanones received a letter from the Archbishop of Saragossa, Cardinal Soldevila, who warned that any alteration of Article 11 would "oblige the prelates to recommend expressly to [the Spanish] that they not vote for the supporters of the reform in the next elections."[28] After the council of bishops endorsed Soldevila's letter on April 1, Romanones backed away from the issue. Three days later the Reformist representative, Pedregal, resigned as Minister of Finance.

The collapse of the coalition after only four months in office disillusioned those who had believed that the inclusion of the Reformists would lead to meaningful change. When the Reformists announced they would continue to support the cabinet without participating in it, they alienated the anticlerical left, who were no less dogmatic than the Spanish bishops.[29] But they also disenchanted those who thought the coalition had sacrificed the opportunity to achieve other necessary reforms because of a doctrinaire attachment to an issue with little popular appeal: as *El Sol* remarked, the Reformists were notorious for raising issues that "ought" to interest public opinion.[30] The key to any successful change in policy was widespread support, as the government's experience in Morocco had demonstrated; in the absence of popular backing, resistance to entrenched interests was impossible. Romanones, whose political prudence was born of the long experience denied the Reformists, merely recognized the division in the country by pulling back on religious reform. But the effect on the cabinet crisis was to discredit parliamentary government as an efficient instrument of national regeneration.

When he called for new elections on April 7, García Prieto reiterated the cabinet's commitment to the other constitutional and administrative reforms, as well as to a reordering of priorities that would place the needs of the peninsula over those of Morocco.[31] But during the electoral period, the Liberals campaigned primarily on the responsibilities question that had propelled them into office in December. The strength of the issue in the country—together with the usual electoral tactics—gave them 203 seats over the Conservatives' 108. More indicative of the national desire for political reform was the large vote given to the parties of protest. The new Cortes contained 20 Reformists (still allied with the Liberal coalition), 22 regionalists, 11 Republicans, and 7 Socialists, including 5 from Madrid. Equally significant, however, was the large percentage of Spaniards who did not vote at all. The abstention rate was 35.5 percent; 23 percent elected deputies under Article 29 for lack of opposition. Nearly three-fifths of the electorate, in other words, were excluded from or had abandoned the political process. Nothing could point more eloquently to the urgency of reform.[32]

The credibility conferred on the government by its electoral victory was short-lived. On May 19, five days before the opening of the Cortes, the coalition broke down again when the War Minister, Alcalá-Zamora, resigned his portfolio. Alcalá-Zamora's grievances were both political and personal. In part, his resignation was merely his ultimate retort to Santiago Alba, who as Minister of State, had single-handedly resolved all issues of colonial policy, often without regard for or deference to the opinions of his colleague.[33] An ambitious man, Alcalá-Zamora had chafed under Alba's overweening presence, but he had waited until the elections had guaranteed him his own coterie of supporters before making an open break.[34] Nonetheless, Alcalá-Zamora's opposition to Alba's Moroccan policy was substantive as well. Both he and the High Commissioner, Luis Silvela, shared the African army's hostility to the halt in military operations. The military situation in the Protectorate had, if anything, deteriorated since the autumn. Al-Raysuni had predictably begun to violate the terms of his pact almost as soon as he had signed it. In the Rif, Abd el-Krim was engaged in a serious effort to construct a modern army and a Moroccan state. Silvela's orders were to reopen negotiations with both rebel leaders in order to stop the harassment of the stationary Spanish forces, but even the skilful General Castro Girona had made no headway with either of them. By spring, it was clear to both Silvela and Alcalá-Zamora that only an active display of military superiority could impose peace in the Protectorate. Alba and a majority of the cabinet remained opposed to a renewal of operations, however, for both political and financial reasons. Alcalá-Zamora had tried unsuccessfully to resign on April 3. When Alba presented the cabinet with a proposal for a new pact with al-Raysuni in May, the War Minister resigned again, this time with success.

The African army applauded the gesture, for their hostility toward the government had mounted since the ransom of the prisoners in January. The army was under assault from every quarter. Along the exposed front lines, daily skirmishes kept military tempers at the breaking point. In Melilla, the junior officers indicted for negligence at Anual were still undergoing prosecution, albeit slowly. Their decisions closely monitored by the vigilantes on the Supreme Military Council in Madrid, commanding officers hesitated to exercise leniency for fear of incurring the disciplinary sentences imposed on the generals who had acquitted the first defendants. The new Commander General, Pedro Vives Vich, had been in Melilla only a few weeks when he began to nag the government to replace him.[35] "One only leaves Melilla embalmed or prosecuted" was the catchword of the day.

The cabinet made a small concession to military feeling by replacing Alcalá-Zamora with the chief of the General Staff, Luis Aizpuru, but otherwise it was determined to adhere to its original program.[36] On May 23 the government opened the Cortes with a "Message from the Crown" that stressed its commitment to constitutional, fiscal, and administrative reforms, the just resolution of the responsibilities issue, and the end of "Moroccan extravagance."[37] As agreed in December, the Conde de Romanones assumed the presidency of the Senate, and Melquíades Álvarez became president of the Congress. The Liberal-Reformist alliance seemed to have regained some of its momentum, but the government immediately squandered it by allowing the Cortes to lapse into its usual wrangling over electoral technicalities and into rhetorical battles over the wording of the parliamentary response to the Message, instead of insisting on immediate consideration of its program. The old habit of "politics as usual" proved difficult to overcome.

Morocco and Catalonia

During the summer of 1923, the Liberals lost the initiative to their critics on both the left and the right. The government's vulnerable points were those of its predecessors: Morocco, Catalonia, and responsibilities. In each case, it seemed essential to respond to the demands for change without unduly offending traditional interests, a task made more difficult by the ambiguity with which some members of the Liberal coalition viewed this assignment. But most crucial to the government's loss of mastery was the hostility of the army.

On June 3 the ambush of a supply convoy to the exposed salient at Tizi Azza cost the Spanish 350 casualties, including the death of the young commander of the Tercio, Lieutenant Colonel Rafael Valenzuela. Heavily exploited in the prowar press, this setback aroused misgivings about the government's policy of pacification, which gave the army the leverage it needed. Its confidence sapped by the two cabinet crises, the government desperately agreed on June 6 to appease military opinion by appointing General Martínez Anido as Commander General of

Melilla. The same day, it promoted the extremely popular Major Franco to lieutenant colonel and made him the new head of the Tercio. The appointment of Martínez Anido was applauded vigorously in the military press, which assured its readers that he would undoubtedly operate with the same disregard for official policy as he had as Civil Governor of Barcelona.[38] The left, too, anticipated a renewal of operations, whatever the government might claim to the contrary, and denounced the appointment of a general so notoriously contemptuous of the principle of civil supremacy.[39] On June 26 Socialists and Republicans in the Cortes called for the immediate abandonment of the Moroccan Protectorate.[40]

Abandonment was the only alternative to military conquest in Morocco, but the government was not confident enough of public support to defy the army, which, since the losses at Tizi Azza, was united in its perception of the Moroccan problem. Not even the government's appointees in the War Ministry could be relied upon to defend its colonial policy; junteros were as indignant as africanistas.[41] The issue that had so long divided Spanish officers had begun to draw them together, making a military pronunciamiento a realistic possibility. Throughout the summer, the military press commented obsessively on the dishonorable policy in Morocco and the iniquity of the politician with whom it was most closely identified, Santiago Alba.

The government could not risk alienating the army because the middle-class consensus that had brought it to power was problematic on every issue except the war. In Barcelona, the situation was increasingly radicalized, though not coherently focused. As usual, the forces of protest were united only in opposition to the status quo; otherwise, they were divided by class interests and by the growing strength of radical nationalism. Catalyst for the latter was Acció Catalana, whose militant separatism appealed to a younger clientele intolerant of the political gradualism and social conservatism of the Lliga Regionalista. Cambó's formal accusation against the Allendesalazar government in December had given the Lliga a majority of Catalan seats in the Cortes elections of April 29, but in the provincial elections of June 10 the Lliga fell into third place behind Acció Catalana and campaigned stridently against Cambó, who, in the interests of the policy of accommodation he had always defended, resigned as director of the Lliga and as a parliamentary deputy on June 11.[42]

Openly hostile to regionalism, the Liberals made no effort to appease Catalan sentiment, whether moderate or radical.[43] As a consequence, they threw away the opportunity to broaden their support among the most dynamic sectors of the Catalan middle class, who might otherwise have proven helpful allies in the struggle with the army over Morocco. Instead, the antagonism of the government contributed to the leftward shift of the Catalan nationalists, who intensified their protests against the centralized state and its instrument, the army. If anything, the Lliga was even less satisfied with the cabinet than the Catalan left. Alba, the advocate of the excess profits tax in 1916, was also an open foe of the highly protectionist tariff of 1922 and was pushing for general fiscal reform in the present cabinet. More important, the government refused to accede to the Lliga's demands for a declaration of martial law to cope with the mounting social disorder.[44]

Divided in their attitudes toward regionalism, the Catalan middle classes were united in their appreciation of the social problem. By 1923 both the Spanish economy and the Spanish working class were recovering from the depressed years of 1921 and 1922.[45] As profits and employment rose, so did the activities—legal and illegal—of the labor organizations and the determination of the Employers' Federation to resist all concessions. Although the number of strikes and acts of terrorism did not rise to the levels of 1919–20, bombings and shootouts claimed an alarming number of victims, including the moderate CNT leader Seguí on March 10 and the Archbishop of Saragossa, Cardinal Soldevila, on June 4.[46] In late May the dismissal of two members of the Sindicato Único of transportation workers sparked the largest work stoppage since the Canadiense strike of 1919—a general transportation strike that brought Barcelona to a standstill, threatening public health as uncollected garbage accumulated in streets and plazas. Unable to negotiate a settlement between unbending adversaries, Raventós resigned as Civil Governor on May 29 and was replaced by a Liberal journalist, Francisco Barber.

If Raventós, a leading member of the Catalan bourgeoisie, had been unable to enlist support for the government's policy of negotiation, Barber had no hope at all. On June 3 the Employers' Federation issued a statement that blamed the government for the prolongation of the strike and for the breakdown of public authority.[47] The assassination of Soldevila in Saragossa the next day won the employers the sympathy of conservative deputies in the Cortes.[48] While attending the public funeral of a murdered Sometenista on June 9, Barber was assailed with cries of "Away with the governor! Away with the representative of the Sindicato Único!" A serious disturbance was narrowly averted by the appearance of General Primo de Rivera, who was able to deflect the hostility toward Barber into a display of support for himself.[49] Nevertheless, on June 11 the government denied yet another request for a declaration of martial law; it was determined to proceed with its plan to "civilianize" governmental authority in Barcelona.[50] Because the Liberals were dependent upon the left and center-left to enact their reform program, both Republicans and Socialists were able to insist that the cabinet retain its commitment to liberal principles.[51] From the point of view of the right, however, the government was being blackmailed by the forces of anarchy.

Mediating the civilian and military discontent in Barcelona was the Captain General, Miguel Primo de Rivera.[52] A notorious beneficiary of the military turno that had collapsed in 1917, Primo had been moderately successful since then in retaining his influence by posing as the champion of juntero interests, particularly within the court and ministry circles to which he was privy. His appointment to the Captaincy General of Catalonia in March 1922 had been a conciliatory gesture to the junteros, whose power in Madrid had waned with the advent of the africanistas. Under the Liberals, however, he had lost some of his influence; the Liberal cacique from Cadiz had prevented his election to the Senate in May.[53]

One of Primo's most extraordinary gifts was his ability to modify his opinions to suit his audience. Though he had twice been forced to resign a post for advocating abandonment of the Moroccan Protectorate, Primo now found it expedient to champion an aggressive military policy to restore the honor of the army. While he had privately congratulated Santiago Alba on the ransom of the prisoners in January, within the Barcelona garrison he had adopted the bellicose language that even junteros now appreciated. Similarly, he listened with sympathy to the grievances of antiseparatist officers while simultaneously expressing respect for the aspirations of moderate Catalan nationalism as represented by the Lliga.[54] The Catalan bourgeoisie in turn viewed Primo de Rivera as their only bulwark against Anarchist terrorism and government incompetence.

On June 13 the Employers' Federation asked the Captain General to settle the transportation strike, which showed no signs of early resolution. In his reply, Primo cautiously remarked that the mediation was entrusted to the Civil Governor, but then proceeded to analyze the points in dispute between labor and management in terms moderate enough to be accepted immediately by the employers and tentatively by the workers.[55] Caught off balance, the government called both Primo and Barber to Madrid; portentously, Primo returned alone to Barcelona on June 23, even though the strike had resumed. Barber's replacement, Manuel Portela Valladares, was appointed five days later, but it was clear that the Captain General was now the real authority in

Catalonia. Neatly circumventing the government's refusal to declare martial law, on June 28 Primo closed the CNT daily, *Solidaridad Obrera*, and arrested Angel Pestaña and twenty-five others for "sedition and incitation to rebellion," crimes over which military courts possessed permanent jurisdiction.[56]

The Quadrilateral

During his brief sojourn in Madrid, Primo began to lay the ground-work for the military dictatorship evoked with increasing frequency by the government's critics on both the left and the right. Upon arriving in the capital on June 18, he had attended a "patriotic" meeting of prestigious senior officers that included Generals Aguilera and Arraiz, both prominent members of the Supreme Military Council.[57] Unable to persuade Aguilera to place himself at the head of a movement, Primo then turned to a rival group of officers, whose resentment was directed as much against the Supreme Military Council as against the government.[58]

The "Quadrilateral," as this group of conspirators was known, met daily in the residence of its leader, General Cavalcanti.[59] Its other members—Generals Dabán, Saro, and Federico Berenguer—commanded the three Infantry regiments stationed in the capital and maintained close relations with the palace. Ardent africanistas, their major grievance against the government was its opposition to a forward policy that would firmly establish Spanish control over North Africa. The conspirators seem to have had no other concrete objectives, although personal motives undoubtedly heightened their sense of injury. Cavalcanti had recently been indicted by the Supreme Military Council for his imprudence during the convoy to Tizza; Berenguer's brother was about to be tried for negligence by the same tribunal. Also rumored to be in touch with the conspirators was a fourth brigadier, General Cabanellas, himself a recent victim of the Juntas, and the Military Governor of Madrid, the Duque de Tetuán, a close confidant of the king.

The Quadrilateral's activities had not gone beyond seditious muttering, for lack of a leader to head a coup. None of them was personally prestigious enough to muster widespread support in the army; the most prominent senior officer in Madrid, General Aguilera, was, for obvious reasons, unacceptable from their point of view. Initially, they were no more favorably inclined toward General Primo de Rivera, because of his political connections, juntero sympathies, and abandonista reputation. But Primo now agreed that the army must be allowed to avenge its honor in Morocco, and the Quadrilateral had overcome some of their misgivings about him by the time he left for Barcelona.

His comings and goings in Madrid reported in the press, Primo made no attempt to hide his intentions, even confessing to the Conde de Romanones that he planned a rebellion sometime in the future.[60] Apparently fearing that Primo's removal from Catalonia would only precipitate matters, the government decided to postpone a confrontation by allowing him to return to Barcelona. From that moment on, they were living on borrowed time. As Primo stepped off the train, he was greeted by crowds cheering "Long live the brave general! Long live the army! Down with the farcical Government! Long live the Somatén!"[61]

The Debate on Responsibilities

The passivity with which the Liberal coalition countenanced the disintegration of its authority in Barcelona and Morocco is understandable only when placed in the context of its disintegrating authority in the Cortes. From the beginning of the sessions, the government had lost the initiative to its critics on both the left and the right, who labeled its policies as, respectively, either hypocritical or pusillanimous. The principal source of the government's weakness was the responsibilities issue, which forced the Liberals to confront the ambiguity of their program of gradual reform from within the system. As during the previous autumn, there was no easy resolution of their problem. Too closely identified with the past history of the regime to avoid implication in its failures, the Liberals clung to political censure of the Conservatives as a compromise that might satisfy a majority of the country.

The demand for a real political accounting was the foundation of the left/center-left coalition, however. From the point of view of the Socialists, the entire reform program depended on a bold resolution of this issue. On June 20 Prieto introduced a new formal accusation against the members of the Allendesalazar and Maura governments for their "omissions and acts" before and after Anual. The inclusion of the Maura government in the accusation made it impossible for the Liberals to support the Socialists' motion, for Romanonists had participated in the Maura cabinet. On the other hand, the Liberal coalition could not afford to abandon the responsibilities issue to the extreme left. To gain time, García Prieto proposed the appointment of a parliamentary "Responsibilities Commission," on the grounds that the findings of the Picasso report were insufficient to support a blanket political indictment. Composed of twenty-one deputies, the Commission was to gather new evidence during the summer recess and to submit a recommendation to the Congress at the opening of the autumn session on October 1. Fearful that rejection of the Liberals' proposal might enable them to avoid the responsibilities question altogether, the Socialists and Republicans voted with the majority in favor of the compromise on July 6.[62]

In the Senate, debate once again revolved around General Berenguer. Interest in military responsibilities had revived in May when Berenguer had published his version of the Moroccan campaign. The documents in his book successfully vindicated his decisions after the disaster but did not quite dispel his negligence prior to Anual.[63] By the summer of 1923, however, the true extent of the former High Commissioner's guilt or innocence mattered less than the general principle of accountability. Sensitive as usual to public opinion, Berenguer had once again asked the Senate to grant the suplicatorio requested by the Supreme Military Council so that he might prove his innocence before the court.[64] Since the government could not oppose the prosecution of Berenguer without abandoning its responsibilities mandate altogether, Romanones grudgingly sponsored the suplicatorio in the Senate.[65] His own position was difficult, for he had been a firm and constant supporter of the former High Commissioner. Freeing his adherents from their obligation to vote with him as a bloc, he allowed them to join the Conservatives and the senior generals in delaying consideration of the motion. By late June it had still not come to a vote.

As the debates dragged on in the Cortes, the stature of the president of the Supreme Military Council, General Aguilera, increased, particularly among the left, who viewed him as the only guarantee that justice would prevail. Aguilera, too, was growing impatient with the political maneuvering in the Senate. In order to obstruct passage of the suplicatorio, "impunista" senators had cast aspersions on the integrity of the Supreme Military Council.[66] In the opinion of Aguilera and other Council members who met to discuss the problem on June 27, the government had been lukewarm in its defense of their honor.[67] Their indignation soared the next day when Joaquín Sánchez de Toca abruptly abandoned his opposition to the suplicatorio and moved that it be granted unanimously "for reasons of state," implying that the Council was preparing a coup. Taking advantage of the surprise, Romanones called for a favorable vote by acclamation and succeeded in obtaining Berenguer's release for trial.[68]

Aguilera, however, was not mollified. Two days later he wrote a highly provocative letter on official stationery to Sánchez de Toca, accusing him of libel and threatening to demand personal satisfaction. Reading the letter in the Senate on July 3, Sánchez de Toca refused to view it as a purely personal matter; instead, he denounced it as an assault on parliamentary inviolability by the president of the highest military tribunal.[69] As president of the Senate, Romanones felt obliged to refer the letter to the civil Supreme Court for adjudication. At the same time, he worked feverishly to promote a reconciliation between the two senators.[70]

Concern for civil supremacy was restricted to the dynastic politicians, for nearly everyone else hailed Aguilera as a national hero. The left interpreted the conflict as part of an impunista maneuver to remove Aguilera from the Council; officers in the Madrid garrison, on the other hand, viewed the Senate action as an affront to military honor. On July 5 both Aguilera and Sánchez de Toca appeared in the Senate surrounded by supporters and journalists anticipating a confrontation. In order to avert a potentially violent scene, Romanones invited Aguilera and the leader of the Conservative party, Sánchez Guerra, to his office, where the conversation soon degenerated into an exchange of insults. When Aguilera suggested an invidious comparison between military and civilian honor, Sánchez Guerra impetuously struck the general, who just as impetuously retaliated. The tussle was quickly ended by Romanones, however, and they were sent back to the Senate after a gentlemanly handshake.

On the floor of the chamber, the battle continued. Insisting that his letter was written as a private individual, Aguilera refused to retract it, adding that if the Senate aimed at removing him from his post, "opinion, and . . . the people, will do me justice." The prime minister, García Prieto, quickly sprang to the defense of civil supremacy, declaring that any opposition would prevail "only over the corpses of all of us." As tension mounted, a fight broke out in the back benches, while Romanones and Sánchez de Toca attempted to persuade Aguilera to retract his letter, without success. On the other hand, Aguilera refused to repeat his earlier challenge to the government. Finally, the session was unceremoniously ended by Romanones.[71]

In Aguilera Spain had not found her Louis Napoleon, but her Boulanger. The violent passions of the three-day affair quickly faded, the *opera buffo* aspects of the scenes in the Senate became clarified, and all that remained was more bad feeling between right and left.[72] But while it divided the civilian politicians, the incident united the army. Sánchez Guerra's assault in the office of Romanones was felt collectively by an officer corps that had experienced a succession of blows

to its corporate pride since the Liberal coalition government took office
in December 1922. Aguilera's unedifying performance in the Senate
was an insult and a challenge that enabled junteros and africanistas,
responsabilistas and impunistas, to transcend their differences and
unite on the basis of their opposition to the government. The pronunciamiento of Primo de Rivera two months later would succeed
because of the nearly universal disaffection of the officer corps from
the parliamentary regime.

Alfonso XIII and the Dictatorship

Observing the panorama of disintegrating civil authority, almost
certainly aware of the rumors of military conspiracy about him, Alfonso
had begun to think seriously of supporting a temporary dictatorship.
Uppermost in his mind was the preservation of his throne, which he believed threatened from two directions—from the Cortes, which might
at any time become "Constituent," and from the army, which might
sweep away the monarchy along with the parliamentary regime. As he
recalled later in exile, he feared the army would mistake his silence for
approval of the government's policies in North Africa and Catalonia.[73]
As the responsibilities debates got underway in the Cortes, the king
let it be known that he was considering a temporary alteration of the
constitution. In a speech in Salamanca on June 26, Alfonso suggested
that dictatorship was admissible "circumstantially and in moments of
extraordinary gravity . . . for a very limited number of days in order to
leave the way clear for Governments that respect the popular will."[74]
A month later he confided to the Minister of Public Instruction, Joaquín
Salvatella, that he was contemplating an interim military government.[75]
After the appointment of the Responsibilities Commission in July, a
defensive movement to save the throne appeared more urgent than
ever. Less than a year earlier, military defeat in Smyrna had led to the
abdication of King Constantine and the formation of a revolutionary
republican regime in Greece. A similar denouement to the responsibilities campaign in Spain was not unthinkable.

In early August Alfonso sought the advice of Antonio Maura, who
responded in a lengthy note a few days later. Maura agreed that the
present situation could not endure. The turno was dead, coalition governments had failed to revive it, and an alternative government that
excluded the traditional political parties would not survive in the absence of any civic sense in the nation. But however necessary to overcome the inertia of the system, a rupture should not be initiated by the

king: "Neither the generosity of the motive, nor constant success, would avoid the inevitable suicide." On the other hand, immediate action was imperative before a rapid return to constitutional normality became impossible. In Maura's opinion, the only alternative open to the king was a temporary military dictatorship. Six years earlier Maura had remarked that "those who do not let others govern should govern themselves." He repeated his advice in 1923:

> It would be less harmful if those who had imposed their will at critical moments would completely assume the governing function under their own responsibility. Even if they did not succeed in overcoming the difficulties, nor even in sustaining themselves, there would be fewer obstacles to a convalescence that, in any case, can only consist in Spaniards' emerging from their abstention and occupying their appropriate place in political life.[76]

Morocco and the Collapse of the Government

Its political vitality spent by eight months of evasion and concession, the Liberal coalition lacked the will to stand up to the army when confrontation over the war in Morocco could no longer be avoided. Goaded into defiance by the unregenerate Martínez Anido, the army took advantage of the cabinet's weakness, a weakness largely of the Liberals' own making. By failing to act decisively in January, when their political support in the nation had been extensive, they had wasted the opportunity to resolve the ambiguities in Spain's colonial policy. Faced with the implications of those contradictions in August, the government found it could not resist the army's demand for new operations. Yet once it had agreed to authorize an advance, its reason for being disappeared.

Arriving in Melilla on June 8, General Martínez Anido had found a demoralized and idle army exposed to continual harassment along the forward line while Spanish negotiators parleyed with Abd el-Krim. Rumor had it that Alba had prohibited the Melilla garrison from even firing a shot in self-defense.[77] Within a few weeks, the new Commander General had transformed expectations and morale. Negotiations with the rebels came to an abrupt halt when the chief negotiator, Idris bin Said, was mysteriously assassinated on June 20. Then in mid-July Martínez Anido submitted a plan for a combined amphibious and overland assault on Alhucemas Bay, accompanied by a warning that he would resign if the plan were not approved. As he made clear to

Silvela, his primary loyalty was to the army of Africa, not to the High Commissioner or the government.[78]

In early August Silvela went to Madrid to discuss the plan with the government. Personally, he supported a renewal of operations, but as his own Military Cabinet had pointed out, the conquest of Alhucemas would necessitate the commitment of twenty thousand additional troops and fifty million pesetas, far more than the nation was prepared to sacrifice. Within the cabinet, only the War Minister, General Aizpuru, favored the plan; the others—particularly Alba, Joaquín Chapaprieta, Rafael Gasset, and Villanueva—wanted to cut Moroccan expenditures even further to free funds for development in the peninsula. Since the existing forward line was clearly untenable, the cabinet voted to order a retreat, disagreeing only on whether the new line should be at Dar Drius and Afrau, or at the Kert River.[79] On August 11 Alba announced that he had asked General Weyler to head a technical commission from the General Staff to assess the situation in the Rif and to recommend on the positioning of the new line.

Public reaction to the government's decision was overwhelmingly favorable, except in the military press, which unanimously condemned the decision as an affront to the honor of the army and a betrayal of the "supreme and true interests of the Fatherland."[80] When Martínez Anido resigned, as he had promised, on August 12, he expressed the collective indignation of the entire officer corps, which was now on the brink of rebellion.[81] In the minds of most officers, the cabinet—especially the nefarious Santiago Alba—was guilty of sacrificing the national interest to personal political ambition. But the ad hominem attacks on Alba disguised a deeper sense of resentment and confusion arising from the government's efforts to transfer the basis of its sovereignty from the army to the Spanish people. The change of policy this transfer implied threatened the power of the army and offended its sense of tradition and purpose. It was an easy step to the assertion that the army must safeguard the nation, whatever the shortcomings of the state.

The confrontation over Morocco was the critical test for the cabinet —and ultimately, for the future of the parliamentary regime. Until the state was assured of the obedience of the army, the possibility of reform was an illusion. Behind the government were the working-class left and most of the middle class, awakened since Anual to the necessity of political change. Yet in the face of mounting military pressure and a new outbreak of revolutionary protest, the will of the cabinet broke. The precipitant of the crisis was a renewal of heavy fighting along the exposed salient in the Rif. Four days after Weyler's arrival in Melilla on August 15, Abd el-Krim shrewdly ordered his haraka to attack the front, causing 339 casualties, including 14 officers, and placing the entire Spanish line in jeopardy. Although there were 60,000 troops in Melilla, the new Commander General, Enrique Marzo, wired for reinforcements, and the government reluctantly mobilized 20,000 additional troops.[82]

In contrast to the patriotic response to Anual, the national mood in August 1923 was bitter. The widespread opposition to further military sacrifice inspired the small Spanish Communist party to attempt a daring reprise of the Tragic Week of 1909. As the troops embarked in Malaga, a Communist corporal, José Sánchez Barroso, set off a mutiny in the Garellano regiment timed to coincide with the outbreak of a general strike in Bilbao. According to the scheme worked out by the Communist leader, Oscar Pérez Solís, the mutiny and the strike would trigger a military coup that would shortly give way to the proletarian revolution.[83] In the event, both the mutiny and the strike were unsuccessful. In Malaga, the troops were soon herded back on board the steamer *Barceló*, the instigators of the mutiny captured and tried by a military court that sentenced Corporal Sánchez Barroso to death. In Bilbao, the Communist strike failed when the Socialists refused to second it, Pérez Solís receiving a wound during a bloody confrontation between strikers and police.

Viewed from a long-term perspective, however, the plot achieved its goals. When the government voted to recommend clemency for Sánchez Barroso on August 28, it definitively alienated a majority of the officer corps. In overruling the verdict of the military court and placing a moratorium on further troop shipments, the government momentarily regained some of its earlier popularity in the country, but it simultaneously convinced the army that it could not or would not defend the principles of military discipline or social order.[84] On August 29 General Primo de Rivera sent the War Minister an "impertinent" telegram protesting the pardon, which Aizpuru read to the cabinet the same day. Alba urged immediate dismissal of the Captain General, whom he later characterized as "the most insurmountable and tenacious obstacle to the normal development of a policy in conformance with that of the Government."[85] But a majority of the cabinet, shaken by the mutiny in Malaga and fearful of precipitating a coup, preferred to do nothing. The traditional reluctance of the dynastic politicians to alienate the military had reasserted itself. Like its predecessors, the Liberal coalition hoped only to stay in office.

When the coalition divided over the renewal of operations on September 1, the dispute was not really over Morocco, but over whether the cabinet should persist in its commitment to the principle of civil supremacy. Returning early from Melilla, General Weyler presented the cabinet with a recommendation to *advance* in the Rif to a line that included the old positions of Anual and Igueriben, a recommendation logical only if the ultimate goal were Alhucemas Bay. Behind his proposal were the combined weight of the king and the army. On August 31 the staunchest supporter of the civil Protectorate, Alba, suddenly announced his decision to accept Weyler's proposal. To do so meant to renounce the government's entire reform program in favor of a new commitment of resources in Morocco; it also meant an end to the attempt to render the regime more responsive to popular opinion. Unwilling to pay such a heavy price, Villanueva, Chapaprieta, and Gasset resigned their portfolios, leaving García Prieto no alternative but to present the resignation of the entire cabinet to the king.

Alfonso, however, ratified his confidence in the prime minister the following day. A Conservative solution was impossible; the Conservatives were too deeply implicated in the Anual disaster to take office one month before the Responsibilities Commission was scheduled to deliver its report. Thus, the search began for Liberals willing to capitulate to the demands of the army. Finally, on September 3, García Prieto announced the formation of a cabinet composed of the followers of Alba, Romanones, and himself;[86] the next day, an official note confirmed that the new government would support the army's plan for an advance.[87]

The cynicism of the final political crisis of the parliamentary monarchy deprived the Liberals of the remnants of their moral authority. The *replâtrage* of September 3 could not disguise that the regime had lost the battle to diminish the power of the army; by 1923 the army had grown too accustomed to its autonomy to surrender without protest. To remain in office under the circumstances seemed hypocritical and debasing, and the democratic left abandoned the government en masse.[88] On September 4 *El Liberal* suggested that the only honorable solution to the crisis of civil authority was resignation, "abandoning power in order for 'those who do not allow others to govern' to govern themselves."[89] For the first time in many years, Antonio Maura and *El Liberal* were in agreement.

CHAPTER TWELVE

The Pronunciamiento

On September 13, 1923, General Primo de Rivera rose against the parliamentary regime in Barcelona; two days later, the king invited him to Madrid to form a military government. The successful military pronunciamiento resolved the struggle over civil supremacy that had opened in 1917 in favor of the army, effectively thwarting the political evolution of Spain for another seven years. The number of active military conspirators in 1923 was small; had they tried to overcome the government with force, the coup would probably have failed. But Primo's pronunciamiento—like its many predecessors in the nineteenth century—was a "negative pronunciamiento," relying less on a display of superior force than on the passivity of a majority of the army and of most significant social groups in the country. By 1923 few Spaniards, civilian or military, felt much loyalty to the parliamentary regime. The hesitant movement toward political reform had achieved too little for some, posed too great a threat for others. Divided in their perceptions of the need and direction of change, most Spaniards were united in their impatience and anger against the state. Bereft of support either in the officer corps or in the country, the parliamentary system could not offer effective resistance to even a handful of determined plotters.

Crucial to the outcome of events was the attitude of the king, Alfonso XIII, since most officers remained loyal to the monarchy whatever their misgivings about the parliamentary regime. The considerable political power granted the Crown under the Constitution of 1876 was never more evident than in 1923, when it became the moderating power between two competing sovereignties, the army and the parliament. By casting his lot with the military, Alfonso thought he was securing his throne. In reality, he placed the Crown in bondage to military opinion. Having destroyed its constitutional underpinnings, the monarchy would lack the means to resist Republican pressure after the army withdrew its support in 1931.

Precipitants of the Revolt

Ironically, the cabinet formed in desperation on September 3 to save the parliamentary system triggered the pronunciamiento by convincing the military conspirators that the regime might continue to stagger from one crisis to the next without succumbing unless the army delivered the coup de grace. Equally important was the rash of antiwar demonstrations in response to the government's announcement of new operations.[1] With the Sánchez Barroso pardon fresh in their minds, Primo de Rivera and the Quadrilateral were not certain that the government would honor its recent commitment to the African army. The politicians of the parliamentary regime seemed at worst capable of any betrayal; at best, incapable of effective leadership. With the army temporarily in control, the war in Morocco would be speedily ended and order restored in the peninsula.

Alongside their concern over Morocco, the impending report of the Responsibilities Commission was of little significance to the military conspirators, partly because it was a divisive issue. Although none of the Quadrilateral was sympathetic to the investigation of responsibilities, many of the junteros who composed Primo de Rivera's clientele in Barcelona were. On the other hand, the outcome of the parliamentary investigation was of exceptional interest to Alfonso XIII, who must have appreciated its implications for the future of the monarchy. Contrary to what has often been asserted, it was clear by September 1923 that the king would not be implicated in the Anual disaster. The Commission had begun to subpoena witnesses in late July, and although the hearings were closed, most of the testimony had been leaked to the press. The parade of military and political officials had been skilfully questioned by the members of the Commission most interested in uncovering political responsibilities—principally, the three Socialists and the Republican, Domingo—but the mountain of testimony had revealed no more than the Picasso report about specific acts of negligence or about the involvement of the king.[2] Like the Picasso report, the Commission's findings indicted an entire system based on apathy and indecision; otherwise, the hearings had provided little more than a forum for the special pleadings of old rivals.

The expectation surrounding the report was not based on anticipation of a spectacular accusation, but on whether any accusation would be made at all. If the Liberals used their majority to support an indictment by the Congress and a formal trial in the Senate, it would mean the destruction of the system of elites that had governed the country since 1875. A new political configuration, skewed to the left, might lead to Constituent Cortes or to a military coup. In either case, the throne would be endangered. It was more likely, however, that the Liberals would lack the courage to vote a bill of indictment. During the September cabinet crisis, the Commission had met to assemble its report. As the skeptics had predicted, the Conservatives had attempted to block any concrete accusations, and the Liberals had continued to show little inclination to provide vigorous leadership. It appeared probable that only the antidynastic minority would support an indictment against the Conservative ministers.[3]

Nevertheless, the Responsibilities Commission still posed a threat to the throne, for an inconclusive outcome would expose the natural limitations of the evolutionary approach to political reform. The antidynastic parties could be counted on to interpret this as further proof of the necessity of revolution, particularly since the Liberals had shown little reluctance to betray their commitments to the left during the previous nine months. Thus, in trying to preserve the traditional system by avoiding a confrontation over responsibilities, the dynastic parties might inadvertently destroy it. The renewal of operations in Morocco might well be the signal for a revolutionary uprising against the regime.

For Alfonso, then, the future was as uncertain as it was for the military conspirators. When, after the formation of the new cabinet on September 3, General Saro informed the king that the army was prepared to end the existing chaos, he received no discouragement. Instructing the prime minister, García Prieto, to deal with the generals, Alfonso discreetly left with Santiago Alba for his summer residence at San Sebastian.[4] Impatient to act, and lacking a better candidate, the Quadrilateral summoned Primo de Rivera to Madrid on September 7. When Primo returned to Barcelona two days later, they had agreed to rise against the government on September 14.

The conspirators had few active supporters in the officer corps. Significantly, however, those in on the secret represented a broad cross-section of military opinion. The heart of the movement in Madrid was the africanista Quadrilateral, which could count on additional support from the Undersecretary, Luis Bermúdez de Castro, and the Military Governor, the Duque de Tetuán, as well as on the official neutrality of two key officers in the capital—the War Minister, General Aizpuru, and the Captain General, Diego Muñoz Cobo.[5] Further africanista support was assured in Morocco and in Saragossa, where General Sanjurjo was Military Governor. In Barcelona, however, Primo's confidants were primarily junteros. Before his trip to Madrid, he had solicited the aid of all colonels with commands in the Barcelona regiments, including the former president of the Infantry Advisory Commission, Colonel Godofredo Nouvilas.[6] After returning to Catalonia, Primo approached the two brigadiers in the garrison, Generals López de Ochoa and Mercader. With his usual opportunism, Primo told López de Ochoa, who had republican and Catalan sympathies, that the army would rule only until a more responsive civil government could be formed, while assuring Mercader, a devoted palaciego, that the rising was necessary to save the king.[7] Both agreed to support the movement.

Absent from the circle of conspirators were the senior generals—either active or retired—whose careers had been made during the palmy days of the turno. "Princes of the militia," like Aguilera, Weyler, Marina, or even Luque, could rally the officer corps on the basis of sentiment and traditional habits of deference; furthermore, several of the senior generals occupied key positions as captains general in the provinces. But the conspirators did not even inform the senior hierarchy of their plans. Too loyal and too well-rewarded to be tempted into rebellion, the Restoration generals were an integral part of the system against which the pronunciamiento was directed. Primo, too, was intimately connected to the network of political and professional favoritism that a younger generation of officers mistrusted. But he was counting less on his uncertain personal prestige than on the widely acknowledged alienation in the officer corps. Officers continued to be divided by professional issues, but they were temporarily united in their sense of injury and impotence. If they abstained from defending the government, the success of the pronunciamiento was assured.

While the conspirators consolidated their support, the government did nothing, choosing to ignore Alfonso's confidential remarks of September 4. On the twelfth, however, Alba, the minister on duty with the king in San Sebastián, received a telegram from a government official in Barcelona, warning him that the imminent rebellion posed a threat to his personal safety.[8] Unable to avoid the unpleasant facts any longer, the cabinet met at 6:00 P.M. and asked the War Minister to dismiss Primo de Rivera at once. Aizpuru, however, refused, promising instead to dissuade him from his plans over the telephone.[9] At eleven o'clock that night he placed the call. At approximately the same hour, in San Sebastián, Alba resigned and made plans to escape. Before leaving, he wrote García Prieto, essentially echoing Maura's advice to Alfonso a month earlier: "their error cannot be appreciated and exposed, even by themselves, except in the course of time. They speak in the name of sentiments that are legitimate in their origin and pose solutions which it would perhaps be best to let them try out, but

'under the public and constitutional responsibility' of those who defend them."[10] The following day, with the benevolence of local military
authorities, he drove across the frontier into France.[11]

The Manifesto of September 13

Alba did well to hasten his departure, for General Aizpuru found
Primo de Rivera totally unamenable to persuasion when he telephoned
him the night of September 12. Indeed, separatist manifestations in
Barcelona had encouraged him to advance his coup by one day to take
advantage of the outrage in the local garrison. On September 10, the
eve of the Catalan national holiday, huge crowds had surged through
the streets shouting *vivas* to Catalonia and the Rif Republic, while at
a nationalist banquet, visiting Basque and Gallegan dignitaries denounced the Spanish state. The following day, thirty people had been
wounded during a confrontation between separatists and police.[12] On
September 12 *La Correspondencia Militar* had exploded:

> No jails, no penitentiaries, no courts-martial. An emergency law,
> approved by the Parliament, under which anyone who writes
> against the Fatherland, delivers separatist speeches, or offers
> cheers that wound national dignity, shall be expelled from Spain,
> with the loss of all rights of citizenship in perpetual exile, con-
> fiscation of property, and with the absolute prohibition against
> possession of property or industries of any kind in Spain.[13]

Primo did not share the antiseparatist fury of his colleagues; on
the contrary, his contacts with the moderate nationalists of the Lliga
had multiplied during the year. When he abruptly terminated his conversation with the War Minister late on September 12, one of the most
influential members of the Catalan bourgeoisie, the Conde de Güell,
was by his side.[14] Nevertheless, he seized the opportunity to exploit
the indignation of his fellow officers. Within three hours after talking
with Madrid, his troops had captured telegraph and telephone offices
in the Catalan capital, and he had issued his first manifesto "to the
country and the army."

In style and content, the manifesto reflected Primo's aspirations
for the new movement as well as the professed motives for his rebellion.[15] In many ways typical of his generation of officers, Primo shared
their frustrations, values, and political notions. If the simplicity and
frankness of the language suggested that his intentions were generally

good, if somewhat misguided, the document also revealed how unprepared the military was to assume the responsibilities of government.

It was immediately apparent that Primo de Rivera envisioned his pronunciamiento as part of the regenerationist movement that had grown out of the crisis in Spanish political life after the defeat of 1898. The first section of the manifesto justified the army's rebellion against the "dense network of the politics of concupiscence" that had ensnared even the royal will. Primo stressed the provisional character of the movement, which would maintain order only until the country could bring forth "just, wise, laborious, and honest" men to govern. The catalog of sins to be redeemed by the army was likely to be approved by most sectors of Spanish opinion: few people favored assassinations, bank robberies, monetary depreciation, suspicious tariff policies, political intrigue, impiety, illiteracy, biased justice, gambling, or separatist propaganda. And only the left—still a political minority—supported what Primo labeled "social indiscipline, communist propaganda, and tendentious passions on the question of responsibilities." On the whole, the list of grievances was one that could be readily adopted by an impatient and disoriented middle class—both civilian and military. The postwar struggle to reform the political system had fostered political instability while diverting national energies from pressing economic and social problems. It was unrealistic to expect decisive action until the political system could be restructured, but neither the officer corps nor the Spanish electorate was in general noted for its political realism. Inexperienced and uninformed after years of turno politics, they succumbed easily to the tempting belief that an iron surgeon and a return to discipline would suffice to solve the national crisis.

The naiveté of the illusion was evident in the manifesto itself. Primo had little concrete to offer as solutions to the most troublesome national problems—social disorder, the Moroccan war, and responsibilities. His panacea for social unrest was the creation of a Great Spanish Somatén, "the reserve and the brother of the Army in everything." Modeled on the Catalan Somatén, from which it would borrow the motto, Peace, Peace, Always Peace, the proposed militia clearly reflected the conviction, shared by the army and the Catalan bourgeoisie, that the social question was merely one of public order. On Morocco, Primo was even more vague, promising only to search for the "swift, honorable, and sensible solution" that had eluded governments since 1909. Africanistas could take little comfort in his assertion that the honor of the army did not depend on a "stubborn persistence in Morocco," an intimation of the abandonista policy he would attempt to implement in 1924. As for responsibilities, Primo pointed out that the collective guilt of the political parties was being discharged by his abolition of them. Specific political crimes would be dealt with promptly by the courts. Revealing his weak grasp of civil rights, Primo guaranteed anonymity to anyone who would inform on "prevarication, bribery, or immorality." He also assured his audience—in particular, the officer corps—that the "cynical and depraved" Santiago Alba would be tried immediately for his crimes. This was no more than a ploy to exploit Alba's lurid reputation in the army for financial and ethical corruption. As Primo undoubtedly knew, Alba was one of the least corrupt of dynastic politicians. Tried in absentia, he would later be absolved of any wrongdoing by the Supreme Court.

Aside from these blemishes, the tone of the manifesto was generally positive. What Primo lacked was not goodwill, but a specific program of reform. Like many officers, Primo believed that honest men could find simple solutions to complex problems; he claimed that only "those whose masculinity is not well-defined" would find little to applaud in his methods. What he failed to perceive was that virility could provide the style but not the substance of reform. The tragic flaw in the Dictatorship was presaged in its first manifesto.

The Subtle Art of Pronunciamiento Politics

At the same time that he issued the manifesto, Primo declared martial law and exhorted his troops to prepare to meet armed resistance with force. Invoking the fallen heroes of the past, Primo dramatically announced that he was willing to die for his cause.[16] But despite the rhetorical bravado, Primo de Rivera was aware that a successful pronunciamiento was a matter of time and patience, not pitched battles. As the government in Madrid discovered during the early morning of the thirteenth, most officers in the peninsula were unwilling to commit themselves one way or the other, for fear of dividing the army against itself. For the cabinet, there were some encouraging signs, to be sure. Artillery officers in the capital had pledged to attack the rebels if ordered to do so; General Weyler, vacationing in Mallorca, had agreed to assume the Captaincy General of Catalonia. The navy having remained loyal to the government, he set sail for Barcelona on the morning of the thirteenth.[17] Shortly afterwards, the cabinet announced its intention to resist the rebellion with force.[18]

The government's attitude, too, was based on bravado, for the future of the regime lay clearly in the hands of Alfonso XIII, who was still in San Sebastian. With the exception of the Captains General of Valencia and Seville, who had sworn loyalty to the government, most officers, including the Captain General of Madrid, Muñoz Cobo, had indicated that they would await the orders of the king. Alfonso, unfortunately, was not willing to throw his support behind the parliamentary regime at the risk of alienating the officer corps. Although his presence in Madrid was urgently required, he lingered in San Sebastian, and, during an afternoon telephone conversation with García Prieto, refused to authorize the dismissal of all the implicated officers unless the prime minister could guarantee the loyalty of the Madrid garrison. When García Prieto hesitated, Alfonso indicated that his primary allegiance was to "his" army.[19] Later in the day, the head of the Military Household, General Milans del Bosch, arrived from San Sebastian to reconnoiter the situation in the capital. His first interviews were with the Quadrilateral and the Captain General, who recommended that the king accept the government's resignation. Thus, owing to Alfonso's dilatory tactics, the waiting game had begun to turn in favor of the conspirators by the evening of September 13.

In the meantime, Primo had used the day to consolidate his support in Barcelona. In spite of the tension provoked by the nationalist demonstrations, the army and the Catalan bourgeoisie were united in their belief that the government's inability to maintain order was the root cause of social unrest in Barcelona.[20] When Primo appeared to inaugurate the Furniture Exposition in place of the Minister of Development (who had been sent back to Madrid on an early train), he was greeted enthusiastically, particularly after a tactful speech in praise of the Catalan language.[21] The same day, the military censor allowed *La Veu de Catalunya* to report that the Captain General had decided to resolve the "internal problem of Spain" by giving "the regions all the strength and all the liberty that are compatible with the existence of state unity."[22] In response, the Promotion of National Labor, representing the Catalan employers, endorsed the pronunciamiento and hailed the proposal for a Great Spanish Somatén as a "sure guarantee of the respect for law and for the tranquility of the citizenry."[23]

Finally arriving in Madrid on the morning of September 14, Alfonso was at last master of the political situation. He had already decided to abandon the government. When García Prieto asked him to sign the decrees dismissing Primo de Rivera and Sanjurjo, he begged for time to consult his military advisers. As he had expected, this provoked the immediate resignation of the entire cabinet. But the king was in no hurry to confer power on General Primo de Rivera. He may have considered governing alone, particularly after General Muñoz Cobo assured him that all his decisions would be supported by the Madrid garrison. In any event, after receiving the resignation of García Prieto, the king informed the Captain General that he was going to solicit the traditional consultative notes from the dynastic parties.[24] Since it was obvious that a normal political solution was out of the question, this could be no more than a pretext to gain time in order to confirm the extent of his support in the army.

Informed by Muñoz Cobo of Alfonso's indecision, Primo quickly cut short the king's dalliance with the idea of personal power. Through Muñoz Cobo, he warned the king that he had hoped to "make the revolution under the sign of the monarchy," but that if opposed, he would not hesitate to consider the alternatives.[25] Lacking the stomach for a test of wills, Alfonso instructed Muñoz Cobo to send for Primo. In the interim, he appointed the Captain General and the four members of the Quadrilateral to a provisional Military Directory. When Primo arrived in Madrid on September 15, he was made president of a formally constituted Military Directory composed of eight relatively unknown brigadier generals.[26] The royal decree characterized the new government as "a brief parenthesis in the constitutional progress of Spain, to be reestablished as soon as the country offers us men uncontaminated by the vices we attribute to political organizations."[27] With this decree, Alfonso deliberately destroyed the parliamentary regime and inadvertently destroyed the monarchy as well.

Later Alfonso would argue that he had saved Spain from civil war by avoiding a confrontation between two factions of the army. He also insisted that he had been forced to deal with a fait accompli, having had no prior knowledge of the coup.[28] Neither argument is convincing. At best, Alfonso was only technically innocent of plotting against the government: if he was unaware of the details of the conspiracy, he had nonetheless been informed on September 3 of the army's intention to act. Far from discouraging the plotters, Alfonso had spared no effort to publicize his own disaffection from the government and to emphasize his solidarity with the army. With every justification, Primo and the Quadrilateral had proceeded as if they had the consent of the king.

Furthermore, Alfonso's contention that he averted a civil war conveniently ignores the fact that the coup might well have failed had the king decisively supported the government from the beginning. Primo was not prepared to fight; he had neither the forces nor the temperament for a bloody coup. His success rested on the refusal of the officer corps to risk a civil war in defense of a political system from which most of them were alienated. By publicizing his own disaffection, the king encouraged their neutrality. Alfonso did not save Spain from a civil war; he destroyed her parliamentary system.

Although Primo de Rivera's pronunciamiento might have been frustrated, a military dictatorship was probably inevitable sooner or later. In retrospect, the turning points seem to have been the successful rebellion of the Juntas de Defensa in June 1917 and the disaster at Anual in July 1921. The failure to assert civilian control over the Juntas encouraged the army as a whole to continue to blackmail the dynastic parties, particularly after the explosion of labor unrest in Barcelona and the renewal of the Moroccan war in 1919. By the time of the defeat at Anual, the dynastic politicians were so dependent on the military that they were unable to alter the relationship. Yet Anual made political reform —particularly with regard to civil-military relations—unavoidable, by awakening large sectors of the middle class to the necessity of meaningful change. Although the dynastic parties made an effort to transform the regime, their efforts were hampered by their lack of broad support in the nation and by the steady resistance of the military to any reduction of its privileged position within the state. Democratic reform and administrative modernization could lead only to personnel cutbacks, smaller budgets, and a reduced role in Morocco. Out of self-preservation, the army had to halt the process of political reform.

Public Reaction to the Pronunciamiento

The military dictatorship was made possible by the alienation of most Spaniards—civilian and military—from the parliamentary regime. Since 1898, but especially since 1917, Spaniards had lived from one crisis to the next: ministerial instability, inflation, scarcity, labor unrest, terrorism, and military disaster—all had contributed to the atmosphere of national crisis and disintegration. On the whole, the traditional political elites had responded poorly to the challenge, defending their right to rule even as they undermined that right by their demonstrated incapacity for change. And the parties of opposition were too divided, by class and regional interests, to provide coherent or effective leadership. United only in their opposition to the status quo, by September 1923 many Spaniards had abandoned hope in the possibility of gradual democratic reform.

Because of the widespread disaffection, the pronunciamiento was welcomed by a broad spectrum of political opinion. Predictably, *La Correspondencia Militar* hailed the movement as a "positive hope of salvation" and invoked the "patriotic and disinterested personality of the unforgettable General Pavía," the only other general in Spanish history to replace civilian government with a military dictatorship.[29] The rest of the right-wing press, which had been clamoring for dictatorship for at least nine months, was also gratified, even though Primo discouraged journalistic attempts to compare him to Mussolini.[30] Among the Catalan bourgeoisie, too, the dictatorship was received warmly, although Cambó, vacationing in Greece, warned the Lliga to remain aloof from the new government.[31] In any event, their enthusiasm was short-lived. Under intense pressure from his fellow officers, Primo would be forced to follow a repressive policy with regard to Catalan nationalism. The Lliga would emerge from the Dictatorship with its moral force spent.

More surprising, perhaps, was the optimism of some of the bourgeois left, which hailed the pronunciamiento of 1923 as it had hailed the Juntas de Defensa in 1917. After years of denouncing militarism, neither *El Sol* nor *El Liberal* sprang to the defense of civil supremacy. *El Liberal* found little of value in the manifesto of September 13,[32] but its renovationist editors seemed to agree with Ortega y Gasset at *El Sol* that

> the system of equilibrium had been broken in 1917; a new one to replace it had not been created. May God grant that it now be achieved, with the coming of a Spain more noble and fertile than the old and ruinous Spain in which we were born. On the Army will fall the honor of having given the final push, and of course [on the Army] falls the responsibility of having initiated the battle and all its consequences. In this initial moment, we ask for swiftness of resolution; any delay is useless and dangerous.[33]

The other social forces that had demanded change since 1917 were too divided in 1923 to offer more than verbal resistance to the Dictatorship.[34] Neither the Socialists nor the Anarchosyndicalists would join the one-day general strike initiated by the Communists in Bilbao. Nor would the Socialists—especially the cautious UGT leaders, Iglesias and Largo Caballero—support the CNT proposal for a general strike to save the regime and to protest the renewal of the war in Morocco. The failure of the working-class left to resist the military usurpation of power was made easier by their ambivalent attitude toward the parliamentary monarchy. It also reflected their own doubts about the revolutionary potential of the Spanish working class. Like the Communist leader Pérez Solís, many leftists believed military dictatorship would provide the necessary incubation period for the proletarian revolution.

The passivity with which the Spanish left greeted the Dictatorship would be followed by seven years of further division and ambivalence. Driven underground, anarchosyndicalism would be captured by the extreme terrorist wing of the movement. The Socialists, on the other hand, would be divided by the decision of the trade union leaders to collaborate with the Dictatorship.[35]

Not unnaturally, those who condemned the pronunciamiento most uncompromisingly were those who had benefited most from the parliamentary regime. Both the dynastic politicians and the political generals were too closely identified with the Restoration system, which had decently hidden the naked reality of military power under the cloak of civil supremacy, to welcome the idea of direct military rule. Since at least 1917, the civilian and military politicians of the turno had been forced to confront the fiction of their own control over the army and had struggled, unsuccessfully, to assert the authority of the state over the unwieldy and obstreperous institution they had created. The pronunciamiento of Primo de Rivera was proof that they had failed.

Still, the dynastic politicians made no effort to resist the coup with force. Repeating Maura's words of 1917 like an incantation, they now agreed that direct military rule would force the army to bear the responsibility for its own decisions. García Prieto had greeted the rebellion with a mixture of cynicism and relief, remarking that he had "a new saint to whom to commend myself: Saint Miguel Primo de Rivera, because he has relieved me of the nightmare of governing."[36] The more responsible dynastic politicians, however, viewed the military dictatorship as an inevitable but temporary evil. Convinced that the army would quickly discredit itself, they preferred to remain aloof until the parliamentary regime could be restored. What they, like Alfonso, failed to recognize was that the old system could never be re-created. Primo's coup had cut short the political transformation of the parliamentary regime. Deprived of its natural growth, the parliamentary monarchy could not serve as an adequate vehicle for the expression of popular sovereignty once the military dictatorship had disappeared.

CHAPTER THIRTEEN

Conclusions

Praetorian intervention in Spain in 1923, like praetorianism elsewhere, grew out of the coincidence of motive and opportunity. What seems important to emphasize is that the military disposition to intervene and the susceptibility of civilian government to intervention interacted in such a way as to make praetorianism not only likely, but nearly constant in the period between 1875 and 1936. Most of the time, the military was content to act merely as a powerful pressure group. But in 1923 and 1936 the military broke through the facade of civil supremacy and asserted its right to govern the nation directly. At all times, however, the army's extraordinary political power derived both from its determination to protect its corporate interests and from the insecurity of the liberal state.

The architect of the Restoration, Cánovas del Castillo, had consciously adopted the British model of civil-military relations: the army was to be small, only moderately professionalized, and apolitical, its leadership cadres drawn from the same social groups that produced the political leadership. Yet like liberalism itself, this model did not transplant well. For one thing, the Spanish officer corps was recruited not from the ruling oligarchy but from the traditional middle class. This meant that the political neutrality of the army would depend on a high degree of professionalization rather than on a similarity of outlook between civilian and military elites. Nevertheless, the dynastic parties attempted to select the military leadership on the basis of political loyalty and patronage rather than merit or expertise, with the result that the large majority of officers believed the state to be the greatest obstacle to military professionalization. Professional standards were further compromised by the size of the officer corps, which kept salaries low, retarded promotions, and prohibited technological modernization. The result was the opposite of what Cánovas had intended—a faction-ridden and demoralized officer corps, the large bulk of which was resentful, politically disaffected, and prone to intervention.

Through the Juntas de Defensa, bureaucratic officers attempted to protect their professional interests by eliminating the political favoritism that undermined institutional autonomy. With the ruling elites dependent on army support, the junteros were successful in imposing their will. Many of their professional grievances remained untreated, however, because military bureaucrats refused to countenance the other military reforms necessary to complete the process of professionalization—most notably, personnel cutbacks and selection promotions based on professional achievement. The efforts of the dynastic politicians to respond positively to military demands were further complicated after the renewal of the Moroccan war in 1919, which created a faction of highly trained officers whose professional interests were diametrically opposed to those of the peninsular bureaucrats. The politicization of the War Ministry and the General Staff made internal resolution of these institutional issues impossible, forcing them instead into the national political arena, where they contributed to political instability.

The army was also politicized by the inability of the traditional elites to adjust to the rapid economic and social changes induced by the world war. The army was the institution by which the dynastic parties repulsed all domestic challenges to their power, especially after the end of the war. Far from being the guarantor of national defense, the army found itself frequently required to adopt the unheroic role of policing social disturbances. At the same time, the opponents of the existing social and political order attacked the regime through the army. Thus, while the civilian politicians reinforced their dependency on the army, the army itself was increasingly alienated from the state.

The military disaster at Anual in 1921 was a turning point for the parliamentary monarchy, for it deprived the dynastic politicians of their traditional support in the middle classes. At the same time, it deepened the factionalism in the officer corps, dramatizing the unreliability of the army as a guarantor of political stability. During the next two years, the dynastic politicians struggled to respond to the national demand for political reform, a task complicated by the heterogeneous character of the protest. While a consensus could be assembled on the need for change, there was little agreement on the degree or direction that change should take. Middle-class democrats envisioned a more responsive parliament, liberated from the control of the traditional interest groups and the king. The working-class parties, on the other hand, viewed political reform as only the first step toward a redistribution of economic and social power. The alliance between these groups, which emerged in 1917 and again after 1921, was at best uneasy. To the

traditional elites in the dynastic parties, it was an unreassuring foundation on which to base the regime. As a result, they were reluctant to
turn their backs completely on their old allies in the military.

In any event, by 1923 the army was unwilling to be shunted aside.
Although Primo de Rivera announced a few days after the pronunciamiento that the army had acted patriotically to prevent "the total
collapse of Spain,"[1] in reality, the army supported the coup to defend
its corporate interests. Like the patriotic language in the Junta manifesto of June 1, 1917, the regenerationist rhetoric of Primo's manifesto
disguised the conservative professional goals of the majority of officers. In 1917, however, the mere threat of a coup had insured that the
Juntas' grievances would receive a hearing. By 1923 the army perceived
that only a military government could be counted on to secure military
interests.

Primo's patriotic phrases were not necessarily hypocritical. Like
military men everywhere, Spanish officers tended to equate their interests with those of the nation. From the belief that the survival of the
state depended on the preparedness and expertise of the military, it
was easy to extrapolate that an injury to the army was, by definition,
an assault on the nation itself. Since officers found it difficult to tolerate
any deviation from their own perception of where the national interest
lay, they could not accept as legitimate the popular demand for a withdrawal in Morocco, nor even the official policy of a reduction in military expenditures. In their view such policies were the equivalent of
treason. If the politicians lacked the will to resist the pressure from the
left, it was up to the army to safeguard vital national interests.

The sense of corporate identity forged during 1923 would endure.
But once the common enemy had been eliminated, corporate solidarity
disappeared. After 1923 many of the conflicts that contributed to the
collapse of the parliamentary monarchy reemerged. This is not the
place for an extended analysis of military policy and military politics
under the Dictatorship and the Second Republic. Nevertheless, the
events of the period under discussion formed the background and
shaped the parameters of the extended constitutional crisis of the 1920s
and 1930s, in which the "military problem" played a significant and
seemingly intractable role. It may be worthwhile, therefore, to conclude this study with some tentative observations about the way in
which the crisis in civil-military relations between 1917 and 1923 prefigured the pattern of events that led to military rebellion and civil war
in 1936.

As a way of understanding the motives and opportunity for military
intervention, it seems useful to stress once again the intimate connec-

tion between military professionalization and political modernization. The key to neutralization of the officer corps was its thoroughgoing professionalization; objective institutional norms to regulate appointments and promotions and financial support for the development of professional expertise would have gone a long way toward eliminating the praetorian tendencies in the Spanish army. Such measures, however, had to be accompanied by extensive personnel cutbacks, which were possible only if the government commanded extensive political support. Without popular backing, no government would dare risk an assault on vested military privilege. Conversely, in the absence of a professionally satisfied army, no regime could consider itself safe from military intervention.

This dilemma was inherited both by General Primo de Rivera and by the provisional Republican government of April 1931. Primo de Rivera in fact possessed few options. Having come to power through the tacit consent of the officer corps and lacking constitutional legitimacy for his new regime, he was no more able than the dynastic politicians to legislate autonomously on military matters. Furthermore, Primo was acutely aware of the military factionalism that had made the formulation of a coherent military policy so difficult. Undeceived by the impressive unity of September 1923, Primo consolidated his support in the peninsular army, where juntero sentiments had survived the dissolution of the Juntas the year before. Merit promotions were not restored, the senior hierarchy was ignored, General Berenguer was convicted (and then quickly pardoned), the General Staff was abolished and the Staff Corps converted into a "service." Military bureaucrats filled lucrative civil posts. Most important of all, Primo decided to withdraw from the interior of Morocco.

At this point, the discontent of the africanistas exploded into near mutiny. After a disastrous retreat from Xauen in 1924, Primo was forced to reverse himself; he had underestimated the degree to which power within the officer corps had shifted across the Straits. After 1925, the dictator pursued a frankly proafricanista policy. The African army, especially the shock units, was retrained and expensively equipped, merit promotions were restored and the closed scale abolished. When the Artillery Corps rebelled, Primo dissolved it and, in an attempt to smooth over intercorps rivalries, revived the General Military Academy.

But factionalism was stronger than institutional solidarity by the late 1920s. Abortive coups were led by Generals Weyler and Aguilera, whose services Primo had disregarded, and by disaffected junior officers, especially in the Artillery Corps, where republicanism was a coef-

ficient of injured privilege. Denied the support of the army, Primo had
no alternative but to resign. His successor, General Berenguer, seemed
most likely to unify military opinion but had no better luck. When the
Republic was proclaimed in April 1931, nearly all of the faction-ridden
officer corps was willing to withhold judgment until the new regime
should reveal its military policy. As in 1923, most officers had few
political ideas beyond the equation of military interests with those of
the nation.

Unlike Primo de Rivera, the new Republican government possessed extensive popular support. Furthermore, the new War Minister,
Manuel Azaña, had retained his early interest in military reform. Using
the democratic foundations of the new government to give him the
leverage he needed, Azaña launched a vigorous attack on the institutional deficiencies that had defied earlier generations of military
reformers. Initially, his program was as popular with officers as it was
with civilians because of his expressed commitment to the complete
professionalization of the Spanish army. Azaña promised to depoliti-
cize military promotions and appointments and to provide the army
with modern equipment and training with the funds released by his
radical reduction of the active list. The Republican army of the future
would be small, efficient, and democratic.

Azaña did not achieve his goal, largely, it seems to me, because his
commitment to military professionalization was compromised by his
desire to "republicanize" the armed forces, a goal that deprived the
military of its institutional autonomy by politicizing the War Ministry.
Advised by officers whose interests had suffered under the Dictatorship, the new War Minister systematically reversed nearly all of Primo
de Rivera's legislation and a large number of his promotions on the
grounds that they had been illegally made. Azaña refused to consider
whether those policies and promotions had been professionally sound,
so eager was he to expunge every trace of the previous regime. This
shortsighted attitude meant that political, rather than professional,
considerations were still the basis for decision making in the Ministry.
As long as this was the case, the professional dissatisfaction that had
nurtured factions of junteros, africanistas, and ministerial favorites in
the past would persist into the future. Once the initial widespread
support for the Republican regime had begun to erode, the way was
clear for a recurrence of praetorianism.

Azaña thus repeated the mistakes of his predecessors under the
parliamentary monarchy. Like them, he distrusted professionalization
as a vehicle for securing the political neutrality of the army. Instead, he
favored a system in which the loyalty of the army was secured through

a high degree of political commitment and identification with the nation as a whole. From his point of view, the political reliability of the army during the first critical months of the new regime was too important to be left to chance. Thus he ignored his own decrees establishing strict seniority in appointments and promotions and placed officers of known Republican sympathies in the most sensitive military posts. In some cases, this led to the elevation of officers whose past careers were less than illustrious; more aggravating to the officer corps, however, was that it isolated a number of the most prestigious and talented officers from the leadership cadres. Many of these officers, africanistas who had risen rapidly during the Moroccan wars of the 1920s, were basically apolitical, willing to serve loyally any government that would respect the professional autonomy of the army. Instead, Azaña provided them with a motive for intervention by stripping them of their merit promotions and enacting "reforms" detrimental to military efficiency, such as the closed scale. At the same time, these policies did not completely satisfy the bureaucratic faction in the officer corps, either. As always, juntero loyalty evaporated at the first sign of professional discontent, which, given the low level of professionalization, was inevitable. By 1933 restless junior officers had joined the Spanish Military Union (UME) in order to protest stagnation, working conditions, and favoritism. In mid-1936 General Francisco Franco warned the prime minister, Santiago Casares Quiroga, that Republican military policies had resuscitated the factionalism and lack of "internal satisfaction" that had nurtured the Juntas de Defensa in 1917. Franco spoke emphatically of the need for justice and equity with regard to promotions and appointments if "civil struggles" were to be averted.[2] The army, in other words, was once again prepared to intervene to protect its corporate interests. A month later, over half the officer corps joined the military rebellion against the government.

Some interesting parallels emerge from a comparison between the origins of the military rebellion of 1923 and that of 1936. In both cases, the opportunity for military intervention was provided by the weakness of civilian government in a country in which uneven economic and social development hindered the formation of a broad consensus on political issues. Out of this basic condition, a similar pattern in civil-military relations emerged. With one political minority attempting to impose its will on other minorities, the temptation to use the army, or a part of it, as a political ally proved irresistible. This stimulated a policy of appeasement, which politicized institutional decisions and encouraged competing groups of officers to influence policymaking. Once it became clear to officers that their professional concerns would be subordinate to political considerations, a defensive military response to protect corporate interests became highly probable. Because the civil-military conflict took place within the context of a constitutional struggle, in each case the military reaction—a pronunciamiento—was cast in ideological terms. Portraying itself as a messianic or regenerative force, the army in fact emerged as the champion of an interpretation of Spanish history that, not surprisingly, included an extensive political role for the military. It remains to be seen whether the social and economic development of the last twenty years will enable Spaniards in the post-Franco era to eliminate praetorianism by constructing a political system based on popular consent and civil supremacy.

Appendixes   Notes   Bibliography   Index

APPENDIX A

Spanish Cabinets, 1900–1923

Prime Minister	Date Assumed Office	Party
Práxedes Mateo Sagasta	March 6, 1901	Liberal
Francisco Silvela	December 6, 1902	Conservative
Raimundo Fernández Villaverde	July 20, 1903	Conservative
Antonio Maura	December 5, 1903	Conservative
Marcelo Azcárraga	December 16, 1904	Conservative
Raimundo Fernández Villaverde	January 27, 1905	Conservative
Eugenio Montero Ríos	June 23, 1905	Liberal
Segismundo Moret	December 1, 1905	Liberal
José López Domínguez	July 6, 1906	Liberal
Segismundo Moret	November 20, 1906	Liberal
Marqués de la Vega de Armijo	December 4, 1906	Liberal
Antonio Maura	January 25, 1907	Conservative
Segismundo Moret	October 21, 1909	Liberal
José Canalejas	February 9, 1910	Liberal
Manuel García Prieto	November 12, 1912	Liberal
Conde de Romanones	November 12, 1912	Liberal
Eduardo Dato	October 27, 1913	Conservative
Conde de Romanones	December 9, 1915	Liberal
Manuel García Prieto	April 19, 1917	Liberal
Eduardo Dato	June 11, 1917	Conservative
Manuel García Prieto	November 3, 1917	Coalition
Antonio Maura	March 22, 1918	Coalition
Manuel García Prieto	November 9, 1918	Liberal
Conde de Romanones	December 5, 1918	Liberal
Antonio Maura	April 14, 1919	Conservative
Joaquín Sánchez de Toca	July 20, 1919	Conservative

Manuel Allendesalazar	December 12, 1919	Conservative
Eduardo Dato	May 5, 1920	Conservative
Gabino Bugallal	March 8, 1921	Conservative
Manuel Allendesalazar	March 13, 1921	Conservative
Antonio Maura	August 14, 1921	Conservative
José Sánchez Guerra	March 8, 1922	Conservative
Manuel García Prieto	December 7, 1922	Liberal

Biographical Appendix

AGUILERA EGEA, FRANCISCO. Born in Ciudad Real in 1857, Aguilera fought in the Carlist wars, in Cuba, and in Morocco, receiving all his promotions through war merits, and rising to lieutenant general at the age of fifty-five. He held several awards for valor. Until his break with the party leadership in 1919, Aguilera was the leading general in the garciaprietista wing of the Liberal party. As president of the Supreme Military Council in 1923, he emerged as a potential leader of a pronunciamiento; in 1926 he participated in the "Sanjuanada," a revolt against the dictatorship of Primo de Rivera. Aguilera died shortly after the proclamation of the Republic in 1931.

ALFAU MENDOZA, FELIPE. Born in 1848, Alfau won his promotions in the Carlist wars, in Cuba, and in Africa. At the same time, he stood out as an intellectual with interests in medicine and North African affairs. As Commander General of Ceuta in 1913, he engineered the bloodless capture of Tetuan, a coup that led to his appointment as first High Commissioner of Spanish Morocco in February 1913. Six months later, the Spanish occupation of Tetuan led to renewed guerrilla warfare, and Alfau was dismissed. Champion of the Juntas de Defensa in 1917, Alfau was passed to the reserve after passage of the reform law of 1918. In 1922 he was elected to the Senate as a Conservative.

AMADO Y REYGONDAUD DE VILLEBARDET, JULIO. Born in 1873, Amado attended the General Military Academy (AGM) and the Superior War College (ESG). As a Cavalry officer, he fought in the Cuban war of 1895–98, receiving a merit promotion to captain in 1896. In 1906 he acquired *La Correspondencia Militar* and in 1911 resigned his commission. Amado sat in the Cortes as an "independent monarchist" from 1910 to 1923.

BERENGUER FUSTE, DÁMASO, Conde de Xauen. Berenguer, the son of a colonial officer, was born in Remedios, Cuba, on August 4, 1873. After attending the AGM, he joined the Cavalry and immediately saw action in Cuba, where he was the aide of General Luque. He served continuously in Morocco between 1909 and 1915, rising from lieutenant colonel to division general in nine years. In 1911 he organized the first units of native troops led by Spanish officers, the Regulars of Melilla. Through Luque, Berenguer affiliated with the Romanonist Liberals and served as Undersecretary of the War Ministry during the National Government of Antonio Maura. In November 1918 he became War Minister, a post he retained when Romanones assumed office a month later. In January 1919 he was appointed High Commissioner in Morocco, where he served until his indictment for negligence at Anual in July 1922. In 1924 the Supreme Military Council found him guilty as charged, but Primo de Rivera pardoned him, named him head of the Military Household in 1924, and in 1927 secured him the title of Conde de Xauen. After the resignation of the dictator in 1930, Berenguer became head of the government. Unable to steer the monarchy back into constitutional channels, he resigned in February 1931. After the proclamation of the Republic, he was tried by the "Responsibilities Tribunal" and remained in prison until the victory of the right in the elections of 1933.

BURGUETE Y LANA, RICARDO. One of three brothers who were officers in the Infantry, Burguete was born in 1871. A graduate of the AGM, he fought in Morocco, Cuba, and the Philippines in the 1890s, and again in Melilla in 1909, receiving the Laurel Wreath of Saint Ferdinand in 1895 and rising rapidly to brigadier by 1913. At the same time, he wrote several books on military theory, in which he insisted upon the superiority of moral factors to technological or "scientific" ones in achieving victory on the battlefield. Burguete also acquired some notoriety for his brutal repression of the Asturian miners' strike in 1917. After the indictment of General Berenguer in July 1922, he was appointed High Commissioner in Morocco, a post he retained until January 1923. As president of the Supreme Military Council in 1931, he was responsible for the light sentences given the Republican conspirators of the previous December. Shortly after the proclamation of the Republic, Burguete retired from the army. He died in 1938.

CABANELLAS Y FERRER, MIGUEL. Born in 1872, Cabanellas attended the AGM, then joined the Cavalry and served in Cuba. Most of his career was spent in Africa. Cabanellas supported the pronunciamiento of

Primo de Rivera in 1923, but he quickly fell out of favor with the dictator. A Mason and a liberal, Cabanellas joined the revolutionary committee formed to work for a republic in 1930. In 1931 he was appointed Commander-in-Chief in Morocco; in 1932 he replaced General Sanjurjo as head of the Civil Guard. In 1936 he somewhat reluctantly supported the military revolt. At his death in 1938, he was Inspector General of the Nationalist army.

CASTRO GIRONA, ALBERTO. Born in the Philippines in 1875, Castro Girona attended the AGM and the ESG, electing after graduation to return to the Infantry Corps as a diplomado. He served almost continuously in Morocco from 1913 until the final pacification of the zone in 1927, when he was promoted to lieutenant general. His africanismo made him the advocate of political pacification rather than of military conquest. In 1929 Castro Girona was briefly involved in the Sánchez Guerra conspiracy against the Dictatorship; his last-minute withdrawal lost him the favor of both the dictator and the opposition. In 1936 Castro Girona supported the military revolt.

CAVALCANTI DE ALBURQUERQUE Y PADIERNA, JOSÉ, Conde de Taxdirt and Marqués de Cavalcanti. The son of a Florentine émigré and his Spanish wife, Cavalcanti was born in Cuba in 1871. He attended the AGM and later the Cavalry Academy with Berenguer and Silvestre. Cavalcanti served in Cuba and Melilla and was a Conservative deputy from La Coruña in 1915. After the Anual disaster of 1921, he was appointed Commander General of Melilla, where he remained until his outspoken opposition to government policy occasioned his dismissal. In 1923, after his indictment by the Supreme Military Council for his rash conduct under fire, he was an active member of the "Quadrilateral" that organized the coup against the Liberal government of García Prieto. Married to a daughter of Emilia Pardo Bazán and a staunch monarchist, Cavalcanti was appointed head of the Military Household in 1923–24; in 1932 he participated in the revolt of General Sanjurjo against the Republic. Cavalcanti also joined the military rebellion of 1936, dying a year later in San Sebastian.

ECHAGÜE Y MÉNDEZ DE VIGO, RAMÓN, Conde de Serrallo. Born in 1852, the son of a general, Echagüe received all his promotions during the Carlist and colonial wars, rising to division general by 1895. One of the inner circle of Restoration generals, Echagüe was head of the Military Household and personal aide to the Queen Regent in 1897. In 1914 he was appointed life senator by the Conservatives. Echagüe served as Minister of War in 1913 and at his death in November 1917 was president of the Supreme Military Council.

FERNÁNDEZ-SILVESTRE, MANUEL. The son of a retired army major, Silvestre was born in Santiago de Cuba in 1871. After attending the AGM, he joined the Cavalry and in 1895 went to Cuba, where his bravery earned him a severe wound and a promotion to major. A favorite of Alfonso XIII before going to Melilla in 1904, he was made gentleman of the chamber in 1909 on his return. In 1911 he became the first commanding officer in Larache. In spite of a record of insubordination while there, he was promoted to brigadier general in 1913. When further insubordination resulted in his dismissal in 1915, he was made head of the king's Military Household. In 1920 he returned to Africa, first to Ceuta, then at his friend Berenguer's request, to Melilla, where he embarked upon the military advance that led to his death at Anual in July 1921.

FRANCO BAHAMONDE, FRANCISCO. The son of a minor naval official, Franco was born December 4, 1892, in El Ferrol. A graduate of the Infantry Academy, he was sent to Africa in 1912, where, as a member of the elite Regulars, he was severely wounded. Franco was head of the Tercio from 1923 until his promotion to brigadier in 1928, when he was made director of the new General Military Academy. In 1931 the Republican government closed the AGM and a year later stripped Franco of the merit promotions he had earned in Morocco during the 1920s. In 1935, Franco was chief of the General Staff under José María Gil Robles; in June 1936 he joined the military conspiracy that rose against the Republic in July, quickly emerging as Commander-in-Chief and head of the new Nationalist state, which he ruled until his death in 1975.

LUQUE Y COCA, AGUSTÍN. Luque was born in Malaga in 1850, the son of an Infantryman. As a young captain, he rose with the Republican Manuel Ruíz Zorrilla in Cadiz. His Republican friends included Nicolás Estévanez and his own father-in-law, the Republican editor of *El Cencerro*. In 1897 Luque was implicated in a conspiracy to overthrow the Regency and establish a republic, but he seems to have been satisfied instead with appointment as Captain General of Seville. During the *¡Cu-cut!* affair of November 1905, rumors again implicated Luque in a republican conspiracy, with the promise of a million pesetas and a Parisian exile should he fail. His appointment to the War Ministry in 1905 marked the beginning of his career as a member of the governing elite. Minister of War with the Liberals four times between 1905 and 1917, he was appointed Director of the Civil Guard in 1917 and head of the Corps of Inválidos in 1918. Passed to the reserve in 1921, Luque died in 1935.

MARINA Y VEGA, JOSÉ. Born into a military family in Gerona in 1850, Marina's influential connections derived from his friendship with Ramón Echagüe and from his wife, a relative of Echagüe's and the daughter of a brigadier. Marina earned his promotions in Puerto Rico, the Philippines, and Cuba, but his professional preeminence was based on his African career. Marina was military governor of Melilla from 1905 until 1909; during the campaign of that year, he was promoted to lieutenant general. High Commissioner from 1913 to 1915, he was dismissed after an incident involving a royal favorite, Manuel Fernández-Silvestre. Briefly a spokesman for the Juntas de Defensa in 1917 and Minister of War in the National Government of 1918, Marina was passed to the reserve in 1919. He died in 1926.

MARTÍNEZ ANIDO, SEVERIANO. Born in El Ferrol in 1862, Martínez Anido fought in Melilla and the Philippines in the 1890s and again in Melilla in 1909, where his bravery caught the eye of General Marina. Displaying his usual fondness for military heroes, Alfonso XIII named him his aide. From then on, his rise was rapid. In 1919 Martínez Anido was made Military Governor of Barcelona; in November 1920 he became Civil Governor of the city. Dismissed in late 1922, Martínez Anido was sent to appease the Melilla garrison during the summer of 1923; that fall, he actively supported the coup of Primo de Rivera against the parliamentary regime. Shortly thereafter, he was appointed Director General of the Security Forces. In exile in France under the Republic, Martínez Anido served as Director of Public Order in the Nationalist zone until his death in 1938.

MILANS DEL BOSCH Y CARRIÓ, JOAQUÍN. A Cavalry officer born in 1854, Milans del Bosch participated in every campaign from the Carlist war to the colonial campaign in Morocco. By 1907 he was a brigadier and an intimate of the king. In 1918 he was appointed Captain General of Barcelona, where he served until his dismissal for insubordination in February 1920. Shortly thereafter, the king made him head of his Military Household, where he served until 1923.

MILLÁN-ASTRAY Y TERREROS, JOSÉ. Millán-Astray was born in La Coruña in 1879, the son of a civil servant who was later Chief of Police in

Barcelona and head of the Model Prison in Madrid. A graduate of the Infantry Academy and a diplomado, Millán-Astray saw service in the Philippines and in Africa. For his exploits as founder and head of the Tercio de Extranjeros, the king made him gentleman of the chamber in 1921; in 1922 he was forced to resign after a public quarrel with the Juntas. Reinstated under Primo de Rivera and promoted to colonel, he was once again made head of the Tercio after Franco's promotion to brigadier in 1928. During his many years in Morocco, he lost an arm and an eye, thus earning the nickname, "El glorioso mutilado." Millán-Astray, who joined the Nationalists during the civil war, died in 1954.

MOLA VIDAL, EMILIO. Born in Plantas, Cuba, in 1887, Mola was a fourth-generation military officer. After graduating from the Infantry Academy in 1904, Mola served in Africa from 1909 to 1925, where he served with distinction in the Regulars. Appointed Director General of the Security Forces by General Berenguer in 1930, Mola was briefly imprisoned and expelled from the army after the proclamation of the Republic in 1931. The right amnestied him and restored him to a command in 1934. Mola was among the chief organizers of the military revolt of 1936. He died in a plane crash in 1937.

PICASSO Y GONZÁLEZ, JUAN. Born in 1857, Picasso initially acquired notoriety as the first Staff officer to break the closed scale in his corps by accepting the Laurel Wreath of Saint Ferdinand and a merit promotion to major during the Melilla campaign of 1893. Subsequently, his rise through the ranks was slow; although he was sixteen years older than Berenguer, he was not promoted to division general until four years after him, in 1921. One of the few Protestants in the Spanish officer corps, Picasso was the uncle of Pablo Ruíz Picasso.

PRIMO DE RIVERA Y ORBANEJA, MIGUEL, second Marqués de Estella. Son of a wealthy retired colonel with landholdings near Jerez de la Frontera, Primo de Rivera was born on January 8, 1870. After four years (1883–87) at the AGM, he entered the Infantry and embarked on a meteoric career that he owed to the prestige and influence of his uncle, the first Marqués de Estella. In Melilla in 1893 he was awarded the Laurel Wreath for bravery and promoted to captain; by 1897 he had received two more promotions while serving as an aide to Martínez Campos and his uncle in Cuba and the Philippines. By 1911, after service in the Kert campaign, Primo was a brigadier, the first graduate of the AGM to rise to that rank. After another brief tour of Morocco in 1913 (when he was promoted to division general), he remained in the peninsula, primarily in Madrid. At his uncle's death in May 1921, he inherited the title of Marqués de Estella. Emerging as the leader of a military pronunciamiento against the parliamentary regime in 1923, Primo ruled Spain as dictator until loss of support in the army forced him to resign in January 1930. He died in exile in Paris a few weeks later.

PRIMO DE RIVERA Y SOBREMONTE, FERNANDO, first Marqués de Estella. Born in Seville in 1831, the Marqués de Estella had a meteoric career, reaching field marshal rank at age forty-one in 1872. In 1875 he was head of the first Military Household; in 1876 he was given his title. A life senator in 1877, he was governor of the Philippines from 1880 to 1883. War Minister under Maura in 1907 and again with Dato in 1917, the Marqués de Estella was also president of the Supreme Military Council from October 1917 until his death in 1921.

RIQUELME LÓPEZ-BAGO, JOSÉ. Born in 1880, Riquelme trained at the Infantry Academy. He spent nearly his entire career in Melilla, where he was an officer in the Native Police. Like his fellow africanista Castro Girona, Riquelme favored political rather than military tactics. He also sympathized with the Juntas, perhaps because his political liberalism inclined him to be critical of the political and military turno. Riquelme participated in the Sanjuanada revolt against the Dictatorship in 1926 and supported the Republic in 1931. The Republicans rewarded him by promoting him to division general. A loyal Republican, after the civil war Riquelme helped reorganize the Agrupación Militar Republicana, with the aim of overthrowing the Franco regime by force.

SANJURJO SACANELL, JOSÉ, Marqués del Rif. Sanjurjo was born into a Carlist family in Pamplona on March 28, 1872. After attending the AGM from 1890 to 1893, he entered the Infantry, serving first in Cuba and later in Melilla, where he was among the first to volunteer for the Regulars organized by Berenguer. In Africa he rose rapidly, receiving three merit promotions and a Laurel Wreath between 1909 and 1916. In the peninsula from 1917 to 1919, he was active in the Infantry Junta during the ESG affair. His return to Africa and promotion to brigadier in 1920 subsequently diluted his enthusiasm for the Juntas. An active supporter of Primo de Rivera in 1923, Sanjurjo was a leading figure in the successful conquest of Morocco after 1925, earning his title in 1927. As head of the Civil Guard in 1931, Sanjurjo did not oppose the proclamation of the Republic. Nevertheless, in 1932 he led an unsuccessful revolt against the Azaña government. Sanjurjo died in a plane crash in July 1936 as he prepared to join the military revolt he had helped to plan.

VARELA IGLESIAS, JOSÉ. The son of a noncommissioned naval officer, Varela was born in the province of Cadiz in 1891. Varela trained in the Naval Academy before entering the Infantry Academy in 1909. From 1916 on, he served in the Regulars of Larache, receiving three merit promotions and two Laurel Wreaths in thirteen years. An uncompromising monarchist, Varela rose with General Sanjurjo against the Republic in 1932 and was a prominent member of the military conspiracy of 1935–36. Varela was a member of Franco's cabinet until 1943, when he was dismissed for his anti-Falangist activities.

WEYLER Y NICOLAU, VALERIANO, Marqués de Tenerife and Duque de Rubí. The son of a military doctor, Weyler was born in Palma de Mallorca in 1838. A Staff officer, he made his career in Santo Domingo and Cuba in the 1860s and in the Carlist war of the 1870s. In 1878, a lieutenant general at thirty-nine years of age, he was sent to the Canary Islands, where his policies earned him the respect of the population and his first title in 1887. A member of the elite political hierarchy, Weyler was named a life senator by the Liberals in 1895. The same year he replaced Martínez Campos as Captain General in Cuba, where his harsh tactics were effective in turning the tide against the Cuban rebels until he was recalled in an abortive effort to conciliate popular opinion in the United States. Minister of War three times (1901, 1905, and 1906), Weyler also served as chief of the General Staff from 1916 to 1921 and again from 1923 to 1925. He was awarded his second title in 1920 after he agreed to replace Milans del Bosch as Captain General of Barcelona. Weyler participated in the Sanjuanada revolt against the Dictatorship in 1926, when he was eighty-nine years of age. He died in 1930.

APPENDIX C

The Law of Jurisdictions of March 23, 1906

(First Five Articles)

Article 1. The Spaniard who takes up arms against the Fatherland under an enemy flag or under the command of those fighting for the independence of a part of Spanish territory will be punished with life imprisonment.

Article 2. Those who verbally or in writing, by means of printing, engraving, prints, allegories, caricatures, signs, shouts, or allusions, offend the Nation, its flag, national anthem, or other emblem of its authority will be punished with correctional imprisonment.

The same punishment will be incurred by those who commit similar crimes against the regions, provinces, cities, and towns of Spain and their flags or coats of arms.

Article 3. Those who verbally or in writing, by means of printing, engraving, or other mechanical means of publication, in prints, allegories, caricatures, emblems, or allusions, insult or offend, overtly or covertly, the Army or the Navy or certain institutions, arms, ranks, or corps of the same, will be punished by correctional imprisonment. The punishments of major detention in the medium and maximum degrees and correctional imprisonment in the minimum degree shall be imposed on those who verbally or in writing, by printing, engraving, or other means of publication, directly incite insubordination in the armed forces or separate from the fulfillment of their military duties persons who serve or who are called to serve in the national forces on land or sea.

Article 4. Defense of the crimes included in this law and of the offenders, shall be punished with major detention.

Article 5. Ordinary courts of law will have jurisdiction over cases brought for any of the crimes referred to in Articles 1, 2, and 4 of this law, provided that the accused do not belong to the Army on sea or land and do not commit a military offense at the same time. Military courts will have jurisdiction over the cases referred to in Article 3.

Paragraph 1 of Case 7 of Article 7 of the Code of Military Justice and Number 10 of Article 7 of the Law of Organization and Attributions of Navy Tribunals, shall be modified as follows:

Article 7. By virtue of the crime committed, military jurisdiction will include those cases brought against any person for:

7. An attack on or disrespect for military authorities, injury or slander against them or against Army institutions or collectivities, whatever the means employed to commit the crime, including the press, engravings, or other mechanical means of publication, with the proviso that said crime refer to the exercise of a military post or command, that it tend to diminish the prestige or to relax the bonds of discipline and subordination in the armed forces, or to encourage those who are serving or are called to serve in that institution to abandon their military duties.

SOURCE: *Gaceta de Madrid* 145 (April 24, 1906), 2: 317–18.

APPENDIX D

The Spanish Officer Corps, 1917

In 1917 there were 18,565 officers on the active and paid reserve lists. The breakdown by corps is as follows:

Active List

Generals	196	Ecclesiastical	280
Staff Corps	338	Auditing	248
Halberdiers	38	Veterinary	242
Infantry	5,942	Inválidos	201
Cavalry	1,520	Military Justice	137
Artillery	1,609	Musicians	92
Engineers	767	Equitation	88
Civil Guard	1,080	Sentries	20
Customs Police	710	Labor and Topographic	18
Medical Corps	908	Brigade	
Quartermaster Corps	781	Transport	5
Military Offices	344	Medical Troops	5
		Total	15,569

Paid Reserve

Generals	212	Customs Police	5
Infantry	1,980	Quartermaster Corps	40
Cavalry	272	Medical Troops	40
Artillery	253	Medical Corps	21
Engineers	157	Military Justice	11
Civil Guard	5	Total	2,996

SOURCE: *Anuario Militar de España*, 1917.

APPENDIX E

The Intervention of the
Army in Social Conflicts

(Document prepared by the Assembly of Junta Presidents, March 27, 1919)

The social and economic disturbance that the last war has produced in the world has had repercussions in Spain and is producing upheavals whose frequency and intensity are growing minute by minute. In order to control them, the public Power is making ample use of the only disciplined and solid force at its disposal; but the action that is imposed on the troops is of such a nature, and the ultimate recourse of mobilization is employed with such freedom, that the moment has arrived for the Army to raise its voice, moved, certainly not by its own interests, but by the sacred interests of the Fatherland.

As an obligatory antecedent, here is an outline of what happens almost daily.

The slightest difference between capital and labor produces a strike, which is not always restricted to a single industry, since at times even State services are involved. Because of the tight link that today exists among all branches of activity, paralysis of work in a given sector affects those in other sectors, gives rise to the intervention of the Syndicates and directing organisms of the proletarian classes, and the movement spreads, grows, and finally threatens, if it does not disturb, public order. Even before this happens, the irregularity provoked in the national, provincial, or local services upsets normal life for a greater or lesser portion of the country. In order to restore it, the Army is used to carry out civilian duties, although subject to military norms and regulations.

It is not taken into account that the action of the Army must generally be limited, in that which concerns these social conflicts, to guaranteeing order. Since the workers do not dispose of any other legal instrument except the strike to achieve their demands and improvements from their employers, when they are replaced by soldiers and the functioning of the industry or service continues, the Army is tacitly placed, although not in an obvious manner, on the side of capital, separating it from that impartiality and unanimity in those internal matters and quarrels that an institution at the service of the nation—"of the whole Nation"—must maintain. It is disregarded, besides, that neither by virtue of its numbers (necessarily insufficient), nor by its professional training, nor by its purpose, nor by its essential nature, is the Army prepared to take charge, with complete probability of success, of the labor done by complex, numerous, skilled, and specially prepared industrial organizations. Thus it turns out that the most diligent zeal, the greatest efforts, the abnegation and the spirit of sacrifice of officers and troops, encounter invincible difficulties.

Improvisation has never been able to replace organization.

In every conflict of this nature, there is unfailingly someone responsible: sometimes the employer, sometimes the worker, sometimes both at once. Well, the Army, which finds itself forced outside its field to resolve problems for which it was not responsible, does not even have "a posteriori" the moral compensation of seeing the guilty ones receive the sanction they deserve. Officers and soldiers abandon workshops, and employers and workers return to them and resume their work as if they were innocent actors and had nothing to do with the damage they have inflicted on the public welfare. It is enough to indicate this point to understand the necessity of reforming the labor legislation. Let others determine if the harm to the country caused by a labor disturbance is less serious than the theft of a roll by a hungry man, but the Army must not continue to be the propitiatory victim of the struggle between labor and capital. This state of affairs is not dignified, nor does it help establish discipline and internal satisfaction in the ranks. Obvious are the risks of partiality in favor of capital, in which the Army, not by its will but because of the functions which it is obliged to carry out, is placed. Since the armed forces are presented as the most powerful, the only effective obstacle, to the demands for betterment of the workers—apart from the right of petition—it is natural that syndicalist and analogous organisms (persuaded that once the Army is disabled, there will be no brake or dike to contain them) should try to undermine the bases upon which its effectiveness rests. Thus, when the Army enters the sphere of public and private labor, against it are incited the passions of the turbulent masses and of the revolutionary elements, who are indirectly invited to undermine discipline and obedience in the ranks. Along this route we are heading toward the rule of anarchy, because the Army finds itself combatted by the most daring, not defended by the rest, and knocked about outside its own sphere.

But is it perhaps being suggested that the Army should always remain at the margin of these conflicts, indifferent to what happens around it, and denying its aid to the higher authorities? Not at all.

In every civilized country, the functioning of public services must be guaranteed, but since in practice, an abusive use of the concept "Public Services" is made, the first thing is to define it and to distinguish which entities ought to watch over them and be in charge of them.

They may belong to (1) the State: communications of all kinds; coal supplies; primary materials and consumer goods necessary to the whole kingdom; (2) regional: sources of energy that serve a region composed of various municipalities; (3) municipal: light, energy, communications, etc., corresponding to a town.

According to this classification, it should be understood that while the State must guarantee services of a general character, it is the responsibility of Diputations and City Governments to watch over those of a regional and local nature. In all three cases, it is necessary to adopt preventive measures. By any reasonable standard, it is inadmissible that a public light company, for example, should enjoy the same autonomy and independence as a carpenter's workshop, and that workers in the former should possess the same right to strike as those in a clothing store (without any restriction other than that of advance warning), as if the abandonment of work in every case only concerned employers and workers and not the entire citizenry. There is no effectively interventionist legislation for the State, and in its absence, to supplement it in intense crises, the Army is brought in, without plan or concrete rules.

Aside from this, if the State must guarantee services of a general nature, it is logical that it be able to employ (if it is necessary and other recourses have failed) the organisms of which it disposes, among them the Army, which has lent itself, and lends itself with pleasure and enthusiasm to that task, in order to redound to the benefit of the country and affect the existence of the Fatherland.

The same does not occur, however, with regard to regional and local services. Of course it is understood that just because the tramways in a town cease to run, or it lacks light, or a few factories close, the entire nation need not rouse itself. Life is not even impossible in the disturbed city itself. It must bear responsibility for the solution; it should have foreseen such an eventuality and taken measures at the appropriate time. Those who learn from experience should cut short the evil, licitly supported to the necessary extent by the Diputation and the State. But since the latter arrives at once with military forces, employed as civilian labor to aid the stricken locality, each and every one has grown accustomed to expect salvation from the State and the Army. The idea that they have such an obligation spreads, and we have finally arrived at the sad extreme in which the Army is almost held to account because, with its scant numbers, it has not instantaneously reestablished normality.

When a strike intensifies and intransigence rules, mobilization is resorted to as an ultimate recourse. The mere fact of decreeing it ratifies the presence of the Army, which is always neutral, on the side of capital (although it is not true). The errors do not stop there: it is lost from sight that obligatory military service is not "obligatory civil labor"; from which it can be inferred that the Army is removed from its bases and its natural foundations and is placed in a false, unstable, or untenable situation.

This cannot and must not be. As if all this were not enough, the weight of the law does not fall upon mobilized workers who have broken it; once the strike is over, a sponge is passed over the faults and crimes committed by the soldiers, and the rigors of discipline and the Code are restricted to those individuals on active duty—precisely the self-sacrificing, the true defenders and saviors of their countrymen— while for the guilty, the wayward, and the provocateurs, there are only considerations, indulgences, respect, and forgetfulness, when not flattery and praise. This is not the way to maintain discipline: the soldier hears, sees, and draws conclusions. A bad example does not fall into a vacuum.

The Army, protector of the law, is resolved that these distinctions shall cease, that the evil practice of mixing it into social conflicts (which in most cases are political at bottom) shall be finished for good, and that accommodating interpretations and compromises shall be terminated. The Army wants to be isolated from these questions and from partisan maneuvers; otherwise it cannot be the safeguard of order. Free, very free, is the constituted Power to act as it understands best; but once the Army intervenes in the conflict, martial law must be applied without differences or attenuations.

In virtue of the above:

Considering: That the Army, upon intervening as an element of labor in social disputes, strays from its mission, operates between the indifference of some, the implicit hostility of others, and the energy of the majority, has to sustain that which is the responsibility of citizen action, which is every day more dormant and selfish, and that if this trend is not cut short with urgency, it [the Army] will soon be useless for those functions that the Fatherland has entrusted to it and that it has sworn to fulfill, "the Assembly of Presidents," representing all arms, corps, and institutes of the Army, agrees:

First. To lend its aid to the legal Power for the functioning of public services of a general nature under all circumstances, once the other instruments that the State possesses have failed.

Second. To provide labor in other cases (regional and local services).

Third. Like the armed force it is, abiding by its strict and pre-emptory regulations, it will defend public order and maintain the Law by means of force, which it will exercise without leniency. Thus it will not allow itself to be given missions to parley, compromise, or temporize. Orders must be concrete, clear, and expressive. Once the troops are in the street, the Army will not be responsible for what might occur.

Fourth. Once partial or total mobilization has been decreed and mobilized workers are subject to the same duties as the regular troops, military law shall apply to all equally, and sanctions must be applied inexorably after mobilization. In this sense, the Army will not admit any exemptions from guilt nor any pardon other than those approved by the Cortes and the King.

Fifth. To invite the constituted Power to consider the suitability of reforming the existing legislation with an eye to: (1) exacting responsibility from those causing social conflicts, depending on the case; (2) intervening administratively with greater efficiency in the organization of services of a general nature; (3) preventing clashes between capital and labor, so that the State, Diputations, and Municipalities will not find themselves at the mercy of disputes between employers and workers in those industries that affect the life of the nation, the province, and the city.

Six. To communicate these accords to the Minister of War, so that they might reach the Government as a whole, indicating to him that in operating in this manner, the Army does not think of itself, but of the Fatherland. . . .

[The end of the document is incomplete.]

SOURCE: *El Liberal*, December 2, 1919, pp. 1–2.

Notes

Abbreviations Used in the Notes

CM / La Correspondencia Militar
DSC / Diario de las sesiones de las Cortes españolas, Congreso de los Diputados
DSS / Diario de las sesiones de las Cortes españolas, Senado
EE / El Ejército Español
MA / Archive of D. Antonio Maura, Fundación Antonio Maura, Madrid
RA / Archive of the Conde de Romanones, Madrid
DNSD / Delegación Nacional de Servicios Documentales, Salamanca
SHM-A / Servicio Histórico Militar, Sección de Estudios Históricos,
      Segundo Negociado: Africa
SHM-GL / Servicio Histórico Militar, Sección de Estudios Históricos,
      Primer Negociado: Guerra de Liberación, Documentación Roja

Preface

1. The fundamental works on Spanish civil-military relations are Stanley G. Payne, *Politics and the Military in Modern Spain*; Eric Christiansen, *The Origins of Military Power in Spain, 1800–1854*; and Raymond Carr, "Spain: Rule by Generals," pp. 135–48. Other useful discussions may be found in Samuel E. Finer, *The Man on Horseback*; Edward Feit, "The Rule of the 'Iron Surgeons'"; Amos Perlmutter, "The Praetorian State and the Praetorian Army," and *The Military and Politics in Modern Times*.

2. Alfredo Kindelán y Duany, *Ejército y política*, pp. 148–49. See also Emilio Mola Vidal, *Obras completas*, p. 945; Jorge Vigón Suerodíaz, *Milicia y política* and *Teoría del militarismo*. A theoretical statement of this viewpoint may be found in Hermann Oehling, *La función política del ejército*.

3. See the remarks of Joaquín Sánchez de Toca in *El Imparcial*, Dec. 26, 1917, p. 1.

4. In Luis de Galinsoga and Francisco Franco-Salgado, *Centinela de occidente*, pp. 203–6.

Chapter 1

1. Cánovas's system has been described, with more or less enthusiasm, in nearly all the general works on contemporary Spain. In my view, the most penetrating analyses are to be found in Luis Sánchez Agesta, *Historia del constitucionalismo español*, pp. 314 ff., and in Juan J. Linz, "The Party System of Spain," pp. 198–282.

2. On the cacique, see Joaquín Costa's classic indictment, *Oligarquía y caciquismo como la forma actual de gobierno en España*. Useful recent analyses include Raymond Carr, *Spain, 1808–1939*, pp. 366–79; Joaquín Romero Maura, "El caciquismo"; and Javier Tusell Gómez, *Oligarquía y caciquismo en Andalucía (1890–1923)*.

3. The concession of permanent Senate membership to captains general was not as generous as it first appeared. Once the original group of Restoration generals had been honored, there were few such promotions, and none at all after those of Camilo García Polavieja and Valeriano Weyler in 1909.

4. See Modesto Sánchez de los Santos, *Las Cortes españolas*. Similar biographical collections are available only for 1910 and 1914. Analysis of military membership for those years reveals results similar to that for 1907.

5. In 1907 there were only 22 army and 9 naval officers in the Senate, out of a total of 360. Two-thirds of them held their seats by right or appointment; 10 of the 31 possessed titles of nobility, 5 of them acquired since the Restoration. Ten had served in the Congress before passing to the Senate, where slightly over half (16 out of 31) voted with the Conservatives. The remainder voted as Liberals or independents. Half of the military senators were over 66 years old; 7 were over the army retirement age of 72. Only 3 were under 50.

In the Congress, only 18 out of 397 deputies possessed a military rank in 1907. Seven of these were inactive and thus not dependent on their army careers for their income. Although 6 of the 18 deputies were generals, 4 of these were members of the support services, somewhat isolated from the regular army hierarchy. As in the Senate, most officers in the Congress voted with the Conservatives. But of the 4 Liberal deputies, 3 were generals, which gave them greater authority.

6. See Articles 6, 26, and 30 of the law of Nov. 29, 1878. All references to military legislation, decrees, and orders are from Ministerio de la Guerra, *Colección legislativa del Ejército*.

7. At his first cabinet meeting in 1902, Alfonso reminded the startled ministers of his prerogative. See Conde de Romanones, *Obras completas*, 3:149–50. In 1904 the king's insistence on exercising that prerogative brought down the government of Antonio Maura. The role of Alfonso XIII in the downfall of the parliamentary monarchy has recently been the subject of sympathetic revision. See Carlos Seco Serrano, *Alfonso XIII y la crisis de la restauración*, and Vicente R. Pilapil, *Alfonso XIII*. The classic critical interpretation is Melchor Fernández Almagro, *Historia del reinado de D. Alfonso XIII*.

8. A royal decree of September 24, 1907, expanded the Military Household

to 16 regular and an unlimited number of honorary members. An attempt was made to provide representation for all army corps in the Household.

9. This tactic was apparent in the appointments of Generals Manuel Fernández-Silvestre in 1915, Joaquín Milans del Bosch in 1920, José Cavalcanti in 1923, and Dámaso Berenguer in 1925.

10. Between 1875 and 1931, the number of titles in Spain more than doubled. Manuel Tuñón de Lara, *Estudios sobre el siglo XIX español*, p. 195.

11. In 1915 a royal decree allowed favored officers to bypass official channels in order to communicate directly with the king. See Fernández Almagro, *Alfonso XIII*, pp. 238–39, n. 1.

12. "Middle class" will be used here to denote a status or reference group rather than a social class with a well-defined relationship to the means of production. There is, in fact, no satisfactory label for the middle sectors of a traditional society in transition. See the discussion in Juan J. Linz and Amando de Miguel, "Within-Nation Differences and Comparisons," pp. 267–319.

13. Military reform is discussed in greater detail in chap. 2.

14. For a list of cabinets between 1900 and 1923, see app. A.

15. Access to the personal service records of twentieth-century army officers, located in the Archivo General Militar in the Alcázar de Segovia, has been generally denied to both civilian and military historians. Until these vital records can be examined, no serious prosopographical study of the Spanish officer corps can be made. Nevertheless, it is clear that by the end of the century, recruitment for all branches except the Artillery and to a lesser extent, the Cavalry, was mainly from the middle classes, especially the military middle class. Daniel Richard Headrick, "The Spanish Army, 1868–1898," pp. 122–23, estimates that by the last third of the century, one-third to one-half of the leading generals were from non-noble military families.

16. Emilio Mola Vidal, *Obras completas*, p. 976.

17. See especially Ricardo Burguete y Lana, *Morbo nacional*; *Mi rebeldía*; and *La guerra y el hombre*.

18. Alfredo Kindelán y Duany, *Ejército y política*, p. 148.

19. See Joseph Harrison, "Catalan Business and the Loss of Cuba, 1898–1914"; "Big Business and the Failure of Right-Wing Catalan Nationalism, 1901–1923"; and "Big Business and the Rise of Basque Nationalism."

20. For these incidents see Fernando Díaz-Plaja, *La historia de España en sus documentos (nueva serie): El siglo XX*, pp. 43–48.

21. See the Cortes debates in ibid., pp. 68, 72–73.

22. *EE*, Nov. 23, 1905, p. 1.

23. The following discussion of the *¡Cu-cut!* incident is based primarily on Gabriel Maura Gamazo, duque de Maura, and Melchor Fernández Almagro, *Por qué cayó Alfonso XIII*, pp. 91–95; Jesús Pabón, *Cambó*, 1:256–68; Maximiano García Venero, *Melquíades Álvarez*, pp. 160–61; Romanones, *Obras*, 3:189–92; Fernández Almagro, *Alfonso XIII*, pp. 78–88; Joaquín Romero Maura, "The Spanish Army and Catalonia"; and a careful reading of the Law of Jurisdictions, the Code of Military Justice, the parliamentary debates, and the military press.

24. On this magazine, see Lluis Solá, *"¡Cu-Cut!"* *(1902–1912)* and Romero Maura, "Spanish Army," pp. 15–18.

25. See the two newspaper accounts in Díaz-Plaja, *Siglo XX*, pp. 100–101.

26. Romero Maura, "Spanish Army," p. 22; Maura and Fernández Almagro, *Por qué cayó Alfonso XIII*, pp. 91–92.

27. *EE*, Nov. 27, 1905, p. 1.

28. Article 258 provided: "Whoever by word, in writing, or in any other equivalent form, injures or offends clearly or covertly the Army, or institutions, corps, ranks, or certain bodies of the same, will incur a correctional prison sentence."

Case 7 of Article 7 gave the military jurisdiction over treason, desertion, military rebellion, and sedition, "insults to sentinels, escorts, and armed forces of the Army and of any Corps militarily organized and subject to military law. . ." (the latter, a reference to the Civil Guard and the provincial militias), and also over "attacks on or disrespect for military authorities, . . . injury or slander against them and against corporations and groups in the Army."

29. Supreme Court decisions of Sept. 19, 1891; Feb. 22, Mar. 15, and July 6, 1892. Law of Jan. 1, 1900.

30. According to Antonio Maura Montaner, "Debate en el Congreso sobre la derogación de la ley de jurisdicciones, los días 10, 11, 12 de junio de 1908."

31. In 1895 junior officers disgruntled by press criticism of their lack of enthusiasm for the Cuban campaign had unsuccessfully pressed a similar demand against the Liberal government of Sagasta. See Carmen García Nieto Paris, "La prensa de Barcelona ante la crisis militar de 1895."

32. Romero Maura, "Spanish Army," pp. 22–26.

33. Romanones, *Obras*, 3:190–92.

34. The phrase is originally in Maura and Fernández Almagro, *Por qué cayó Alfonso XIII*, p. 91, and is repeated with approval by Seco Serrano, *Alfonso XIII*, p. 73.

35. A brief biography of Luque and other prominent officers may be found in app. B.

36. The element of blackmail in Luque's republican posturing could not be ignored; as the Portuguese poet Guerra Junqueiro observed, "It's curious! Every time I come to Madrid, I find as Minister of War the general whom on my last journey I met at the house of [the Republican leader] Salmerón" (quoted in Pabón, *Cambó*, 1:266).

37. *DSS* (1905–06), 1:472.

38. To allow the dissenters (Manuel García Prieto, Víctor Concas, and Amós Salvador) to remain in the cabinet, the government introduced a compromise measure in the Congress that retained civil jurisdiction over press offenses while speeding up trial procedures at the expense of due process. Meanwhile, a Senate committee was to prepare independently the bill the army wanted.

39. See app. C for the first five articles of the Law of Jurisdictions.

40. Alejandro Rosselló in *DSC* (1905–06), 7:2625.

41. Ibid.

42. Ibid. (Feb. 19, 1906), 7:2682–87.

43. Ibid. (Feb. 17, 1906), 7:2655.

44. See Romero Maura, "Spanish Army," p. 29, n. 30.

45. The Republican deputy, Marcelino Domingo, for example, was indicted under the Law of Jurisdictions 45 times in 1917–18, but the Congress denied each time the military prosecutor's petition for removal of his immunity.

46. See the comments of Melquíades Álvarez in *DSC* (Feb. 17, 1906), 7:2658–59.

47. For example, Jorge Vigón Suerodíaz, *Milicia y política*, p. 270.

48. Quoted in Stanley G. Payne, *Politics and the Military in Modern Spain*, p. 60.

49. Article 7, Cases 3, 4, and 7 of the Code of Military Justice.

50. For a discussion of conscription during the Restoration, see Pío Suárez Inclán, *El problema del reclutamiento en España*. See also Nuria Sales de Bohigas, "Sociedades de seguros contra las quintas (1865–1868)," pp. 109–25.

51. A helpful, although perhaps overly generous, summary of the role of Martínez Campos in the early years of the Restoration can be found in Miguel Alonso Baquer, *El ejército en la sociedad española*, pp. 173–80.

52. Two eulogistic biographies of Weyler are Julio Romano, *Weyler, el hombre de hierro*, and Valeriano Weyler y López de Puga, *En el archivo de mi abuelo*.

53. The most influential exposition of the army's social mission was published in the *Revue des Deux Mondes* in 1891 by the future French marshall, Hubert Lyautey. See "Du rôle social de l'officier." Lyautey's article inspired similar essays in Spanish professional journals and an occasional book. See especially Enrique Ruíz Fornells, *La educación moral del soldado*, a textbook used in the Infantry Academy.

54. See, for example, Joaquín Fanjul y Goñi, *Misión social del ejército*, p. 6.

55. There is a brief biography of General Marvá in León Martín-Granizo, *Biografías de sociólogos españoles*.

56. Professor Joan Connelly Ullman has informed me of a case in 1903 when General Zappino threatened to remove his troops if mine owners in Bilbao did not negotiate with workers on strike.

57. For the Tragic Week, its background, and its aftermath, see Joan Connelly Ullman, *La Semana Trágica*.

58. The Moroccan involvement is described below, pp. 22–25.

59. Payne, *Politics and the Military*, p. 106.

60. Ullman, *Semana Trágica*, pp. 512–13, 508.

61. For the political consequences of the Tragic Week, see ibid., pp. 555–63.

62. Maura and Fernández Almagro, *Por qué cayó Alfonso XIII*, p. 264.

63. Gerald Meaker, *The Revolutionary Left in Spain, 1914–1923*, p. 7.

64. There is a vast bibliography on Spain's involvement in Morocco. For an introduction to the question, the reader may consult Carlos Hernández de Herrera and Tomás García Figueras, *Acción de España en Marruecos*; Víctor Ruíz Albéniz, *España en el Rif*; Estado Mayor Central, Servicio Histórico Militar, *Ac-*

ción de España en Africa; Pabón, *Cambó*, 2:233–375; J. A. Chandler, "Spanish Policy toward North Morocco, 1908 to 1923"; Shannon E. Fleming, "Primo de Rivera and Abd-el Krim," pp. 1–108; Payne, *Politics and the Military*, pp. 102–23, 152–87; David S. Woolman, *Rebels in the Rif*; and Víctor Morales Lezcano, *El colonialismo hispanofrancés en Marruecos (1898–1927)*. See also Edmund Burke III, *Prelude to Protectorate in Morocco*.

65. For Costa, the Spanish colonization of Morocco represented the validation of Spain's credentials as a modern European nation as well as the repayment of an historic debt. See Angel Flores Morales, ed., *Africa a través del pensamiento español*, p. 165. This book contains selected passages from the principal apologists for Spanish intervention in Morocco.

66. The 1904 treaty is in Servicio Histórico Militar, *Acción de España*, 3:122–25.

67. See Morales Lezcano, *Colonialismo*, pp. 69–89.

68. See the Marina-Maura correspondence in Ruíz Albéniz, *España en el Rif*, pp. 93–106.

69. Testimony of Colonel José Riquelme before the Responsibilities Commission. Congreso de los Diputados, Comisión de responsabilidades políticas, *La Comisión de responsabilidades*, p. 113.

70. On the Kert campaign, see Gonzalo Calvo, *España en Marruecos, 1910–1913*.

71. The Franco-Spanish treaty of 1912 is in Servicio Histórico Militar, *Acción de España*, 3:115–18.

72. Manuel García Prieto, Minister of State, in *DSC* (Dec. 13, 1911), 17:5886. García Prieto was awarded the title of Marqués de Alhucemas in 1913 for his role in the treaty negotiations. For a summary of the ratification debates in December 1912, see Diego Sevilla Andrés, "Los partidos políticos y el Protectorado."

73. Álvaro López Mora in *DSS* (Dec. 20, 1912), 11:3034.

74. The final vote on December 17, 1912, was 216 to 22 in favor of ratification.

75. *DSC* (May 26 and 27, 1914), 4:887–97, 915–19.

Chapter 2

1. For a good general discussion of military professionalization, see Bengt Abrahamsson, *Military Professionalization and Political Power*.

2. There were 24,000 officers in 1899, including 578 colonels and 499 generals. Eduardo Aunós Pérez, *España en crisis (1874–1936)*, pp. 229–30; Stanley G. Payne, *Politics and the Military in Modern Spain*, p. 87.

3. Comandante Beta, *Apuntes para historiar tres años de reformas militares (1915–1917)*, pp. 38–39.

4. See the articles in *CM* on Feb. 24, 1917, and Aug. 24, 1916. During 1916, 1917, and 1918, this was an almost daily demand.

5. Even the General Staff, which was not always sensitive to grievances in

the lower ranks, sympathized with this view. See its report in 1905 in Beta, *Reformas militares*, pp. 174–75.

6. "La organización del ejército español mirada por un prusiano," 10:201.

7. Paul-Marie de La Gorce, *The French Army*, p. 49.

8. See the comparison between Spanish and French officers' salaries in *CM*, Nov. 29, 1919, p. 1.

9. "Organización mirada por un prusiano," 10:198. Augusto Vivero in *El Mundo*, Jan. 18, 1918, p. 1, published the following figures for 1917:

Officers with rank above major per 100 lieutenants, by corps:

Engineers	149.8	Cavalry	105
Infantry	145.4	Artillery	101.2

10. For the reserve, see Antonio Sánchez Bravo, *Apuntes para la historia de la escala de reserva del ejército*.

11. La Gorce, *The French Army*, pp. 82–85.

12. The period of military obligation was distributed as follows: 3 years active duty (in practice, much less; to save money, half were released after a few weeks' training and the rest at the end of 2 years); 5 years in the first reserve; 6 years in the second reserve; and 4 years in the territorial reserve, or national guard.

13. See Conde de Romanones, *El ejército y la política*, p. 51, and Pío Suárez Inclán, *El problema del reclutamiento en España*, p. 155.

14. The number of quota soldiers rose from 6,599 in 1912 to 16,242 in 1920. Romanones, *Ejército y política*, p. 143.

15. After being drafted, 35 or 40 percent of the conscripts were dismissed as unfit for service. Romanones, *Ejército y política*, p. 150. In part, this was the result of corruption in the local recruitment centers. Caciques intervened to obtain physical exemptions for the sons of their clients, while the less fit and the less favored filled the local quotas. Joaquín Romero Maura, "El caciquismo," p. 31.

16. *Memorial de Infantería* 10 (1917): 284–85.

17. *CM*, Feb. 26, 1916, p. 1. Literacy statistics vary according to source and method of calculation. Official government statistics for 1916 indicate that 36.6 percent of the conscripts could neither read nor write. Ministerio de Instrucción Pública y Bellas Artes, Dirección General del Instituto Geográfico y Estadístico, *Anuario estadístico de España* (1917), p. 374.

18. According to Romanones, *Ejército y política*, p. 65, only 26 sessions in the Congress were devoted to discussion of the military budget between 1906 and 1917. An examination of the indexes of the debates for these years confirms that there was generally little discussion of the military budget.

19. *Anuario estadístico* (1917), p. 385; (1919), p. 219; Ministerio de Trabajo, Comercio e Industria, Dirección General de Estadística, *Anuario estadístico de España* (1921), p. 217.

20. Ibid. (1917), p. 290.

21. A. J. P. Taylor, *The Struggle for Mastery in Europe, 1848–1918*, p. xxix.

22. Payne, *Politics and the Military*, p. 88.

23. Actual expenditures in 1917 would total 244 million pesetas.

24. Appointment to the major politico-military and technical posts carried pay supplements of up to 5,000 pesetas a year, ostensibly to maintain the "dignity of the office." The handful of officers who wore the Cross of Military Merit, the Cross of María Cristina, and the Laurel Wreath of Saint Ferdinand, received pensions of up to 10,000 pesetas a year, according to their rank. See Eduardo San Martín Losada, *Sueldos, haberes y gratificaciones del personal del ejército*.

25. Up to the rank of lieutenant colonel, officers received an annual supplement of from 480 to 900 pesetas after 10 years in grade. The Cross of Saint Hermenegild, awarded for longevity of service, carried an optional pension of 600 to 2,000 pesetas a year.

26. I am grateful to Captain Alfonso de Carlos Peña of the Servicio Histórico Militar for pointing this out to me.

27. See the letter of Lieutenant Colonel Francisco de Artiñano in *Los sucesos de agosto ante el parlamento*, pp. 321–24.

28. *El Liberal*, Oct. 13, 1917, p. 1.

29. I am grateful to Colonel Ramón Salas Larrazábal for this information.

30. *CM*, May 26, 1917, p. 1.

31. A civil servant of equivalent rank in the Finance Ministry earned 3,500 to 4,000 pesetas a year; a bank clerk with 20 years of service, about 3,700. See Ministerio de Hacienda, *Presupuestos generales del Estado para el año económico de 1917*, and Wenceslao Fernández-Flórez, *Impresiones de un hombre de buena fé*, 2:35.

32. The social sensitivity of the officer corps is illustrated by these typical complaints in *La Correspondencia Militar* in 1916:

"The living problem for the officer corps is complicated especially by the lack of lodgings suitable to the dignity with which an officer should live. . . . In this we are truly more democratic than the most advanced republics, and we allow our subalterns to live and eat in houses frequented by social classes that, if they are their equals or superiors in salary, are their inferiors by virtue of their rank in society" (*CM*, July 28, 1916, p. 1).

"The social situation of the officer obliges him to travel in second class, at least, and to transport his family in the same class. . . . The luster of the uniform does not allow him to wear a forty-peseta suit and travel in cheap trains without running the danger of meeting one of his subordinates, to the detriment of military discipline" (*CM*, Aug. 18, 1916, p. 1).

33. See the observations of Emilio Mola Vidal in *Obras completas*, p. 971.

34. For the Artillery Corps, the standard work is Jorge Vigón Suerodíaz, *Historia de la artillería española*.

35. Proof of nobility in the Infantry had first been abolished in 1811 and disappeared definitively in 1836. Proof of racial purity and legitimacy was demanded of all academy-trained officers until 1865. Santiago Otero Enríquez, *La nobleza en el ejército*, p. 16.

36. For a brief history of the Staff Corps, see Julio Busquets Bragulat, *El*

militar de carrera en España, pp. 229–36. For contemporary evaluations of the Corps, see Tomás Peire, *Una política militar expuesta ante las Cortes Constituyentes*, pp. 27–35; Capitán Equis, *El problema militar en España*; Comandante Beta, *Reformas militares*; and Pío Suárez Inclán, *Organización del cuerpo de estado mayor, 1810–1910*. See also Miguel Alonso Baquer, *Aportación militar a la cartografía española en la historia contemporánea*, p. 187. This doctoral dissertation offers a general analysis of the controversial role of the Staff Corps in the nineteenth-century Spanish army. Created in 1811, the Corps had originally been used by both Progressives and Moderados to provide a check on independent-minded field commanders. In 1851 Narváez had ordered that cadets at the War College be recruited from the civilian population, instead of from the regiments or from the other academies. Beginning in 1886, Staff officers were recruited from the General Military Academy.

37. For example, between 1843 and 1847, aides-de-camp had received 50 percent of all promotions awarded in the Infantry and Cavalry, even though they comprised only 1 percent of all officers in those corps. Vigón, *Artillería*, 2:279, n. 113.

38. In 1868 Staff officers had comprised only 6.7 percent of the generals in the Spanish army. By 1884 this percentage had risen to 14.6 percent. In contrast, the percentage of generals of Infantry origin had fallen from 58.8 to 43.2. See Daniel Richard Headrick, "The Spanish Army, 1868–1898," p. 129. See also Alonso Baquer, *Cartografía*, pp. 137–40.

39. Busquets, *Militar de carrera*, p. 231.

40. The reform initiative came from General Manuel Cassola y Fernández, who was appointed War Minister in the Sagasta cabinet in 1887. Cassola was unsuccessful in securing passage of his controversial reform bill in the Cortes, but some of its features were incorporated into the Ley Constitutiva del Ejército of July 19, 1889. See Fernando-María Puell de la Villa, "Las reformas militares del general Cassola."

41. R.D. of Oct. 17, 1889.

42. From 1891 on, graduating Artillery cadets were required to sign the following pledge:

> The artillerists who sign this album want to conserve in the Corps and transmit by example to those who will later serve in it, the traditional spirit of honor, union, and fellowship that they received from their forerunners and that led to the glory and prestige that the Corps enjoys, both for the well-being of the Fatherland and the honor of its members.
>
> And whereas the closed scale is the indispensable condition for the attainment of such exalted goals, they resolve to maintain it among themselves, offering on their honor to renounce (in a legal manner) any promotion within the Corps or to a generalship assigned to it, that is not awarded on the basis of seniority. [Vigón, *Artillería*, 2:134–35, 236]

43. The first Staff officer to accept a wartime merit promotion was Major Juan Picasso González, who won the Laurel Wreath of Saint Ferdinand (the

highest decoration in the army) and a promotion in 1893. Picasso later acquired prominence as the author of the *Expediente Picasso*. For the subsequent deluge of Staff Corps promotions, see Marcelino Domingo in *La Lucha*, June 17, 1917, p. 1.

44. R.D. of Feb. 8, 1893, discussed in Busquets, *Militar de carrera*, pp. 123–25.

45. Some diplomado privileges were purely symbolic, but others were material: a 20 percent salary increase and preference in promotion to general and in appointments to the academies, foreign missions, and aides-de-camp. Capitán Equis, *Problema militar*, pp. 136–37.

46. Some of the brightest young officers became diplomados, including Alberto Castro Girona, Santiago González-Tablas, José Millán-Astray, Angel Rodríguez del Barrio, Vicente Rojo, Leopoldo Ruíz Trillo, and Andrés Saliquet.

47. The Colegio General Militar was created on paper by a royal decree of July 12, 1904.

48. Capitán Equis, *Problema militar*, pp. 51–55. For the defects of the General Staff, see also Comandante Beta, *Reformas militares*.

49. *Anuario estadístico* (1922–23), pp. 237–39.

50. A royal decree of February 27, 1913, outlined the organization of the Protectorate without clarifying the respective jurisdictions of the two ministries. The Ministry of State was assigned "all of the affairs of the zone of influence that are not related to the organization and functioning of the military and naval forces," a definition that proved to depend on the War Ministry and its subordinates. The quiet but bitter struggle between the two ministries blurred the source of ultimate authority in the zone and forestalled the creation of a civilian Protectorate. In 1915 Manuel González Hontoria, a career diplomat with a long-standing interest in Morocco, denounced this dualism in an essay entitled *El Protectorado francés en Marruecos y sus enseñanzas para la acción española*. In 1919 Joaquín Sánchez de Toca resigned the presidency of the Liga Africanista Española for the same reason.

51. A royal order signed by the Minister of State on April 24, 1913, gave the High Commissioner authority over "the direction of the Spanish action in the totality of the zone," and over "all consular and military authorities . . . without losing sight of the fact that the peculiarities of the various territories into which the zone is divided will require different procedures in each." This order, while recognizing the heterogeneity of the zone and the absence of easy communication between regions, sanctioned the de facto autonomy of the commanders general, and thus undermined the goal of a centrally controlled civil Protectorate. Three weeks after the order was signed, the High Commissioner, General Alfau, wrote Romanones to complain of this anomaly. RA, legajo 98, no. 131.

52. For popular opposition to the war, see Conde de Romanones, *Obras completas*, 3:299–300; RA, leg. 53, no. 27 and leg. 98, no. 131.

53. In 1915 General Silvestre's outspoken contempt for pacification inspired his subordinates to assassinate one of al-Raysuni's agents. The govern-

ment demanded the resignations of Silvestre and the High Commissioner, General José Marina, whose replacement, General Francisco Gómez Jordana, quickly signed a pact with al-Raysuni (on September 25, 1915) that guaranteed peace in the western sector until the end of the war. Silvestre's reward was appointment as head of the Military Household. On the relations between al-Raysuni and Silvestre, see particularly Víctor Ruíz Albéniz, *Ecce homo*, pp. 55–76; Rafael López Rienda, *Frente al fracaso*, pp. 1–159; David S. Woolman, *Rebels in the Rif*, pp. 51–54; and Payne, *Politics and the Military*, pp. 116–21. See also the letter from the High Commissioner, General Alfau, to Romanones on May 22, 1915, in RA, leg. 98, no. 131.

54. See Alan Scham, *Lyautey in Morocco*.

55. R.O. of July 1, 1911. See Emilio Mola, "Los primeros Regulares," *Revista de Tropas Coloniales*, June 1924, no page.

56. The Regulars, envied and resented by other officers, were accused of receiving fraudulent merit promotions. In fact, they saw most of the military action in the zone and seem to have earned most of their promotions legitimately. Ambitious young officers without connections, like Emilio Mola and Francisco Franco, recognized the opportunity and seized it. For an early complaint against the Regulars, see the letter to Maura's secretary, Prudencio Rovira, from his brother, an officer, in 1912, in MA, legajo 91.

57. R.O. of Apr. 28, 1914.

58. *España*, Aug. 17, 1916, pp. 4–5.

59. Corruption is discussed in Rafael López Rienda, *El escándalo del millón de Larache*. See also a report from the War Ministry in 1922, "Sobre abono de la administración militar de Marruecos," in RA, leg. 28, no. 17; the personal experiences of Arturo Barea in Africa in *La forja de un rebelde*, pp. 254–59; and the files of Marcelino Domingo in DNSD, Madrid: Sección Político-Social, carpeta 2202.

60. For Domingo's denunciations, see *DSC* (Dec. 12, 1916), 9:3757–61. The findings of the Ministry's investigations were read aloud by him in the Congress on November 20, 1918. See ibid., 2:3159–63. In the interim, the War Ministry had issued two royal orders prohibiting officers from all business activities except property ownership. R.O. of Mar. 12, 1917, and July 28, 1917.

61. *ABC*, Jan. 15, 1910, quoted in *CM*, Jan. 15, 1910, p. 1.

62. *DSC* (Dec. 20, 1911), 17:6050.

63. According to one general, 236,718 wartime merit promotions and decorations were awarded between 1909 and 1917. Jorge Vigón Suerodíaz, "Breves notas para la historia de las juntas de defensa y de la dictadura," p. 6.

64. One officer confided to Maura's secretary, Rovira, in July 1913: "All officers of good faith believe that one solution, or at least part of one—a practical measure—would be the suppression of campaign promotions. There would be fewer military actions, and casualties would decrease. The current acts of arms in many cases lean toward the flashy and the glorification of their directors" (MA, leg. 91).

Chapter 3

1. Spanish neutrality was first announced in the *Gaceta de Madrid* on July 30, 1914, then reconfirmed on August 7.

2. Dato to Maura, Aug. 25, 1914, in Gabriel Maura Gamazo and Melchor Fernández Almagro, *Por qué cayó Alfonso XIII*, pp. 470–71.

3. See "Neutralidades que matan," *Diario Universal*, Aug. 20, 1914, quoted in Conde de Romanones, *Obras completas*, 3:337.

4. Maura and Fernández Almagro, *Por qué cayó Alfonso XIII*, p. 471.

5. Romanones, *Obras*, 3:341–42.

6. An excellent description of the divisions caused by World War I can be found in the account of a longtime Madrid journalist sympathetic to the democratic left: Luis Bello, *España durante la guerra*. A perceptive discussion of the ideological debate is in Gerald Meaker, *The Revolutionary Left in Spain, 1914–1923*, pp. 17–61. See also Jesús Longares Alonso, "La guerra de propagandas en España, 1914–1918."

7. *CM*, June 15, 1917, p. 1.

8. For references to Gibraltar, see ibid., Aug. 5, 1916; Jan. 30, Feb. 23, and Dec. 1, 1917; Jan. 29 and Apr. 5, 1918. In 1915 Germany offered Spain Tangier, Gibraltar, and a free hand in Portugal in exchange for Spanish belligerency, but the offer was refused. Romanones, *Obras*, 3:343.

9. Ibid., Mar. 25, 1917, p. 1.

10. Ibid., Aug. 15, 1916, p. 1.

11. *España*, Aug. 17, 1916, pp. 4–5.

12. See, for example, *CM*, Jan. 30, 1917, p. 1.

13. According to the pro-Allied daily *El Liberal*, Feb. 3, 1917, p. 1, the blockade had destroyed 35,000 tons of Spanish shipping between August 1914 and January 1, 1917. Five more ships had been lost in January 1917.

14. The note is in ibid., Feb. 8, 1917, p. 1. A list of all Spanish ships sunk before May 12, 1917, is in ibid., May 14, 1917, p. 1.

15. See *CM*, Feb. 23, 1917, p. 1, and the germanófilo circular signed by "Dos Jinetes" in MA, leg. 215.

16. *DSC* (1917), 2:501.

17. Ibid., pp. 505–6.

18. For a summary of this dispute, see Joseph Harrison, "Big Business and the Failure of Right-Wing Catalan Nationalism, 1901–1923."

19. Alba's viewpoint may be found in Maximiano García Venero, *Santiago Alba*.

20. To compensate for the drastic reductions of imported coal, domestic coal production increased by 56 percent between 1913 and 1918, only to drop by nearly 20 percent by 1920, after the end of the war. Coal *prices*, however, rose by nearly 350 percent during the same years. See Santiago Roldán and José Luis García Delgado, *La formación de la sociedad capitalista, 1914–1920*, 2:118–19. Similarly, iron production increased only 10.3 percent and steel production remained constant, while iron prices rose by 265 percent in the same period. Manuel Tuñón de Lara, *La España del siglo XX*, p. 18.

21. There were 35 new banks created between 1915 and 1922, including the powerful Banco Urquijo and the Banco Central. Private bank reserves quintupled between 1915 and 1922, while their investments more than quadrupled. See Roldán and García Delgado, *Sociedad capitalista*, 2:222, 231.

22. Gerald Meaker rejects F. G. Bruguera's estimate of a 60 percent increase in industrial workers during the war and suggests a 20 percent increase is more plausible. *Revolutionary Left*, p. 32.

23. *Anuario estadístico* (1922–23), p. 359. See also the analysis in Alberto Balcells, *El sindicalismo en Barcelona, 1916–1923*, pp. 12–15, and Roldán and García Delgado, *Sociedad capitalista*, 1:127–87. The annual expenditure for a working-class family rose from 2,099 pesetas in 1914 to 2,941 pesetas in 1917, and 3,443 in 1919. Manuel Tuñón de Lara, *El movimiento obrero en la historia de España*, p. 562.

24. *DSC* (1916), 2:380, app. 4.

25. Cambó's speech is summarized in Jesús Pabón, *Cambó*, 1:460–62.

26. Taxes on profits rose by only 4 million pesetas between 1914 and 1918. Tuñón de Lara, *Siglo XX*, p. 19.

27. Andrés Saborit, *La huelga de agosto de 1917*, p. 48.

28. The manifesto of March 27 is in *El Liberal*, Mar. 28, 1917, p. 1.

29. See his account in *Obras*, 3:348–49.

30. *CM*, Mar. 28, 1917, p. 1.

31. *El Liberal*, Mar. 2, 1917, p. 2.

32. The PSOE did not officially participate because the revolutionary intent of the meeting had not been made explicit. Juan José Morato, *El Partido Socialista Obrero*, p. 291.

33. The speeches are reported in *El Liberal*, Supplement of May 27, 1917, pp. 1–2.

34. *DSC* (1915), 1:16, apps. 1, 2, 3, 4.

35. Ibid. (1916), 9:3511, app. 6.

36. Nearly 2,400 more had no assignment whatever; they were divided into "supernumeraries" (no pay), "substitutes" (half-pay), and "involuntary unassigned" (four-fifths pay). See app. D for a breakdown of the officer corps by corps in 1917.

37. In the Infantry, the percentage of officers with active, rather than bureaucratic, commands ranged from a high of 84 percent of the first lieutenants to a low of 29.6 percent of the colonels. See the article by Augusto Vivero in *El Mundo*, Jan. 18, 1918, p. 1. Similar articles appeared on Jan. 8 and 12, 1918.

38. *CM*, Jan. 13, 1917, p. 1.

39. The rise of the Juntas is described in Benito Márquez-Martínez and José-María Capo, *Las juntas militares de defensa*, first published in Havana as J.-M. Capo, *Las juntas militares de defensa*; José Buxadé, *España en crisis*; Emilio Mola Vidal, *Obras Completas*, pp. 997–1021; Stanley G. Payne, *Politics and the Military in Modern Spain*, pp. 123–51; Jorge Vigón Suerodíaz, "Breves notas para la historia de las juntas de defensa y de la dictadura"; Romanones, *Obras*, 3:366–71; and Juan Antonio Lacomba Avellán, *La crisis española de 1917*, pp.

103–60. The following discussion is principally based, however, on the documents in SHM-GL.

40. See the account in Mola, *Obras*, pp. 998–1000.

41. See above, p. 37.

42. Alfredo Kindelán y Duany, *Ejército y política*, p. 197.

43. Mola, *Obras*, p. 1000.

44. A summary of Luque's reforms appeared in *CM*, Aug. 19, 1916; each section was then presented and justified with supporting data throughout the month of September.

45. Mola, *Obras*, p. 1001.

46. For the full text of the principal articles of the statutes, see Gabriel Martínez de Aragón y Urbiztondo, *Las juntas militares de defensa*, pp. 20–35.

47. The pledge is in Mola, *Obras*, pp. 1001–2.

48. *El Liberal*, June 7, 1917, p. 1.

49. SHM-GL, legajo 73, carpeta 2.

50. Alfau to Luque, Jan. 8, 1917, ibid.

51. Ibid.

52. Buxadé, *España en crisis*, p. 40.

53. Romanones, *Obras*, 3:368.

54. SHM-GL, leg. 73, carp. 2.

55. Romanones, *Obras*, 3:353.

56. SHM-GL, leg. 73, carp. 2.

57. Alfau to Luque, Mar. 11, 1917, in ibid.

58. Ibid.

59. Ibid.

60. Jorge Vigón Suerodíaz, *Historia de la artillería española*, 3:246.

61. Ibid., pp. 240–44.

62. Ibid., pp. 245–47.

63. The circular is in *El País*, June 8, 1917, p. 2.

64. The Staff Corps pledge stressed that the "first condition it is necessary to establish and proclaim is the existence of the Corps as such. . . . " (SHM-GL, leg. 72, carp. 12).

65. See the letter of Colonel Carlos García Alonso in ibid.

66. Ibid., leg. 73, carp. 2.

67. Ibid.

68. Olegario Díaz Rivero, an Infantry colonel attached to the Supreme Military Council, to Colonel Márquez, May 24, 1917, in ibid., leg. 72, carp. 13.

69. Ibid.

70. Ibid.

71. Vigón, *Artillería*, 3:247.

72. The order is in Mola, *Obras*, p. 1003.

73. SHM-GL, leg. 72, carp. 13. The letter is also reproduced in *Sucesos de agosto*, pp. 24–26.

74. SHM-GL, leg. 72, carp. 13.

75. Ibid.

76. Ibid.

77. The imprisoned members of the Superior Junta included Colonel Márquez, Lieutenant Colonel Silverio Martínez Raposo y Real, Major Rafael Espino Pedrós, Captains Manuel Álvarez Gilarranz and Miguel García Rodríguez, and Lieutenants Emilio González Unzalu and Marcelino Flores. Mola, *Obras*, pp. 1003–4. Flores is named Suárez in Buxadé's account, *España en crisis*, p. 45.

78. The "shadow" Superior Junta included Colonels José Hechevarría y Limonta, José Molina Salazar, and Leoncio Moratinos; Lieutenant Colonels Andrés Saliquet Zumeta and Mariano Bretón; and Captain Leopoldo Pérez Pala.

79. Buxadé, *España en crisis*, pp. 62–63.

80. There is a eulogistic biography of Marina that deals with his career up to 1916: Luis Antón del Olmet and Arturo García Carraffa, *El general Marina*.

81. R.D. of May 30, 1917.

82. Márquez and Capo, *Juntas de defensa*, p. 37, n. 1.

83. SHM-GL, leg. 72, carp. 13.

84. The manifesto is in *El País*, June 5, 1917, pp. 1–2, and has been reproduced in Buxadé, *España en crisis*, pp. 51–53; Lacomba, *Crisis de 1917*, pp. 128–30; Mola, *Obras*, pp. 1005–8.

85. Mola, *Obras*, p. 1005.

86. See Buxadé, *España en crisis*, pp. 58–59.

87. Márquez and Capo, *Juntas de defensa*, pp. 38–39.

88. Ibid., p. 38.

89. Their statement is in Mola, *Obras*, pp. 1008–9.

90. *CM*, June 4, 1917, p. 1.

91. *El País*, June 3, 1917, p. 2.

92. Ibid.

93. Buxadé, *España en crisis*, pp. 75–82.

94. The new government included: Interior, José Sánchez Guerra; Finance, Conde de Bugallal; State, Marqués de Lema; Justice, Manuel Burgos y Mazo; Public Instruction, Rafael Andrade; Development, Vizconde de Eza; and Navy, Vice-Admiral Manuel Flórez.

95. This account is based on Maximiano García Venero, *Eduardo Dato*, pp. 273–74; and Maura and Fernández Almagro, *Por qué cayó Alfonso XIII*, pp. 300–302.

96. See the interview in Fernando Soldevilla, *Tres revoluciones*, p. 36.

Chapter 4

1. Conde de Romanones, *Obras completas*, 3:371.

2. *El Imparcial*, June 13, 1917, p. 1.

3. The manifesto is in *El País*, June 17, 1917, pp. 1–2.

4. *El Liberal*, June 17, 1917, p. 1.

5. The June 7 declaration contained the following points:

First. That everything that occurs is the fault of the arbitrary regime of the Governments of the Monarchy, both in what concerns civil life as well as in the military.

Second. That by neglecting the prestige of the civil Power, the Government is making a shameful and contemptible spectacle.

Third. That [the Madrid Socialist Group] will oppose with all its forces, at whatever cost, any solution that tends to diminish the sovereignty of the civil Power, or to place at the head of the country's destiny the men who embody reaction, and particularly, a government led by Maura. [*El País*, June 9, 1917, p. 2]

On June 12 the Madrid Socialist Group issued a five-point declaration:

First. Declare that in the latent military question there is a socio-political aspect that it is necessary to clarify.

Second. In the confusion, favoritism, and disorganization of the Army, the military is not free from fault, because they are represented in every government.

Third. Faced with the seditious attitude and indiscipline of the officer corps, the people should be ready to defend civil supremacy.

Fourth. The responsibility for what is happening does not extend to the most recent governments alone, but to all institutions.

Fifth. Protest one more time against the Law of Jurisdictions and against Maura. [*CM*, June 13, 1917, p. 1]

6. See Luis Araquistáin Quevedo, *Entre la guerra y la revolución*, p. 105.

7. *El País*, June 16, 1917, p. 1.

8. Alejandro Nieto, *La retribución de los funcionarios de España*, pp. 209–10.

9. *Mundo Gráfico*, Apr. 10, 1918, p. 4.

10. The manifesto of the Defense Junta of Taxpayers is in *Sucesos de agosto*, pp. 175–76, and Juan Antonio Lacomba Avellán, *La crisis española de 1917*, p. 425.

11. *CM*, June 6, 1917, p. 1.

12. *El País*, June 13, 1917, p. 2.

13. Emilio Mola Vidal, *Obras completas*, pp. 1001, 1011, 1015.

14. Letters in Gabriel Maura Gamazo and Melchor Fernández Almagro, *Por qué cayó Alfonso XIII*, pp. 303–5, 486.

15. The complete manifesto is in José Buxadé, *España en crisis*, pp. 98–113, and is partially quoted in Lacomba, *Crisis de 1917*, pp. 434–47, and in Alejandro Lerroux, *Al servicio de la república*, pp. 106–10.

16. *El Liberal*, June 7, 1917, p. 1.

17. *La Acción*, June 7, 1917, p. 4.

18. Benito Márquez-Martínez and José-María Capo, *Las juntas militares de defensa*, pp. 180–81.

19. See *CM*, June 24, 1917, p. 1.

20. Law of July 15, 1912. See above, pp. 28–29.

21. The full text is in SHM-GL, leg. 73, carp. 4.

22. In ibid.

23. *La Lucha*, June 20, 1917, p. 1. See also the account in Marcelino Domingo, *En la calle y en la carcel*, pp. 13–33.

24. The manifesto appeared in *La Acción, El Mundo*, and *La Correspondencia de España*.

25. *El País*, June 28, 1917, p. 1.

26. Guillermo Cabanellas, *Militarismo y militaradas*, pp. 63–64.

27. SHM-GL, leg. 73, carp. 4.

28. See *El País*, June 27, 1917, p. 1, for the censorship list and the decree suspending guarantees.

29. An overly sympathetic, but nevertheless very useful biography of Cambó is Jesús Pabón, *Cambó*. Despite some tactful omissions, these volumes are among the best available on Catalan regionalism and the Spanish parliamentary system at the beginning of the twentieth century.

30. Pabón, *Cambó*, 1:503–5. The official response of the government is in *El Liberal*, July 9, 1917, p. 1.

31. Maura and Fernández Almagro, *Por qué cayó Alfonso XIII*, pp. 488–89.

32. In Márquez and Capo, *Juntas de defensa*, pp. 184–87; Pabón, *Cambó*, 1:527–30; and Lacomba, *Crisis de 1917*, pp. 459–61.

33. In Buxadé, *España en crisis*, pp. 168–71; Fernando Soldevilla, *Tres revoluciones*, pp. 138–41; and Lacomba, *Crisis de 1917*, p. 157, n. 134.

34. Márquez and Capo, *Juntas de defensa*, p. 50; Maximiano García Venero, *Eduardo Dato*, pp. 282–83.

35. García Venero, *Dato*, p. 284.

36. *El Liberal*, July 16, 1917, p. 1.

37. Márquez and Capo, *Juntas de defensa*, p. 54.

38. The Assembly is fully described in Pabón, *Cambó*, 1:512–19, and Gerald Meaker, *The Revolutionary Left in Spain, 1914–1923*, pp. 70–76.

39. Lacomba, *Crisis de 1917*, p. 202.

40. See Márquez and Capo, *Juntas de defensa*, pp. 204–8, and Lacomba, *Crisis de 1917*, pp. 441–45.

41. The proposed cabinet included: President, Whomever His Majesty designates; Interior, General José Marvá; War, General Alberto de Borbón; State, Santiago Alba; Development, Francisco Cambó; Finance, Angel Urzáiz; Justice, Melquíades Álvarez; Public Instruction, Santiago Ramón y Cajal; Labor, Leonardo Torres Quevedo (in 1917 there was no Ministry of Labor).

42. Márquez and Capo, *Juntas de defensa*, pp. 66, 68, n. 1.

43. Accounts of the general strike of August 1917 may be found in Meaker, *Revolutionary Left*, pp. 76–98; Andrés Saborit, *La huelga de agosto de 1917*; Jacinto Martín Maestre, *Huelga general de 1917*; Fernanda Romeu Alfaro, *Las clases trabajadoras en España (1898–1930)*; Lacomba, *Crisis de 1917*, pp. 213–84; Pabón, *Cambó*, 1:536–45; and Manuel Tuñón de Lara, *El movimiento obrero en la historia de España*, pp. 581–602.

44. Saborit, *Huelga de agosto*, p. 63.

45. Manuel Tuñón de Lara, *La España del siglo XX*, pp. 44, 49.

46. The CNT manifesto is in Lacomba, *Crisis de 1917*, pp. 472–75.

47. The two men accused of working secretly for the government were Felix Azzati, the leader of the Valencia Republican movement, and Ramón Cordoncillo, secretary of the Southern Federation of Railworkers and a relation of Julio Amado, the editor of *La Correspondencia Militar*. Saborit, *Huelga de agosto*, p. 12.

48. *El Liberal*, Aug. 10, 1917, p. 1.

49. See the "Instructions for the Strike" in Saborit, *Huelga de agosto*, p. 73.

50. Ibid., pp. 72–73.

51. See Alberto Balcells, *El sindicalismo en Barcelona, 1916–1923*, pp. 39–43.

52. Cordoncillo and Amado were blamed for crippling the railway strike once it was underway.

53. Manifesto in Buxadé, *España en crisis*, pp. 268–71, and Lacomba, *Crisis de 1917*, pp. 511–12.

54. Pabón, *Cambó*, 1:454.

55. García Venero, *Dato*, p. 289; Márquez and Capo, *Juntas de defensa*, pp. 58–59.

56. Meaker, *Revolutionary Left*, p. 88.

57. Domingo, *En la calle*, pp. 104–55.

58. See the account in Saborit, *Huelga de agosto*, pp. 109–10, and Manuel Llaneza, "La huelga de agosto en Asturias," *España*, Nov. 1, 1917, pp. 7–8.

59. *El País*, Oct. 19, 1917, p. 2.

60. Tuñón de Lara, *Siglo XX*, p. 55.

61. Amadeu Hurtado, *Quaranta anys d'avocat*, 1:295.

62. *El Liberal*, Aug. 21, 1917, p. 2.

63. The trial proceedings are in ibid., Sept. 28–Oct. 5, 1917.

64. Mangada, an ardent Republican and Esperantist, was involved in a famous incident with General Manuel Goded in 1932. He remained loyal to the Republic in 1936.

65. The prosecution of senators and deputies was regulated by Article 47 of the constitution and a law of Feb. 9, 1912. See *El Liberal*, Sept. 15, 1917, p. 1.

66. Ibid.

67. *ABC*, Oct. 20, 1917, pp. 8–9.

68. Minutes of the assembly are in Buxadé, *España en crisis*, pp. 297–99, 300–302, and in Márquez and Capo, *Juntas de defensa*, pp. 71–75, n. 2.

69. *El Liberal*, Sept. 28, 1917, p. 1.

70. Maura and Fernández Almagro, *Por qué cayó Alfonso XIII*, p. 505.

71. *ABC*, Oct. 20, 1917, p. 8; *El Liberal*, Oct. 22, 1917, p. 1.

72. General Marina to Captain General Barraquer in Barcelona, Oct. 20, 1917, and reply of Superior Junta on Oct. 22, 1917, SHM-GL, leg. 73, carp. 5. See also *CM*, Oct. 18, 1917, p. 1.

73. *El Liberal*, Oct. 18, 1917, p. 1.

74. *ABC*, Oct. 23 and 24, 1917, pp. 13, 12.

75. The message is in Márquez and Capo, *Juntas de defensa*, pp. 210–23, and Lacomba, *Crisis de 1917*, pp. 534–38.

76. SHM-GL, leg. 73, carp. 5; Gustavo Peyra to Maura, Oct. 26, 1917, in Maura and Fernández Almagro, *Por qué cayó Alfonso XIII*, pp. 505–6; *El Liberal*, Oct. 25, 1917, p. 1.

77. *El Heraldo de Madrid*, Oct. 24, 1917, p. 1.

78. *El Liberal*, Oct. 27, 1917, p. 2.

79. The notes are in *ABC*, Oct. 29, 1917, pp. 8–11.

80. Quoted in Pío Zabala y Lera, *Historia de España y de la civilización española en la edad contemporánea*, 2:400.

81. Pabón, *Cambó*, 1:559.

82. See Márquez's letter of self-justification, published in *El Mundo*, Jan. 30, 1918, after his resignation as president of the Superior Junta. The account in his book varies rather markedly. Márquez and Capo, *Juntas de defensa*, pp. 71–78.

83. Juan de la Cierva (1864–1938) was a powerful cacique from Murcia. The saying went, "Kill the king and go to Murcia." The proverb referred to La Cierva's enormous influence in his home province, but it seems to have originated early in his career as a criminal lawyer with a formidable record of acquittals. In 1909 La Cierva had acquired an infamous reputation on the left for his harsh repression of the Tragic Week. Since then, like his political ally Antonio Maura, he had been kept at the margin of Conservative party politics.

84. See Juan de la Cierva y Peñafiel, *Notas de mi vida*, pp. 187–90.

85. For Cambó's view of the crisis, see Pabón, *Cambó*, 1:568–75.

86. The García Prieto government of November 3, 1917, included: Interior, Vizconde de Matamala (without affiliation); Justice, Joaquín Fernández Prida (Maurist); War, Juan de la Cierva (Ciervist); Finance, Juan Ventosa (Lliga Regionalista); Navy, Amalio Gimeno (Romanonist); Development, Niceto Alcalá-Zamora (Democrat); Public Instruction, Felipe Rodés (Catalan Left).

Chapter 5

1. Gerald Meaker, *The Revolutionary Left in Spain, 1914–1923*, pp. 99–116.

2. *El Sol*, Dec. 9, 1917, p. 1.

3. *El Imparcial*, Dec. 26 and 27, 1917, p. 1.

4. SHM-GL, leg. 73, carp. 2. Examination of the indexes to the Cortes debates gives a general idea of the frequency with which military courts presented petitions for removal of parliamentary immunity.

5. *CM*, Dec. 17, 1917, p. 1.

6. Ibid., Dec. 18, 1917, p. 1.

7. *EE*, Nov. 27, 1917, p. 2; *El Liberal*, Dec. 5, 1917, p. 1.

8. In Benito Márquez-Martínez and José-María Capo, *Las juntas militares de defensa*, pp. 223–25.

9. This and what follows is based on Márquez's letter of self-justification in *El Mundo*, Jan. 30, 1918, pp. 1–2.

10. The composition of the new Infantry Superior Junta is in *EE*, Feb. 7, 1918, p. 1.

11. The manifesto is in *El Liberal*, Jan. 5, 1918, p. 1.

12. Márquez and Capo, *Juntas de defensa*, p. 93; Juan de la Cierva y Peñafiel, *Notas de mi vida*, p. 195.

13. La Cierva, *Notas*, pp. 194–96, and *CM*, Jan. 5, 1918, p. 1.

14. The account is in *El Liberal*, Jan. 5, 1918, pp. 1–2.

15. *CM*, Jan. 4, 1918, p. 1.

16. Ibid., Jan. 5, 1918, p. 1.

17. For example, Ortega y Gasset in *El Sol*, Jan. 6, 1918, p. 1.

18. On the AGM banquet, see La Cierva, *Notas*, pp. 197–99, and the Spanish press on Feb. 20 and 21, 1918, which gave ample coverage to the banquet.

19. See the analysis in Miguel Martínez Cuadrado, *Elecciones y partidos políticos de España (1868–1931)*, 2:807–11.

20. The figures in *La Época*, Feb. 24, 1918, indicated that the combined Conservative factions had won 154 seats, the Liberal factions, 161. The left had won 30 seats; the regionalists, 29; and the far right, 12.

21. Romanones had written García Prieto on March 1 to warn him that he would withdraw his support for the government if the bill were not submitted to the Cortes. RA, leg. 5, no. 4.

22. *El Liberal*, Mar. 3, 4, and 8, 1918, p. 1.

23. La Cierva, *Notas*, p. 203.

24. *El Liberal*, Mar. 9, 1918, p. 1.

25. The declaration of the Madrid Socialist Group was as follows:

> 1. Its most energetic protest against the abuse of parliamentary rights and constitutional precepts that the resigning Government carried out upon approving the military reforms by decree.
>
> 2. Its intention to combat energetically the militaristic policies represented by La Cierva, and La Cierva himself.
>
> 3. Its readiness to fight with the necessary determination the military dictatorship it glimpses.
>
> 4. Its desire that the Socialist deputies in the Parliament struggle ceaselessly to restore to its position the indispensable sovereignty of the civil Power and the necessary dissolution of the Juntas de Defensa, rebellious and irresponsible organisms that the Constitution and the civilian spirit together reject. [*El Liberal*, Mar. 9, 1918, p. 2]

26. The reform bill of Mar. 7, 1918, is summarized in *CM*, Mar. 9, 1918, pp. 1–2. It is complete in *DSC* (1918), 3:785, app. 1.

27. A critique of the reform bill by Augusto Vivero appeared in *El Mundo* on Mar. 24, 1918, p. 1.

28. Retirement ages were as follows: lieutenant generals, 70; division generals, 66; brigadiers, 64; colonels, 62; lieutenant colonels and majors, 60; captains, 56; lieutenants, 51.

29. The number of brigadier generals was fixed at 102, in the following proportions: Infantry, 51; Artillery, 18; Cavalry, 13; Engineers, 10; Staff Corps, 10.

30. See *CM*, Mar. 14, 1918, p. 1; the telegram from General Barraquer, Captain General of the Fourth Region, to La Cierva, Mar. 4, 1918, in SHM-GL, leg. 73, carp. 6; and Márquez and Capo, *Juntas de defensa*, pp. 104–8.

31. Márquez and Capo, *Juntas de defensa*, pp. 133–34, n. 1.

32. Ibid., p. 134, n. 2.

33. Ibid., pp. 147–52.

34. See the letter from Márquez to the Spanish press in 1920 in Fernando Soldevilla, ed., *El año político* (1920), pp. 26–27.

35. Soldevilla, *Año político* (1918), p. 70; José Luis Coello de Portugal, *Las juntas de defensa*, p. 58.

36. The events can be followed in Fernando Díaz-Plaja, *La historia de España en sus documentos (nueva serie): El siglo XX*, pp. 385–95.

37. *CM*, Mar. 14, 1918, p. 1.

38. *EE*, Mar. 15, 1918, p. 1.

39. In *CM* and *EE*, Mar. 18, 1918.

40. Conde de Romanones, *Obras completas*, 3:374–75; Gabriel Maura Gamazo and Melchor Fernández Almagro, *Por qué cayó Alfonso XIII*, p. 312.

41. La Cierva, *Notas*, pp. 206–7.

42. See *EE*, Mar. 23, 1918, p. 1, and La Cierva, *Notas*, pp. 207–8.

43. Maura and Fernández Almagro, *Por qué cayó Alfonso XIII*, p. 311.

44. The cabinet included: State, Eduardo Dato; Interior, Manuel García Prieto; Justice, Conde de Romanones; Finance, Augusto González Besada; Development, Francisco Cambó; Public Instruction, Santiago Alba; Navy, Admiral José Pidal y Rebollo; and War, General José Marina.

45. See the speech of Marcelino Domingo in *DSC* (Apr. 22, 1918), 2:564.

46. See ibid., p. 567, and Indalecio Prieto, ibid. (Apr. 23, 1918), 2:596–603.

47. See the speeches in *Los sucesos de agosto ante el parlamento*, especially the speech of Julián Besteiro on May 28.

48. Indalecio Prieto in *DSC* (June 6, 1918), 4:1509; Joaquín Llorens, ibid., p. 1512.

49. See *CM*, May 27, 1918, p. 1.

50. Ibid., May 24, 1918, p. 1.

51. *EE*, May 25, 1918, p. 1.

52. *DSC* (1918), 5:1582. The complete speech by Alcalá-Zamora is reproduced in *Las reformas militares*.

53. See the humorous view of the debates on the military reform bill in Wenceslao Fernández-Flórez, *Acotaciones de un oyente*, pp. 291–92.

54. In Maura and Fernández Almagro, *Por qué cayó Alfonso XIII*, p. 313.

55. *CM*, July 2, 1918, p. 2.

56. Ibid., July 9, 1918, p. 1.

57. See the disapproving article in ibid., July 4, 1918, p. 1.

58. R.D. of July 12, 1918. See *CM*, July 16 and 18, 1918, p. 1.

59. See Alejandro Nieto, *La retribución de los funcionarios de España*, pp. 212–14.

60. See the letters from Gustavo Peyra to Maura's secretary, Pedro Rovira, on July 16, 21, and 27, 1918, in MA, leg. 82; the undated notes in leg. 215; and *CM*, July 13, 1918, p. 1.

61. Particularly galling were the promotions of Luis Bermúdez de Castro, Ricardo Burguete, Manuel Fernández-Silvestre, and Manuel Montero Navarro. Bermúdez de Castro and Burguete had incurred the wrath of the Juntas the previous summer. Silvestre was a part of the king's camarilla and had been Alfonso's personal aide since 1915. Montero was the brother-in-law of the High Commissioner in Africa, General Gómez Jordana.

62. Peyra wrote Rovira on July 27, 1918: "General Berenguer, whatever his merits might be, is the genuine representative of the policy of favoritism that the Juntas, and with them, the Army, repudiate" (MA, leg. 82).

63. *CM*, July 12, 1918, p. 1.

64. *EE*, Aug. 28, 1918, p. 1.

65. For the fall of the National Government, see Jesús Pabón, *Cambó*, 1:647–78; Maura and Fernández Almagro, *Por qué cayó Alfonso XIII*, pp. 316–17; Romanones, *Obras*, 3:379–82; and Raymond Carr, *Spain, 1808–1939*, pp. 506–7.

66. This is insisted upon by the principal historian of the period, Pabón, *Cambó*, 1:647–78.

67. Alba was criticized for resigning over an issue of secondary importance. Yet the situation of schoolteachers was pathetic. Salaries for the 10 ranks ranged from 1,000 to 4,000 pesetas a year. Eighty-five percent of the personnel received 1,375 pesetas or less a year. *El Liberal*, July 17, 1917, p. 1.

Chapter 6

1. Gerald Meaker, *The Revolutionary Left in Spain, 1914–1923*, p. 133.

2. The government included: State, Conde de Romanones; Finance, Santiago Alba; Interior, Luis Silvela; Justice, José Roig y Bergadá; Public Instruction, Julio Burell; Provisioning, Pablo Garnica; Navy, Admiral José-María Chacón; War, General Dámaso Berenguer.

3. Jesús Pabón, *Cambó*, 2 (1):20.

4. See the manifesto in Fernando Díaz-Plaja, *La historia de España en sus documentos (nueva serie): El siglo XX*, pp. 389–404.

5. The account of Cambó's interview with Alfonso on November 14, 1918, is in Pabón, *Cambó*, 2 (1):15–17.

6. In Manuel de Burgos y Mazo, *El verano de 1919 en Gobernación*, app., pp. 16–23.

7. The campaign for autonomy is described in Pabón, *Cambó* 2 (1):3–95.

8. The government included: Interior, Amalio Gimeno; Justice, Alejandro Rosselló; Finance, Fermín Calbetón; Development, Marqués de Cortina; Public Instruction, Joaquín Salvatella; Provisioning, Baldemero Argente; Navy, Admiral Chacón; and War, General Berenguer. Romanones continued in State in addition to presiding over the government. Berenguer was appointed High Commissioner in Morocco in December and was replaced by General Diego Muñoz Cobo.

9. See the telegram of the Captain General of Barcelona, General Milans del Bosch, to the War Minister, General Muñoz Cobo, on Dec. 13, 1918. RA, leg. 20, no. 5.

10. Benito Márquez-Martínez and José-María Capo, *Las juntas militares de defensa*, pp. 151–52.

11. The transcripts of their telephone conversations, which were apparently monitored by the government, are in RA, leg. 20, nos. 5 and 18.

12. *El Liberal*, Jan. 17, 1919, p. 1.

13. *CM*, Jan. 18, 1919, p. 1.

14. Espino to Amado, Jan. 27, 1919, RA, leg. 20, no. 18.

15. Espino to Amado, Jan. 28, 1919, ibid.

16. Pabón, *Cambó*, 2 (1):95.

17. On the labor movement, 1918–21, see Meaker, *Revolutionary Left*; Manuel Tuñón de Lara, *El movimiento obrero en la historia de España*; Alberto Balcells, *El sindicalismo en Barcelona, 1916–1923*; Maximiano García Venero, *Historia de las Internacionales en España*, 2:233–411; Manuel Buenacasa, *El movimiento obrero español, 1886–1926*, pp. 64–115; F. Baratech Alfaro, *Los Sindicatos Libres de España*; Francisco Madrid, *Ocho meses y un día en el gobierno civil de Barcelona*; Fernanda Romeu Alfaro, *Las clases trabajadores en España (1898–1930)*, pp. 143–65; Gerald Brenan, *The Spanish Labyrinth*, pp. 66–74. On agrarian unrest in Andalusia, see Juan Díaz del Moral, *Historia de las agitaciones campesinas andaluzas–Córdoba*, pp. 265–376.

18. *Anuario estadístico* (1919), pp. 358–59.

19. Between January and August 1919, 427.6 million tons of foodstuffs were exported. Fernando Soldevilla, ed., *El año político* (1920), p. 30.

20. Balcells, *Sindicalismo en Barcelona*, p. 65.

21. Díaz del Moral, *Agitaciones campesinas*, p. 309.

22. Meaker, *Revolutionary Left*, p. 139.

23. See Balcells, *Sindicalismo en Barcelona*, pp. 51–64.

24. According to Jorge Nadal, quoted in Pabón, *Cambó*, 2 (1):138.

25. *Solidaridad Obrera*, June 9, 1918, p. 1.

26. Buenacasa, *Movimiento obrero español*, p. 67.

27. Pabón, *Cambó*, 2 (1):94–95.

28. Conversation between Milans del Bosch and Muñoz Cobo, Feb. 17, 1919, RA, leg. 98, no. 131.

29. Milans del Bosch to Muñoz Cobo, Mar. 19, 1919, in ibid.

30. See the strike committee's instructions for mobilized workers in Baratech Alfaro, *Sindicatos Libres*, p. 54.

31. Telegraphic correspondence with General Milans del Bosch, Mar. 12, 13, and 15, 1919. RA, leg. 20, no. 5, and leg. 98, no. 131.

32. Meaker, *Revolutionary Left*, p. 160.

33. The proposals of the CNT and the counterproposals of the company are in Conde de Romanones, *Obras completas*, 3:397–98.

34. Fernando Primo de Rivera y Sobremonte, marqués de Estella, *Opiniones emitidas ante un redactor del periódico "El Ejército Español" con motivo del problema de orden público en los actuales momentos*, p. 30.

35. Jorge Vigón Suerodíaz, "Breves notas para la historia de las juntas de defensa y de la dictadura," p. 27.

36. RA, leg. 98, no. 131.

37. In *El Liberal*, Dec. 2, 1919, pp. 1–2. See app. E for the complete text.

38. See the article in *CM*, Mar. 18, 1919, p. 1; the speech in the military casino by General Federico Ochando (the Captain General of Madrid), reported in *El Sol*, Apr. 6, 1919, p. 2; and General José Marvá y Mayer, *El ejército y la armada y la cultura nacional*.

39. In agreeing to address the document to the king alone, the Assembly of Presidents reaffirmed "the inviolability of the principles maintained in the document, . . . which does not allow variation in either substance or form. . . " (Vigón, "Breves notas," pp. 26–27).

40. Papers were prohibited from discussing attacks on institutions, military discipline, troop movements, or strikes. *EE*, Mar. 29, 1919, p. 1.

41. Pabón, *Cambó*, 2 (1):114–15.

42. The decree is in Díaz-Plaja, *Siglo XX*, pp. 443–45.

43. For the Montañés and Doval affair, see principally, Romanones, *Obras*, 3:389–98, and the letter from Milans del Bosch in MA, leg. 263.

44. See *La Tribuna*, Feb. 18, 1919; *El Debate*, Mar. 8, 1919; and *CM*, Mar. 11, 1919.

45. See Thomas Granville Trice, "Spanish Liberalism in Crisis," p. 169.

46. The letter is in both *CM* and *EE*, May 12, 1919, p. 1.

47. The cabinet included one Romanonist, the Minister of State, Manuel González Hontoria. The rest were all Maurists: Interior, Antonio Goicoechea; Finance, Juan de la Cierva; Development, Angel Ossorio y Gallardo; Justice, Vizconde de Matamala; Provisioning, Tomás Maestre; Public Instruction, César Silió; Navy, Vice-Admiral Miranda; and War, General Luis Santiago Aguirrevengoa.

48. Meaker, *Revolutionary Left*, pp. 168–78.

49. See the correspondence between Maura and Milans del Bosch in MA, leg. 263.

50. Díaz del Moral, *Agitaciones campesinas*, pp. 325–27; MA, leg. 229.

51. The election is analyzed in Miguel Martínez Cuadrado, *Elecciones y partidos políticos de España (1868–1931)*, 2:820–28. Overall, the Liberals won 32.5 percent of the vote, the Conservatives, 49.3 percent, and the left, 7.3 percent. See also the analysis of Maura's 1919 government by his own son in Gabriel Maura Gamazo and Melchor Fernández Almagro, *Por qué cayó Alfonso XIII*, pp. 330–32.

52. The cabinet included: State, Marqués de Lema; Interior, Manuel Burgos y Mazo; Justice, Pascual Amat; Finance, Gabino Bugallal; Development, Abilio Calderón; Public Instruction, José Prado Palacios; Provisioning, Marqués de Mochales; Navy, Admiral Manuel Flórez; and War, General Antonio Tovar Marcoleta.

53. Burgos y Mazo wrote an account of his months in the Ministry of the Interior: *Verano de 1919*.

54. Interview with *La Veu de Catalunya*, quoted in *CM*, July 3, 1919, p. 1.

55. Burgos y Mazo, *Verano de 1919*, p. 461; García Venero, *Internacionales*, 2:284.

56. Interview with General Milans del Bosch in *CM*, Sept. 4, 1919, p. 1.

57. See Gonzalo Redondo, *Las empresas políticas de José Ortega y Gasset*, 1:422.

58. The agreement is in Burgos y Mazo, *Verano de 1919*, pp. 518–20.

59. See chap. 7.

60. Burgos y Mazo, *Verano de 1919*, p. 597. General Tourné is identified as General Turner.

61. See Baratech Alfaro, *Sindicatos Libres*.

62. The Allendesalazar coalition government of December 12, 1919, included: State, Marqués de Lema; Interior, Joaquín Fernández Prida; Justice, Pablo Garnica; Finance, Gabino Bugallal; Development, Amalio Gimeno; Public Instruction, Natalio Rivas; Provisioning, Francisco Terán; Navy, Admiral Flórez; and War, General José Villalba y Riquelme.

63. See Mariano Sánchez Roca, *La sublevación del cuartel del Carmen*.

64. *DSC* (Jan. 12, 1920), 6:1715.

65. Conde de Limpias in *DSS* (Feb. 5, 1920), 4:1358.

66. Bertrán y Musitú in *DSC* (Feb. 11, 1920), 7:2404.

67. See, for example, Antonio Fernández de Rota y Tournán, *¡Salvemos a España!*, and Ramón Donoso-Cortés Navarro, "El ejército y la cuestión social," *Memorial de Infantería* 19 (1921): 26–32.

68. For example, Rogelio Gorgojo, "Cuestiones que debe tratar el oficial en sus conversaciones con la tropa," *Memorial de Infantería* 17 (1920): 290–302.

69. The government included: State, Marqués de Lema; Interior, Francisco Bergamín; Justice, Gabino Bugallal; Finance, Lorenzo Domínguez Pascual; Development, Emilio Ortuño; Public Instruction, Luis Espada; and War, Vizconde de Eza.

70. See the statement of Carlos Bas in Madrid, *Ocho meses*, pp. 79–93.

71. Meaker, *Revolutionary Left*, pp. 225–313.

72. Balcells, *Sindicalismo en Barcelona*, pp. 152–53.

73. For a sympathetic biography by his aide-de-camp, see Juan Oller Piñol, *Martínez Anido, su vida y su obra*.

74. See Meaker, *Revolutionary Left*, pp. 338–45, for a relatively sympathetic appraisal of Martínez Anido's policies.

75. Baratech Alfaro, *Sindicatos Libres*, pp. 86–91.

76. For statistics on strikes and labor violence in this period, see José-María Farré Morego, *Los atentados sociales en España*.

77. *DSC* (1921), 2:354–415.

78. The Conservative victory was aided by caciquismo and by a 40 percent abstention rate. The Conservatives won 232 seats; the Liberals, 103; and the left, 29. Martínez Cuadrado, *Elecciones*, 2:829–33.

79. Soldevilla, *Año político* (1921), p. 105.

80. Quoted in Pabón, *Cambó*, 2 (1):212.

81. The Allendesalazar government of 1921 included: State, Marqués de Lema; Interior, Gabino Bugallal; Justice, Pío Vicente de Piniés; Finance, José Agustín Argüelles; Development, Juan de la Cierva; Public Instruction, Fran-

cisco Aparicio; Labor, Eduardo Sanz Escartín; Navy, Joaquín Fernández Prida; and War, Vizconde de Eza.

82. *CM*, Jan. 24, 1921, p. 1.

Chapter 7

1. Staff officers were well aware of the danger. See the letter of Dec. 24, 1917, in SHM-GL, leg. 72, carp. 12.

2. The pledge is in Gabriel Martínez de Aragón y Urbiztondo, *Las juntas militares de defensa*, app. 8, p. 48, n. 1.

3. The following account is drawn primarily from Martínez de Aragón, *Juntas militares*, and José Luis Coello de Portugal, *Las juntas de defensa*. The latter was one of the 23 ESG students; the former, the father of one of them.

4. The emissary who conveyed the order to the ESG lieutenants was the head of the regional Infantry Junta in Madrid, Colonel José Sanjurjo, later a determined opponent of the Juntas and a prominent africanista.

5. *DSC* (July 29, 1919), 2: app. 10.

6. "Ponencia de Infantería, Caballería, Artillería e Ingenieros" by the Asamblea de Presidentes de Juntas del Ejército in MA, leg. 229.

7. "A nuestros compañeros del Ejército," in ibid.

8. The resignation is in Martínez de Aragón, *Juntas militares*, app. 8, p. 47; their pamphlet, "Al Arma de Infantería," dated Oct. 16, 1919, is in RA, leg. 3, no. 1.

9. *EE*, Nov. 8, 1919, p. 1.

10. *DSC* (Nov. 14–19, 1919), 4:1167–1203; 5:1224–31.

11. *DSS* (Nov. 18, 1919), 1:app. 1.

12. *DSC* (Nov. 26, 1919), 5:1355.

13. Ibid. (Nov. 19, 1919), 5:1230–31.

14. Martínez de Aragón, *Juntas militares*, p. 152; Melchor Fernández Almagro, *Historia del reinado de D. Alfonso XIII*, p. 366; Fernando Soldevilla, ed., *El año político* (1919), p. 342; Esmé Howard, *The Theatre of Life*, 2:421–22.

15. Martínez de Aragón, *Juntas militares*, pp. 146–49.

16. The Minister of the Interior, Manuel de Burgos y Mazo, argued strenuously for resistance. See *El verano de 1919 en Gobernación*, pp. 615–21; see also his note in Soldevilla, *Año político* (1919), pp. 345–46.

17. Burgos y Mazo, *Verano de 1919*, p. 621, and Soldevilla, *Año político* (1919), p. 346.

18. Coello de Portugal, *Juntas de defensa*, p. 134.

19. In *CM*, Jan. 2, 1920, p. 1. The decree appeared in the *Gaceta* on this date.

20. Dues, which had been 1 *real* a month in 1917, were 2 pesetas a month by 1919. Coello de Portugal, *Juntas de defensa*, pp. 11, 136.

21. SHM-GL, leg. 73, carp. 6.

22. Discussion of the budget is in *DSC* (1919), 10:5156–5344. The budget as approved is in ibid., 13:6195, app. 1.

23. The new salary levels (which were enacted by royal decree on May 20, 1920) were as follows:

Colonel	12,000 pesetas	Captain	6,000
Lieutenant colonel	10,000	First Lieutenant	4,000
Major	8,000	Second Lieutenant	3,000

According to length of service, subofficials would receive 1,700 to 3,110 pesetas per year; brigades, 1,600 to 2,731; and sergeants, 1,227 to 2,241.

24. *DSC* (Mar. 26, 1920), 10:5297–98; *DSS* (Apr. 15, 1920), 7:2423.

25. *DSC* (Mar. 22, 1920), 10:5202.

26. See, for example, Marcelino Domingo in ibid. (Mar. 24, 1920), 10:5314.

27. Jorge Vigón Suerodíaz, "Breves notas para la historia de las juntas de defensa y de la dictadura," p. 34.

28. See Cándido Pardo González, *Al servicio de la verdad*.

29. The Directory first attempted to secure a merit promotion for its president, Colonel Martínez Raposo; then, when this proved unsuccessful, it tried to force the government to waive the retirement age, arguing that the colonel was still at "the height of his powers." Emilio Mola Vidal, *Obras completas*, pp. 1016–17; *CM*, June 23, 1921, p. 1.

30. Mola, *Obras*, p. 1017.

31. *CM*, July 24, 1920, p. 1.

32. His report is in Dámaso Berenguer y Fuste, conde de Xauen, *Campañas en el Rif y Yebala, 1919–1921*, 2:99–108.

33. Mola, *Obras*, pp. 1017–18.

34. *CM*, Apr. 13, 1922, p. 2.

35. *El Socialista*, Aug. 23, 1921, p. 1.

36. Manuel Azaña Díaz, *Obras completas*, 1:437–41.

37. Ibid., pp. 259–434.

38. Ibid., p. 262.

39. Luis Araquistáin Quevedo, *España en el crisol*, pp. 169–70.

40. Luis Araquistáin Quevedo, *Entre la guerra y la revolución*, p. 105.

41. The essay first appeared as a serial insert in *El Sol* in 1920–21.

42. See, for example, *El Debate*, Mar. 8, 1919, p. 1; *CM*, Mar. 11, 1919, p. 1; the references in *España*, July 3, 1919, pp. 4–5; and the article by Marcelino Domingo, also in España, Jan. 29, 1921, p. 1.

43. *El Sol*, Feb. 20, 1920, p. 1.

44. The speech of May 23, 1921, is quoted in Gonzalo Redondo, *Las empresas políticas de José Ortega y Gasset*, p. 362. A slightly different version is in Pedro Rodríguez de Toro y de Mesa, conde de los Villares, *Estudios del reinado de Alfonso XIII*, p. 52.

45. See the report of the British ambassador Howard on Alfonso's attempt to bargain directly and without the knowledge of his government for the cession of Tangier and an Anglo-Spanish defense of Gibraltar. Howard, *Theatre of Life*, 2:427–28. See also the recollections of Niceto Alcalá-Zamora y Torres, *Memorias*, pp. 74–78.

46. The story on the Cordova speech in *La Época* appeared hidden in small print on p. 2 on May 24, 1921.

47. Diego Sevilla Andrés, *Historia política de España (1800–1967)*, pp. 391–92.

48. Argüelles was replaced by Mariano Ordoñez in Finance; Piniés, by Julio Wais in Justice.

Chapter 8

1. See above, p. 39.

2. Dámaso Berenguer y Fuste, conde de Xauen, *Campañas en el Rif y Yebala, 1919–1921*, 1:17.

3. *Anuario estadístico* (1917), p. 385.

4. His letter is in Berenguer, *Campañas*, 1:12–23.

5. Conde de Romanones, *Obras completas*, 3:292.

6. The platform of the National Republican Directory, dated Nov. 19, 1918, contained the following plank on Morocco:

> At one time it could be discussed whether the solution to the problem of our Protectorate in Morocco was abandonment. This occurred when there was no hope that it would cease to be, as it is, in its exploitation, occupation, and administration, a great shame, a great ignominy, as were the last days of our colonial administration.
>
> But things are going to change. The Republic will not abandon this piece of earth. . . . The Republic, which will follow a path in international politics that unites peoples through racial affinity, common boundaries, and harmony of interests, will negotiate with its natural allies, the democracies of the western nations, to fortify with their support and sympathy the moral standing of Spain, her integral independence, viewed from Tangier without remorse, not from Gibraltar, which oppresses and alters the beat of the national heart. [Fernando Díaz-Plaja, *La historia de España en sus documentos (nueva serie): El siglo XX*, pp. 398–404]

7. Romanones in *DSC* (Nov. 14, 1921), 8:4159–60.

8. Berenguer, *Campañas*, 1:35.

9. There is one biography of Berenguer by Juan de Alfarache, *Berenguer*. A better understanding of the man can be derived from his military and political memoirs: *Campañas*; *Campañas en el Rif y Yebala, 1921–1922*; and *De la dictadura a la república*.

10. From Gallieni's *La guerre dans les colonies*, quoted in Dámaso Berenguer y Fuste, *La guerra en Marruecos*, p. 43.

11. For Lyautey's methods, see Alan Scham, *Lyautey in Morocco*.

12. The following discussion is based primarily on Berenguer's account, *Campañas*.

13. Ibid., 1:69.

14. Ibid., p. 73.

15. See *El Sol*, Oct. 6 and 21, 1919, p. 1.

16. Marqués de Lema to Burgos y Mazo, Sept. 2, 1919, and an intelligence report to the Interior Ministry, in Manuel de Burgos y Mazo, *El verano de 1919 en Gobernación*, pp. 327–28.

17. *La Época*, Oct. 15 and 19, 1919, pp. 2, 1.

18. *El Sol*, July 13, 1919, p. 1.

19. Berenguer, *Campañas*, 1:156.

20. Rodríguez del Barrio to an aide of Berenguer's, Aug. 22, 1919, quoted in Francisco Gómez Hidalgo, *Marruecos, la tragedia prevista*, p. 136.

21. Rodríguez del Barrio was dismissed from his post and charged with responsibility for the incident; he was absolved, however, in May 1922 and was promoted to brigadier. It appears likely the absolution was the work of Berenguer's enemies on the Supreme Military Council, including Generals Domingo Arraiz and Luis Aizpuru.

22. See, for example, *España*, July 17, 1919, p. 1.

23. According to Indalecio Prieto in *El Liberal*, Aug. 4, 1921, p. 1.

24. Silvestre to Berenguer, Aug. 17, 1919, in Berenguer, *Campañas*, 1: 206–10.

25. Ibid., pp. 210–22.

26. Ibid., 2:38.

27. Berenguer, *Campañas, 1921–1922*, p. 4.

28. Berenguer to the Vizconde de Eza, June 4, 1920, in Berenguer, *Campañas*, 2:92–93.

29. Berenguer officially delegated his authority to Silvestre in a General Order of Sept. 4, 1920.

30. For the Moroccan budget of 1920–21, see *DSC* (1919), 13:6195, app. 1.

31. Berenguer, *Campañas*, 1:123.

32. Law of June 9, 1921, and R.D. of July 4, 1921.

33. See Joaquín Fanjul in *DSC* (Mar. 22, 1920), 10:5202, and Marcelino Domingo in ibid. (Mar. 24, 1920), 10:5314.

34. Compare the tone and contents of Berenguer's telegram to Lema on Nov. 1, 1920, in *Campañas*, 2:212; his letters to Eza on Nov. 5, 1920, and Feb. 4, 1921, in ibid., pp. 212–14, 232–46; and his press interview in *CM*, Nov. 8, 1920, p. 1.

35. There is a list of all the materiel sent to Morocco between January 1919 and July 1921 in Luis Marichalar y Monreal, vizconde de Eza, *Mi responsabilidad en el desastre de Melilla como ministro de la Guerra*, pp. 14–15.

36. The report is in Berenguer, *Campañas*, 2:99–108.

37. R.D. of Aug. 31, 1920, and R.O. of Sept. 4, 1920. Spanish volunteers (who comprised the majority) received 700 pesetas enlistment bonus; foreigners, 600. All received 4.50 pesetas a day in addition to food, lodging, and uniforms. Officers volunteering for service in the Tercio received an annual supplement of 1,500 pesetas.

38. For a description of the Tercio by its founder, see José Millán-Astray Terreros, *La Legión*.

39. Report of Carlos Lamela, the head of the Bureau of Moroccan Affairs in the War Ministry, Aug. 27, 1920, in Eza, *Mi responsabilidad*, p. 96.

40. Berenguer to Eza, Feb. 4, 1921, in *Campañas*, 2:232–46.

41. See the correspondence between Gómez Jordana and Berenguer in ibid., 1:12–23, 192–93; 2:220–21.

42. R.D. of Sept. 13 and Oct. 5, 1920. Salaries were raised by 125 to 175 pesetas a month.

43. *El Sol*, Oct. 21, 1919, p. 1.

44. *CM*, Aug. 23, 1919, p. 1.

45. The article appeared a year later in Franco's book, *Marruecos*, pp. 76–77.

46. "While the officer tells the soldier that he fights in Africa for civilization and progress, when officers die valiantly for an idea, there is an *intellectual* who believes that civilization and progress are in the other band, in the Riffians. And these are the same ones who incited the allies against Germany in the name of civilization, and today will push the Bolsheviks against the allies. The Germans, not the Riffians, are the savages; scientific and industrial progress always came from the Rif" (*CM*, Aug. 11, 1919, p. 1).

47. Silvestre's letter of Oct. 29 and his telegram of Nov. 15, 1920, are in Berenguer, *Campañas*, 2:248–51.

48. For a biography of Abd el-Krim, see David S. Woolman, *Rebels in the Rif*, pp. 74–82; Rupert Furneaux, *Abdel Krim*; and Shannon E. Fleming, "Primo de Rivera and Abd-el Krim," pp. 57–65.

49. For Abd el-Krim's mining interests, see *El Liberal*, Oct. 27 and 30, 1921, pp. 1–2; *El Debate*, Oct. 29, 1921, p. 1.

50. Morales's report is in Berenguer, *Campañas*, 2:269–75.

51. *CM*, Apr. 9 and 12, 1921, p. 1.

52. See the testimony of Sr. Corbella, president of the Centro Hispano-Marroquí, before the Responsibilities Commission. Typed transcript in SHM-A, 4-1-11-24.

53. Julián Cortes Cavanillas, *Confesiones y muerte de Alfonso XIII*, pp. 64–65.

54. Berenguer, *Campañas, 1921–1922*, p. 242.

55. According to Manuel Ciges Aparicio, *España bajo la dinastía de los Borbones, 1701–1931*, p. 429.

56. The number of books on Anual and the atmosphere in Melilla just prior to the disaster is seemingly endless. Contemporary accounts include the Expediente Picasso and the report of the Responsibilities Commission; Berenguer, *Campañas, 1921–1922*; Juan Guixé, *El Rif en sombras*; Eduardo Rubio Fernández, *Melilla, al margen del desastre (mayo-agosto, 1921)*; Víctor Ruíz Albéniz, *España en el Rif* and *Ecce homo*; Eduardo Ortega y Gasset, *Annual*. Recent studies include Stanley G. Payne, *Politics and the Military in Modern Spain*, especially pp. 159–72; Woolman, *Rebels in the Rif*; Jesús Pabón, *Cambó*, 2 (1): 275–96; J. A. Chandler, "Spanish Policy toward North Morocco, 1908 to 1923"; and Shannon E. Fleming, "The Disaster at Annual."

57. Testimony of the son of Gabriel Morales before the Responsibilities Commission. Typed transcript, SHM-A, 4-1-11-24.

58. Letter from Morales's son in *CM*, July 26, 1921, p. 1.

59. Telegram in Berenguer, *Campañas, 1921–1922*, pp. 235–36.

60. Eza, *Mi responsabilidad*, p. 311; *CM*, June 6, 1921, p. 1.

61. On July 4 Morales wrote a friend in the peninsula about the growing danger of an attack. Francisco Hernández Mir, "El proceso de las responsabilidades," p. 24.

62. See their statements to the press in *CM*, July 1 and 4, 1921, p. 1.

63. For Silvestre's press interviews and official reports in July 1921, see Hernández Mir, "Responsabilidades," p. 24; Eza, *Mi responsabilidad*, p. 278; Berenguer, *Campañas, 1921–1922*, pp. 243–45.

64. The telegrams are in Berenguer, *Campañas, 1921–1922*, pp. 235–43, and Eza, *Mi responsabilidad*, pp. 445–53.

65. Congreso de los Diputados, Comisión de responsabilidades políticas, *La Comisión de responsabilidades*, pp. 81–82.

66. There are no conclusive estimates of the casualties, partly because the total number of troops in the sector prior to the disaster is uncertain. See the debate between the Vizconde de Eza and Indalecio Prieto in *DSC* (Oct. 25–27, 1921), 8:3742–3832. Prieto placed the number of European casualties at 8,668; Eza, at 10,126. Other sources suggest total losses of 12,000 to 14,000 Spaniards. See Julio Repollés de Zayas, "Resumen de los sucesos acaecidos en la Comandancia General de Melilla entre los días 1 de junio y 9 de agosto de 1921, y actuación del regimiento de Cazadores de Alcántara durante su desarrollo," p. 10; and Woolman, *Rebels in the Rif*, p. 96.

67. Ruíz Albéniz, *España en el Rif*, p. 228.

68. Ricardo de la Cierva y de Hoces, *Historia de la guerra civil española*, p. 73.

69. Gabriel Martínez de Aragon y Urbiztondo, *Las juntas militares de defensa*, p. 230. See the reports on the expeditionary forces in Berenguer, *Campañas, 1921–1922*, pp. 249–51.

70. Juan Mariscal del Gante in *CM*, Aug. 12, 1921, p. 1.

71. Eza, *Mi responsabilidad*, pp. 295–96.

Chapter 9

1. Juan de la Cierva y Peñafiel, *Notas de mi vida*, p. 237.

2. See the interview with Eza in *CM*, July 25, 1921, p. 1.

3. *El Socialista*, July 26, 1921, p. 1.

4. See the remarks of Lerroux in ibid., Aug. 17, 1921, p. 1.

5. *El Debate*, Aug. 14, 1921, p. 2.

6. The material in this paragraph is based on a reading of the major dailies and a popular illustrated weekly, *Mundo Gráfico*.

7. See, for example, *El Socialista*, July 23, 1921, p. 1; the letter of Marcelino Domingo in ibid., Aug. 25, 1921, pp. 1–2.

8. For a critical view of this strategy, see María-Rosa de Madariaga, "Le Parti socialiste espagnole et le parti communiste d'Espagne face à la révolte rifaine."

9. Quoted in *CM*, Aug. 26, 1921, p. 1.

10. See General Luque's two-part article in *El Sol*, Aug. 2 and 3, 1921, p. 1.

11. *CM*, July 23, 1921, p. 1.

12. See Indalecio Prieto in *El Liberal*, Aug. 4, 1921, p. 1.

13. *CM*, Aug. 5, 1921, p. 1.

14. See ibid., July 25, 1921, p. 2; *El Sol*, Aug. 3, 1921, p. 1.

15. *El Debate*, July 29, 1921, p. 1.

16. Burguete's campaign began in ibid., July 31, 1921, p. 1, and ran through the fall and winter.

17. La Cierva, *Notas*, p. 268.

18. See ibid., p. 244; *El Heraldo*, Oct. 23, 1921, p. 3.

19. *DSS* (Nov. 25, 1921), 5:2039.

20. In Jesús Pabón, *Cambó*, 2 (1):297.

21. In Cortes, *El Expediente Picasso*, p. 606.

22. MA, leg. 248.

23. The cabinet included: State, Manuel González Hontoria; Finance, Francisco Cambó; War, Juan de la Cierva; Interior, Conde de Coello de Portugal; Development, Tomás Maestre; Public Instruction, César Silió; Labor, Leopoldo Matos; Navy, Marqués de Cortina.

24. See Maura to his son Gabriel, July 29, 1921, in Gabriel Maura Gamazo and Melchor Fernández Almagro, *Por qué cayó Alfonso XIII*, p. 350.

25. *El Heraldo*, Aug. 3, 1921, p. 1.

26. *Diario Universal*, Aug. 25, 1921, pp. 1–2.

27. La Cierva, *Notas*, pp. 243–44; *Diario Universal*, Aug. 26 and 27, 1921, p. 1.

28. This correspondence is in Cortes, *Expediente Picasso*, pp. 606–10.

29. *CM*, Nov. 21, 1922, p. 1.

30. R.O. of Aug. 22 and Sept. 2, 1921.

31. Dámaso Berenguer y Fuste, conde de Xauen, *Campañas en el Rif y Yebala, 1921–1922*, pp. 110–11.

32. Francisco Franco Bahamonde, *Marruecos*, p. 279.

33. *El Liberal*, Oct. 22, 1921, p. 3.

34. *Diario Universal*, Sept. 9, 1921, p. 1.

35. *El Debate*, Sept. 28 and Oct. 1, 1921, p. 1; *El Heraldo*, Oct. 20, 1921, p. 1.

36. *El Liberal*, Oct. 21 and 23, 1921, pp. 3, 1.

37. *El Mundo, La Tribuna, El Heraldo*, and *Diario Universal*.

38. *El Liberal*, Oct. 23, 1921, p. 1; *El Socialista*, Oct. 24, 1921, p. 1; *El Heraldo*, Oct. 23, 1921, p. 3.

39. *CM*, Oct. 24, 1921, p. 1.

40. *El Liberal*, Oct. 25, 1921, p. 1.

41. Ibid., Oct. 23 and 25, 1921, p. 1.

42. Cabanellas was charged with violation of Articles 258, 300, and 329 of the Code of Military Justice. *CM*, Nov. 14, 1921, p. 1.

43. *El Heraldo*, Nov. 14, 1921, p. 3.

44. SHM-A, 1-4-8-21.

45. *El Debate*, Sept. 28, 1921, p. 1.

46. Maura in *DSC* (Oct. 20, 1921), 7:3670.

47. Pabón, *Cambó*, 2 (1):303–6.

48. *DSC* (1921), 7:3669–73.

49. Ibid., 8:4165–66.

50. See especially the Marqués de la Viesca (Captain Arsenio Martínez Campos) in ibid. (Oct. 21, 1921), 7:3694–3710; Marcelino Domingo in ibid. (Oct. 27, 1921), 8:3824–30.

51. See Indalecio Prieto and Julián Besteiro in ibid. (Oct. 27 and Nov. 3, 1921), 8:3819–32, 3938–48.

52. Ibid., 8:3734, app. 2.

53. *CM*, Nov. 10, 1921, p. 1.

54. *El Liberal*, Nov. 3, 1921, p. 1.

55. *DSC* (1921), 9:4488–94.

56. See the correspondence in December 1921 between General Emilio Barrera and La Cierva in SHM-A, 1-4-8-21.

57. *CM*, Dec. 20, 1921, p. 1.

58. *DSC* (1921), 9:4562.

59. Ibid. (Dec. 7, 1921), 9:4657–59.

60. Ibid.

61. Congreso de los Diputados, Comisión de responsabilidades políticas, *La Comisión de responsabilidades*, pp. 20–21.

62. On December 5 a "mother's commission" petitioned La Cierva, and the Federation of Municipal Workers and Employees of Madrid held a pro-ransom meeting. *El Liberal*, Dec. 4 and 6, 1921, p. 1; *El Socialista*, Dec. 5, 1921, p. 1. A typical attitude is expressed by Miguel de Unamuno, "El rescate, principio de la civilización," *El Liberal*, Dec. 8, 1921, p. 1.

63. *El Debate*, Dec. 6, 1921, p. 1.

64. Quoted in ibid., Dec. 15, 1921, p. 1; *El Heraldo*, Dec. 15, 1921, p. 2.

65. On conditions in the African army, see Eduardo Ortega y Gasset in *DSC* (Nov. 8, 1921), 8:4001–9; *El Heraldo*, Jan. 2, 1922, p. 1; Francisco Hernández Mir, *Del desastre al fracaso*; Ernesto Giménez Caballero, *Notas marruecas de un soldado* (for which the author was imprisoned in September 1923); José Díaz-Fernández, *El blocao*; and Arturo Barea, *La forja de un rebelde*.

66. See especially, *CM*, Aug. 12, 1922, p. 1; Juan Guixé, *El Rif en sombras*.

67. Berenguer, *Campañas, 1921–1922*, p. 167.

68. *ABC*, Apr. 1, 1922, p. 9.

69. Berenguer had originally opposed Sanjurjo's appointment. SHM-A, 1-4-8-21.

70. Division General Neila went on indefinite sick call. *CM*, Dec. 19 and 29, 1921, pp. 1–2, 1.

71. *El Liberal*, Jan. 10, 1922, p. 1.

72. Ibid., Jan. 5, 1922, p. 1.

73. La Cierva, *Notas*, p. 268.

74. MA, leg. 275.

75. R.D. of Jan. 16, 1921.

76. Alfonso was reported to have sent a messenger to the Juntas with a note saying, "Be calm. If the decree is presented, since I am quite dull witted, I will have to study it for several days" (*El Heraldo*, Jan. 12, 1921, p. 2).

77. The note is in *El Liberal*, Jan. 12, 1922, p. 1.

78. Ibid., Jan. 13, 1922, p. 1.

79. Ibid., Jan. 15, 1922, p. 1.

80. *CM*, Jan. 12, 1922, p. 1.

81. Ibid., Jan. 14, 1922, p. 1.

82. La Cierva, *Notas*, p. 269.

83. See the testimony of Colonel Riquelme and General Berenguer in Congreso, *Comisión de responsabilidades*, pp. 199–200, 314; and *CM*, July 28, 1922, p. 1.

84. Their official notes are in *El Liberal*, Jan. 17, 1922, p. 1.

85. For an excellent discussion of the individual views of the cabinet members, see Pabón, *Cambó*, 2 (1):328–40.

86. Military officials present at the Pizarra Conference included the chief of the General Staff, General Luis Aizpuru, the Commander of the Fleet in Morocco, Admiral Juan B. Aznar, their aides, and the Undersecretary for War, General Julio Ardanaz.

87. Berenguer, *Campañas, 1921–1922*, pp. 252–53.

88. *El Liberal*, Feb. 21, 1922, p. 1.

89. *DSC* (1922), 1:41–43.

90. Ibid., pp. 44–46.

91. Julián Besteiro in ibid., pp. 52–53.

92. *La Época*, Mar. 8, 1922, p. 2.

Chapter 10

1. The cabinet included: State, Joaquín Fernández Prida; War, José Olaguer-Feliú y Ramírez; Interior, Pío Vicente de Piniés; Justice, José Bertrán y Musitú; Finance, José Bergamín; Development, Agustín Argüelles; Public Instruction, César Silió; Labor, Abilio Calderón; Navy, Mariano Ordoñez. After the resignations of Bertrán y Musitú and Silió on March 31, Ordoñez went to Justice and was replaced at Navy by Admiral Rivera, while Tomás Montejo y Rica took Public Instruction.

2. Romanones in *El Liberal*, Nov. 5, 1922, p. 2.

3. See ibid., Mar. 11 and 30, 1922, pp. 2, 1.

4. Congreso de los Diputados, Comisión de responsabilidades políticas, *La Comisión de responsabilidades*, pp. 70–71.

5. *ABC*, Apr. 23, 1922, p. 15. Berenguer also expelled one of his most acerbic critics, Francisco Hernández Mir, correspondent for Alba's paper *La Libertad*. SHM-A, 1-4-9-24.

6. The complete accords are in *CM*, Apr. 13, 1923, pp. 1–2. Abbreviated versions appeared in most of the daily press around this date.

7. In Gabriel Martínez de Aragón y Urbiztondo, *Las juntas militares de defensa*, pp. 242–43, and Jorge Vigón Suerodíaz, "Breves notas para la historia de las juntas de defensa y de la dictadura," pp. 44–45.

8. *El Heraldo*, May 10 and 12, and June 1, 1922, p. 1.

9. *La Época*, Apr. 5, 1922, p. 1.

10. *DSC* (1922), 2:901–6, 940–50.

11. Indalecio Prieto in ibid. (May 5, 1922), 2:1163.

12. The bill is in ibid. (1922), 2:1063, app. 4.

13. *DSS* (May 30, 1922), 3:915–16.

14. *DSC* (1922), 7:2798, app. 7.

15. Indalecio Prieto in ibid. (July 20, 1922), 10:3947.

16. Ibid. (1922), 6:2453. For the ESG affair, see chap. 7.

17. See *El Liberal*, July 2, 1922, pp. 1–2; July 4, p. 1; and July 9, p. 2. The court declared itself competent on the grounds that the disputed honor court had been formed in compliance with a royal order and not with the Code of Military Justice.

18. Ibid., July 12 and 13, 1922, pp. 3, 1.

19. Ibid., Aug. 2, 1922, p. 3.

20. *DSC* (June 29, 1922), 8:3174.

21. See the figures presented by the Reformist Augusto Barcia in ibid. (June 28, 1922), 8:3102–5.

22. Cortes, *El Expediente Picasso*, pp. 1–300. This volume also contains the report of the Supreme Military Council of July 10, 1922.

23. Ibid., p. 307.

24. Ibid., p. 314.

25. Ibid., pp. 387–88.

26. *El Liberal*, July 9, 1922, p. 1.

27. Ibid., July 18, 1922, p. 3.

28. Ibid., July 20, 1922, p. 1.

29. Ibid., July 9, 1922, p. 1.

30. *DSS* (1922), 6:1724–58.

31. See, for example, *CM*, July 15, 1922, p. 1.

32. See *El Liberal*, July 14, 1922, p. 1; Gerald Meaker, *The Revolutionary Left in Spain, 1914–1923*, pp. 437–38.

33. According to Gerald Meaker, "the Communist Party was nearly as much a victim of the Moroccan conflict as the army of General Fernández Silvestre" (*Revolutionary Left*, p. 438). Marcelino Domingo was arrested under the Law of Jurisdictions on July 16, and organizers from the Madrid Socialist Youth were arrested for scheduling an antiwar meeting in the Casa del Pueblo on July 29. *El Liberal*, July 18 and 19, Aug. 1, 1922, p. 1.

34. The Picasso Commission included 10 Conservatives (Sres. Rodríguez de Vigurí, Lazaga, Sáiz Pardo, Sánchez de Toca [D. Fernando], Marfil, Canals, Lequerica, Marín Lazaro, Estrada, and Matos); 7 Liberals (Sres. Álvarez Arranz, Nicolau, Alvarado, Rosselló, Armiñán, Alcalá-Zamora, and Sala); 1 Reformist (Pedregal); 1 Catalan (Bastos); 1 Republican (Lerroux); and 1 Socialist (Prieto).

35. *El Sol*, June 11, 1922, p. 3.

36. *El Liberal*, July 16, 1922, p. 1.

37. *CM*, July 20, 1922, p. 1.

38. Burguete's harangue is in *El Liberal*, Aug. 26, 1922, p. 1.

39. *El Heraldo*, Aug. 30, 1922, p. 1.

40. *CM*, Sept. 1, 1922, p. 1.

41. The decree abolished the Office of Native Affairs and created two new offices, Civil Inspection and Khalifal Services, and General Inspection of Military Intervention and Khalifal Troops, both under the jurisdiction of the Ministry of State.

42. Most of what follows is taken from Rafael López Rienda, *El escándalo del millón de Larache*.

43. "Ministerio de la Guerra. Informe sobre abono de la administración militar de Marruecos." RA, leg. 28, no. 17.

44. See Sánchez Guerra's instructions to Burguete in SHM-A, 1-4-8-21.

45. *El Heraldo*, Sept. 22, 1922, p. 1.

46. Ibid., Sept. 27, 1922, p. 1.

47. Ibid., Sept. 29, 1922, p. 1.

48. See the insubordinate remarks of the Commander General of Melilla, General Carlos de Lossada, in *El Liberal*, Sept. 9, 1922, p. 1.

49. Ibid., Oct. 10, 1922, p. 2.

50. Ibid., Nov. 7, 1922, p. 1.

51. See *EE*, July 17, 1922, p. 1; *El Heraldo*, Aug. 3, 1922, p. 2; and Francisco Madrid, *El ruidísimo pleito de las juntas de defensa y Millán-Astray*.

52. *El Liberal*, Oct. 18, 1922, p. 3.

53. *El Heraldo*, Oct. 18, 1922, p. 1.

54. *EE*, Oct. 18–21, 1922, p. 1.

55. *El Liberal*, Oct. 19 and 22, 1922, p. 1, and *España*, Oct. 21, 1922, pp. 3–4.

56. Amadeu Hurtado, *Quaranta anys d'avocat*, pp. 422–23. See also *El Liberal*, Feb. 12, 1922, p. 1.

57. *EE*, Aug. 8, 1922, p. 1; *El Liberal*, Aug. 8 and 11, 1922, p. 3.

58. *El Liberal*, Oct. 28, 1922, p. 1. One was Captain Rafael Espino, a member of the original Infantry Superior Junta.

59. *El Sol*, June 11, 1922, p. 3.

60. Conde de Romanones, *Obras completas*, 3:411.

61. In *El Liberal*, Nov. 1, 1922, pp. 1–2.

62. In *ABC*, quoted in ibid., Nov. 5, 1922, p. 2.

63. *CM*, Nov. 10, 1922, pp. 1–2.

64. *El Liberal*, Nov. 12, 1922, p. 1.

65. *CM*, Nov. 13, 1922, pp. 1–2.

66. *El Liberal*, Nov. 12, 1922, p. 1.

67. *DSC* (Nov. 14, 1922), 11:4016, app. 1. The bill as passed is in ibid. (Nov. 23, 1922), 11:4295, app. 1.

68. Berenguer was charged with violation of Article 275 of the Code of Military Justice: "The governor or commander who loses the military garrison

or post under his command because he has not taken preventative measures or has not asked in time for the means necessary for defense when he becomes aware of the danger of attack, will incur the punishment of life imprisonment."

69. *El Heraldo*, Oct. 28, 1922, p. 3.

70. See the motion and speech of the Maurist Tomás Maestre in *DSS* (Dec. 1, 1922), 8:2144.

71. *El Liberal*, Nov. 19, 1922, p. 1.

72. *CM*, Nov. 29, 1922, p. 1.

73. *DSS* (1922), 8:2169–70.

74. *DSC* (1922), 11:4089, app. 2.

75. Prieto's report is in ibid., p. 4128, app. 1; he spoke in its defense on Nov. 21–22, 1922, in ibid., pp. 4186–4204, 4225–46.

76. Ibid., p. 4089, app. 3.

77. *El Liberal*, Nov. 26, 1922, p. 1.

78. Sánchez Guerra hailed Maura's position as "the only possible parliamentary and constitutional doctrine." *DSC* (Nov. 30, 1922), 12:4459.

79. Ibid., pp. 4471–72.

80. See Jesús Pabón, *Cambó*, 2 (1):405–6.

81. For the events of December 5, 1922, see *DSC* (1922), 12:4511–33. See also La Cierva's interpretation of the responsibilities debate in *Notas de mi vida*, pp. 283–89.

Chapter 11

1. See Amadeu Hurtado, *Quaranta anys d'avocat*, 1:436.

2. The cabinet included representatives from each of the principal Liberal factions. Romanones took the Justice portfolio until becoming president of the Senate, when he was replaced by the Conde de López Muñoz; his man, Joaquín Salvatella, took Public Instruction. García Prieto's faction, the Democrats, included Luis Silvela in Navy and the Duque de Almodóvar del Valle in Interior. After Pedregal's resignation in April, Miguel Villanueva became Minister of Finance. A former Democrat, Niceto Alcalá-Zamora, in the War Ministry, was now an independent with his own following. Another independent, Rafael Gasset, took Development. Santiago Alba, leader of the third great Liberal faction, became Minister of State; his man, Joaquín Chapaprieta, was in Labor.

3. *El Heraldo*, Dec. 10, 1922, p. 1.

4. *El Liberal*, Dec. 22, 1922, p. 1. Echevarrieta, owner of *El Liberal* of Bilbao, had once employed the Socialist deputy Indalecio Prieto as a private secretary.

5. Burguete's report is in Congreso, *Comisión de responsabilidades*, app., pp. 69–101.

6. *El Liberal*, Dec. 26, 1922, p. 1.

7. Quoted in Jesús Pabón, *Cambó*, 2 (1):421.

8. R.D. of Jan. 17, 1923; R.O.C. of Feb. 19, 1923; R.D. of Mar. 28, 1923; R.O.C. of Feb. 24, 1923.

9. *El Liberal*, Jan. 28, 1923, p. 1.

10. *El Heraldo*, Dec. 29, 1922, p. 1.

11. *El Liberal*, Dec. 28, 1922, p. 1.

12. See *El Sol*, Feb. 7 and 20, 1923, p. 1; *Ejército y Armada*, Feb. 7 and 11, 1923, p. 1; *CM*, Feb. 7–16, 1923, p. 1; Niceto Alcalá-Zamora y Torres, *Memorias*, p. 72.

13. The letter is in Santiago Alba, *L'Espagne et la Dictature*, pp. 30–51.

14. *El Liberal*, Feb. 14, 1923, p. 1; *EE*, Feb. 14, 1923, p. 1.

15. *CM*, Feb. 20, 1923, p. 2.

16. Quoted in Gabriel Maura Gamazo and Melchor Fernández Almagro, *Por qué cayó Alfonso XIII*, pp. 361–62. According to Alcalá-Zamora, the king had been considering a personal dictatorship since December, or abdication in favor of his son should this fail. *Memorias*, pp. 89–90.

17. *El Sol*, Mar. 3, 1923, p. 3.

18. Gerald Meaker, *The Revolutionary Left in Spain, 1914–1923*, p. 459.

19. *El Liberal*, Mar. 18, 1923, p. 3.

20. *El Heraldo*, Mar. 24 and Apr. 9, 1923, pp. 1, 3.

21. Pabón, *Cambó*, 2 (1): 449–50.

22. *El Liberal*, Apr. 6 and 8, 1923, p. 1.

23. *Ejército y Armada*, Feb. 11, 1923, p. 1.

24. *El Heraldo*, Mar. 28, 1923, p. 1.

25. *El Sol*, Jan. 14, 1923, p. 1.

26. Gambling was prohibited everywhere except in the military casino, the Circle of Fine Arts, the Grand Club, and the Casino of Madrid; i.e., it was prohibited to all but the privileged.

27. The decree is in Conde de Romanones, *Obras completas*, 3:418–19.

28. *El Sol*, Mar. 30, 1923, p. 1.

29. See *España*, Mar. 31, 1923, pp. 2–3, and in subsequent issues throughout the spring of 1923. As of January 1, the new editor was Manuel Azaña.

30. *El Sol*, Apr. 4, 1923, p. 1.

31. *El Liberal*, Apr. 7, 1923, p. 1.

32. For an analysis of the elections, see Miguel Martínez Cuadrado, *Elecciones y partidos políticos de España (1868–1931)*, 2:840–45.

33. *DSC* (May 30, 1923), 1:102–10. See also Alcalá-Zamora's memoirs, *Memorias*, pp. 86–91, where he argues that the king also desired his resignation.

34. See the critical remarks in *España*, June 2, 1923, p. 5.

35. See his correspondence with the government in SHM-A, 1-4-8-21, and in DNSD, Madrid: Sección Político-Social, carp. 848, leg. 740. See also Silvela's testimony before the Responsibilities Commission, typed transcript in SHM-A, 4-1-11-24.

36. On the search for a replacement for Alcalá-Zamora, see *El Heraldo*, May 25, 1923, p. 1. According to Alcalá-Zamora, the docile Aizpuru was the king's candidate. *Memorias*, p. 88.

37. *DSS* (May 23, 1923), 1:12–14.

38. *EE*, June 7, 1923, p. 2.

39. See *España*, June 16, 1923, pp. 1–2; Indalecio Prieto in *DSC* (June 14, 1923), 2:380–84, 388–89.

40. *DSC* (1923), 2:547.

41. *El Liberal*, June 1 and 9, 1923, p. 1; *El Heraldo*, June 7, 1923, p. 1.

42. His letter of resignation is in Pabón, *Cambó*, 2 (1):434–36.

43. See the Lliga's amendment to the Message to the Crown and the Liberals' response in *DSS* (June 21, 1923), 1:266–78, and *DSC* (June 22, 1923), 2:493, app. 1.

44. Conveyed through the Captain General, Primo de Rivera, during a trip to Madrid. *El Liberal*, May 23, 1923, p. 1.

45. Manuel Tuñón de Lara, *El movimiento obrero en la historia de España*, pp. 723–28.

46. According to Gerald Meaker, there were 34 deaths and 76 injuries between December 1922 and May 1923. *Revolutionary Left*, p. 458.

47. *El Liberal*, June 3, 1923, p. 2.

48. See La Cierva in *DSC* (June 5, 1923), 1:175–76, and Sánchez de Toca, who rejected "outdated liberalisms" as a solution to the problem of terrorism, in *DSS* (June 5, 1923), 1:60.

49. *El Liberal*, June 10, 1923, p. 1.

50. *DSC* (June 5, 1923), 1:176–77.

51. See, for example, Rafael Guerra del Río, ibid. (June 1, 1923), 1:130–36; Marcelino Domingo, ibid. (June 21, 1923), 2:481–86.

52. For Primo's background and early career, see Francisco Cimadevilla, *El general Primo de Rivera*.

53. Gabriel Maura Gamazo, duque de Maura, *Bosquejo histórico de la dictadura, 1923–1930*, pp. 23–24; Francisco Hernández Mir, *La dictadura ante la historia*, pp. 34–35.

54. See his letter to Cambó in January 1923 in Pabón, *Cambó*, 2 (1):427.

55. The correspondence is in *El Sol*, June 16, 1923, p. 3.

56. *El Liberal*, June 29, 1923, p. 1.

57. Miguel Primo de Rivera y Orbaneja, *La obra de la dictadura*, p. 12.

58. *El Heraldo*, June 23, 1923, p. 1.

59. Hernández Mir, *Dictadura*, p. 30.

60. Romanones, *Obras*, 3:420.

61. *El Liberal*, June 24, 1923, p. 3.

62. See *DSC* (1923), 2:663, 805. The Responsibilities Commission, elected July 10, included 7 Liberals (Sagasta, Morote, Fernández Jiménez, Palacios, García Inza, Zancada, and Soto Reguera); 4 Conservatives (Rodríguez de Vigurí, Ruano, Alas Pumariño, and Taboada); 2 Ciervists (Díez de Revenga and Rodríguez Valdés); 1 Maurist (Lequerica); 1 Traditionalist (García Guijarro); 2 Republicans (Domingo and Rodés); 2 Socialists (Prieto and De los Ríos); and 2 Independents (Tejero and Martínez Campos). Ibid., 3:847. The Socialist Julián Besteiro was elected to replace Rodés on July 20.

63. Dámaso Berenguer y Fuste, conde de Xauen, *Campañas en el Rif y Yebala, 1921–1922*. It was reviewed critically by Manuel Azaña in *España*, July 14–Sept. 15, 1923.

64. *El Liberal*, Apr. 26, 1923, p. 1.

65. *DSS* (June 5, 1923), 1:56.

66. See Tomás Maestre in ibid. (June 27, 1923), 1:359–74.

67. El Liberal, June 28, 1923, p. 2.

68. DSS (June 28, 1923), 1:402–8.

69. Ibid. (July 3, 1923), 1:424.

70. See RA, leg. 5, no. 5; Romanones, Obras, 3:420–22.

71. DSS (July 5, 1923), 2:474–79. The Aguilera-Sánchez de Toca incident has been examined by Ricardo de la Cierva y de Hoces in "La dialéctica de las bofetadas."

72. See El Liberal, July 7, 1923, p. 1; El Heraldo, July 6, 1923, p. 1; EE, July 9, 1923, p. 1.

73. Manuel Tuñón de Lara, La España del siglo XX, p. 121, n. 2.

74. El Liberal, June 26, 1923, p. 1.

75. Ramón Martínez Sol, De Canalejas al tribunal de responsabilidades, pp. 54–55.

76. Gabriel Maura Gamazo, Bosquejo histórico de la dictadura, pp. 20–21.

77. Manuel Aguirre del Cárcer, Glosa del año 23, p. 177.

78. El Liberal, Aug. 14, 1923, p. 1; the plan of operations is in RA, leg. 58, no. 37.

79. El Liberal, Aug. 5, 1923, p. 1.

80. CM, Aug. 31, 1923, p. 1.

81. See, for example, the remarks in EE, Aug. 14, 1923, p. 1.

82. El Liberal, Aug. 19–23, 1923, p. 1.

83. Meaker, Revolutionary Left, pp. 469–72.

84. See El Liberal, Aug. 29, 1923, p. 1; CM, Sept. 1, 1923, p. 1.

85. Alba, Dictature, pp. 23–24.

86. The three dissenting ministers were replaced by Manuel Portela Valladares in Development, Felix Suárez-Inclán in Finance, and Luis de Armiñán in Labor.

87. El Liberal, Sept. 5, 1923, p. 1.

88. See Pablo Iglesias in ibid., Sept. 4, 1923, p. 1; El Sol, Sept. 4, 1923, p. 1.

89. El Liberal, Sept. 4, 1923, p. 1.

Chapter 12

1. El Liberal, Sept. 7, 1923, p. 1.

2. The report of the Responsibilities Commission was published in 1931 by the Constituent Cortes of the Republic. There is also a typewritten transcript in SHM-A, 4-1-11-24. I was unable to compare the two texts together, in toto, but a study of my notes suggests that they are identical.

3. See El Liberal, Sept. 5, 1923, p. 1.

4. Sir Charles Petrie, King Alfonso XIII and His Age, pp. 172–73.

5. Ramón Martínez Sol, De Canalejas al tribunal de responsabilidades, p. 71.

6. CM, Sept. 1, 1923, p. 2, reports a meeting of these officers in the Captaincy General of Barcelona on August 29.

7. Eduardo López de Ochoa, De la dictadura a la república, pp. 24–26.

8. Santiago Alba, L'Espagne et la Dictature, pp. 13–14.

9. Aizpuru later denied his involvement in the conspiracy before the

Responsibilities Commission of the Second Republic. See Martínez Sol, *De Canalejas al tribunal*, p. 51.

10. In Alba, *Dictature*, pp. 17–19.

11. Ibid., pp. 24–29. Alba's escape was aided by two Artillery officers, colleagues of his brother.

12. *El Sol*, Sept. 11 and 12, 1923, pp. 2, 1.

13. *CM*, Sept. 12, 1923, p. 1.

14. Manuel Tuñón de Lara, *Estudios sobre el siglo XIX español*, p. 222.

15. The complete manifesto is in *CM*, Sept. 13, 1923, pp. 1–2.

16. Ibid., p. 2.

17. Julio Romano, *Weyler, el hombre de hierro*, p. 182.

18. *CM*, Sept. 13, 1923, p. 1.

19. Petrie, *Alfonso XIII*, p. 174.

20. The moderate Anarchosyndicalist leader, Angel Pestaña, later believed that Anarchist terrorism was a primary cause of the Dictatorship. Gerald Meaker, *The Revolutionary Left in Spain, 1914–1923*, p. 459.

21. Manuel Ribé, *Memorias de un funcionario*, p. 115.

22. Francisco Hernández Mir, *La dictadura ante la historia*, p. 111.

23. Joaquín Maurín, *Los hombres de la dictadura*, pp. 123–24.

24. Carlos Seco Serrano, *Alfonso XIII y la crisis de la restauración*, p. 160.

25. Ibid., p. 161.

26. The Directory contained one brigadier general for each military region: Adolfo Vallespinosa Vior, Luis Hermosa Kith, Luis Navarro y Alonso de Celada, Ramiro Rodríguez Pedré, Antonio Mayandía Gómez, Francisco Gómez-Jordana Souza, Francisco Ruíz del Portal y Martínez, and Mario Muslera Planes. Secretary of the Military Directory was Colonel Nouvilas, the former president of the Infantry Junta. *CM*, Sept. 17, 1923, p. 1.

27. Ibid.

28. Julián Cortes Cavanillas, *La caída de Alfonso XIII*, p. 67.

29. *CM*, Sept. 13, 1923, p. 1.

30. *El Liberal*, Sept. 14, 1923, p. 1.

31. Jesús Pabón, *Cambó*, 2 (1):459–60; Maurín, *Hombres*, p. 124.

32. *El Liberal*, Sept. 14, 1923, p. 1.

33. *El Sol*, Sept. 14, 1923, p. 1.

34. See the joint PSOE-UGT manifesto in *El Liberal*, Sept. 14, 1923, p. 1.

35. Meaker, *Revolutionary Left*, pp. 472–77.

36. Quoted in Gabriel Maura Gamazo and Melchor Fernández Almagro, *Por qué cayó Alfonso XIII*, p. 435.

Chapter 13

1. *CM*, Sept. 17, 1923, p. 2.

2. Luis de Galinsoga and Francisco Franco-Salgado, *Centinela de occidente*, pp. 203–6.

Bibliography

Manuscript Sources

Spain

Estado Mayor Central. Servicio Histórico Militar, Sección de Estudios Históricos, Madrid.
 Primer Negociado: Guerra de Liberación
 Segundo Negociado: Africa
Papers of D. Antonio Maura, Fundación Antonio Maura, Madrid.
Papers of the Conde de Romanones, in the possession of the Marqués de Santo Floro, Madrid.
Presidencia del Gobierno. Delegación Nacional de Servicios Documentales, Salamanca.
 Barcelona: Sección Político-Social
 Madrid: Sección Político-Social

Printed Sources

Official Publications

Great Britain

Foreign Office. *Spanish and Italian Possessions: Independent States.* Historical Section Peace Handbooks, vol. 20. New York: Greenwood Press, 1969.

Spain

Congreso de los Diputados. Comisión de responsabilidades políticas. *La Comisión de responsabilidades: Documentos relacionados con la información instruída por la llamada "Comisión de responsabilidades" acerca del desastre de Anual.* Madrid: J. Morata, 1931.
Cortes. *Diario de las sesiones de las Cortes españolas.* 1917–1923.
————. *El Expediente Picasso: Las responsabilidades de la actuación española en Marruecos. Julio 1921.* Madrid: J. Morata, 1931.
Instituto de Reformas Sociales. Dirección General del Trabajo e Inspección. *Movimiento de los precios al por menor en España durante la guerra y la post-*

guerra, 1914–1922. Madrid: Sobrinos de la Sucesora de M. Minuesa de los Ríos, 1923.

————. Sección Tercera, Técnico-Administrativa. *Coste de la vida del obrero: Estadística de los precios de los artículos de primera necesidad en toda España, desde 1909 a 1915*. Madrid: Est. Tip. de Felipe Peña Cruz, 1916.

Ministerio de la Guerra. *Anuario militar de España*. Madrid: Imprenta y lit. del Depósito de la Guerra, 1915–23.

————. *Colección legislativa del Ejército*. Madrid: Imprenta y lit. del Depósito de la Guerra, 1878–1923.

Ministerio de Hacienda. *Presupuestos generales del Estado*. Madrid: Sobrinos de la Sucesora de M. Minuesa de los Ríos, 1917–23.

Ministerio de Instrucción Pública y Bellas Artes. Dirección General del Instituto Geográfico y Estadístico. *Anuario estadístico de España*. Madrid: Sobrinos de la Sucesora de M. Minuesa de los Ríos, 1912–20.

Ministerio de Trabajo, Comercio e Industria. Dirección General de Estadística. *Anuario estadístico de España*. Madrid: Sobrinos de la Sucesora de M. Minuesa de los Ríos, 1921–23.

Handbooks and Yearbooks

Código de justicia militar. Madrid: Est. Tip. de Pedro Nuñez, 1890.

Escobar y Huerta, Ramón, ed. *El código de justicia militar al día*. 4th rev. ed. Madrid: Imprenta Clásica Española, 1927.

Estirado, Restituto, ed. *Almanaque del empleado para el año de 1917*. Vol. 49. Madrid: Imp. y Encuad. de Julio Cosano, 1916.

Guía oficial de España. Madrid: Sucesores de Rivadeneyra, 1917–23.

San Martín Losada, Eduardo. *Sueldos, haberes y gratificaciones del personal del ejército*. 3d ed. Madrid: Imprenta del Patronato de Huérfanos de Intendencia e Intervención Militares, 1929.

Sánchez de los Santos, Modesto. *Las Cortes españolas: Las de 1907. Las de 1910. Las de 1914*. 3 vols. Madrid: Est. tip. de Antonio Marzo, 1908, 1910, 1914.

Contemporary Periodicals

ABC (Madrid). Monarchist daily.

La Acción (Madrid). Maurist daily.

La Correspondencia Militar (Madrid). Military daily sympathetic to the Juntas de Defensa.

El Debate (Madrid). Conservative Catholic daily.

El Diario Universal (Madrid). Romanonist daily.

Ejército y Armada (Madrid). Daily representing the views of noncommissioned officers.

El Ejército Español (Madrid). Military daily with ties to General Agustín Luque and the Liberal party.

La Época (Madrid). Daily voice of the "*idóneo*" faction of the Conservative party led by Eduardo Dato.

España (Madrid). Biweekly magazine, pro-Allied, pro-Republican.
El Heraldo de Madrid. Daily affiliated with the newspaper syndicate known as "the Trust." Voice of the Liberal party.
El Imparcial (Madrid). Independent daily affiliated with the newspaper syndicate "the Trust."
El Liberal (Madrid). Pro-Republican daily affiliated with "the Trust."
La Lucha (Barcelona). Republican daily of Marcelino Domingo.
Memorial de Infantería (Toledo). Official journal of the Infantry Corps.
El Mundo (Madrid). Pro-Maura daily.
Mundo Gráfico (Madrid). Popular illustrated weekly.
El País (Madrid). Republican daily.
Revista de tropas coloniales (Ceuta). Political organ of the africanistas, founded in 1924.
El Socialista (Madrid). Daily of the PSOE.
El Sol (Madrid). Independent "renovationist" daily.
Solidaridad Obrera (Barcelona). Daily of the Anarchosyndicalist CNT.
La Tribuna (Barcelona). Independent daily.

Memoirs, Collections of Speeches and Documents, Contemporary Essays, and Eyewitness Accounts

Aguirre del Cárcer, Manuel. *Glosa del año 23*. Madrid: Editorial Pace, 1944.
Alba, Santiago. *L'Espagne et la Dictature: Bilan-Prévisions-Organisation de l'avenir*. Paris: Librairie Valois, 1930.
––––––. *Para la historia de España: Artículos publicados en mayo de 1930 por "El Sol."* Madrid: Diana, 1930.
––––––. *Problemas de España*. Madrid: Editorial Hesperia, 1916.
Alcalá-Zamora y Torres, Niceto. *La crisis de las ideas en los fundamentos del ejército: Conferencia pronunciada el 12 de abril de 1919 en el Centro del Ejército y de la Armada*. Madrid: Imprenta Gráfica Excelsior, 1919.
––––––. *Memorias: (Segundo texto de mis memorias)*. Barcelona: Editorial Planeta, 1977.
Antón del Olmet, Luis, and García Carraffa, Arturo. *El general Marina*. Madrid: Imprenta Cervantina, 1916.
Araquistáin Quevedo, Luis. *Entre la guerra y la revolución: (España en 1917)*. Madrid: N.p., 1917.
––––––. *España en el crisol: (Un estado que se disuelve y un pueblo que renace)*. Barcelona: Editorial Minerva, 1921.
Azaña Díaz, Manuel. *Obras completas*. Edited by Juan Marichal. 4 vols. Mexico, D.F.: Ediciones Oasis, 1966.
Azpeitua, Antonio. *Marruecos, la mala semilla: Ensayo de análisis objetivo de cómo fue sembrada la guerra en África*. Madrid: Imprenta Clásica Española, 1921.
Barado y Font, Francisco. *Literatura militar española*. Barcelona: Tipografía la Academia, 1890.
Baratech Alfaro, F. *Los Sindicatos Libres de España: Su origen, su actuación, su ideario*. Barcelona: Talleres Gráficos Cortel, 1927.

Barea, Arturo. *La forja de un rebelde*. 4th ed. Buenos Aires: Editorial Losada, 1966.

Barrios y Carrión, Leopoldo. *La milicia como elemento político contemporáneo*. Madrid: Librería Fernando Fé, 1897.

Bastos Ansart, Francisco. *El desastre de Annual: Melilla en julio de 1921*. Barcelona: Editorial Minerva, 1921.

Bello, Luis. *España durante la guerra: Política y acción de los alemanes, 1914–1918*. Vol. 1. Madrid: Editorial Europea, 1919.

Berenguer y Fuste, Dámaso, conde de Xauen. *Campañas en el Rif y Yebala, 1919–1921*. 2 vols. Madrid: Ediciones Ares, 1948.

———. *Campañas en el Rif y Yebala, 1921–1922: Notas y documentos de mi diario de operaciones*. Madrid: Sucesores de R. Velasco, 1923.

———. *De la dictadura a la república*. Madrid: Editorial Plus Ultra, 1946.

———. *La guerra en Marruecos: Ensayo de una adaptación técnica*. Madrid: Librería Fernando Fé, 1918.

Bermúdez de Castro y Tomás, Luis. *Teoría militar y deberes cívicos*. Madrid: Sucesores de Rivadeneyra, 1903.

Buenacasa, Manuel. *El movimiento obrero español, 1886–1926: (Historia y crítica.) Figuras ejemplares que conocí*. Paris: Familia y amigos del autor, 1966.

Burgos y Mazo, Manuel de. *Páginas históricas de 1917*. Madrid: Casa Editorial de M. Núñez Samper, 1918.

———. *El verano de 1919 en Gobernación*. Cuenca: Tip. Emilio Pinós, 1921.

Burguete y Lana, Ricardo. *La guerra y el hombre: Psicología de las tropas. (Melilla, 1909–1910)*. Madrid: Saénz de Jubera Hnos., 1911.

———. *Mi rebeldía: "Mane-Thecel-Phares."* Madrid: Sucesores de Rivadeneyra, 1904.

———. *Morbo nacional: Vida defensiva*. Madrid: Imprenta de Fortanet, [1904].

[Burguete y Lana, Ricardo]. *El problema de Marruecos: Un cuarto a espadas*. Madrid: Imprenta Hélenica, 1914.

Buxadé, José. *España en crisis: La bullanga misteriosa de 1917*. Barcelona: Imprenta de B. Bauzá, 1918.

Cabanellas, Guillermo. *Militarismo y militaradas: (Acotaciones de la historia político-militar de España)*. Madrid: Editorial Castro, 1933.

Calvo, Gonzalo. *España en Marruecos, 1910–1913*. Barcelona: Casa Editorial Maucci, 1913.

Capitán Equis [pseud. of Germán León y Lores]. *El problema militar en España: Apuntes para un estudio sincero y al alcance de todos*. Burgos: Imprenta J. Saíz y Compañía, 1916.

Capo, José-María. *Las juntas militares de defensa*. Havana: Imprenta "Los rayos X," 1923.

Castillo Puche, José Luis, ed. *Diario íntimo de Alfonso XIII*. Madrid: Biblioteca Nueva, 1960.

Cebreiros, Nazario. *Las reformas militares: Estudio crítico*. Santander: Talleres tip. J. Martínez, 1931.

Cierva y Peñafiel, Juan de la. *Notas de mi vida*. 2d ed. Madrid: Instituto Editorial Reus, 1955.

Ciges Aparicio, Manuel. *El libro de la crueldad: Del cuartel y de la guerra*. Madrid: Imprenta de Bernardo Rodríguez, [1906].

Coello de Portugal, José Luis. *Las juntas de defensa: Cómo perdí mi carrera militar*. Madrid: Librería de Alejandro Pueyo, 1922.

Comandante Beta [pseud. of José García Benítez]. *Apuntes para historiar tres años de reformas militares (1915–1917)*. Part 1. Madrid: Imprenta de Bernardo Rodríguez, 1917.

Costa, Joaquín. *Oligarquía y caciquismo como la forma actual de gobierno en España: Urgencia y modo de cambiarla*. Madrid: Imprenta de los hijos de M. G. Hernández, 1902.

Dato Iradier, Eduardo. *El movimiento revolucionario de agosto de 1917: Discursos pronunciados en el Congreso de los diputados por los excmos. señores D. Eduardo Dato Iradier y D. José Sánchez Guerra en las sesiones de los días 29 y 31 de mayo de 1918*. Madrid: Imprenta de Fortanet, 1918.

Díaz del Moral, Juan. *Historia de las agitaciones campesinas andaluzas—Córdoba: (Antecedentes para una reforma agraria)*. 1929. Reprint. Madrid: Alianza Editorial, 1973.

Díaz-Fernández, José. *El blocao: Novela de la guerra marroquí*. Madrid: Historia Nueva, 1928.

Díaz-Plaja, Fernando. *España, los años decisivos: 1917*. 2d ed. Esplugas de Llobregat: Plaza y Janés, 1970.

————. *La historia de España en sus documentos: El siglo XIX*. Madrid: Instituto de Estudios Políticos, 1954.

————. *La historia de España en sus documentos (nueva serie): El siglo XX*. Madrid: Instituto de Estudios Políticos, 1960.

————. *La historia de España en sus documentos: El siglo XX. Dictadura . . . república, 1923–1936*. Madrid: Instituto de Estudios Políticos, 1964.

Domingo, Marcelino. *En la calle y en la carcel: Jornadas revolucionarias*. Madrid: Renacimiento, 1921.

España, Juan de [pseud. of José Rimblas]. *La actuación de España en Marruecos: Apuntes de historia y estudios sobre la política y situación actual del problema hispano-marroquí*. Madrid: Imprenta de Ramona Velasco, 1926.

Estella, Fernando Primo de Rivera y Sobremonte, marqués de. *Continuación a las opiniones y contestación a comentarios habidos en la prensa con el resumen de la idea*. Guadalajara: Est. Tip. Colegio de Huérfanos, 1919.

————. *Opiniones emitidas ante un redactor del periódico "El Ejército Español" con motivo del problema de orden público en los actuales momentos*. Guadalajara: Est. Tip. Colegio de Huérfanos, 1919.

Eza, Luis Marichalar y Monreal, vizconde de. *Mi responsabilidad en el desastre de Melilla como ministro de la Guerra*. Madrid: Gráficas Reunidas, 1923.

Fanjul y Goñi, Joaquín. *Misión social del ejército*. Madrid: Imprenta de Eduardo Arias, 1907.

Farré Morego, José-María. *Los atentados sociales en España*. Madrid: Artes Gráficas, 1922.

Fernández de Rota y Tournán, Antonio. *¡Salvemos a España!* Saragossa: Est. Tip. de G. Casanal, 1920.

Fernández-Flórez, Wenceslao. *Acotaciones de un oyente*. Madrid: Librería de la viuda de Pueyo, 1918.

———. *Impresiones de un hombre de buena fé*. 2 vols. Madrid: Espasa-Calpe, 1964.

Flores Morales, Angel, ed. *África a través del pensamiento español: (De Isabel la Católica a Franco)*. Madrid: Consejo Superior de Investigaciones Científicas, Instituto de Estudios Africanos, 1949.

Franco Bahamonde, Francisco. *Marruecos: Diario de una bandera*. Madrid: Editorial Pueyo, 1922.

García Alonso, Carlos. "El ejército y el socialismo." *Revista Científica Militar* 3 (4th ser.) (1892): 118–21.

García Nieto, María Carmen; Donézar, Javier M.; and López Puerta, Luis. *Crisis del sistema canovista, 1898–1923*. Bases documentales de la España contemporánea, vol. 5. Madrid: Guadiana, 1972.

Giménez Caballero, Ernesto. *Notas marruecas de un soldado*. Madrid: Imprenta de Ernesto Giménez, 1923.

Gómez Hidalgo, Francisco. *Marruecos, la tragedia prevista*. Madrid: Imprenta de Juan Pueyo, 1921.

González Hontoria y Fernández Ladreda, Manuel. *El Protectorado francés en Marruecos y sus enseñanzas para la acción española*. Madrid: Residencia de Estudiantes, 1915.

Guixé, Juan. *El Rif en sombras: (Lo que yo he visto en Melilla)*. N.p., [1921].

Hernández Mir, Francisco. *Del desastre al fracaso: Un mando funesto*. Madrid: Editorial Pueyo, 1922.

———. *La dictadura ante la historia*. Madrid: Compañía Iberoamericana de Publicaciones, 1930.

———. "El proceso de las responsabilidades: Artículos publicados en *La Libertad* de Madrid entre el 22 de julio y el 4 de diciembre de 1931." Mimeographed. Madrid: Biblioteca Nacional, Colección García Figueras.

Hidalgo de Cisneros, Ignacio. *Cambio de rumbo*. Vol. 1. Bucarest: Coleción Ebro, 1970.

Howard, Esmé. *The Theatre of Life*. Vol. 2. *Life Seen from the Stalls, 1905–1936*. London: Hodder & Stoughton, 1936.

Hurtado, Amadeu. *Quaranta anys d'avocat: Història del meu temps*. 2 vols. Barcelona: Ediciones Ariel, 1969.

Isern, Damián. *De la defensa nacional*. Madrid: Imprenta de la sucesora de M. Minuesa de los Ríos, 1901.

Larrea, Francisco. *Fortalecimiento y mejora del ejército español*. Madrid: Imprenta de Eduardo Arias, 1906.

Lerroux, Alejandro. *Al servicio de la república*. 2d ed. Madrid: Ediciones Morata, 1930.

———. *Mis memorias*. Madrid: Afrodisio Aguado, 1963.

López de Ochoa, Eduardo. *De la dictadura a la república*. Madrid: Editorial Zeus, 1930.

López Rienda, Rafael. *El escándalo del millón de Larache: Datos, antecedentes y derivaciones de las inmoralidades en Marruecos*. Madrid: Imprenta Sáez Hnos., 1922.

_____. *Frente al fracaso: Raisuni, de Silvestre a Burguete*. Madrid: Sociedad General Española de Librería, 1923.

[Lyautey, Hubert]. "Du rôle social de l'officier." *Revue des Deux Mondes*, Mar. 15, 1891, pp. 443–58.

Madrid, Francisco [pseud. of Carlos Madrigal]. *Ocho meses y un día en el gobierno civil de Barcelona: (Confesiones y testimonios)*. Barcelona: Las Ediciones de la Flecha, 1932.

_____. *El ruidísimo pleito de las juntas de defensa y Millán-Astray*. Barcelona: Gráficos Costa, 1922.

Márquez-Martínez, Benito, and Capo, José-María. *Las juntas militares de defensa*. Barcelona: Librería Sintes, 1923.

Martínez de Aragón y Urbiztondo, Gabriel. *Las juntas militares de defensa: Los alumnos de la Escuela de Guerra. Los hombres públicos de España. La soberanía de la ley*. Madrid: Librería de Alejandro Pueyo, 1923.

Martínez de Campos y Serrano, Carlos, duque de la Torre. *Ayer: 1892–1931*. Madrid: Instituto de Estudios Políticos, 1946.

Marvá y Mayer, José. *El ejército y la armada y la cultura nacional: Conferencia pronunciada el sábado 22 de febrero de 1919*. Madrid: Imprenta Editorial Ibérica, 1919.

Maturana Vargas, Carlos. *La trágica realidad: Marruecos (1921)*. Barcelona: Editorial Cervantes, 1921.

Maura Montaner, Antonio. "Debate en el Congreso sobre la derogación de la ley de jurisdicciones, los días 10, 11, 12 de junio de 1908." Madrid: N.p., 1908.

Mendaro del Alcázar, Eduardo. *Recuerdos de un periodista de principios de siglo*. Madrid: Prensa Española, 1958.

Millán-Astray Terreros, José. *La Legión*. Madrid: V. H. Sanz Calleja, 1923.

Mola Vidal, Emilio. *Obras completas*. Valladolid: Librería Santarén, 1940.

Morato, Juan José. *Pablo Iglesias: Educador de muchedumbres*. 1931. Reprint. Barcelona: Ediciones Ariel, 1968.

_____. *El Partido Socialista Obrero: Génesis, doctrina, hombres, organización, desarrollo, acción, estado actual*. Madrid, Biblioteca Nueva, 1918.

Navascués, Felipe de. *La próxima guerra: Estudios político-militares sobre la Europa contemporánea y reorganización del estado militar de España*. Madrid: Sucesores de Rivadeneyra, 1895.

"La organización del ejército español mirada por un prusiano." *Revista Técnica de Infantería y Caballería* 10–11 (1910–11).

Ortega y Gasset, Eduardo. *Annual: (Relato de un soldado e impresiones de un cronista)*. Madrid: Sucesores de Rivadeneyra, 1922.

Ortega y Gasset, José. *España invertebrada*. 1921. Reprint. Madrid: Revista de Occidente, 1971.

Otero Enríquez, Santiago. *La nobleza en el ejército: Estudio histórico de legislación nobiliario-militar (1500–1865)*. Madrid: Sucesores de Rivadeneyra, 1915.

Pardo González, Cándido. *Al servicio de la verdad: Las juntas de defensa militares. El protectorado de Marruecos y Alhucemas. Dictadura del segundo Marqués de Es-*

tella. *Aportaciones para un estudio crítico de la dictadura del general Primo de Rivera*. Madrid: Rehyma, 1930.

———. *El problema militar de España: Su resolución más racional, económica y nacional*. Madrid: Rehyma, 1934.

Peire, Tomás. *Una política militar expuesta ante las Cortes Constituyentes*. Madrid: Vallinas, 1933.

Pérez Solís, Oscar. *Memorias de mi amigo Oscar Perea*. Madrid: Compañía Iberoamericana de Publicaciones, [1931].

Posada, Adolfo. *España en crisis: La política*. Madrid: Caro Raggio, 1923.

Prieto, Indalecio. *Convulsiones de España. Pequeños detalles de grandes sucesos*. Madrid: Ediciones Oasis, 1967.

Primo de Rivera y Orbaneja, Miguel. *La obra de la dictadura: Sus cuatro últimos artículos*. Madrid: Imprenta Sáez Hnos., 1930.

Queipo de Llano, Gonzalo. *El general Queipo de Llano perseguido por la dictadura*. Madrid: J. Morata, 1930.

———. *El movimiento reivindicativo de Cuatro Vientos*. Madrid: Tip. Yagües, 1933.

Recapitulación de pensamientos antimilitaristas. Barcelona: Publicaciones de la Escuela Moderna, 1903.

Ribé, Manuel. *Memorias de un funcionario*. Barcelona: Ediciones Marte, 1963.

Romanones, Álvaro Figueroa y Torres, conde de. *El ejército y la política: Apuntes sobre la organización militar y el presupuesto de la Guerra*. Madrid: Renacimiento, 1920.

———. *Obras completas*. 3 vols. Madrid: Editorial Plus Ultra, 1949.

Rovira y Virgili, Antoni, ed. *Anuari de Catalunya: Crònica de la vida política, literaria, teatral artística, universitaria, social, corporativa, científica, economica, i deportiva, a les terres de llengua catalana durant l'any*. Barcelona: Editorial Minerva, 1917.

Royo Villanova, Antonio. *La misión educativa del ejército*. Madrid: Imprenta Gráfica Excelsior, 1919.

Rubio Fernández, Eduardo. *Melilla, al margen del desastre (mayo-agosto, 1921)*. Barcelona: Editorial Cervantes, 1921.

Ruíz Albéniz, Víctor. *Ecce homo: Las responsabilidades del desastre. Prueba documental y aportes inéditos sobre las causas del derrumbamiento y consecuencias de él*. Madrid: Biblioteca Nueva, 1922.

———. *España en el Rif: Estudios del indígena y del país. Nuestra actuación de doce años. La guerra del veintiuno*. Madrid: Biblioteca Hispana, [1921].

Ruíz Fornells, Enrique. *La educación moral del soldado*. Toledo: Imprenta y Librería de la viuda y hijos de Juan Peláez, 1894.

Saborit, Andrés. *La huelga de agosto de 1917: (Apuntes históricos)*. Mexico, D.F.: Editorial "Pablo Iglesias," 1967.

———. *Julián Besteiro*. Buenos Aires: Editorial Losada, 1967.

Saínz de Varanda, Ramón, ed. *Colección de leyes fundamentales*. Saragossa: Acribia, 1957.

Sánchez Bravo, Antonio. *Apuntes para la historia de la escala de reserva del ejército*. Cuenca: Tip. Ruíz de Lara, 1930.

Sánchez de Toca, Joaquín. *La crisis de nuestro gobierno constitucional: Desde 1 de junio de 1917 a. . .* Madrid: Isidoro Perales, 1918.

Sánchez Roca, Mariano. *La sublevación del cuartel del Carmen: (Unas horas de gobierno soviético en Zaragoza).* Madrid: Prensa Gráfica, [1920].

Sevilla Andrés, Diego. *Constituciones y otras leyes y proyectos políticos de España.* Vol. 1. Madrid: Editora Nacional, 1969.

Soldevilla, Fernando, ed. *El año político.* Vols. for 1917–23. Madrid: Imprenta de R. Rojas, 1917–23.

―――. *Tres revoluciones: (Apuntes y notas).* Madrid: Imprenta de Julio Cosario, 1917.

Solidaritat Catalana. *Discursos contra la ley de las jurisdicciones en el Senado y en el Congreso: Año 1906.* Barcelona: Tipografía El Anuario de la Exportación, 1906.

Soriano, Rodrigo. *¡Guerra, guerra, al infiel marroquí!* Madrid: T. Tip. "El Día de Cuenca," 1921.

Suárez Inclán, Pío. *Organización del cuerpo de estado mayor, 1810–1910.* Madrid: Talleres del Depósito de la Guerra, 1912.

―――. *El problema del reclutamiento en España.* Madrid: Est. Tip. "El Trabajo," 1905.

Los sucesos de agosto ante el parlamento: (Discursos parlamentarios de Largo Caballero, Anguiano, Saborit, Prieto, Besteiro, Marcelino Domingo, y Barriobero). Madrid: Tip. Artística, 1918.

Tapia, Luis de. *Coplas del año (1919).* Madrid: Renacimiento, 1920.

Téllez de Sotomayor, Comandante. *El odioso ejército.* Madrid: Imprenta Gráfica Excelsior, 1918.

Vivero, Augusto. *El derrumbamiento: La verdad sobre el desastre del Rif.* 2d ed. Madrid: Caro Raggio, 1922.

Weyler y Nicolau, Valeriano, duque de Rubí. *Valor de la historia en el arte militar: Discursos leídos en la Real Academia de la Historia.* Madrid: Talleres del Depósito de la Guerra, 1925.

Secondary Sources

Abrahamsson, Bengt. *Military Professionalization and Political Power.* Sage Series on Armed Forces and Society, vol. 2. Beverly Hills, Calif.: Sage Publications, 1972.

Aguado Bleye, Pedro, and Alcázar Molina, Cayetano. *Manual de historia de España.* Vol. 3. 8th rev. ed. Madrid: Espasa-Calpe, 1959.

Alcázar, Mariano del. *López Domínguez.* Los Presidentes del Consejo de la Monarquía, 1874–1931, vol. 12. Madrid: Editorial Purcalla, 1946.

Alfarache, Juan de. *Berenguer.* Los Presidentes del Consejo de la Monarquía Española, 1874–1931. Madrid: Editorial Purcalla, 1949.

Alonso, José Ramón. *Historia política del ejército español.* Madrid: Editora Nacional, 1974.

Alonso Baquer, Miguel. *Aportación militar a la cartografía española en la historia contemporánea: Siglo XIX.* Madrid: Consejo Superior de Investigaciones

Científicas, Instituto de Geografía Aplicada del Patronato "Alonso de Herrera," 1972.

———. *El ejército en la sociedad española*. Madrid: Ediciones del Movimiento, 1971.

Ambler, John Steward. *Soldiers against the State: The French Army in Politics*. Garden City, N.Y.: Doubleday Anchor, 1968.

Armiñán, Luis de. *Excmo. sr. general D. Gonzalo Queipo de Llano, jefe del Ejército del Sur*. Héroes de España, no. 3. Avila: Imprenta Católica y Enc. Sigirano Díaz, 1937.

Arrarás Iribarren, Joaquín, ed. *Historia de la cruzada española*. 7 vols. Madrid: Ediciones Españolas, 1940.

Aunós Pérez, Eduardo. *España en crisis (1874–1936)*. Buenos Aires: Librería del Colegio, 1942.

———. *Primo de Rivera: Soldado y gobernante*. Madrid: Editorial Alhambra, 1944.

Balcells, Alberto. *El sindicalismo en Barcelona, 1916–1923*. Barcelona: Editorial Nova Terra, 1965.

Ballesteros y Beretta, Antonio. *Historia de España y su influencia en la historia universal*. Vol. 8. 2d rev. ed. Barcelona: Salvat Editores, 1956.

Bertrán Güell, Felipe. *Caudillo, profetas y soldados*. Madrid: Editorial Juventud, 1939.

Blanco y Pérez, Carlos. *La dictadura y los procesos militares*. Madrid: J. Morata, 1931.

Brenan, Gerald. *The Spanish Labyrinth: An Account of the Social and Political Background of the Spanish Civil War*. 2d ed. Cambridge: At the University Press, 1960.

Burke, Edmund, III. *Prelude to Protectorate in Morocco: Precolonial Protest and Resistance, 1860–1912*. Chicago: University of Chicago Press, 1976.

Busquets Bragulat, Julio. *El militar de carrera en España: Estudio de sociología militar*. 2d rev. ed. Barcelona: Ediciones Ariel, 1971.

Carr, Raymond. *Spain, 1808–1939*. Oxford: The Clarendon Press, 1966.

———. "Spain: Rule by Generals." In *Soldiers and Governments: Nine Studies in Civil-Military Relations*, edited by Michael Howard. London: Eyre & Spottiswoode, 1957.

Carrasco Verde, Manuel, et al. *Cien años en la vida del ejército español*. Madrid: Editora Nacional, 1956.

Carsten, Francis Ludwig. *The Reichswehr and Politics, 1918 to 1933*. Oxford: The Clarendon Press, 1966.

Chandler, J. A. "Spanish Policy toward North Morocco, 1908 to 1923." Master's thesis, University of Keele, 1971.

Christiansen, Eric. *The Origins of Military Power in Spain, 1800–1854*. London: Oxford University Press, 1967.

Cierva y de Hoces, Ricardo de la. "La dialéctica de las bofetadas." *Historia y Vida* 2 (1969): 137–41.

———. *Francisco Franco: Un siglo de España*. Madrid: Editora Nacional, 1972–73.

———. *Historia de la guerra civil española*. Vol. 1. *Perspectivas y antecedentes, 1898–1936*. Madrid: Librería Editorial San Martín, 1969.

Ciges Aparicio, Manuel. *España bajo la dinastía de los Borbones, 1701–1931*. Madrid: M. Aguilar, 1932.

Cimadevilla, Francisco. *El general Primo de Rivera*. Madrid: Afrodisio Aguado, 1944.

Cortes Cavanillas, Julián. *La caída de Alfonso XIII: Causas y episodios de una revolución*. 4th ed. Madrid: Imprenta de Galo Sáez, 1932.

_____. *Confesiones y muerte de Alfonso XIII*. Madrid: Colección ABC, 1951.

Craig, Gordon A. *The Politics of the Prussian Army, 1640–1945*. New York: Oxford University Press, 1955.

Crozier, Brian. *Franco: A Biographical History*. London: Eyre & Spottiswoode, 1967.

Demeter, Karl. *The German Officer-Corps in Society and State, 1650–1945*. Translated by Angus Malcolm. New York: Frederick A. Praeger, 1965.

Doorn, Jacques van, ed. *Armed Forces and Society: Sociological Essays*. The Hague: Mouton, 1968.

_____. *Military Profession and Military Regimes: Commitments and Conflicts*. The Hague: Mouton, 1969.

_____. *The Soldier and Social Change*. Comparative Studies in the History and Sociology of the Military, vol. 7. Beverly Hills, Calif.: Sage Publications, 1975.

Echeverría, Tomás. *Sobre la caída de Alfonso XIII: Errores y ligerezas del propio rey que influyeron en su destronamiento*. Sevilla: Editorial Católica Española, 1966.

Estado Mayor Central del Ejército. Servicio Histórico Militar. *Acción de España en África*. 3 vols. Madrid: Imprenta y talleres del Ministerio de la Guerra, 1935–41.

_____. *Historia de la guerra de liberación (1936–1939)*. Vol. 1. *Antecedentes de la guerra*. Madrid: Imprenta del Servicio Geográfico del Ejército, 1945.

_____. *Historia de las campañas de Marruecos*. 2 vols. Madrid: Imprenta del Servicio Geográfico del Ejército, 1947.

Esteban Infantes, Emilio. *General Sanjurjo: (Un laureado en el Penal del Dueso)*. Colección "La epopeya y sus héroes." Barcelona: Editorial AHR, 1957.

Feit, Edward. "The Rule of the 'Iron Surgeons': Military Government in Spain and Ghana." *Comparative Politics* 1 (1969): 485–97.

Fernández Almagro, Melchor. *Historia del reinado de D. Alfonso XIII*. 2d ed. Barcelona: Montaner y Simón, Editores, 1934.

_____. *Historia política de la España contemporánea*. 3 vols. Madrid: Alianza Editorial, 1968–70.

Ferrer, Joaquim. *Layret (1880–1920)*. Barcelona: Editorial Nova Terra, 1971.

Finer, Samuel E. *The Man on Horseback: The Role of the Military in Politics*. London: Pall Mall Press, 1962.

Fleming, Shannon E. "The Disaster at Annual: Spanish Colonial Failure in Northern Morocco, 1902–1921." Master's thesis, University of Minnesota, 1969.

_____. "Primo de Rivera and Abd-el Krim: The Struggle in Spanish Morocco, 1923–27." Ph.D. dissertation, University of Wisconsin, 1974.

Furneaux, Rupert. *Abdel Krim: Emir of the Rif*. London: Secker & Warburg, 1967.

Galinsoga, Luis de, and Franco-Salgado, Francisco. *Centinela de occidente: (Semblanza biográfica de Francisco Franco)*. Barcelona: Editorial AHR, 1956.

Gárate, José María. *España en sus héroes*. 2 vols. Madrid: Ornigraf, n.d.

García Escudero, José-María. *De Cánovas a la república*. Madrid: Ediciones Rialp, 1951.

García Figueras, Tomás. *La acción africana de España en torno al 98 (1860–1912)*. 2 vols. Madrid: Consejo Superior de Investigaciones Científicas, Instituto de Estudios Africanos, 1966.

———. *Biografía del general Fernández Silvestre y su labor desarrollada en la zona de Larache*. Ceuta: Imprenta "Tropas Coloniales," 1929.

———. *Marreucos: La acción de España en el norte de África*. 4th ed. Madrid: Ediciones FE, 1955.

García Nieto Paris, Carmen. "La prensa de Barcelona ante la crisis militar de 1895." *Estudios de Historia Moderna* 4 (1954): 441–89.

García Venero, Maximiano. *Antonio Maura, 1907–1909*. Madrid: Ediciones del Movimiento, 1953.

———. *Eduardo Dato: Vida y sacrificio de un gobernante conservador*. Vitoria: Diputación Foral de Álava, Consejo de Cultura, 1969.

———. *El general Fanjul: Madrid en el alzamiento nacional*. Madrid: Ediciones Cid, 1967.

———. *Historia de las Internacionales en España*. Vol. 2. *(Desde la primera guerra mundial al 18 de julio de 1936)*. Madrid: Ediciones del Movimiento, 1957.

———. *Melquíades Álvarez: Historia de un liberal*. Madrid: Editorial Alhambra, 1954.

———. *Santiago Alba: Monárquico de razón*. Madrid: Aguilar, 1963.

Girardet, Raoul. *La Société militaire dans la France contemporaine, 1815–1939*. Paris: Plon, 1953.

González Ruano, César. *El general Primo de Rivera*. Madrid: Ediciones del Movimiento, 1954.

Gordon, Harold J., Jr. *The Reichswehr and the German Republic, 1919–1926*. Princeton, N.J.: Princeton University Press, 1957.

Harries-Jenkins, Gwyn. "The Development of Professionalism in the Victorian Army." *Armed Forces and Society* 1 (1975): 472–89.

———, and Doorn, Jacques van, eds. *The Military and the Problem of Legitimacy*. Sage Studies in International Sociology, no. 2. Beverly Hills, Calif.: Sage Publications, 1976.

Harrison, Joseph. "Big Business and the Failure of Right-Wing Catalan Nationalism, 1901–1923." *The Historical Journal* 19 (1976): 901–18.

———. "Big Business and the Rise of Basque Nationalism." *European Studies Review* 7 (1977): 371–91.

———. "Catalan Business and the Loss of Cuba, 1898–1914." *The Economic History Review, Second Series* 27 (1974): 431–41.

Headrick, Daniel Richard. "The Spanish Army, 1868–1898: Structure, Function and Politics." Ph.D. dissertation, Princeton University, 1971.

Hennessy, Charles A. M. *The Federal Republic in Spain: Pi y Margall and the Federal Republican Movement, 1868–74*. Oxford: The Clarendon Press, 1962.

Hernández de Herrera, Carlos, and García Figueras, Tomás. *Acción de España en Marruecos*. 2 vols. Madrid: Imprenta Municipal, 1929.

Howard, Michael, ed. *Soldiers and Governments: Nine Studies in Civil-Military Relations*. London: Eyre & Spottiswoode, 1957.

Huntington, Samuel P. *Changing Patterns of Military Politics*. International Yearbook of Political Behavior Research, vol. 3. Glencoe, Ill.: The Free Press, 1962.

————. "Civilian Control of the Military: A Theoretical Statement." In *Political Behavior: A Reader in Theory and Research*, edited by Heinz Eulau, Samuel J. Eldersveld, and Morris Janowitz. Glencoe, Ill.: The Free Press, 1956.

————. *Political Order in Changing Societies*. New Haven: Yale University Press, 1968.

————. *The Soldier and the State: The Theory and Politics of Civil-Military Relations*. Cambridge, Mass.: Harvard University Press, Belknap Press, 1957.

Irribaren, José-María. *Mola: Datos para una biografía y para la historia del alzamiento nacional*. Saragossa: Librería General, 1938.

Janowitz, Morris. *The Professional Soldier: A Social and Political Portrait*. Glencoe, Ill.: The Free Press, 1960.

Johnson, John J. *The Military and Society in Latin America*. Stanford, Calif.: Stanford University Press, 1964.

Julien, Charles André, ed. *Abd el-Krim et la République du Rif: Actes du colloque international d'études historiques et sociologiques, 18–20 janvier 1973*. Paris: Francois Maspero, 1976.

Jutglar, Antoni. *Ideologías y clases en la España contemporánea*. 2 vols. Madrid: EDICUSA, 1971.

Kern, Robert W. *Liberals, Reformers and Caciques in Restoration Spain, 1875–1909*. Albuquerque: University of New Mexico Press, 1974.

Kindelán y Duany, Alfredo. *Ejército y política*. Madrid: Ediciones Ares, n.d.

————; Martínez de Campos y Serrano, Carlos; et al. *El ejército como problema*. Madrid: Euramérica, 1961.

Lacomba Avellán, Juan Antonio. *La crisis española de 1917*. Madrid: Editorial Ciencia Nueva, 1970.

La Gorce, Paul-Marie de. *The French Army: A Military-Political History*. Translated by Kenneth Douglas. New York: George Braziller, 1963.

Larson, Arthur D. "Military Professionalism and Civil Control: A Comparative Analysis of Two Interpretations." *Journal of Political and Military Sociology* 2 (1974): 57–72.

Linz, Juan J. "The Party System of Spain: Past and Future." In *Party Systems and Voter Alignments: Cross-National Perspectives*, edited by Seymour M. Lipset and Stein Rokkan. New York: The Free Press, 1967.

————, and de Miguel, Amando. "Within-Nation Differences and Comparisons: The Eight Spains." In *Comparing Nations*, edited by Richard L. Merrit and Stein Rokkan. New Haven: Yale University Press, 1966.

Longares Alonso, Jesús. "La guerra de propagandas en España, 1914–1918." *Tiempo de Historia* 3 (1977): 86–99.

López-Campillo, Evelyne. "Ortega, *El Imparcial* y las Juntas." *Revista de Occidente*, no. 75 (1969): 311–17.

Madariaga, María-Rosa de. "Le Parti socialiste espagnole et le parti communiste d'Espagne face à la révolte rifaine." In *Abd el-Krim et la République du Rif*, edited by Charles André Julien. Paris: Francois Maspero, 1976.

Madariaga, Salvador de. *Spain: A Modern History*. New York: Praeger, 1958.

Martín-Granizo, León. *Biografías de sociólogos españoles*. Madrid: Imprenta Nacional del Boletín Oficial del Estado, 1963.

Martín Maestre, Jacinto. *Huelga general de 1917*. Madrid: Editorial ZYX, 1966.

Martínez Cuadrado, Miguel. *La burguesía conservadora (1874–1931)*. Historia de España Alfaguara, no. 6. Madrid: Alianza Editorial, 1973.

———. *Elecciones y partidos políticos de España (1868–1931)*. 2 vols. Madrid: Taurus Ediciones, 1970.

Martínez de Campos y Serrano, Carlos, duque de la Torre. *España bélica: El siglo XIX*. Madrid: Aguilar, 1961.

Martínez Sol, Ramón. *De Canalejas al tribunal de responsabilidades: (Anecdotario inédito de la disolución de un reinado)*. Madrid: Dédalo, 1933.

Maura Gamazo, Gabriel, duque de Maura. *Bosquejo histórico de la dictadura, 1923–1930*. 5th rev. ed. Madrid: Tip. de Archivos, 1930.

———. *Historia crítica del reinado de Don Alfonso XIII durante su menoridad bajo la regencia de su madre Doña María Cristina de Austria*. 2 vols. Barcelona: Montaner y Simón, Editores, 1919.

———, and Fernández Almagro, Melchor. *Por qué cayó Alfonso XIII: Evolución y disolución de los partidos históricos durante su reinado*. Madrid: Ediciones Ambos Mundos, 1948.

Maurín, Joaquín. *Los hombres de la dictadura*. Madrid: Editorial Cénit, 1930.

Meaker, Gerald. *The Revolutionary Left in Spain, 1914–1923*. Stanford, Calif.: Stanford University Press, 1974.

Morales Lezcano, Víctor. *El colonialismo hispanofrancés en Marruecos (1898–1927)*. Madrid: Siglo XXI de España Editores, 1976.

———. "Las minas del Rif y el capital financiero peninsular: 1906–1930." *Moneda y Crédito* 135 (1975): 61–79.

Nieto, Alejandro. *La retribución de los funcionarios de España: (Historia y actualidad)*. Madrid: Revista de Occidente, 1967.

Oehling, Hermann. *La función política del ejército*. Madrid: Instituto de Estudios Políticos, 1967.

Olivar Barallat, Coruna. "Datos político-sociales de España (1915–1917)." *Cuadernos de Historia de España* 43–44 (1967): 261.

Oller Piñol, Juan. *Martínez Anido, su vida y su obra*. Madrid: Librería General de Victoriano Suárez, 1943.

Olmedo Delgado, Antonio, and Cuesta Monero, José. *General Queipo de Llano: (Aventura y audacia)*. Barcelona: Editorial AHR, 1957.

Ossorio y Gallardo, Angel. *Diccionario político español, histórico y biográfico (desde Carlos IV hasta 1936)*. Buenos Aires: Editorial Mundo Atlántico, 1945.

Pabón, Jesús. *Cambó*. 3 vols. Barcelona: Editorial Alpha, 1952, 1969.

Payne, Stanley G. *Politics and the Military in Modern Spain*. Stanford, Calif.: Stanford University Press, 1967.

Perlmutter, Amos. *The Military and Politics in Modern Times: On Professionals, Praetorians, and Revolutionary Soldiers*. New Haven: Yale University Press, 1977.

———. "The Praetorian State and the Praetorian Army: Toward a Taxonomy of Civil-Military Relations in Developing Polities." *Comparative Politics* 1 (1969): 382–404.

Petrie, Sir Charles. *King Alfonso XIII and His Age*. London: Chapman & Hall, 1963.

Pilapil, Vicente R. *Alfonso XIII*. Twayne's Rulers and Statesmen of the World. New York: Twayne Publishers, 1969.

Poblet, Josep M. *Aquell any 1917. . . . (Les assemblees de parlamentaris. La vaga general. Les juntes de defensa militars. La mort de Prat de la Riba)*. Barcelona: Editorial Pòrtic, 1971.

Prieto, Tomás. *Soldados en España: Datos para la historia*. Madrid: Ediciones Tormes, 1946.

Puell de la Villa, Fernando-María. "Las reformas militares del general Cassola." Memoria de Licenciatura, Universidad Complutense de Madrid, 1975.

Ralston, David, ed. *Soldiers and States: Civil-Military Relations in Modern Europe*. Boston: D. C. Heath, 1966.

Rapoport, David C. "The Political Dimensions of Military Usurpation." *Political Science Quarterly* 83 (1968): 551–72.

Redondo, Gonzalo. *Las empresas políticas de José Ortega y Gasset: "El Sol," "Crisol," "Luz" (1917–1934)*. Vol. 1. Madrid: Ediciones Rialp, 1970.

Repollés de Zayas, Julio. "Resumen de los sucesos acaecidos en la Comandancia General de Melilla entre los días 1 de junio y 9 de agosto de 1921, y actuación del regimiento de Cazadores de Alcántara durante su desarrollo." Mimeographed. Madrid: Servicio Histórico Militar, Sección de África, 1967.

Rojo Lluch, Vicente. *El ejército como institución social*. Madrid: Editorial ZYX, 1968.

Roldán, Santiago, and García Delgado, José Luis. *La formación de la sociedad capitalista, 1914–1920*. 2 vols. Madrid: Confederación Española de Cajas de Ahorro, 1973.

Romano, Julio [pseud. of Hipólito González y Rodríguez de la Peña]. *Sanjurjo: El caballero del valor*. Madrid: Imprenta de la viuda de Juan Pueyo, 1940.

———. *Weyler, el hombre de hierro*. Vidas españolas e hispanoamericanos del siglo XIX, no. 44. Madrid: Espasa-Calpe, 1934.

Romero Maura, Joaquín. "El caciquismo: tentativa de conceptualización." *Revista de Occidente*, no. 127 (1973): 15–44.

———. "The Spanish Army and Catalonia: The 'Cu-cut! Incident' and the Law of Jurisdictions, 1905–1906." Sage Research Papers in the Social Sciences (Contemporary European Studies Series, no. 90–933). Beverly Hills, Calif.: Sage Publications, 1976.

Romeu Alfaro, Fernanda. *Las clases trabajadoras en España (1898–1930)*. Madrid: Taurus Ediciones, 1970.

Ropp, Theodore. *War in the Modern World*. Durham, N.C.: Duke University Press, 1959.

Salas López, Fernando de, and Nestares Guillén, Fernando. *Literatura militar*. Madrid: Imprenta de Juan Bravo, 3, 1954.

Sales de Bohigas, Nuria. "Sociedades de seguros contra las quintas (1865–

1868)." In *La revolución de 1868: Historia, pensamiento, literatura*, edited by Clara E. Lida and Iris M. Zavala. New York: Las Américas, 1970.

Sánchez Agesta, Luis. *Historia del constitucionalismo español*. 2d ed. Madrid: Instituto de Estudios Políticos, 1964.

Scham, Alan. *Lyautey in Morocco: Protectorate Administration, 1912–1925*. Berkeley and Los Angeles: University of California Press, 1970.

Seco Serrano, Carlos. *Alfonso XIII y la crisis de la restauración*. Barcelona: Ediciones Ariel, 1969.

Sevilla Andrés, Diego. *Antonio Maura: La revolución desde arriba*. Barcelona: Editorial Aedos, 1954.

————. *Canalejas (1854–1912)*. Barcelona: Editorial Aedos, 1956.

————. *Historia política de España (1800–1967)*. Madrid: Editora Nacional, 1968.

————. "Los partidos políticos y el Protectorado." *Archivos del Instituto de Estudios Africanos* 65 (1963): 61–86.

Solá, Lluis. *"¡Cu-cut!" (1902–1912)*. Barcelona: Editorial Bruguera, 1967.

Stepan, Alfred. *The Military in Politics: Changing Patterns in Brazil*. Princeton, N.J.: Princeton University Press, 1971.

Suero Roca, Teresa. *Los generales de Franco*. Barcelona: Editorial Bruguera, 1975.

Taylor, A. J. P. *The Struggle for Mastery in Europe, 1848–1918*. Oxford: The Clarendon Press, 1954.

Termes Ardévol, Josep. *Anarquismo y sindicalismo en España: La primera Internacional, 1864–1881*. Barcelona: Ediciones Ariel, 1972.

Trice, Thomas Granville. "Spanish Liberalism in Crisis: A Study of the Liberal Party during Spain's Parliamentary Collapse, 1913–1923." Ph.D. dissertation, University of Wisconsin, 1974.

Trythall, J. W. D. *El Caudillo: A Political Biography of Franco*. New York: McGraw-Hill, 1970.

Tuñón de Lara, Manuel. *La España del siglo XX*. Paris, Librería Española, 1966.

————. *Estudios sobre el siglo XIX español*. Madrid: Siglo XXI de España Editores, 1971.

————. *Historia y realidad del poder: El poder y las élites en el primer tercio de la España del siglo XX*. Madrid: EDICUSA, 1967.

————. *El movimiento obrero en la historia de España*. Madrid: Taurus Ediciones, 1972.

Tusell Gómez, Javier. "La descomposición del sistema caciquil español (1902–1931)." *Revista de Occidente*, no. 127 (1973): 75–93.

————. *Oligarquía y caciquismo en Andalucía (1890–1923)*. Barcelona: Editorial Planeta, 1976.

Ullman, Joan Connelly. *La Semana Trágica: Estudio sobre las causas socioeconómicas del anticlericalismo en España (1898–1912)*. Translated by Gonzalo Pontón. Barcelona: Ediciones Ariel, 1972.

Vagts, Alfred. *A History of Militarism, Civilian and Military*. Rev. ed. New York: Meridian Books, 1959.

Valdesoto, Fernando de [pseud. of Joaquín Valdés Sancho and Fernando Soto Oriol]. *Francisco Franco*. Madrid: Afrodisio Aguado, 1943.

Vigón Suerodíaz, Jorge. "Breves notas para la historia de las juntas de defensa y de la dictadura." Mimeographed. Madrid: Servicio Histórico Militar, Sección de Estudios Históricos, Primer Negociado: Guerra de Liberación, n.d.

————. *El espíritu militar español: Réplica a Alfredo de Vigny*. Madrid: Ediciones Rialp, 1950.

————. *Historia de la artillería española*. 3 vols. Madrid: Consejo Superior de Investigaciones Científicas, Instituto Jerónimo Zurita, 1947.

————. *Milicia y política*. Madrid: Instituto de Estudios Políticos, 1947.

————. *Un personaje español del siglo XIX: (El cuerpo de artillería)*. Madrid: Compañía Iberoamericana de Publicaciones, 1930.

————. *Teoría del militarismo*. Madrid: Ediciones Rialp, 1955.

Villares, Pedro Rodríguez de Toro y de Mesa, conde de los. *Estudios del reinado de Alfonso XIII*. Madrid: Ediciones Jordán, 1948.

Weyler y López de Puga, Valeriano. *En el archivo de mi abuelo: Biografía del capitán general Weyler*. Madrid: Industrias Gráficas, 1946.

Woolman, David S. *Rebels in the Rif: Abd el Krim and the Rif Rebellion*. Stanford, Calif.: Stanford University Press, 1968.

Zabala y Lera, Pío. *Historia de España y de la civilización española en la edad contemporánea*. Vol. 5, pt. 2. *Historia de España y de la civilización española*, by Rafael Altamira y Crevea. Barcelona: Sucesores de Juan Gili, 1900–1930.

Index

Military officers are identified by their highest rank prior to September 1923.